SECOND EDITION

VIOLENCE ASSESSMENT AND INTERVENTION

THE PRACTITIONER'S HANDBOOK

JAMES S. CAWOOD, CPP
MICHAEL H. CORCORAN, PH.D.

CRC Press
Taylor & Francis Group
Boca Raton London New York

CRC Press is an imprint of the
Taylor & Francis Group, an **informa** business

CRC Press
Taylor & Francis Group
6000 Broken Sound Parkway NW, Suite 300
Boca Raton, FL 33487-2742

© 2009 by Taylor & Francis Group, LLC
CRC Press is an imprint of Taylor & Francis Group, an Informa business

No claim to original U.S. Government works
Printed in the United States of America on acid-free paper
10 9 8 7 6 5 4 3 2 1

International Standard Book Number-13: 978-1-4200-7112-2 (Hardcover)

Visit the Taylor & Francis Web site at
http://www.taylorandfrancis.com

and the CRC Press Web site at
http://www.crcpress.com

Contents

Section I
INTRODUCTION

1 Fusion   3

Section II
ASSESSMENT

2 Information Gathering   17

3   The Informative Discussion   63

4   Formula for Assessment   103

5   Assessment Tools   151

6   The Victim's Role   175

Section III
MANAGEMENT

7 Organizational Influences — Personal and Professional   203

8 Post-Secondary School Violence   219

Preface

Welcome to our Second Edition. We are writing this book for you, the practitioner, who is confronted on a regular basis with calls from frightened people who want you to keep them safe. It doesn't matter if you are a mental health practitioner, security professional, human resources professional, attorney, police officer, probation or parole officer, or risk evaluator in the mental health field. When you receive that call you realize you do not have the luxury of having perfect information, but you may still need to act now. This book is for you.

The two of us have handled such phone calls for a total of more than 50 years in a variety of contexts. This includes experience in federal law enforcement, municipal law enforcement and as consultants to federal agencies, state agencies and private and public corporations. We continue to handle them on a daily basis as part of our practice. Even though this book is written with the primary focus being anchored in North American laws and nuances, both of us have worked and continue to work internationally. From this experience, we have learned that core assessment and resolution principles, being behaviorally based, are universal, regardless of culture or geography.

We have structured the book into three main sections for the purpose of addressing different approaches to the material and to provide us an opportunity to show different aspects of the entire process. The first section, "Introduction," and Chapter 1, "Fusion," will show the process and flow of our violence assessment model from the perspective of the initial call or "notice event," and the essential steps to initially quantify the situation as well as make the first decisions concerning proper and immediate response. We will illustrate in this section it is in managing this "notice event" and understanding its place in the continuum of the behavior (what has come before and what may come after) that success or failure of the resolution may be found. You may find this section reflects the most similarity with what you do every day and will serve as an overview for the entire guide.

Section II, "Assessment," has been structured to provide information concerning the essential informational components and processes required to provide a thorough and accurate assessment. The chapters in this section cover information gathering, victimology, formulas for assessment, and tools for violence risk assessment. In the appendices of these chapters are practical tools developed by the authors and others for use in guiding the assessment process, speeding information gathering, and providing actuarial frameworks for information analysis. We have not attempted in this section to provide a detailed log of every available instrument or other tool that we may have used or understand may prove to be valuable to you as our intent is not to make judgments. We simply want to provide you with practical information we personally know to be useful and effective based on our day-to-day work.

In Section III, "Management," we cover organizational influences, ethics, security issues, consultation issues and the laws related to violence assessment. We have also added a chapter on violence risk assessment in a post-secondary educational environment, as both of us have been drawn in to do more of that work, both before and after the Virginia Tech shooting. In this section we want to cover not only the obvious issues, but provide a perspective that may allow you to go beyond your current perception of these elements and acquire new appreciation and understanding of how these areas can provide better case outcomes.

For the mental health professionals, lawyers and other professionals reading this guide, we have attempted to provide references to the literature, when applicable. However, we do not intend this guide to be a detailed academic work that attempts to reflect the breadth of literature available for assessing potential violent behavior. We want this book to provide practical, proven ideas and tools for case evaluation and management. If you come away with at least one new idea, tool or practical solution to an assessment or intervention problem, we have accomplished our goal in writing this handbook.

We would also hope that reading and using this book would motivate you to share your knowledge with others, whenever and however you can. Only in the sharing of practical, effective methods of violence assessment and intervention can we continue to increase the safety of the people each of us is responsible for protecting.

We hope that you enjoy this guide and continue to be interested in improving the safety of the communities you serve.

Acknowledgments

The second edition of this book could not have been possible without the efforts of a great many people. We both would like to acknowledge some people for helping us reach this point of our careers and helping this edition of our book emerge from our minds and collective experiences. This second edition provided its own host of challenges, given the rapid acceleration in the volume of research being done and information being provided in the field and the emphasis that particular events have had in driving a new wave of development concerning intervention and response protocols. Some of this has been constructive and some has just added noise to the discussion. We are reminded again and again that practical experience in the management of actual assessments and dynamic incidents of violence, especially in uncontrolled environments (e.g., streets, businesses, schools, etc.) is rare for most people who have been contributing to the research side of the discussion and if that continues, then the research, and the discussion of it, will become less valuable over time. We hope that does not occur. We both continue to do the work every day, throughout North America, and continuing into the European Union and the Near and Far East. And we hope that our ongoing focus on practical, real-world strategies for assessment and intervention will benefit those who are doing or want to do the same.

First, I would like to acknowledge my wife, who has worked with me for the last 22 years and has continually provided her encouragement, expertise and direct feedback when needed. Thanks to Steve McIntire, who was there at the beginning of the work and is a brother to continue to grow with — even though we never have enough time to stay caught up. Thanks to various colleagues who have continued to teach, encourage and collaborate along the way — Bill Zimmerman for his friendship and practical advice; Sue Ann Van Dermyden, Esq., who has provided legal consultation and significantly collaborated across a wide range of areas, including training development and delivery, as well as case work; Dr. Glenn Lipson, who has generously provided his support and insight; Dr. Stephen D. Hart, who has always been generous with his time; Dr. P. Randall Kropp; Dr. Mario Scalora, who has not only provided opportunities to participate in new research of interest but also case insight, assessment and management expertise; Mike Prodan, Rachel Solov, Esq., Dr. Brenda Frechette, and myriad others, too numerous to name. Last, but not least, thanks to my co-author,

Dr. Mike Corcoran, for working through this project with me — again — which always ensures a better product, and our editors for their interest, trust, patience and guidance.

James S. Cawood

An acknowledgment is a recognition, and in our first book I tried to acknowledge everyone I could think of, which included the usual nod to my wife, my parents, many of my esteemed colleagues and numerous researchers of this topic as well. My acknowledgment of their value, support and education that enhanced my abilities has not changed and so I must again say I could not have done it without them. But I also want to acknowledge those who are out there doing violence risk assessments who have the courage and understanding to know they do not do this all the time and therefore must at times depend on experts such as the authors. Those in the educational arena, corporate security, human resources, law enforcement and the medical/mental health field — those are the people whom I must also acknowledge for they have consistently given me pause for reflection in almost every case I work on to ensure I have considered all aspects.

Last, I again want to publically acknowledge the tenacity, perseverance and in-depth assessment principles my co-author, Jim Cawood, has brought to the table. I am often asked, "So did you write the chapter on …," as people try to determine which of us has the better ability to research and express the views and facts of this topic. Instead of trying to determine which of us did what and who is therefore the more qualified "expert," as the order of our authorship has changed in this text, it is the order of importance the reader should look to concerning who is the more astute and better capable violence risk assessment expert. For this book, I am along for the ride and I thank Jim, my colleague and long-time friend, for allowing me to participate.

Michael H. Corcoran

Authors

James S. Cawood, CPP, is president of Factor One, a California-based corporation specializing in violence assessment, security consulting and investigations. He has worked in the area of violence assessment and prevention, security analysis and incident resolution for the last 23 years, with a total security career spanning more than 29 years. He has successfully assessed and managed more than 4000 violence-related cases for federal and state government agencies, public and private corporations and other business entities throughout the United States. Mr. Cawood has also provided consultation and training to these same types of organizations on the design and implementation of threat assessment and incident response protocols. This included participation in the development of the POST (Peace Officers Standards and Training) telecourse on workplace violence for California and Arizona law enforcement, as well as participation in the development of a threat assessment protocol by the California District Attorney's Association for use in training judges, district attorneys and others in the California justice system. He also has served as an expert witness in dozens of cases involving questions concerning investigative and security issues, including threat assessment and violence in the workplace.

Mr. Cawood is the current association president of the Association of Threat Assessment Professionals (ATAP). He has served as the president of the Northern California Chapter of the Association of Threat Assessment Professionals; as secretary of the American Society of Industrial Security Foundation Board; and as the chairman of the board of the California Association of Licensed Investigators, where he also has served as chairman of its legislative committee and vice-president for security.

Mr. Cawood is a graduate of the University of California at Berkeley and has served on the faculties of Golden Gate University, in its Security Management degree program; and the University of California, Santa Cruz extension, teaching Threat Management. He is a Certified Protection Professional (CPP), Professional Certified Investigator (PCI), Physical Security Professional (PSP), Certified Security Professional (CSP), Certified Professional Investigator (CPI), Certified Fraud Examiner (CFE), Certified International Investigator (CII), and Diplomate, American Board of Forensic Examiners. He has written articles, book chapters, and co-authored book chapters for various professional publications including *Security*

Management magazine, the *Protection of Assets Manual,* the *Accident Prevention Manual for Business & Industry — Security Management*; *Safety, Health and Asset Protection: Management Essentials, 2nd Edition*; and *The Psychology of Stalking: Clinical and Forensic Perspective.*

Michael H. Corcoran, Ph.D., currently president of Henley-Putnam University, the only online accredited institution to offer bachelor's, master's and doctoral degrees in the areas of Intelligence Management, Counterterrorism Studies and the Management of Personal Protection, and the first ever Doctorate of Strategic Security. He is also the president of The Workthreat Group, LLC, specializing in identifying and handling potentially violent subjects since 1970. He provides violence risk assessments, determinations of the true potential of violence and criminal profiling for government, law enforcement agencies, businesses, school districts and private individuals around the world. In the law enforcement field since 1968, Dr. Corcoran has served in the U.S. Secret Service and as a municipal police officer.

Dr. Corcoran has taught classes on how to recognize, confront and control suicidal and mentally ill substance abusers or combative populations at various colleges, law enforcement academies and Fortune 500 companies across the country. He has established protocols for evaluating and dealing with personnel; either pre- or post-hiring to avoid conflict, assess the potential of violence and to determine truthfulness. He has also assisted in designing, implementing, training and advising hostage or crisis negotiation teams for local law enforcement agencies and private concerns.

One of the original founding members and a national board member of the Association of Threat Assessment Professionals, Dr. Corcoran has helped write policies and procedures and has consulted on these workplace violence issues for the Police Officers Research Association of California, the International Association of Chiefs of Police, the Department of Justice, the American Red Cross and numerous other organizations across the country. He frequently travels across the United States to lecture and conduct training seminars for businesses and school districts on the elements of workplace violence, including identifying and handling the potentially violent subject.

Introduction I

Fusion

1

The Call

Every case begins with a "call." An assessment professional could be notified by phone, radio, e-mail, memo or letter. The people on the other end of such communications may be emotional, factual or in shock. But they have decided you need to know what is going on in a situation involving the potential for ongoing or future violence. Therefore, the first step you must take is to narrow your focus to that particular communication to the exclusion of all other business.

Practically, this will be the most difficult step you need to take. In today's working world, with all its demands and distractions, it is very difficult to focus on one issue. However, in the area of violence assessment, we have found that only by redirecting our attention to that one "notice event" do we begin the process of engaging all of our senses and knowledge for the purpose of violence assessment. Your ability of putting yourself into this mode, of trying to put yourself into the mind of the communicator, will determine your success in the immediate understanding of the situation for proper assessment of the event and decisions concerning the immediate next steps. This is true, not only because violence assessment requires your attempt to place yourself into the world of any communicators, but also because the communicators must immediately feel they have a connection with you. Your undivided attention validates that connection for communicators and allows them to communicate more subtle and intimate clues that might provide essential information for successful management of the situation. It is not critical for you to have the experience and ability of a trained professional to accomplish this connection because just trying to understand is generally perceived by others as more attention than they are used to receiving anyway.

Think of how you have felt when calling colleagues on the phone to talk about something of importance and have heard them clicking away on their computers. Similarly, remember the frustration felt when calling colleagues on their cell phones and having them continually disengage from the conversation to interact with others in their immediate environment. Recall how distracting this was and how negative emotions might have been stimulated even though these communications probably were not life-threatening.

During initial contacts several important elements should be noted. If the notice event is verbal, were communicators direct or indirect witnesses to the notice event and what is their immediate concern? What is their current emotional level of engagement? Are they communicating clearly or in a confused fashion? What is your immediate impression concerning their ability to follow directions? If the communication is written, many of these same impressions will have to be monitored. But your ability to know whether the individual will follow directions will have to be reserved for direct contact.

Each of these pieces of information is important because they provide immediate means to allow you to guide the process. If the individual is not a direct witness to the notice event, you will need to note this immediately and begin to collect the names of others who have been or could have been direct witnesses to the event. If the calling individuals are direct witnesses, they may provide you with valuable information concerning the incident itself as well as the context in which the event occurred.

The significance of whether communicators are direct or indirect witnesses is not just found in understanding the clear context of the act as discussed above, but also in determining whether they can serve as witnesses in any following actions that might involve law enforcement or the courts. Clearly, direct witnesses of actions are going to be of greatest value in an investigatory, disciplinary or prosecutorial situation. There may be times when hearsay testimony (testimony from third parties) may be admissible due to exceptions to the hearsay rule, but that will depend on the location of your jurisdiction and will need to be discussed with legal counsel.

After we determine whether they are direct or indirect witnesses, we consider their apparent level of emotional engagement. This is to determine the accuracy of their accounts. The more emotionally elevated communicators are, the less likely the first report of the events will be accurate. When elevated emotion is combined with second- and third-hand reports or possibly tainted by perceptions of "payback," the more important it will be to quickly seek direct witnesses to obtain more accurate information. Everyone has experienced the phenomenon of telling a story to other people, their passing it on to another and so on, until the final story repeated bears little resemblance to the original tale. This demonstrates the problem of significant distortion of vital information that takes place in the transmission of information. Bad information leads to bad assessments, which lead to bad interventions.

Coupled with this, you must also consider the power that outside sources, such as an organization, may have on an individual reporting this information. Is there a culture that might cause undue pressure one way or another when chronicling potential problem behaviors? Or are there ulterior motives influencing the account?

In monitoring the clarity of the communication, you are assessing whether the individuals communicating with you are doing so on more of a cognitive level as opposed to the emotional. It has long been recognized (Goleman, 1995; Ekman, 2003) in this area that it is virtually impossible to be processing both emotionally and cognitively at the same time. Hence, if it is possible to convince communicators to report the event on the more factual or "thinking" level, the complications of emotional interference will be greatly reduced. Or, if the direct witness can be queried on the factual level, the information obtained will be more reliable for these same reasons.

The consideration as to whether individuals can take direction provides two valuable pieces of information. First, if you can engage them cognitively and they comply, you have the ability to decrease their emotional engagement and thus increase the likelihood of their accurately communicating both with you and others. From a practical perspective, individuals who are incapable of taking directions cannot be effectively utilized to gather additional information or be a part of the initial response that may need to occur. It can be disastrous to give clear direction of what will need to be done immediately upon the receipt of the communication without having ascertained whether the individuals are capable of doing what they need to do. In most of these situations, you are going to be receiving the notification from a source who may be just across town, but possibly is across the country, so it will be necessary to rely — at least in the initial stage of the case — on other people to act for you in accomplishing initial tasks (see Chapter 4, Appendix 4.1, "Witness Interview Form").

Notification

After you have done your initial information gathering, the next question to be answered is who needs to be notified of this situation who doesn't already know. The most obvious question in some cases is whether 911 should be called. This question goes to the heart of the immediacy of the needed response. If the answer is yes, then you should have already gathered the necessary information to provide answers to the questions the emergency operator will ask. Also, you should then have the ability to activate an evacuation plan for those individuals who are at risk for immediate physical harm. This could involve one person or an entire office, building or campus, depending on the circumstances. Even if it is necessary to call 911 and evacuate personnel, it is important to understand that the assessment process is not over. It is being placed on suspension while the more immediate physical risk is addressed. If subjects are diverted, arrested or even killed, the assessment process will still need to continue after those actions have occurred. If the individuals are diverted, the continued assessment will be important considering the if, when and where they might reengage in potentially violent behavior. If arrested, the same questions need to be addressed after they are released. In the case of death, there may still be exposure or risk associated with allies, friends or family members of the individuals, as well as the need for post-incident assessment for the protection of the threatened organization or individuals from a liability perspective.

In the vast majority of cases, when you received the notification, you will determine that a 911 call is not necessary. You will have sufficient time to conduct other information-gathering activities as well as notify other necessary personnel who will usually provide additional skills to the process and may include more senior human resources, security staff, legal counsel, senior management or administration and resources outside the immediate organization. The consideration in terms of priority of notification will need to be established ahead of time as a part of the development of an incident management plan in each organization. In our experience, the priority of notification is made on a case-by-case basis, depending on who has the most direct link to the behavioral or situational information needed as the assessment evolves. Most often, this means the initial notification will be made with human resource and security people, who usually have the most direct access to individuals and information in each organization (see Figure 1.1).

Assessment

After the initial immediate decision has been made as to whether the situation calls for a 911 response, the strategy of assessment becomes the compiling of as much behavioral and situational information as can be found. While actually still in the early stages of the assessment process, gathering necessary information at this point is crucial to a clear understanding of the potentials of violence or danger to others. For example, communicators may initially be anonymous or want to remain anonymous, as they are concerned about potential retaliation by the instigator.

Based upon our collective experience, we have come to the conclusion all violent behavior is caused by the need to establish control. Hence, we can identify three elements and their relationship to one another to understand motivational factors of violence both in the current situation and as projected into future possible situations:

1. The individuals have reached the point where they desperately need to establish control.
2. There is a target or targets for their actions that, when acted against, will provide the individuals that needed sense of control.
3. They believe the environment in which they are acting allows them to commit the act.

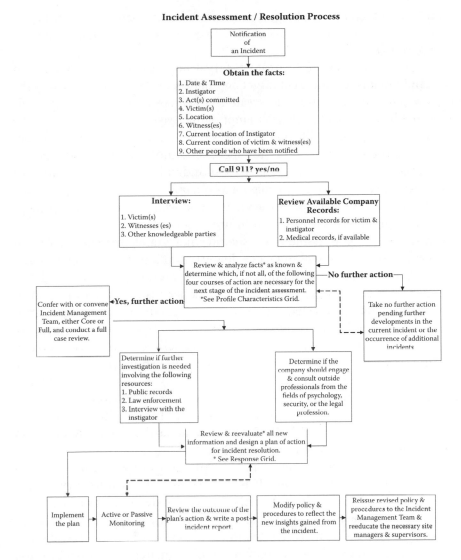

Figure 1.1 Incident flow chart.

By understanding each of these elements, we have the keys of intervening, mitigating or preventing the violent act.

If threat assessment professionals understand the instigators' perception pertaining to the need for control, they can influence this perception directly or indirectly. Direct influence can be delivered through establishing a rapport with instigators if there is the opportunity to contact them personally. If direct contact is not possible, for reasons of logistics or concerns of case consequences, the professional can have an indirect influence over the instigators' situational perception by controlling the actions that are taken around the instigators by family members, law enforcement, legal action and therapeutic intervention. The goal is to alter the instigators' motivation so that they can "discover" nonviolent ways to establish or reestablish their lost sense of control.

By understanding the instigators' target population, professionals can divert individuals to a different target population or remove the access to the target population. The aim is to create the perception that the individuals would not be successful in their attempt by increasing the security to make access to the target more difficult, or altering the activities in the environment to decrease the perceived ability for successful connection with the target. Each of these elements must be understood (individual, target, environment) to successfully understand the behavior as not only done by the perpetrators, but also how it was perceived by the victims and what that intent and perception will mean in terms of potential future actions.

In this stage of assessment, we should understand that every question asked and action taken will influence downstream intervention options and the effectiveness of the intervention. Ultimately, it is not enough just to determine whether the instigator poses an immediate risk of physical harm to those who are being protected. There must be intervention to stop them from taking action, monitoring for any possibility of reengagement and calming of the protectees or their organization so they can believe they are safe and can return to their normal activities. Only by accomplishing each one of these goals can we claim that the process was completely successful. With that in mind, it is important to always tell the truth to everyone involved. However, the truth for any specific individuals may not need to encompass the whole truth of the situation but must be the truth in areas that are related to them (see Chapter 10, "Duty to Warn" section).

An example of this would be individual witnesses who come forward but wish to remain anonymous. It is important to be truthful with these individuals, informing them that, although you understand their desire for anonymity, it is not going to be possible. The best case scenario is to limit the knowledge of the individuals' identity to a small group of people (possibly the incident management team) but they will still ultimately be known by these people. Even then, it will be important to inform the witnesses that they could still be exposed, not by you or your colleagues, but through the perception of the instigators. There have been numerous cases in our experience where the identity of the witnesses has been successfully held in confidence by the incident management team, but the instigators have determined the identity of the witnesses on their own. This honest interaction with each one of the witnesses during the assessment is actually essential to maintaining the trust and compliance of these individuals with the process of assessment, intervention and monitoring. Even though it would appear that educating the witnesses and other parties to the variety of their exposures could scare them and make them less likely to cooperate, our experience has shown exactly the opposite. People do not like being surprised by outcomes. The more transparent professionals can be in educating them to their real exposure, even if it appears to be initially frightening, the more likely they will trust them throughout the entire course of events.

Another example where this is important is when dealing with paranoid thinking. We have learned that the only successful way in dealing with paranoid thinking is to be as open as possible. This can diffuse the natural inclination of individuals who have this outlook, allowing them to be more comfortable participating in both the assessment and resolution of a potentially violent incident. However, if people with this outlook are not treated with openness and honesty, their paranoia will be reinforced and the ensuing mistrust will prevent them from being part of a successful assessment process.

Sources of information for the assessment will be found in individuals who have interacted with the instigator. Records of interaction with individuals (field interviews, police reports, employee evaluations, personnel actions, etc.) who are witnesses to specific incidents and public records (court records, financial records, property records, etc.) are the deepest and most accessible sources of behavioral information. Care should be taken in recognizing that the closer the instigator is to a personal source of information, the greater its potential value, but the higher the risk of exposing the process to the instigator. Also, a close source may provide information skewed by emotions, including ideas of loyalty.

The behavioral information we are seeking involves what an instigator has specifically done, verbally and physically. Specific descriptions of physical behavior and capturing of exact wording can make a tremendous difference in the accuracy of the assessment. There is a significant difference between a person hitting someone in the face with a closed fist versus a slap. There is a significant difference between a person saying, "I *would like* to hurt you" and "I *will* hurt you." Surprisingly, this exact information is often not sought, nor is it appreciated when found. Professionals should constantly strive for that level of exact detail in the information gathering process. We all understand that the best predictor of future behavior is past behavior. Knowing the exact past behavior creates the only true basis for accurate interpretation of the current behavior, thereby allowing for successful projection of future behavioral possibilities.

Security
As the assessment process progresses, the security strategy revolves around addressing both immediate and long-term needs. Security is driven by assessment. This means the immediate security needs of each case are indexed on the initial assessment of the exhibited behavior, but a safety margin is always added to anticipate rapidly escalating events. Given that it takes time to gather and deploy security personnel and equipment, the normal security

strategy at the onset of a problem will be a rapid identification of current available personnel and equipment and their current placement. When this has been accomplished, the security practitioner will supplement the current assets as needed.

An example of this would be a case involving threats of violence against company personnel from an outside individual. The threats are that the individual is going to come to a location and assault the personnel. The current security configuration at this location is a card-activated access control system, a reception area for visitors controlled by a receptionist and two contract security officers roaming the site. This security configuration is not adequate for stopping a determined individual — with or without a weapon — from entering the building and assaulting staff members. Consequently, the security practitioner will need to augment this configuration as quickly as possible. Since notifying building employees to maintain access control procedures alone will not be effective, the only viable short-term strategy is to supplement the on-site security personnel with others trained to manage emotionally destabilized people who might possibly have weapons. These personnel could come from the contract guard service, from other security companies that have a relationship with the company or from local law enforcement agencies that allow use of their personnel. We suggest that, in this example, a minimum of two trained persons should be added, so they could act as a response team should the individual come to the site. The choice could be made to place them in the reception area, as that is the most likely place for an outside individual to attempt entrance to the facility. The issue of how these personnel, the receptionist and the current contract security personnel will identify the instigator will need to be quickly addressed. If the name of the instigator is known and the level of threat is sufficient, a photo of the instigator might be made available by local law enforcement. However, if the instigator is not known, the behavior of all visitors would have to be monitored in an attempt to identify subjects and respond to them as appropriate for their level of behavior. Confrontation is rarely effective with highly motivated people. Calm, attentive, responsive interaction is the most effective way to manage the widest range of destabilized people.

Due to the cost of this limited short-term solution, the long-term security strategy could revolve around strengthening of the controls in the reception area (e.g., creating an enclosed reception area, modifying sign-in and identification procedures and training reception personnel to better manage and respond to destabilized visitors). The timeline for implementation of this long-term strategy would be determined by the level of continuing risk, available resources and the commitment of the company to implementing these changes.

One concept needs to be remembered during this time. All security strategies must address the potential for a dynamic incident of violence. This means that static security systems (e.g., locks, alarms, closed-circuit television

(CCTV) and access procedures) will never by themselves be adequate to address violent behavior. The 101 California St. case in San Francisco and the Columbine High School case are dramatic examples of the failure of static security systems. In both of these incidents, the instigators circumvented or passed through established static security procedures and initiated their acts of violence. In both cases, the instigators killed themselves long before law enforcement was positioned to control the situation. Consequently, security planning needs to address the actual physical barriers needed to stop committed, violent, armed offenders. This process requires new thinking that addresses actual attack behavior and does not assume compliance.

Legal

During the initial assessment process, legal counsel plays a vital role in monitoring issues of privacy, confidentiality and organizational and individual communications, and providing advice concerning the various legal and liability exposures that the organization and individuals face. This monitoring process provides a level of legal privilege, assistance in managing employment issues, the drafting of legal documents such as cease-and-desist letters and restraining orders, and including communications with local government agencies, community organizations and instigators.

In our experience, though we have worked with competent corporate attorneys, we have found our most successful collaborations have been with employment or family-law attorneys, either available within the community organization or contracted by the organization. Employment or family law is often involved with potentially violent situations, either directly, because instigators or victims are in a relationship or are employees of the organization, or indirectly, because the actions of the organization may impact the employment of many of the parties involved. Also, these counsels often have experience in dealing with emotional individuals and can bring a level of sensitivity to the legal oversight of the process that is extremely beneficial to the success of the overall process.

The time required for the development of legal documents (i.e., restraining orders, cease-and-desist letters, etc.) or utilization of confidential resources in the beginning stages of assessment strategies may require time to develop and implement. Therefore, the need for rapid engagement of legal counsel is similar to the engagement of security. Hence, the importance of prior identification of currently available legal personnel and their willingness to be a part of this total process cannot be overemphasized.

Interventions and Monitoring

Once the initial information gathering, assessment, security and legal components have been initiated and a threshold assessment has been completed, consideration of interventions can begin. Before these components are in place, any attempt at intervention has a higher potential for failure, thereby increasing the risk of potential physical harm as well as exposing the assessor and other concerned parties to claims of negligence.

Interventions can include single actions or combinations of actions, direct or indirect, all focused on diverting the instigator from continuing on a trajectory toward violent action. Direct actions could include:

- Instigator interview
- Employer discipline, including termination
- Cease-and-desist letter
- Protective or restraining order
- Law enforcement contact, with or without arrest
- Involuntary commitment in a mental health facility

Indirect actions could include:

- Victim relocation or removal
- Security enhancements
- Interaction with family members, friends or associates
- Countersurveillance

Optimally, the selection of interventions is matched to the instigator's perception and motivators, starting with the least intrusive that will effect a desirable change. The presentation of these interventions is most effective when delivered in a "carrot and stick" format. This means that each direct intervention is explained to the instigator as the preferred option and that avoidance of greater consequences can be achieved through compliance. As an example, in a cease-and-desist letter, a request for compliance can also discuss that this letter is not public information and if the instigator chooses to comply with the request to end contact, no knowledge of this situation will become known to others, including future employers. However, should the instigator choose not to comply and if the victim should seek a restraining or protective order, these actions will be available in the public record and could impact the future options of the instigator. This type of approach maximizes the possibility that instigators will act in their own self-interest, which, ulti-mately, is the strongest motivator for the vast majority of people.

Another example of utilizing an instigator's self-interest would be when an employer is considering the instigator's termination. This situation does not allow for much compliance prior to taking the actions, but during the interview with the instigator, the assessor can "preview" this possibility with him and explore his potential reactions to this event and alternative responses to inappropriate behavior. These alternatives could include legal action against the employer, success at a future job to prove the employer wrong, or as an opportunity to find an employer who is more appreciative of the instigator's talents and abilities. Alternatively or in conjunction with this, an employer could decide to terminate and provide a severance package contingent on appropriate behavior. This money would be paid out over a set period of time, in regular installments, based on continued good behavior. However, this option may not be available due to the type of termination (e.g., termination for cause) or because there is concern that it will establish a legal or behavioral precedent. Paying people off for bad behavior can be counterproductive, in that it might lead them to believe that if they continue to act badly they will make more money. So, choosing any of these options or approaches needs to be done with a view to long-term results and in conjunction with both legal and behavioral analysis.

Once an intervention has been initiated, monitoring its results creates an essential feedback loop for continued assessment. Monitoring is the single most neglected process of violence assessment. The assessor or assessment team must create an active or passive monitoring system to feed ongoing information regarding the behavior of the instigator to the assessment process for analysis. This means identifying the people or organizational elements that the instigator will most likely contact and determining how to learn whether they have been contacted and what the nature of the contact is, as quickly as possible. These contacts are behavioral cues that will let the assessor know whether instigators are complying with the boundaries established by the intervention or are escalating their behavior in a harmful direction.

Active monitoring means that the assessor or members of the assessment team actively seek this information from the identified people or organizations on an established schedule (e.g., twice a day, once a day, once a week, etc.). This type of monitoring is used when the assessor believes that the situation is currently of moderate or high risk or the parties acting as "sensor points" for the process will not initiate a notification of behavior on their own.

Passive monitoring means waiting for the sensor parties to contact the assessor, because it is believed that the situation will most likely not escalate quickly enough to require the time and expense of active monitoring.

The reason this monitoring process is neglected is that it can be required for months or years. Participants get distracted or fatigued or a new person is assigned to the caseload and inadequately briefed or loses track. The result is that the case is no longer monitored. This loss of monitoring leads to missing behavioral cues that, in retrospect, could have alerted victims to the fact that the instigator was building up to an inappropriate act. Certainly anyone with even a reasonable caseload understands the difficulty of maintaining contact with any individual case. Computers can be very helpful in this area by using personal information managers (PIMs) to help manage case monitoring. Microsoft Outlook, GoldMine, Act and other PIMs have alarm functions that can remind assessors, assessment team members and victims of critical dates, regular monitoring calls and other events that could easily be missed.

Summary

We have covered the essential elements of an assessment and intervention process that can be efficiently used by practitioners responsible for determinations of potential risk for physical violence. This process includes intake, notification, assessment, security, legal, intervention and monitoring elements. The rest of this book will further develop each of these elements and provide practical, usable, defensible methodology for successful violence assessment.

Assessment

Information Gathering

2

Introduction

Information is the central axis of all violence risk assessment, and behavioral information is the most important information of all because "actions speak louder than words." The depth and accuracy of the behavioral information that is obtained are directly correlated to the quality and accuracy of the assessment. In every assessment, a dynamic balance of time, resources and intervention must be reached and maintained for optimum safety. This means that the information-gathering process will be done under varying degrees of pressure, usually intense.

While the push in a situation involving the possibility of violence will be to "act" as quickly as possible, information gathering does not appear to be acting. However, nothing could be farther from the truth. In violence risk assessment, we try not to set events in motion that we cannot significantly control — like the medical profession, first we try to do no harm. A rush to action from limited information increases the likelihood of making some type of operational or tactical mistake. The information in this chapter will help speed the information-gathering process, while also increasing the quantity and quality of the information gathered.

Information can be gathered from three general categories: people, records and forensic evidence. For the purposes of this chapter, the focus will be on gathering information from people and records, the sources most often used in violence risk assessment.

Once the information has been gathered, it must be organized and analyzed for the purposes of assessment. In terms of organizing data collection, we have found that some forms and question outlines can be very helpful. Therefore, in Appendix 2.2, we have included forms A through E, which will help keep track of incident management team (IMT) contact information, incident flow, and victim, witness and instigator information. We have also included a witness interview form in Appendix 4.1. In regard to analysis of information, we have found the use of meta-chronologies, or several different chronologies woven together, to be the best method of organizing information for assessment. It not only provides for a natural format for behavior-related data, but this type of organization more easily enables cause-and-effect analysis, which is also helpful. We will discuss this in the "Information Organization" section later in this chapter.

During the information-gathering process, it should never be forgotten that, prior to seeking information from any source, we should consider how the process of gathering information from that source might change the violence dynamic. That means weighing each source of information for value on a risk or reward scale and determining what adverse consequences might arise from approaching and interacting with that source of information and whether the information we might obtain justifies the risk. If the initial assessment is that the benefit does not outweigh the risk, we do not approach that source. If the assessment is that the information is of sufficient importance, then the next step is to plan the approach and the information-gathering process to minimize the possible adverse consequences and maximize the quality and quantity of the information that we receive. In other words, develop a well-crafted information-gathering strategy prior to approaching the source. Any time spent on planning usually returns a premium over the initial investment, either in time saved from not having to return to the source(s) or in managing events that can arise out of a poorly planned interaction.

An example of this information-gathering strategy can come up in cases involving domestic violence or violence in the workplace. In a domestic violence scenario, a current boyfriend or husband may threaten a woman. Information gathering from public records reveals that this individual has a prior girlfriend who has filed a restraining order or other case against the instigator. The question arises whether approaching this prior victim would be of value in a violence risk assessment. Certainly, depending on the type of information that is already on file, we may wish to contact her, as she might be a rich source of information concerning past behavior (e.g., past use of violence, family relationships, medical conditions, criminal history, mental health, weapons use, substance use, etc.). However, what are the risks in making such a contact? Might the former love interest warn the instigator out of love, fear or revenge? Would the information be reliable or tainted? If the instigator were to learn of the contact, how would he react? Would it escalate or deescalate his behavior? Toward whom? Would he believe that we were "hunting" him and would that justify in his mind an escalated response against the current love interest or organization the violence assessor is trying to help? All of these questions should be considered prior to deciding whether to approach. A similar situation arises concerning the behavior of employees in the workplace; should we contact their former employer? A similar process of consideration should be followed before action is taken.

In general, records research, with the exception of records that require notification of the subject, such as when obtaining permission to run credit reports, is the safest form of initial information gathering that can be done. Once the process involves talking to people, each person becomes a possible source of process exposure and elevated risk.

Interview Structure

Violence assessors must develop an interviewing style that is compatible with their individual strengths and weaknesses. However, in addition, each assessor should incorporate new methodology that might maximize their effectiveness. After more than 20 years in the field, we were introduced to an interviewing methodology called Enhanced Cognitive Interviewing (ECI),[1] which incorporates several elements of our normal interviewing process while adding some valuable tools. ECI is a semistructured interviewing process that makes use of the knowledge obtained from hundreds of human cognition and interviewing studies. It is meant to allow investigators to interview victims and witnesses in a way that increases the quality of the information that these sources provide, while decreasing the need for follow-up interviews and the likelihood that inaccurate information is being given to the interviewer. The ECI process is broken into seven stages:

1. Greeting the witness and personalizing the interview; establishing rapport
2. Explaining the aims of the interview
3. Initiating a free report
4. Direct questioning
5. Varied and extensive retrieval (if necessary)
6. Summary
7. Closure

We would encourage all readers of this book to learn more about ECI for the benefit of their work, but even if you choose not to use ECI, it is important to learn how people encode information into their memories and how interviewers can enhance their ability to retrieve that information without tainting it. Some important points we picked up follow.

The neurophysiological ability to retrieve information from memory is reduced when people feel anxiety. So anything we can do to reduce anxiety by enhancing rapport will increase the quality and quantity of information from a neurophysiological perspective. This includes greeting people by name, telling them who you are and why you are talking with them and, at the beginning of the interview, investing time in letting them talk about the things most important to them.[2]

Avoid creating a question-and-answer dynamic with victims or witnesses before they have been able to tell their whole story from beginning to end, because interrupting the narrative significantly reduces the amount of information that is learned. That means not asking for personal or contact information from them at the beginning of the interview, or interrupting the interview each time you have a question about what they said at that moment. Instead, let them provide an uninterrupted free narrative of their information, then use their own words to go back and explore what they meant. As an example, if victims said, "Then he hurt me," make a note of that and, when they are finished relating the narrative, you have a list of questions from what they had said to return to and clarify before continuing with other questions. The question for the above statement might be phrased like, "When you mentioned what happened in the kitchen that night you said, 'He hurt me.' What does that mean?" This gives people a chance to clarify using their own words, including correcting their statement, if necessary, without creating a question-and-answer dynamic. You learn what "hurt" means to them (e.g., stinging slap, punch, kick, teeth knocked out, etc.) without coloring the testimony. If such victims were then to say, "He hit me," a follow-up might be, "Tell me about that," rather than "Did he punch you, kick you, slap you or what?" See more on this in the next section.

Be careful about how you phrase a question to make certain you don't skew the answer, such as the difference between saying, "Did you see the blue car?" and "Did you see any vehicles?" The first question raises several barriers to the witnesses' information because they may not have seen any vehicles, or seen a truck, or seen a green car, but the investigator is "saying" by his question that there was a blue car, so the witness may say no and decide not to say anything else or he may say yes to please the investigator or to get the interview over more quickly. Regardless of the reason for the answer, valuable information was lost that the second question has a higher probability of revealing.

Studies have shown that police investigators who used the ECI format spent more time during each individual interview, but spent less time overall on the investigation because of the enhanced quality of the information obtained during the interview process and the reduced need to follow up with the interview subjects.

Interview Sources

Your interview sources can be grouped into subcategories of victims, witnesses, collateral informants and instigators. In our assessments, the two most important sources of information are the victims and the instigators. Witnesses and collateral informants are essential for providing information to corroborate or enhance information provided by the victims or instigators, but the direct information provided by victims and instigators concerning their individual dynamics and perceptions of each other provides the richest source of information that can be used for projection of future behavior and, therefore, intervention planning.

Victim Interview

It takes a victim and an instigator to create a violence dynamic, and that dynamic is what we need to understand before we can successfully intervene. The victim is usually the first person to be interviewed, which has some distinct advantages. Interviewing the victim first offers an opportunity to not only learn about the chronology of the violence process, but also to begin the process of building a relationship that will allow monitoring of the situation in the future and tracking of any boundary probing or escalation. If a relationship cannot be successfully built with the victim, opportunities for continued intelligence are diminished, which will lead to decreased opportunities to alter intervention strategy and successfully deescalate the violence in any given situation. This would force an increase in surveillance of the victims' activities (e.g., monitoring voicemails, e-mails, visits to them at work and home, etc.) to maintain the same level of intelligence and strengthen the possibility of knowing of any inappropriate attempt to approach or contact the victims, which adds an additional burden to resource use (e.g., time, telephone, transportation, etc.). Thus, successfully building a relationship with victims increases the likelihood of success for the process, while decreasing the use of limited resources necessary to succeed.

Some readers may now be thinking that they do not have a responsibility to work to gain the victims' trust. The thinking is that this is the victims' problem and, if they do not choose to cooperate, then they, the victims, have the most to lose. This is only partially true. These thoughts are particularly comforting in situations where resources are limited and caseload is abundant; however, this is not a justifiable position, merely an attempt to make the assessor feel more comfortable. If you are responsible for these victims and they get hurt, you pay a price emotionally, psychologically and, possibly, in your career. If you are doing this work and trying to do it well, you know that victims have their own perspectives and their own motivations. You know that they may be reluctant to tell you the truth and follow your advice. They are going to do what they *believe* is best to protect their safety, even if they are wrong and their choices elevate the possibility that harm will come to themselves and others. However, in most cases, you will still be held responsible if harm comes to them. It is the nature of the work. Consequently, it is in the best interest of both victims and violence assessors that a relationship be established that enhances communication and the likelihood that the victims will follow your advice to increase the probability of a safe outcome for both. For the violence assessor, it might be considered enlightened self-interest.

Following the ECI style of interviewing, we normally introduce ourselves in a very quick way and then turn control of the interview over to the victims. It might go something like this: "Hello (name of victim), my name is Jim and I am a consultant to human resources on sensitive personnel issues. I have been asked to help understand this situation and provide advice about how to resolve it safely for everyone. Why don't you tell me what you think I need to know?" No matter where they go from here, I am learning about:

- How they think
- How emotional they are
- Whether they seem to be telling the truth
- Whether I believe they are experiencing any cognitive distortion
- What they are sensitive about
- How they process the world (the order of importance in seeing, hearing, tactile or kinesthetic input)
- What their preferred mode of expression is (e.g., emotional [feeling] or logical [thinking])
- What their body language is (for use in mirroring), do they exhibit any tells (e.g., involuntary body movements that can be tied to particular actions, including attempts at diversion or deception)
- What their rhythm and tone of speaking are (so I can begin to mirror it to enhance rapport)

In addition to learning this information, the interviewer is giving the victim a sense of control, something most victims have lost or have begun to lose as their fear increases. This reinforcement of their sense of control can help reduce their anxiety, thereby decreasing their emotional level, which increases their cognitive functioning and their ability to remember what has happened and in what sequence. High emotion is known to decrease cognitive processing.[3]

After the victims have had an opportunity to divulge, in their own way, all the information they think the interviewer should know, the interviewer then goes back and asks them clarifying questions concerning what they have related. The questions should be as general as possible and care should be taken not to, by tone or action, imply any doubt in the information provided. An example of this might be that during their dialogue, they stated, "Then he hurt me." If they are interrupted at that time and asked a clarifying question, the interviewer is taking control of the interview and breaking the rhythm of their account. This would not only disrupt their developing sense of control, but it would disrupt the interviewer's ability to let them show how they link ideas and concepts. The interviewer should wait until they are completely finished with their account and then, referring to the notes made during the recital of events, would ask a question using their exact words, such as, "You mentioned he hurt you?" indicating by question and tone of voice that they should provide more information. If they just say "yes," the interviewer would then say, "Tell me about that." What we should be getting from victims are the exact actions and words of the instigators (behavioral information) in response to what was said or done by the victims, to the best of the victims' capability to tell us. What, exactly, instigators said or did, in what sequence, in response to what stimulus, provides us the richest possible understanding of that moment in time. Hitting people with an open or closed fist, hitting them once or repeatedly, hitting them while they are down on the floor, walking away at some point or continuing to hit them until exhausted — all such details provide important information to the assessment process concerning that particular incident, how they might relate to prior incidents and what might happen in future incidents.

Once interviewers have clarified all the questions they had from the victims' account, they will then progress to questions that have not been touched on. These questions cover a range of behaviors that have been linked to violence by scientific study[4] and the experiences of violence assessors to the present time. These questions will include:

- The instigators' and victims' relationship history, if any
- The instigators' and victims' criminal history, if any
- Their respective past histories of violence, if any, including their history of violence together, with other partners, family members or in the community, if any
- Their use of alcohol and drugs (both prescription and nonprescription)
- Their interest in, training with and use of weapons
- Medical history, including mental health, diagnosis and treatment and any history of head trauma
- Employment histories, both instigators' and victims'
- Future possibilities of contact: when, where and why

After interviewers have completed this portion of the interview and have clarified, once again in the victim's own words, any questions they might have had, it is time to move on to the next step of the interview process. If interviewers still lacked certain detail in important areas, they might use a change-of-perspective technique (e.g., reverse chronology process, activation of other senses [smell, touch, hearing], etc.) in a particular part of the narrative to stimulate different parts of the brain to reveal other memories. If there are no unanswered questions, they would move into a summary phase, where interviewers would tell victims that they wanted to make certain that they understood what they had been told, so it would provide a complete account of what the victims had told them, starting at the beginning of their chronological knowledge of the events and the instigators through to the present moment. Before interviewers begin the summary, they should encourage victims to concentrate and to interrupt at any time if the summation did not state what they wanted to communicate. It is very important to tell them that it is common for them to remember new things and that they need to correct any mistakes because it could affect the accuracy of the assessment and, therefore, their safety. If victims are not given permission to add new information or correct the interviewers' account, they most likely will be reluctant to do so, because they might believe it will appear that they had not been initially truthful with the interviewers.

After the summary narrative is completed and the corrections made, wrap up with any formal written or verbal statement from the victims, assuming that one is desired.

Finally, close the process with them by capturing any future contact information and any personal information that would allow the interviewer to complete his report or file. Return interviewees to a neutral emotional state by answering any questions they have on how the process will proceed, encouraging them to contact the interviewer with any information they think of in the future, telling the interviewer of future contacts with the instigator and asking permission to contact them in the future if there are any further questions. If they say they do not want any contact in the future, then the interviewer has failed in a significant way to establish and nurture rapport.

Taking Notes

Finally, let us address the idea of note taking. All assessors will have their own style, but our preferred style is taking "burst notes." These are phrases of exact language captured in quotes, if possible, in a time-delayed manner — that is, written with no correlation to their speaking. This leaves the interviewer with pages of quotes, in a chronological order that reflects the flow of the interview, but does not allow interviewees to learn, by watching the timing of the writing, what the interviewer finds to be important enough to capture or not. Some interviewees will talk very quickly and, if interviewers hurry to write down what they said, they may slow down and wait until the writers catch up. Therefore, burst-note taking helps us recall the flow of the interview and capture critical information in the subject's own words, while minimizing the possibility that the act of note taking will influence the interviewee in a way that negatively impacts the process. Interview mechanics should be managed so that they do not overshadow content.

This also raises the question of whether interviewers should ask permission to take notes. When video- or audiotaping an interview, legal requirements generally obligate interviewers to notify the subject that the interview is being recorded and, in most (noncriminal) cases, to seek their permission to tape the interview. However, note taking is another matter, and there is no need to request permission. Some professionals believe that asking permission to take notes gives interviewees a needed sense of control and therefore helps establish rapport. But what do you do if they say no? You either have to convince them to change their mind, which can devalue their sense of control, or you must have an extraordinary memory for detail or risk a confrontation by explaining that you need to take notes anyway and your question was only a social courtesy. This is an example of a general theme in our assessment process; if at all possible, we do not want to allow ourselves to initiate a process we cannot control. Lawyers are taught never to ask a question of a witness that they do not already know the answer to. This type of situation is congruent to that advice. Notes are a vital part of capturing all the details obtained during an interview and having those details available in the future for possible use in a variety of venues in which extemporaneous notes are an important evidentiary item. Notes are also going to protect interviewers from allowing new case facts to mutate the information provided by any individual witness, allowing for comparing and contrasting accounts given by various parties. Finally, our notes are the basis for defending our actions in the future, by showing an appropriately diligent investigative style of practice that can be relied upon for accurate information. Memory alone, particularly across a normal caseload, is not adequately defensible.

Taking notes can make interviewees uncomfortable, so keeping the note pad tilted up in your lap so they cannot see the notes being taken diminishes their awareness of the process. In addition, during very sensitive narratives, or when it appears that they are reluctant to say something, interviewers can suspend note taking so interviewees know the interviewer is paying attention to them and not just writing it down. This suspension of process usually encourages them to continue. Also, if some interviewees ask you to stop taking notes during certain parts of the narrative, a good reply is, "I understand. I will stop for now." Notice that we did not say, "Okay, I will not take notes on this," or "Okay, I will stop taking notes." Either of these answers could imply that we would *never* write down what they are about to tell us and could, therefore, raise questions in the future that could taint the process. Interviewers can just draw a box on their note pad and go back later to fill in what was said during that part of the interview, returning to normal note taking after it is believed we have passed through the sensitive part. In this way, you preserve the rapport during the interview, but do not sacrifice the accuracy of the information in your notes or allow the interview process to be compromised.

The Witness Interview

Witness interviews should be handled in the same general manner as victim interviews; however, the interviewer can usually be a little more directive. During a witness interview, interviewers could use a similar opening to the victim interview, but, instead of saying, "Why don't you tell me what you think I should know?" they might say, "Why don't you tell me about the X incident?" meaning the incident interviewees have witnessed. The interviewer still allows them a free narrative and follows up for clarification in their own words, but could be a little less flexible with allowing them to stray outside the boundaries of the incident they have allegedly witnessed.

It is important to remember that witnesses are not as invested in the situation, in most cases, as either the victims or instigators and, therefore, we have less actual control over what they do with the information from the interview, including the information provided by the types of questions asked. Therefore, unless individual witnesses have a long-time connection with victims or instigators, the interviewer should be very careful not to explore anything other than what interviewees have experienced directly. In those cases where the witnesses do have such an association, after the incidents of interest are explored, they could talk about their knowledge of the parties involved, but only after weighing whether their information would be so valuable as to outweigh the risk of having it given to the victim or instigator, who might possibly take actions that would be detrimental to the informants' safety.

Rarely, if ever, would we provide witnesses with information about what the rest of the assessment process will be, though we would give them the ability to contact us in the future and would encourage them to do so if they think of anything else they believe is related to what we have discussed.

Collateral Interviews

These are interviews of individuals who can provide us additional information on specific occurrences or facts for the purpose of clarification or corroboration. In a violence risk assessment, these individuals can be law enforcement personnel, doctors, lawyers, former romantic partners, educational institutions or instructors, former or current employers or their representatives, neighbors, friends, former or current opposing parties in litigation, etc. As with witness interviews, with these parties you always weigh risk and reward before approaching them and asking any questions at all, due to the possible risks of exposing your interest at an inappropriate time. In some cases, if we believe that the information is important but are concerned about alerting instigators to the process, we will delay the contact until after we have talked to instigators or have ascertained whether they know the process is in progress. Delay in contacting collateral witnesses can increase the risk that certain information can be destroyed and certain individuals are warned not to talk with you. However, with the exception of past romantic partners and friends, most instigators will not be able to control the actions of all the other possible sources of collateral information, assuming they could even anticipate the range of people you may attempt to contact.

During collateral interviews, in general, we usually just ask a series of questions meant to confirm or deny information that we already have in our possession. If, during the interview, we sense any hesitancy on the part of interviewees to release certain information, or if they seem to have other information that they want to share with us, that should be addressed in a manner that will encourage them to interact with us. In the case of reluctance to share information, finding out if the reasons are legal or personal and then attempting to help evaluate the first and explore the latter can, in many cases, relieve their concerns and allow them to provide information. If they have other information they would like to provide, encourage them to do so by saying something like, "If, at any time, you think of something that we should know or you believe is connected, we would be interested in hearing it." Then we explore what we learn as needed.

Rarely in these interviews, with the exception of doctors, lawyers and clergymen, do we start by explaining why we are calling them or explaining in any detail who we are. Most parties who are approached, often over the telephone, with a warm tone and a direct manner that communicates that the information you're requesting is appropriate for you, the interviewer, to know, will just tell you what you want to know. This means that, with collateral informants, interviewers share only information about what they are doing when it is necessary to do so and only to the extent that it is believed a benefit to their work versus the risk of process exposure. If, during an interview, the risks of the interview begin to outweigh the benefits of the information, be prepared to end the interaction in an appropriate manner and move on.

Doctors, lawyers and clergymen have guidelines that must be met for the release of information under their control, so a more thorough explanation is usually required. Even if they agree to talk, they may have to delay the conversation until they have reviewed the files in question. Doctors might not be able to tell you anything at all without a release, but you can provide them with information. Because violence risk assessment is a safety issue and most doctors are interested in the safety of their patients and others, you might try asking whether a doctor would be willing to discuss a "hypothetical" situation. This relieves the doctor of an obligation to act on certain information and also opens the way to bounce certain information off them for consideration and comment. An example of this conversation might be,

"Doctor, I am a violence assessor representing X and I am calling in regard to a series of behaviors involving Y, who I understand you have treated. I realize your constraints to talking with me without a release, however, due to the very serious concerns I have involving the safety of others, I thought it might be valuable to contact you." Pause to see if the doctor will jump in and give you some idea how you could proceed, while meeting his obligations. "Could I tell you a series of behaviors that I have learned about and could you tell me whether this information surprises you?

"In a hypothetical case involving these behaviors and an individual similar to your client, would this situation rise to the level of a Tarasoff[5] warning for you? In this hypothetical case, might there be other factors that you would need to consider as a part of your analysis, which might not be obvious to the untrained person?"

It is important in these conversations to be very sensitive to nuance and innuendo, as these may be the only things that doctors, if they are willing, are able to provide to steer you to an understanding of what they know. We are not relying on doctors to provide a diagnosis and, like any interaction with doctors, we should not trust their impressions or information without personal knowledge of their training, experience and judgment. What we are doing is attempting to obtain information about instigators' past behavior and treatment, including any psychotropic medications. Also, we are placing doctors on notice that we have a concern about a patient and they might wish to reevaluate their diagnosis on the basis of the new information we have provided. In one case, this "reevaluation" led the doctor to call the patient, set up an appointment for that afternoon and then transport the patient to a locked mental health facility for treatment. This was best for the patient and best for the potential victims.

Similar approaches, interaction models and lines of questioning can be developed for each type of collateral witness, so that anticipated objections or concerns can be smoothly addressed and the opportunity for information flow maximized.

The Instigator Interview

This interview is generally the most important information source of all. Who better to tell you how they are thinking and feeling, what they are planning to do, how they are planning to do it and when, than the instigators themselves? A number of experienced violence assessors believe that direct interview of instigators should be done rarely, or not at all, because, either it elevates the emotional energy in a case and the risk is not worth the reward, or these people are just going to lie to you and revealing your interest in them just increases the danger to the possible victim. Others, including one co-author of this book, believe that, based on their extensive experience, they can conduct these interviews over the phone and, to their credit, they have successfully done telephone interviews in hundreds of cases and no one has been hurt.

Those practitioners who believe in the personal interview start with the assumption that the value of the information provided by these people, both verbally and physically, is the richest and best possible source of information available. They also want to interview subjects personally because, from a process credibility and, therefore, a liability-avoidance perspective, the fact that someone interviewed instigators, especially in a workplace violence risk assessment where an employee is involved, helps show that the process did not just rely on records or the observations of others, but allowed the people to communicate their side of the story directly to assessors so they could provide an objective assessment of future violence risk, based on all knowable information.

Regarding interviewing instigators, one should always be concerned that the process of interviewing may stir up emotions and lead to impulsive or predatory acts. If the best-trained people to identify and deescalate these possibilities (a professional assessor) are taking the risk of setting these events in motion by conducting the phone interview, but are not on site with the client (or potential victims) to help manage a safe outcome if trouble arises, they may be doing their client a disservice. We recognize that physical violence in most settings, and particularly in a workplace, is a not a common event, but violence assessors have come into existence because societies would like to lower their incidence even further by understanding and preventing some of these violent events. Therefore, using a process that allows for maximum control of the instigator, physically, psychologically and emotionally, seems to be the most valuable course of action to achieve physical safety and some protection from ongoing liability. In most assessment cases, that would seem to support a face-to-face interview with instigators.

After starting from the position that we want to physically interview the instigator, we weigh the disadvantages in any given case to decide whether, on balance, in this particular case, the value of the possible information gained directly from the instigator and our ability to use that contact to help control the situation is outweighed by other factors. In cases where physical violence has not yet occurred, points to consider are:

- *Is there physical access to the instigator that will not increase risk to my client?* The concern here is that surprising the instigator by our involvement can create a new target focus, with no benefit to the assessment. In a case of potential workplace violence, where instigators are members of the client's workforce, access to them is easy and the interest in them is generally understood. However, if the individuals have already been fired, are spouses of employees or are customers, clients or vendors, then further situational assessment must take place. If the behavior that has raised concern and initiated the assessment process has been directed at the business or organization the assessor represents, there is reason to contact instigators directly to "understand" their perspective. Access can be easily accomplished in a variety of locations that can be mutually agreed upon, including the organization's offices, the instigator's home (a "knock and talk") or some other location.[6] However, if instigators have threatened individuals at the business, such as spouses, friends or acquaintances, and we are hearing about the behavior from spouses, co-workers or others (e.g., a Tarasoff warning, etc.) and the organization is not directly involved, we must decide whether having the organization, through its violence assessor, step in and reveal that an interest in the instigators is a good idea. Maybe it would be better to initiate action through other parties, such as the spouse or law enforcement, rather than reveal the interest of the organization and create an additional target fixation that was not there before, increasing the risk to heretofore unexposed parties.

- *Are there legal issues that would overshadow our contact with instigators?* In some cases, concerns about claims of harassment, invasion of privacy, discrimination and other claims or torts might overshadow the value of talking to the instigator. As the level of perceived violence risk escalates up the scale, these considerations usually begin to recede, because, on balance, it is "better to be tried by 12 than be carried by six" (sued with a 12-person jury versus carried by six pallbearers).

- *Is the behavior demonstrated by instigators at this point of the assessment at such a low level of concern that introducing an assessor to instigators would create more disturbance than value to the process?* In these situations, it may be better to have a correctly selected and trained company representative contact instigators with a prepared script to gather additional factual and behavioral information. After assessing the information provided by that contact, it might be determined that contact by an assessor is now appropriate, or it could be delayed until additional behavior shows an escalation that warrants an assessor's contacting the instigator directly.

If physical violence has already occurred, the issue of whether to expose the client's interest in instigators is still relevant, but some other issues also become important.

- *Are the acts of the instigator so violent that their examination is all that is necessary to complete the assessment, because the intervention required by the acts already should be using all available resources?*

One of the main purposes of assessment is to understand the risk of future violent behavior so that appropriate allocation of limited resources is made. In some cases, the assessor is introduced to the case when repeated, high-intensity, physically violent acts have already occurred. These may involve murder, rape, torture, extensive battery, etc. If these acts have already occurred, an analysis of the acts themselves can help identify whether the assessor's protectees are a target population for the violence, assuming they have not already been attacked. If they are a target population, or have already been a victim of high-intensity violence, assessment is no longer strictly necessary — response is. Once instigators are in custody, assessment may play another role for the purpose of bail or provisional release, but using all available resources to get them into custody should be the focus, not whether to interview them.

- *If the people are in custody, is interviewing them going to provide a quality of information that is more important than revealing that the client is still thinking about them?* Remember, we are discussing situations in which there is an option to interview instigators. In court-ordered and incarceration-related assessments this is not an issue, since direct interview is mandated but in other cases it is not. In one case, a subject had been sentenced to federal prison for threatening to kill federal officers. He had also made prior threats to kill my client's employees, and now was being released. We were asked to conduct a violence risk assessment to determine risk to the employees upon his release. However, when we were approached to conduct the assessment, we were told that two of the client's employees had already contacted the prison and requested permission to talk to the subject. We counseled against this action because of our concern that the value of the interview (the employees were a psychiatrist and psychologist who had treated the subject and wanted to assess his current level of risk) was going to be outweighed by the problems in letting the subject know that these individuals were still thinking of him, which might make him feel more powerful. The good news was he refused to see them (prisoners in the United States have the right to refuse to talk to anyone, including law enforcement); the bad news was that it did elevate his interest in the client's employees he had threatened. He had his lawyer claim that they were trying to continue to harass him by seeking contact with him, probably enjoying that he still was a part of their consciousness and that he could "tweak" them.

Personal factors also need to be admitted by assessors and openly addressed as a part of the process. If assessors just do not like to travel, or are afraid to directly interview an instigator, then those issues need to be

personally acknowledged and openly be a part of the decision-making process concerning direct interviews during the assessment. It is a disservice
to the client to have these issues be the main reasons that assessors suggest
a particular course of action, rather than reasons that have the best interest
of the client in mind. In either case, the engagement of another assessor who
does not have these concerns, to review the case and consult on this part of
the assessment recommendation, might be the best solution to work through
these issues, both from the client's perspective and considering the liability of
the assessor. As my valued colleague, Dr. Stephen G. White of Work Trauma
Services, has often said, "When in doubt, confer."

In terms of the format of the instigator interview, it is unlike the victim
and witness interviews. The plan for this interview must acknowledge that
the assessor may get only one opportunity to interview instigators, for a
variety of reasons including legal representation, unwillingness of instigators to subject themselves to this type of interview in the future and the reality that instigators are learning a great deal in this interview about what the
assessor is interested in and, even if they agree to a future interview, their
information may be less reliable due to possible conscious manipulation.
Consequently, the planning for this interview must be very well developed
prior to starting it. We suggest constructing a general outline based on what
the victims and witnesses have told the assessor and adding in the general
areas of information that the assessor knows are of interest for violence
risk assessment investigations. In general, the more serious the behavior
that has led to the interview, the quicker the interview plan moves into the
first behavioral incident. This is based on the idea that the more serious the
behavior, the more likely that interviewees know why the assessor is there
talking to them; and, therefore, the more direct the assessor appears to be
in approaching them about the topic, the more likely they will perceive the
assessor as being straightforward and honest. This perception increases the
likelihood of their engaging in a manner that provides the assessor with
some authentic response to the questions and the process. Therefore, after a
fairly quick introduction phase and a short rapport-building phase, which
really is a short anxiety reduction phase where the assessor might ask them
to give a short history of themselves or their job, the assessor might say
something like:

> "Bob, thank you for providing me with that brief history so that I have some
> background to work with. As I said at the beginning, I am interested in under-
> standing what has been going on and I believe that being direct is the best way
> to move forward in situations like this. In that spirit, last Monday, you and
> your wife had a pretty emotional disagreement. Can you tell me what that was
> about?"

"When she said that to you, what do you remember doing?"
"How did you feel when you did that?"
"What happened then?"

After the assessor has gotten through that particular incident, having instigators provide their version and then directly exploring all the behavior that the assessor has learned from the interview with the victims and the witnesses that might have been involved, you then move on to the next incident, doing the same thing until all the incidents are covered. When that part of the interview has been completed, you will use different segments of the accounts to loop into other areas that you are interested in. This might be done like:

"Bob, when you were talking about the time last May when you hit Denise, you mentioned that was the first time you had hit her with your fist. What other ways have you hit Denise? Have you ever shown her a weapon? What type of weapons do you own? When you bought your last handgun, why did you buy that one?"

Eventually, if the interview runs its full course, it will cover all the areas of interest for assessment, including medical history, psychological history, weapons ownership and use, history of violence and criminality, family relationships, past significant relationships, employment history, use of drugs and alcohol, perception of the victim, co-workers and other significant individuals and plans for future activities and what would activate those plans. We have done hundreds of interviews with instigators and, so far, we have only had one subject who would not speak to us. Most of these individuals, particularly those who have exhibited the most serious behavior, seem to want to tell their stories and have someone understand what they are going through. In some cases, it is the first time they have had someone ask them why they did certain things, rather than just telling them what would happen to them if they did that again. The role of the assessor is not to judge, but to understand how instigators plan, make decisions and act the way they do. This provides the information necessary to begin to project future behavior, given certain possible future events.

Private Records

Information concerning victims, witnesses and instigators may be available in certain private records that can be legally accessed for different cases, depending on both your relationship to the case and the legal powers you have available for use. The most likely source of obtainable private records will be employment records, particularly when you are working for the victims' or instigators' employer. A variety of employment records might be of interest, including:

- Applications for employment
- Records of disciplinary actions
- Periodic employment evaluations
- Records of any investigations involving the victim, witnesses or instigator
- Benefits records that list the use of various benefits, if allowed by company policy, regulation or law
- Incident reports that did not result in an investigation
- Records of any legal actions involving the parties, including wage garnishments, subpoenas for records, notification of other legal actions

The information of interest in these records is any behavioral data that can be synthesized. That would include the lies on their applications; their responses to requests for performance improvement or behavioral change; any claims of harassment, stress or discrimination; their interaction style during previous investigations; handling of privileges or new responsibilities, etc. All cause-and-effect–based information can be helpful in building a picture of how the person is internally structured, which can aid in prognostication of their future behavior.

Public Records

All the following sources of information are available in the United States and in some areas of the world, depending on the quality of the repository's records and how they handle privacy issues. In any given case, at any given location, obtaining all the records legally available will strengthen the assessment and protect the assessor from claims of negligence. Because the time to instigator action, if action is ever going to occur at all, is never known at the outset of an assessment, speed of information gathering is always a paramount consideration. All the sources listed below can be accessed by hand search (versus computer search) and 80% or more of the results can normally be researched in 72 hours of available archive time, if the assessor has established a process and resources to start the work in that jurisdiction. In our work, we access records throughout the United States and Canada in this time frame, but there can be further delays for records accessed in the European Union and other foreign countries. We have the records hand searched at the county and local levels because of the significant drop-off rate between the number of available automated records and available records at the county and local levels. The U.S. Department of Justice stated that, in 1999, 40 states reported that more than 75% of their criminal history records were automated, compared with only 26 states in 1992.[7] This is a wonderful improvement, but this would mean that relying on an automated records search by law enforcement systems, if they are available to your case, could mean a failure to locate available prior criminal history information 20% or more of the time. We have learned that private data services have failure rates about equal to this. When you look at individual states, the results can be even more problematic. Kansas reported in 1999 that only 46% of their criminal records were automated and North Dakota reported only 37%.[8] This difference between what is available by computer search and what might be available at the local level has caused us to standardize to hand searches of all records, both criminal and civil. My company is not comfortable with the prospect of attempting to defend our assessment without a hand search, knowing that any information that is located could change the outcome of the assessment and, therefore, the decision to change intervention strategy to prevent violence. This particular issue associated with information gathering strategy is something all assessors have to address as they establish their procedures.

Care will have to be taken in any employment-related cases in how to gather this information without crossing over certain guidelines for the U.S. Fair Credit Reporting Act, or similar state consumer information laws. See Chapter 10 for more information.

Internet Information

- Personal Web sites
- Social networking sites (e.g., MySpace, Facebook, etc.)
- Usenet
- Message boards
- Chat rooms

Running name searches in these areas of the Internet can reap rewards concerning the attitudes and activities of any search target. Normally, I would use an escalating search structure, starting with a fast search engine like Google. com or AlltheWeb.com, and then move to a metasearch engine like Dogpile. com and finally, possibly use a proprietary metasearch engine like Intelliseek's Bullseye, which was designed not only to search intelligently, but also to help process the information that it finds for easy management by the searcher. Each search engine has its own way of searching and various strengths and weaknesses for certain types of data, so time should be spent learning about the strengths and weaknesses for various search engines so that the assessor can select the ones most useful in locating the type of information that is reflected in the majority of their case load. Also, time invested in learning how to conduct effective Internet searches and compiling results will be time well spent when faced with a case that requires a quick response.

Department of Motor Vehicles

- Driver's license information — photo and history
- Automated name index (ANI) — vehicle description and registration

This information can lead an assessor to other areas of the country or state when a driver's license record shows vehicle violations or accidents in other jurisdictions. It can provide information on behaviors of interest such as substance abuse (e.g., drunk or impaired driving), behavioral attributes (e.g., reckless driving, speeding, hit-and-run, etc.) and more serious crimes such as vehicular manslaughter and vehicular homicide. It can also provide information concerning how the people in question handle their social contract concerning the privilege of driving. If the subjects have several Failures to Appear (FTAs) on their license, which are usually issued with a warrant for arrest or with a license suspension when someone has made a promise to appear for court and then does not appear or pay the bail amount, it provides a behavioral indication that they do not care about breaking rules or agreements. This can be important information for case management. We encountered a case in Colorado in which we pulled a traffic citation that had been issued to the instigator and looked at the back of the ticket for the officer's comments.[9] In this case, the officer had written a detailed note that showed the instigator had willfully refused to cooperate during the stop and had become hostile and aggressive for no apparent reason. This provided insight into how the instigator might handle confrontations with other authority figures and our assessment was that it illustrated that obtaining a restraining order in this case would probably not stop the instigator's actions, but would exacerbate them. Based on the entire assessment, the client decided not to pursue a restraining order at that time, but to wait and see what further behavior developed. This is a classic example of not just noting available information in a catalog format, but digging further into that piece of data to uncover any available behavioral information that might be present.

Criminal Court Records

This is an obvious category of interest and *all* behavior in this area is of interest, not just felonies and convictions. Many cases in the criminal justice system are "pled down" to lower charges during plea bargaining. Consequently, many misdemeanors involving violence may have started out as felonies[10] and been pled down. For assessment purposes, convictions for felonies or misdemeanors should not matter; the behavior during the offense is what matters. It is important to pull the records and read the files, including the court transcripts of how the individual testified concerning certain crimes. It is in the specific details of the crime, how it unfolded and how the individual acted during the entire process, including the trial, that we gain the behavioral knowledge that we need.

Civil Court Records

- Prior restraining orders that may have been dropped from a system like California's DVROS (Domestic Violence Restraining Order System) or possibly have been filed and never served
- Current restraining orders
- Divorce records, including alleged conduct during the marriage
- Financial cases
- Other torts involving violence, harassment, etc.

Many times assessors check the criminal records, but not the civil records. This could be because they are unfamiliar with how to research civil records or they do not know the value of the records. Either way, a large source of potential information is untapped if these records are not utilized. Particularly of interest are those records that show behavior and stressors, such as management of financial obligations, proceedings in divorce or child custody matters, prior restraining orders and the behavior that led to them and claims brought by them or against them of harassment or discrimination. All of this information should be located and incorporated into a complete assessment package.

Federal Court Records

- Bankruptcy — what they owned, who they owed and how much
- Civil
- Criminal

Often assessors neglect to check for federal cases and information. Some 20 or 30 years ago, this source of information may have been perceived as having a limited value to assessors because federal prosecution priorities did not generally encourage the management of case types that assessors would find of value. However, in the 1990s, the priorities began to change and a significant number of cases are now being prosecuted involving weapons, drugs, interstate stalking and other crimes that will have value for the assessment. Consequently, these records should now be checked to make certain that relevant material is not missed for evaluation.

County Recorder's Office

- Debts, including those from other jurisdictions
- Property records
- DD214 records — discharge papers from military service can show military training and type of separation
- Birth, death and marriage records

Records available at this office, sometimes called the County Clerk's office, primarily deal with debts, liens and judgments. This information is valuable for providing an insight into financial pressures, including debts that have been incurred in other counties that the assessor did not know to check, that have been registered in the instigator's county of residence for the purpose of collection. Also, DD214 documents may be registered with the county, though it is not required. If military information is desired, see below for more information. Obviously, birth, death and marriage records may be relevant to complete an understanding of the instigator's past relationships and family history.

Miscellaneous Records

- Local premises' history of calls for service to the residence(s)
- Military records

Checking law enforcement records for calls to the current and past residence(s) of the instigator can provide some valuable information that would not otherwise be available. In most jurisdictions in the United States and in many overseas, every time a law enforcement officer is dispatched on a call, a record is made of the call and the address. Many individual calls per day result in activity that does not require a report, because law enforcement officers, already overwhelmed with paperwork, will often attempt to manage as many calls as they can without having to produce a report. This means that the only record of their response to a particular address may be in the "run" log or history of calls for service. By requesting access to reports for the several years prior to the departure of the instigator from that address, valuable information can be learned. This works especially well when the instigator lived in single-family residences or in locations where each unit had its own street address. Apartment complexes and public housing complexes are the least productive for this type of search because many calls for service are cleared without designating which units of these complexes were contacted. In numerous cases, we have located records of contacts between law enforcement and instigators that would not have been located any other way.

We have then followed up with contact officers and learned their impression of the instigator and behavioral information from their interaction that has proven valuable.

Military information can be acquired by several routes. If the instigator is currently serving in the military and there is a base nearby, the Provost Marshal's Office or equivalent may be a quick and useful source to contact for information concerning the instigator. If the instigator is not currently serving, information can be requested through a Freedom of Information Act (FOIA) request. This normally is done by using a "Request Pertaining to Military Records" form (Standard form 180, prescribed by NARA [36 CFR 1228 162(a)]). This one-page form, with instructions on the back, is sent to one of 14 repositories of records of the five branches of the U.S. military (Air Force, Coast Guard, Marine Corps, Army and Navy) depending on certain criteria. Starting in late 1998 and increasing after September 11, 2001, information received from these types of requests has been significantly reduced. However, in several dozen cases that my company has handled, data from military records, particularly training, stationing and court martials, have proven to be very significant to an assessment. Before you submit the form, it will be necessary to know which branch of service the subject served in and the general time frame. Prior to the early 1970s, the service number of a military person was uniquely assigned; however, the Social Security Number (SSN) has become the service number since that time, so including the SSN and the instigator's date of birth (DOB) will increase the ability to get information. This type of request can take months to return results, but, given the cost (e.g., the price of a postage stamp) and the fact that some cases have long monitoring periods after initial assessment and intervention, these types of requests can be extremely beneficial. Obviously, if you have more-immediate access to these records, based on employment or other assessment personnel who are involved, it will be better for you.

Restricted Records (United States)

- National Crime Information Center (NCIC)
- Federal Bureau of Prisons
- State crime information indexes (e.g., CII in California, etc.)
- State restraining order systems (e.g., DVROS in California, etc.)
- Federal and state weapons registration
- County mental health services
- Child Protective Services (CPS) — listed by child's name (Welfare and Institutions Code Section 827 sets forth method by which prosecutors, school officials, parents of the named minors, court personnel and select others may review juvenile case files for W&I 300, 601

602 case files and others. This list includes, under W&I 827(a)(1)(K), "any other person who may be designated by court order of the judge of the juvenile court upon filing a petition." Juvenile case files are defined under W&I Code Section 827(e)).

- Law Enforcement Automated Data System (LEADS) or equivalent — All California Department of Corrections (CDC) information: tattoos, street moniker, current pictures, release photos, family and gang affiliations
- Department of Corrections records as needed
- Reports of correctional institution rules violations — negative behavior by prison inmates, results of inmate disciplinary hearings — stored in inmate's central or "C-file" (e.g., "115s" in California, etc.)
- Parole violation reports, State Board of Prison terms reports, activity reports (continued on parole, perhaps with outside agency referral); stored by parole region for central files — field files are at the local parole unit's office — special parole conditions noted here
- Intelligence
- Gang validation
- Local jail records
- Local criminal history in jurisdictions of residence (local files not uploaded to state level)
- Similar records to 115s for CDC exist at virtually every correctional facility (look for "inmate behavior" write-ups)
- Probation reports (probation field files list prior behaviors, current contacts, special conditions of probation and more)
- Local law enforcement intelligence, including drugs, gangs, etc.

The number of restricted information sources is almost endless and keeps changing as old resources are consolidated and new ones are created. These sources are available for access only by federal, state, county or local law enforcement personnel who are actively working a case that meets their department's criteria for access to these records. An assessor with access to these records needs to track the information that becomes available about the instigator and then choose which resources are best for providing detail in those areas. In almost every assessment, NCIC, state criminal index records, a check for prior restraining or protective orders and a weapons registration check are going to be warranted. Should any jail, prison or involuntary mental health commitments show up, then further checking should be pursued in those areas to the fullest extent possible. In the area of mental health, assessors may not be allowed to access a treatment record, but they may be able to identify the instigator's doctor(s) and talk with them concerning their information and seeing whether that elicits a Tarasoff-type[11] warning from the doctor.

The goal of the assessor is to gather as much information as possible, as fast as possible, because more information maximizes the possibility of a valid, defensible assessment that allows for a more accurate intervention strategy, possibly saving lives and limited resources.

Information Organization

As the information is being gathered from all the sources listed above, the assessor needs to have a means to organize it so that the data can be related to themselves and other sets of data for comparison, which enhances behavioral pattern development and recognition. In other words, the data can be transformed into knowledge.

A form of data organization we have found to be the best for violence risk assessment is a metachronology, which is made up of three different types of chronologies woven together:

1. A chronology of each incident internal to itself
2. A chronology of the entire relationship between the victim and instigator
3. A chronology of the whole life of the instigator

The first step is to create these three types of chronologies using the information collected and organizing it by date of occurrence. Then each chronology is reviewed for the behavioral information that can be learned by looking for any stimulus and resultant behavior (cause and effect) during the period covered by that chronology. After that knowledge is captured and all the chronologies are combined, a metachronology is created that weaves together all available data in past events and makes note of the cause-and-effect behavioral knowledge. Any new knowledge of other stimulus and resultant behavior that had not been identified within the individual chronologies (e.g., behavior by the instigator in the community that seemed to trigger or follow behavior in the relationship between the instigator and victim(s), etc.) is of special interest, because it provides insight into other variables that need to be considered during the projection of future behavior and the development of the intervention.

After all of these patterns have been identified and captured, the result can then be used to hypothesize about the possible ranges of the instigator's future behavior given certain variables and interventions. As others have said, this works because, in human behavior, the best predictor of future behavior is past behavior.[12]

In terms of projection of behavior and interventions, we have found some simple and effective ways to proceed. After reviewing the past behavior of the instigator, we factor in what an incremental extension of the current behavior might be if conditions remain the same. This becomes a low range of possible behavior. We have to anticipate that human beings, if they choose to act, are not going to remain satisfied with a prior level of behavior; they tend to want to exceed prior behavior because it provides more stimulation, including a sense of increased mastery and control over the circumstances. Consequently, if the instigator has threatened to hurt the victim on several occasions and the behavior in the threats is becoming more detailed (e.g., "I am going to smack you" becomes "I am going to punch you right in the eye so it swells shut"), then the low end of the range of behavior becomes a physical blow. If the intervention and security strategy is capable of managing a physical blow, then it can manage another verbal threat. To get a sense of the upper end of the range, we take a look at our experience and the experience of others in similar cases and project what a "quantum leap" in the behavior curve might look like, given a confluence of all the current case "stressors" escalating at the same time. This gives us our upper end of the range. Then we factor in how fast the case has escalated to this point; I call this *case velocity* and make an estimate of the range of the speed at which we believe events will unfold. The low-end range of velocity is set as a value slightly ahead of the current pace. An example is an instigator who has threatened his wife periodically over the last 2 years with increasing specificity and frequency over the last 2 weeks. He is about to lose his job and he thinks she will leave him. Low end on velocity is an act of physical violence within 2 to 3 months; high end is in the next week, prior to the actual loss of his job. Given this example, the intervention would best occur prior to his job loss, with a security plan to manage his reaction to his wife for a minimum of 72 hours after the time of the intervention.[13] The security plan should be centered on limiting the instigator's ability to have physical proximity to the victim without a third party present and to have a safety plan to aid the victim in removing herself from his area of activity in the case of significant escalation. The suggested intervention itself, given these limited case facts, could center around family members or friends who are respected by the instigator, suggesting that they approach the instigator with a scripted conversation to see if he is aware of what is going on and whether he has a reasonable plan for managing the impending crisis. In a worsening case, it might be discovered that the instigator has developed the justification for escalation of his violence, but not for working through the possible job loss. This might lead to a more direct intervention involving professionals to provide alternatives to the use of violence and known consequences if pursued (e.g., carrot-and-stick).

Projection of future behavior, followed by the development and implementation of interventions, is the art of violence risk assessment and intervention. It is learned by working with other talented people and dealing with many caseloads. But the art cannot be practiced without a foundation in all the previous behavioral information that can be gathered about instigators, their victim(s) and an organization of that behavior into a form that can provide knowledge by showing a rich, four-dimensional (length, width, height and time) picture of the behavior in a cause-and-effect rendering.

Summary

Behavioral information is the soul of violence risk assessment. The more behavioral information that is learned about the instigator, victim and situational dynamics, the more accurate the assessment. More accurate assessment allows for more precise and timely intervention. Better intervention provides greater safety to the victim. Therefore, more productive interviews, increased information from records and better analysis of gathered information provide the assessor a richer database and context for use in assessing current levels of risk, projecting the trajectory and velocity of future behavior and providing guidance for any intervention.

Endnotes

1. This process is defined in more detail in *Investigative Interviewing: Psychology and Practice*, by Rebecca Milne and Ray Bull, John Wiley & Sons, New York, 1999, ISBN 0-471-98728-X.
2. I was a part of a panel that put together an assessment process outline for the California District Attorney's Association, as part of a threat management video project. See Appendix 2.1 for a copy of this outline.
3. For more on the neurophysiology of this emotion and cognitive interaction, see *Emotional Intelligence: Why It Can Matter More Than IQ*, by Daniel Goleman, Bantam Books, New York, 1995, ISBN:0-553-37506-7. It is a wonderful book for providing an introduction to the scientific literature available on this interaction.
4. See Chapters 4 and 5, in which assessment instruments are discussed and their literature is explored.
5. See Chapter 7 for an explanation of Tarasoff.
6. Obviously, the issue of security for the assessor, as well as possible third-party liability in case of a violent event occurring during the interview, will have to be addressed before this type of interview can take place. See Chapter 9 for further detail on these issues.
7. *Use and Management of Criminal History Record Information: A Comprehensive Report, 2001 Update*, U.S. Department of Justice, Office of Justice Programs, Bureau of Justice Statistics, NCJ 187670.
8. *Ibid.*, Appendix 11, Table 2, page 142.
9. Police officers often write comments about the traffic stop on the back of the ticket to remind themselves of particular events in case of court action. This is especially critical for traffic officers who may write dozens of tickets a day and may not get to court on any given ticket for 30 or more days.

10. The difference between misdemeanor and felony is the difference in penalty defined by the legislative body that enacted the law. Generally, any crime with a penalty of 1 year in county jail or less is a misdemeanor and those with a penalty of more than 1 year in county jail or time in prison are felonies. Crimes that have both a lower and higher penalty depending on certain case facts are called "wobblers."

11. Check Chapter 10 for more information on this.

12. I have no idea what the origin of this phrase or underlying concept is. My research on this statement has led me backward in time to the late 1960s, and most articles quote the concept as a generally accepted principle. Who first made this statement or under what circumstances is unknown to me, and, it seems, to many others as well.

13. We have been taught that the highest probability of a physically violent event for an affectively violent person is the 24–72 hours preceding and following a significant event (e.g., anticipating a court hearing, going to prison or jail, etc. or after a court hearing, disciplinary meeting or job termination). The next statistical window of significant probability is 14 days after a significant event. After that, re-engagement or "probing" behavior most likely will occur (calls, letters, e-mails, physical approaches with attempted confrontations, etc.), as the subject has to reescalate emotionally prior to committing a physical act of violence.

APPENDIX 2.1

The Threat Assessment Process:
An Outline

This outline was developed by the advisory group to the production of the CDAA video *Threat Assessment and Management: A New Way of Thinking*. Special thanks go to Jim Cawood, CPP, who served as a core advisor to the project. Mr. Cawood is currently president of the Northern California chapter of the Association of Threat Assessment Professionals.

The process of threat assessment is driven by information concerning the behaviors of the involved individuals. In general, the more information provided to the assessment process, the higher the quality (accuracy) of the assessment. This, in turn, provides the best use of intervention strategies to promote safety and correctly allocate and spend public resources of professional time, equipment and facilities. Finding the balance between information gathering, available resources and assessment time will be a constant challenge, but, in this type of process, small amounts of additional information can pay large dividends to the safety of the victims and the community. These dividends continue to accrue as new interactions with the instigator occur and additional agencies may become involved.

The long-term goal of this project is to provide a standard framework and understanding of the threat assessment process. This framework includes the gathering of information so that agencies can build on the work of others as cases pass from, or expand into, other jurisdictions. This will allow for increased safety and shared cost savings. The following information should not be considered an exhaustive insight into the process, but should provide enough information to allow for a competent, basic understanding of the process and resources that can be considered for use and intervention possibilities.

I. Preliminary act: Victim or other person comes forward to report
II. The initial information gathering process
   A. Victim(s) interview: consider policy guidelines — e.g., releases in a victim advocate interview, methods of information recording (audio, video), etc. Consider interview dynamics — objectivity, tone and question style affect how the subject will answer your questions. Elements to assess concerning the interviewee: credibility (e.g., reporting party could be instigator), mental health (e.g., stability, etc.), emotional health (e.g., ability to follow through on process, need for support, etc.)
      a. First explore the victims' initial priorities
         – Incident(s)
           (1) What are their concerns?
           (2) Where do they start the narrative?
         – Safety
           (1) What are their concerns for level of violence?
           (2) Who do they believe will be targets? Under what circumstances?
         – Current resources available
           (1) Who?
              (i) Family
              (ii) Friends
              (iii) Co-workers
              (iv) Community resources (cultural, religious, other)
           (2) What?
              (i) Money
              (ii) Transportation
              (iii) Time
      b. Develop detailed incident histories
         – Current victim or current instigator (suspect/aggressor)
           (1) Intimidation
           (2) Threats
           (3) Assaults
           (4) Batteries

　　　　　(5) Injuries
　　　　　(6) Cultural issues
　　　　– Current victim or other attacker(s)
　　　　– Current instigator (suspect) or other victims
　　　　　(1) Others
　　　　　(2) Self
　　　　　(3) Animals
　　c. Weapons (both victim and current instigator)
　　　　– Knowledge
　　　　– Training
　　　　– Possession or access
　　　　– Appropriate use
　　　　– Inappropriate use
　　d. Substance use or abuse and behavior associated (both victim
　　　　and current instigator)
　　　　– Alcohol
　　　　– Cocaine
　　　　– Methamphetamine
　　　　– Narcotics
　　e. Mental health (both victim and current instigator)
　　　　– Use of counseling
　　　　– Diagnosis
　　　　– Treatment
　　　　– Medication
　　　　– Any adverse experiences
　　f. Current employment status (both victim and current
　　　　instigator)
　　　　– Current employer
　　　　– Length of employment
　　　　– Location
　　　　– Employee benefits that may be available
　　g. Hobbies or interests (both victim and current instigator)
　　h. Stability issues (factors that could help stabilize or destabilize
　　　　the situation)
　　　　– Employment status
　　　　– Financial situation
　　　　– Family or relationship issues
　　　　– Children
　　　　– Cultural issues
　　　　– Current or recent losses
　　i. Future interactions
　　　　– Pending
　　　　– Anticipated

    j. Resource referral
- Shelter
- Counseling
- Legal services (legal issues)
- Local law enforcement
- Employment resources
    - (1) Human Resources (HR) or Employment Relations (ER)
    - (2) Employee assistance programs (EAP)
    - (3) Corporate security
- Community or cultural resources
- Schools

B. Further information development — both victim and instigator (aggressor or suspect)
    a. Automated information histories
- NCIC
- CII
- Local criminal history or local report history
- Local premises' history or calls for service to the residence(s)
- DMV
    - (1) California driver's license (CDL) — photo and history
    - (2) Automated Name Index (ANI) — vehicle description and registration •
- Restraining Order System (DVROS)
- Weapons registration
- County mental health services use
- Child Protective Services (CPS) — listed by child's name (Welfare and Institutions Code Section 827 sets forth method by which prosecutors, school officials, parents of the named minors, court personnel and select others may review juvenile case files for Welfare and Institutions Code Sections 300, 601 and 602 cases. Under Welfare and Institutions Code Section 827(a)(1)(K), this list includes "any other person who may be designated by court order of the judge of the juvenile court upon filing a petition." Juvenile case files are defined in Welfare & Institutions Code Section 827(e).)
- Law Enforcement Automated Data System (LEADS): All California Department of Corrections information — tattoos, street moniker, current pictures, release photos, family and gang affiliations

b. Other histories
  - Criminal court records
  - Civil court records
    (1) Prior restraining orders that may be from
        California's Domestic Violence Restraining Order
        System (DVROS) or filed and never served
    (2) Divorce records, including alleged conduct during
        the marriage
    (3) Financial cases
    (4) Other torts involving violence, harassment, etc.
  - Federal court records
    (1) Bankruptcy — what they owned, who they owed
        and how much
    (2) Civil
    (3) Criminal
  - County Recorder's Office
    (1) Debts, including those from other jurisdictions
    (2) Property records
    (3) DD214 records — separation documents from mili-
        tary service can show military training and type of
        separation
  - Military records — as needed
    (1) Prior records can be obtained under the Freedom of
        Information Act
    (2) Current records can be obtained by contacting the
        local provost marshal
  - California Department of Corrections records — as needed
    (1) 115s — reports of institutional rules violations —
        negative behavior by prison inmates, results of
        inmate disciplinary hearings — stored in inmate's
        central or "C-file"
    (2) Parole violation reports, Board of Prison Terms
        reports, activity report (continued on parole, per-
        haps with outside agency referral) stored by parole
        region for central files. Field files are at the local
        parole unit's office. Special parole conditions would
        be noted here.
    (3) Intelligence
    (4) Gang validation
  - Local jail records
    (1) Similar records to 115s for CDC exist at virtually
        every correctional facility. Look for "inmate behav-
        ior" write-ups.

(2) Probation reports and probation field files list prior behaviors, current contacts, special conditions of probation and more.

(3) Intelligence

(4) Gang affiliation

- Internet information

(1) Personal web sites

(2) Usenet

(3) Message boards

(4) Chat rooms

c. Collateral interviews

- Other victims of instigator
- Other witnesses
- Family members, if appropriate

III. Information analysis

A. Chronology development: In this process of listing data by date of occurrence, first by creating the chronologies listed below and then combining all the chronologies together, you are weaving together all available information looking for any patterns of stimulus and resultant behavior (cause and effect) in past events. From these identified patterns, a hypothesis of future behaviors can be developed and tested using chosen interventions and interactions that will further refine the working hypothesis of the instigator's behavior. Remember, "the best predictor of future behavior is past behavior."

a. A chronology of each incident internal to itself

b. A chronology of the entire relationship between the victim and instigator

c. A chronology of the whole life of the instigator

d. Weave all three chronologies together to assist in projecting potential behavior in the future based on cause and effect from the past.

B. Use of assessment tools: Using assessment tools checks the information gathering process for thoroughness and provides objective analysis of risk. These tools are used at the end of the process because they have value only if the information gathering and early analysis have been done. If used too early in the process, the results could be skewed and mislead individuals to the level of risk. The tools that might be considered for use are listed below:

a. SARA — Spousal Assault Risk Assessment Guide (Kropp, Hart et al.)

b. HCR-20 ver. 2 (Webster, Douglas, Eaves, Hart)

    c. PCL-R/SV — Psychopathy Check List, Revised or Short Version (Hare, Hart)

    d. MOSAIC (de Becker et al.)

    e. Assessment and response grids (White and Cawood)

IV. Intervention: All of the items listed below are potential courses of action; none is mandatory. Their use should be based on a case-by-case analysis of what will increase safety. Before any of these interventions are started, victim notification of the "threshold assessment" (current assessment of risk given all the known information) and the starting date and time of the direct intervention process are important considerations. This information will allow the victims to understand what is currently known and provide them the opportunity to take whatever steps they feel are appropriate to help safeguard their safety as the process continues. In certain settings, this notification would fall under the "duty to warn" expectations of certain statutes and case law. The first two items (e.g., Instigator Interview and "Knock and Talk") provide the opportunity to clearly establish boundaries of acceptable conduct. If conducted by law enforcement personnel, these interviews should be tape recorded or videotaped.

  A. Instigator interview

  B. "Knock and talk" by law enforcement or other trained personnel (interview of the subject in a natural environment, e.g., home, office, etc., rather than a law enforcement location)

  C. Letter from legal counsel

  D. Protective or restraining orders

  E. Arrest

  F. 5150 Health and Safety Commitments ("danger to self and/or others")

  G. Target (victim[s])relocation or removal

  H. Security enhancements for victim(s)

    a. Security hardware

    b. Training (e.g., situational awareness, self-defense training, behavior modification, etc.)

  I. Administrative remedies (e.g., suspension, termination, etc.)

  J. Federal level issues

    a. Interstate restraining orders

    b. Weapons tracing

    c. Weapons charges

    d. Immigration and Naturalization Service (e.g., detention, deportation, etc.)

Thanks to the following development team that made this project possible: Nancy Bassett, Greg Boles, Kimberly Briggs, James Cawood, Judy Cornick,

Scott Gordon, Kate Killeen, Patricia Lenzi, Greg Peters, Phil Reedy, Jane Shade, Carole Taverna, Kristina Thompson, Kerry Wells, Steve Weston, Jim Wright and David Wysuph.

APPENDIX 2.2

Threats and Violent Incident Resource List (Form A)

Legal Representative:

Name: _____

Phone: _____ Home Phone: _____

Direct Extension: _____ Pager: _____ Fax: _____

Address: _____

Alternative Contact Person: _____

Phone: _____ Home Phone: _____

Direct Extension: _____ Pager: _____ Fax: _____

Address: _____

Human Resources Representative:

Name: _____

Phone: _____ Home Phone: _____

Direct Extension: _____ Pager: _____ Fax: _____

Address: _____

Alternative Contact Person: _____

Phone: _____ Home Phone: _____

Direct Extension: _____ Pager: _____ Fax: _____

Address: _____

Site Security Representative:

Name: _____

Phone: _____ Home Phone: _____

Direct Extension: _____ Pager: _____ Fax: _____

Address: _____

Alternative Contact Person: _____

Phone: _____ Home Phone: _____

Direct Extension: _____ Pager: _____ Fax: _____

Address: _____

Corporate Security Representative:

Name: _____

Phone: _____ Home Phone: _____

Direct Extension: _____ Pager: _____ Fax: _____

Address: _____

Alternative Contact Person: _____

Phone: _____ Home Phone: _____

Direct Extension: _____ Pager: _____ Fax: _____

Address: _____

Corporate Communications Representative:

Name:_____

Phone: _____ Home Phone: _____

Direct Extension: _____ Pager: _____ Fax: _____

Address: _____

Alternative Contact Person: _____

Phone: _____ Home Phone: _____

Direct Extension: _____ Pager: _____ Fax: _____

Address: _____

Local Law Enforcement Contacts:

Primary

Name:_____

Agency:_____

Phone: _____ Home Phone: _____

Direct Extension: _____ Pager: _____ Fax: _____

Address: _____

Secondary

Name:_____

Agency:_____

Phone: _____ Home Phone: _____
Direct Extension: _____ Pager: _____ Fax: _____
Address: _____

Threat Assessment Professional:

Name: _____
Company: _____
Phone: _____ Home Phone: _____
Direct Extension: _____ Pager: _____ Fax: _____
Address: _____

Alternative Contact Person: _____

Phone: _____ Home Phone: _____
Direct Extension: _____ Pager: _____ Fax: _____
Address: _____

Telephone Company Contact:

Name: _____
Agency: _____
Phone: _____ Home Phone: _____
Direct Extension: _____ Pager: _____ Fax: _____
Address: _____

Alternative Contact Person: _____

Phone: _____ Home Phone: _____
Direct Extension: _____ Pager: _____ Fax: _____
Address: _____

Additional Security/Protection Contacts: (Form A)

Name: _____
Company: _____
Phone: _____ Home Phone: _____
Direct Extension: _____ Pager: _____ Fax: _____
Home Phone: _____
Address: _____
Services: _____

Name: _____
Company: _____

Phone: _____ Home Phone: _____
Direct Extension: _____ Pager: _____ Fax: _____
Home Phone: _____
Address: _____
Services: _____

Name: _____
Company: _____
Phone: _____ Home Phone: _____
Direct Extension: _____ Pager: _____ Fax: _____
Home Phone: _____
Address: _____
Services: _____

Name: _____
Company: _____
Phone: _____ Home Phone: _____
Direct Extension: _____ Pager: _____ Fax: _____
Home Phone: _____
Address: _____
Services: _____

Incident Log (Form B)

Subject (Instigator): _____

Date of Birth: _____ SSN: _____
Date of Hire, if Employee: _____

Victim: _____

Date of Birth: _____ SSN: _____
Date of Hire, if Employee: _____

Witness(es): _____
_____
_____

Brief Description of Incident: (date, time, place, act, etc.)
_____
_____
_____
_____
_____

Police Report: _____

Date Filed: _____ Report Number: _____
Law Enforcement Agency: _____
Address: _____

Copy Attached: _____ yes _____ no

Background Check:

Date Assigned: _____ Date Completed: _____
Assigned to: _____
Department: _____
Phone Number: _____
Results: _____
_____
_____
_____

Report Attached: _____ yes _____ no

Probation/Parole Officer Contact:

Name: _____

Phone: _____

Agency: _____

Date & Time of Initial Contact: _____

Information Obtained: _____

_____

_____

_____

Threat Assessment: (Form B)

Assessor: _____

Phone: _____ Address: _____

Initial Assessment Date: _____

Final Assessment Date: _____

Assessment: _____

_____

_____

Psychological/Psychiatric Assessment:

Evaluator: _____

Phone: _____ Address: _____

Initial Evaluation Date: _____

Final Evaluation Date: _____

Assessment: _____

_____

_____

_____

Restraining Order:

Date Applied for: _____ Date Issued: _____

Date & Location Served: _____

Reaction of Subject: _____

_____

Copy Attached: _____ yes _____ no

Date of Court Hearing: _____

Did Subject Appear in Court for Hearing: _____ yes _____ no

Permanent Order Issued: _____ yes _____ no

Date Order Expires: _____

Date & Location Permanent Order Served: _____

Reaction of Subject: _____

Disposition:

Terminated: _____ yes _____ no. If yes, date: _____
Transferred to: _____
Shift Change to: _____
Retired: _____ yes _____ no. If yes, date: _____
Arrested: _____ yes _____ no. If yes, date: _____
Time:_____ Charge(s): _____
Arresting Agency: _____
Convicted: _____ yes _____ no. If yes, date: _____
Charge(s): _____
Sentence: _____

Other: _____

Victim Information Synopsis (Form C)

Name: _____   **Check One:**

Nicknames: _____   Employee: _____

Work Phone: _____ Ext.: _____   Contractor: _____

Fax:_____ Pager: _____   Visitor: _____

Dept: _____   Other: _____

Employer: _____   _____

Job Title: _____

Physical Location of Work Area: _____

Building:_____ Room: _____

Address: _____

Supervisor: _____

Supervisor's Phone: _____ Ext.: _____

Physical Description: Ht. _____ Wt. _____ M/F Hair _____ Eyes _____

Glasses-Y/N

Distinguishing Characteristics: _____

_____

Photograph Available: _____ yes _____ no

Date of Hire: _____

Date of Birth: _____ SSN: _____

Driver's Lic.: _____

Residence Address: _____

_____

Home Phone: _____

Mobile Phone: _____

Pager: _____

Vehicles: (make, model, year, color)   **License Numbers:**

_____

_____

Family:_____ single _____ married _____ divorced _____ separated

Spouse's Name: _____

Address: _____

Work Phone: _____ Home Phone:_____

Children's Name/Ages: _____

_____

Children's Schools/Addresses:

_____

_____

_____

Witness Information Synopsis (Form D)

Witness #: _____   **Check One:**
Name: _____   Employee: _____
Nicknames: _____   Contractor: _____
Work Phone: _____ Ext.: _____   Visitor: _____
Fax: _____ Pager: _____   Other: _____
Dept.: _____   _____
Employer: _____
Job Title: _____
Physical Location of Work Area: _____
Building: _____ Room: _____
Address: _____
Supervisor: _____
Supervisor's Phone: _____ Ext.: _____
Date of Hire: _____
Date of Birth: _____ SSN: _____
Driver's Lic.: _____
Residence Address: _____
Home Phone: _____
Vehicles: (make, model, year, color)   **License Numbers:**

_____

_____

Witness #: _____   **Check One:**
Name: _____   Employee: _____
Nicknames: _____   Contractor: _____
Work Phone: _____ Ext.: _____   Visitor: _____
Fax: _____ Pager: _____   Other: _____
Dept: _____   _____
Employer: _____
Job Title: _____
Physical Location of Work Area: _____
Building: _____ Room: _____
Address: _____
Supervisor: _____
Supervisor's Phone: _____ Ext.: _____
Date of Hire: _____
Date of Birth: _____ SSN: _____
Driver's Lic.: _____
Residence Address: _____
Home Phone: _____
Vehicles: (make, model, year, color)   **License Numbers:**

_____

_____

Instigator Information Synopsis (Form E)

Name: _____   **Check One:**

Aliases: _____   Employee: _____

_____   Contractor: _____

Work Phone: _____ Ext.: _____   Visitor:_____

Fax: _____ Pager: _____   Other: _____

Dept: _____   _____

Employer: _____

Job Title: _____

Extent of Site Access: _____

Keys Issued: _____

Physical Location of Work Area: _____

Building: _____ Room: _____

Address: _____

Supervisor: _____

Supervisor's Phone: _____ Ext.: _____

Physical Description: Ht. _____ Wt. _____ M/F Hair _____ Eyes _____

Glasses-Y/N

Distinguishing Characteristics: _____

_____

Photograph Available: _____ yes _____ no

Date of Hire: _____

Date of Birth: _____ SSN: _____

Driver's Lic.: _____

Residence Address: _____

_____

Home Phone: _____

Mobile Phone: _____

Pager: _____

Vehicles: (make, model, year, color)   **License Numbers:**

_____

_____

_____

Weapons (known or rumored): _____

_____

_____

Past Activities Related to Violent Behavior:

(past incidents, arrests, convictions, police reports, restraining orders, court
case numbers, etc.)

_____

_____

_____

_____

_____

Family: _____ single _____ married _____ divorced _____ separated

Spouse's Name: _____

Address: _____

Work Phone: _____ Home Phone:_____

Children's Names/Ages: _____

_____

Children's Schools/Addresses:

_____

_____

Parents: _____

Phone/Address:_____

Ex-Spouse's Name: _____

Phone/Address: _____

Children's Names/Ages: _____

Past Employers: Name, Location, Phone, Comments

_____

_____

_____

_____

_____

Work Performance/Evaluations:

_____

_____

_____

_____

Related Medical Evaluations or Conditions:

_____

_____

_____

_____

Financial Condition:

(liens, judgments, delinquent child support, unlawful detainers, bankruptcies, etc.)

_____

_____

_____

_____

Additional Information/Factors Relevant to Subject's Current State of Mind:

_____

_____

_____

_____

_____

The Informative Discussion

3

Introduction

We, the authors, agree and instruct regularly in our individual seminars about collecting data and the type of data necessary to conduct successful violence risk assessments. We refer to or suggest what information will be or should be forthcoming from collateral information, available records, background checks, witnesses, victims and even the subjects of concern. However, we have not yet addressed in depth the real "how" in soliciting or attaining that information when it comes to individuals — how to talk and listen or, in essence, how to have the optimum informative discussion. This chapter is shared in the hopes of illuminating our experiences in our most successful interviews.

Almost everyone has his own style of talking to people and there is no one style that is necessarily more correct than others. There are obvious processes that are better suited to talking to people in order to solicit information and many of those elements are easily discussed. Additionally, we all know individuals who seem capable of getting so much more information out of people than others that we often find ourselves relying more on them to talk to others than ourselves. Furthermore, the location, time, environment and distractions during the conversation process can make all the difference in what is said, heard or shared during the interview process. Last, there is the distinct difference inherent in the interview versus the interrogation process that must be considered. All of these concerns beg the question as to what exactly is the most successful process to obtain necessary information from victims, witnesses and/or the subject of concern in a violence risk assessment case.

Interview versus Interrogation

The first consideration must be how one is going to present oneself and operate within the discussion sphere. Essentially, it must be decided if this is going to be an interview or an interrogation. Additionally, it must be understood that an interview could turn into an interrogation if that is the goal.

The most commonly accepted difference between the two is that an interview is a non-accusatory format in which specific questions can be directed to stimulate or elicit behaviorally oriented responses, while an interrogation involves accusing the individual of some form of involvement in a particular incident or situation. In violence risk assessment interviews, behavioral dynamics seem to dictate that for witnesses and victims, the interview process is more appropriate than an interrogation. Yet there are times when a witness (one who is trying to get someone into trouble, for example) and/or a victim (one who is seeking revenge on another, for example) should be interrogated.

Many individuals in the private sector will use the word "interview" when in fact they are conducting an interrogation. Those in law enforcement and even the military will often mislabel these two as well, simply for the psychological advantage of deception and hope for better compliance — at least initially. However, for this dialog and instructional format, the interview process will be stressed for all discussions with individuals during the violence risk assessment process.

The Interview

One of the primary reasons any discussion involving the assessment process should be conducted in the interview mode is because a fact-gathering process not only allows questions to be asked in a non-accusatory manner, but in general, witnesses, victims and potential perpetrators feel more in control as they do most of the talking. Also significant is the fact that only they have the information we need. There are many concerns with this style of discussion, however, that every good interviewer must be aware of and be looking for. For example, are there personal biases or prejudices on the part of the interviewee? The interviewee could give erroneous or inaccurate information without intentionally doing so. Of course, the interviewee may be giving erroneous or inaccurate information intentionally.

The interviewee may have other inappropriate motivations for revealing information, such as revenge or dislike for the company, law enforcement or whomever the interviewer represents. Omission, evasion and attempts to conceal information, especially when talking to potential perpetrators, are always concerns. Hence, misleading or misdirecting the interviewer must be recognized as a possible tactic by some interviewees.

The key to mitigate most of these issues is what we have been preaching throughout this text — *plan your work and work your plan*. Consider all background information, never make false allegations and create a supportive environment for the interview to take place. Make notes about specific points that are germane to the research. Write specific questions that may be helpful to glean this insight. Although the actual use of these questions will be dependent upon your specific interview process (asking questions face-to-face is often hindered if the interviewee is reading from a "script" and it often alerts the subject of specific "interests"), the psychological impact of comfort and control for the interviewer in developing and actually writing these questions ahead of time can be substantial to the successful outcome of the interview.

The background information about an interviewee allows for one to not only gain some insight as to the type of person the interviewer is going to question, but it allows for the possible ascertaining of common interests. Capitalizing on these interests may allow the interviewer to provide a supportive environment to the interviewee, thus allowing the discussions to flow more easily. Through establishment of enhanced rapport it is also the time to determine the relationship between the interviewee and all the others involved in this matter. By determining such a relationship, natural biases, prejudices and other issues may be exposed, especially knowing this information as the discussion process unfolds. Always remember, the key to a successful violence risk assessment depends on you establishing the relationship dynamics among the victim, the potential perpetrator and the environment; hence, this background information adds critical data to those interconnecting issues. (For more on this, see Chapter 4, "Formula for Assessment.")

Environmental Considerations

The Location

While it is not always possible to find the perfect location for the interview, the location is one of the most critical components to a successful dialog. Ideally, the setting should be private, with a minimal amount of surrounding distractions, so that the main focal point of the meeting is the discussion. Interruptions should be guarded against, thus appropriate arrangements to ensure use of the room for this entire process must be made. The room should be neither cold and uninviting, as interrogation rooms of old, nor cozy and warm, with lots of pictures and knick-knacks that distract from the actual interview. Thus, a typical office space or small conference room often represents the best balance in achieving the right environment. This will also add to the psychological feeling of the interviewee that this is going to be more of a business meeting than a confrontational experience.

Contents of the Location

Next, what should be in or not in this environment? Obviously, enough chairs for all participants. At the very least, there will be the interviewer and the interviewee, and at times, there may be an additional witness or witnesses. It is not unusual for someone in the business setting to request the presence of a "representative." If it is a union shop, allowances should be made for those instances where this is the accepted norm (i.e., Weingarten Rights). Other times the number of people involved can be limited very easily. For example, thought should go to whether there should be two people present who are both potential interviewers, one as the primary interviewer and one as a witness/note-taker.

For one thing, two interviewers does allow for an extra pair of eyes and ears to observe and listen to the interviewee. Second, if the decision is made ahead of time that it would be wiser to make the interview process continual as opposed to stop and start for breaks that happen as a matter of course, then a second interviewer present in the room can contribute to this style of discussion. While primarily reserved when interviewing a potentially hostile or difficult person of interest, consideration should be given for using this technique when there is a suspicion that the witness and/or the victim may have a hidden agenda or may not be completely forthcoming. In any case, the secondary interviewer does not enter into the conversation until indicated to do so by the primary interviewer, lest the tone of the discussion change dramatically from an interview to an interrogation.

It is also important to make sure any potential weapons are removed prior to the interview. While this may seem rather practical, it is surprising the amount of ingenuity people can muster when they perceive they are being threatened and want to lash out at the person with whom they are upset. We have seen pens, letter openers, scissors, and even a "pet rock" (yes, we're dating ourselves here — but it's true) used as effective weapons by individuals in a close office setting. Hence, a little forethought and common sense will go a long way in determining what is safe and not so safe to leave within reach of those involved in this discussion process.

Positioning

Next, a discussion of where to sit is always raised, with many interviewers having their own personal preferences for a variety of reasons. Remember, this is a non-accusatory discussion to solicit as much information as possible; hence the need for as many psychological tools as one can use seems appropriate. While it is practical to have a desk present in order to "hold" necessary papers and other things needed for the interview, the position of the interviewee and the interviewer can make a difference in cooperation and a rapport-building environment.

First, the interviewer should never be standing while the interviewee is sitting. If anyone should be standing, it should be the interviewee. Psychologically this gives him or her a sense of power and control, which leads to less fear and anger. Second, sitting directly across from one another can seem confrontational to many individuals, and if a desk is in-between the two subjects, it is often perceived as a barrier that prevents sufficient rapport building. Hence, it is recommended that the chairs be positioned at a 10 and 2 position, often with just the corner of a table sticking a bit into the free space between the two subjects to afford a place to put things — including a relaxing arm or elbow that adds to the comfort of the individual. Spacing, too, should be considered, as being too close can seem intimidating or invasive.

Last, consideration of the positioning of the interviewee and interviewer in relationship to the door must be discussed. Psychologically, if the interviewee feels he has to go through someone or something in order to get to the door, he often feels he is being contained or prevented from freely leaving. Practically speaking, the interviewer must also consider what is going to be the safest position for him to make the quickest exit in time of need, lest the interviewee becomes hostile or violent. Thus the most viable position for both subjects is where both seem to have a fairly equal distance from where they are to the door and that either one could easily get up and exit if necessary.

If the room were such that this is impractical, then the determination of who should be closer and who should have his back more to the door than the other becomes one of individual comfort and belief. In any event, the interviewer should literally not have his back to the door, but in some room configurations, it is difficult to prevent this completely. If the interviewer had more of his or her back to the door and were closer to the door than the interviewee, it should be in a manner such that the interviewee can see he has a fairly clear and unobstructed path to the door while talking to the interviewer. The argument here is that the interviewer is thus ensured that a quick exit only requires a quick turn as opposed to worrying about having to go anywhere near the interviewee when exiting.

On the other hand, many interviewers would maintain it is better that the interviewee has more of his back to the door than the interviewer. The contention is that, before one even enters the interview, a certain part of the assessment process has been completed. Hence there should now be an informative understanding on the part of the interviewer of the potential for violence, and if there is any hint of this, an arrangement would be made to ensure that appropriate security is already in place. So if the interviewee does become volatile, the interviewer can still try to maintain some control of the interview, yet through some pre-arranged signal, the "protection" previously arranged by the interviewer can be initiated. By having the interviewee with his back to the door more than the interviewer, the interviewee will not be as aware when security enters the room and the interviewer is not in the way of security. The belief by the interviewer is that he still has adequate space within the room to move out of the way if necessary and thus maintain a safe distance from the subject.

The Interviewer's Appearance

While not usually discussed in most texts, care should also be taken at this time regarding the appearance of the interviewer. Many interviewers believe they should go into a discussion of this nature looking very professional and business-like, dressing up in a suit and tie with meticulous grooming and spit-shine shoes. Of course, there are certain circumstances where this is true, especially if the interviewer is trying to portray a specific image in order to better solicit information. Nevertheless, care must be taken not to be perceived as being "better" than the interviewee. To dress as an equal decreases the subject's defensiveness.

It is also important that consideration be given to the style of dress. For example, a woman who is conducting an interview with a man must take care that the opening of her blouse or dress is not revealing where it could be deemed a distraction — and unfortunately that level of exposure differs for every individual. Hence, a high neckline style of dress, blouse or sweater would be more appropriate in the interview process.

For both men and women, the matter of colors and patterns of dress are important. A brightly colored outfit or a mixture of stripes and checks may prove to be entirely too diverting. The actual color of dress may have some influence as there are many studies that suggest that certain colors can actually increase or decrease the agitation level of the viewer. For example, there was the study years ago of how the color pink seemed to decrease a subject's level of disturbance, so much so that some incoming detention cells were purposely painted pink to place volatile offenders with the initial achievement of diminished commotion. Unfortunately, after a few months of really observing the results of this experiment it was soon discovered that after a few hours the precise opposite effect began to take place — the incarcerated subject became even more disturbed and angry than when originally placed in this cell.

Many books address the "dress for success" concept, suggesting that certain colors are "power" colors while others represent warmth and understanding. Deciding exactly what to wear can often be thought of as quite a challenge, yet the more important aspect is that the interviewer look to that kind of clothing that is not "loud" and out of place, is not showy or flashy, is comfortable for the interviewer and does not make the interviewee feel he is being looked down upon or "outclassed." In general, darker colors are better than lighter ones; browns, dark grays and dark blues may be the best choice.

The last concern in this area is any and all kinds of jewelry, including glasses. The idea is to be conservative first and foremost, but the real key is to consider what might be a distraction to someone else. Jewelry is generally purchased by someone because he or she is attracted to the piece, or at the very least feels that it will enhance his or her look. Hence it is an easy leap to understand that another person may look at the same piece of jewelry in a similar manner and be thinking of that as opposed to concentrating on the matter at hand. Simple jewelry such as an ankle bracelet on a woman or a necklace or earring on a man is often seen as having some sexual undertones. And, of course, the biggest mistake is the individual who keeps his sunglasses on while talking to a person of interest. Many interviewers choose to wear no jewelry while conducting an interview but some modification of what one normally wears may want to be considered in order to make sure that the interviewee concentrates on the questions and not on something entirely unrelated.

Last Thoughts

Thoughtfulness and reflection on the needs of the person to be interviewed can pay large dividends. Those versed in the art of counterintelligence and solicitation of information could write volumes concerning how the behavioral approach to the interview/discussion is paramount to a successful fact-gathering task. Planning on the likely demeanor and attitude of the interviewees, gaining as much background information about them as possible through review of files or personal interviews of those who may know them, and care on the dress and environment of the interview all play a role in countering the subjects' objections and fitting into the needs of the people for more comprehensive discussions. This is the role of a good interviewer, the goal of an informative discussion and therefore the ultimate goal to acquire the maximum amount of information for the violence risk assessment.

Rapport — The Primary Need for an Informative Discussion

It seems that everyone knows that rapport is necessary to be successful; however, most texts do not explain how to achieve this — yet it is the most critical component of the successful interview. It is the same principles we use in instructing hostage negotiators, and in fact that is exactly what any interviewer should believe he is if he is going to achieve the desired results — a negotiator. In the violence risk assessment process the interviewer is negotiating between the rights and needs of the individual and the safety of others. By entering into the discussion procedure with this kind of mind set, the interviewer is more mindful of his responsibility to gather all the facts possible so that an easy and successful outcome can be negotiated for all. The ultimate goal is that everyone walks away a winner — the proverbial "win–win" scenario.

First step — establish common ground. The first 5 minutes of the discussion should be focused on this principle. What is some common interest or activity that is shared? If this can be found, it psychologically tells the other person that you must be similar to him. Similar interests or activities almost always translate into a belief of similar character traits and thus there is a connection. This connection can be employed to encourage the individual to talk more about himself, which we all subconsciously like to do. It also allows for an easy escape into a non-threatening arena when the interviewer senses some resistance or hostility in the interviewee.

It may seem somewhat out of place if you have not utilized this technique, but after a brief introduction describing the purpose of the interview as well as the interviewer, it is not out of place to open with some common questions as a matter of course as if meeting anyone for the first time. "I noticed you wear Nike's MayFly running shoes — do you jog?" Or, "It looks like you stay in pretty good shape — how do you stay fit?" The interviewee may logically understand that these questions really have nothing to do with the situation, yet subconsciously he feels the human attempt at a connection and is more likely than not to reciprocate.

Staying within the framework of the environment can be used just as easily. "I see you are an electrical engineer. Where did you get your degree?" Or, "So do you have a long drive to work or do you live fairly close?" Remember, the idea is to stimulate data that you might have a chance to relate to — again confirming the need to do some background work prior to conducting the interview. You might discover that the person you are going to interview went to the same college you went to, or that your best friend went there, that he has a long drive to work as do you, or that he loves to jog as do you. Regardless of the hook you may find, it is this type of beginning dialogue that can subliminally be very attractive to the interviewee, who is already looking for direction and guidance on how to react in this setting.

Second, your presentation can be the end of any discussion. In the law enforcement field they refer to it as having "command presence" and oftentimes interviewers feel this is the proper demeanor to exhibit in an interview. But the truth of it is, the more the interviewer can demonstrate a sincere and interested demeanor, the more he or she can display a relaxed and comfortable manner, and the greater the intent is to allow the interviewee to perceive he is in control of the discussion, then it is the interviewer who is going to gain the most information from the subject being questioned.

It starts with watching your words. Common terms used in one environment may prove foreign in another. Slang terms may promote confusion and thus anxiety. The tone and fluctuation of the interviewer's words may also promote feelings of nervousness or concern. The simple solution — KISS. Yes, the old adage of Keep It Simple Stupid applies completely in these cases. This is not the time to show how you have been successful in improving your vocabulary — no one will be impressed in this setting. Additionally, add a smile. Try feeling angry or upset when forcing a smile. Besides, there is research that shows that people with a smile on their faces were perceived by others to be more friendly and trustworthy than those who had no expression.

Next, remember that you are a mirror. Anytime you go to interview someone, especially for the first time, that person is not sure what to expect and is looking for clues. He is sizing you up, listening to your words and watching your behavior. It simply makes good sense that people are going to feel more comfortable around someone who looks, acts and talks like they do. Think about when you were growing up and tried to look like your friends. Why did you do that? To fit in, to be accepted and to feel comfortable, you found yourself using the same language and more times than not acting in the same way. As much as you wanted to be considered an individual, the truth of the matter was you were doing everything you could to "mirror" those you felt would be good role models so you could fit into the group.

So observe the interviewees' demeanor and posture, be aware of how they act toward you and their gestures, and concentrate on their speech patterns and delivery. The quicker you are able to gauge all of this, the quicker you are going to be able to match the outward affect of the other person. This is the ultimate goal of mirroring — to reflect what the other person is expressing so the person will feel a connection with you. This will also allow you to "lead" the interviewee into a more desirable frame of mind. For as you gain the trust and confidence of the interviewee, the easier it will be for you to modify your behavior and draw him into a deeper rapport, which makes a more open and honest discussion possible.

Of course, there are notes of caution, as one does not want to appear to be mimicking the subject. In addition, if you are not aware of this process, it is critical to understand that even if it is at an unconscious level the interviewee is going to be aware of it. At least he is going to respond to the interviewer as he perceives the interviewer is presenting himself or herself. He is reading your mirror. Remember, he is looking for how to act and what is expected of him. Hence, if the interviewer is acting professional and business-like, the interviewee will do likewise and the rapport process will be minimal if at all.

Additionally, if the person is skilled at any level of "reading" people, he can very easily detect if there are some issues that are of greater concern than others during the interview process and can have the advantage over the interviewer of knowing when to share information and when not or to mislead the interviewer. Many others are equally skilled at "reading" another to the extent they will actually mirror back the demeanor and behavior of the interviewer. Hence, while the interviewer is trying to present a comfortable

and trustworthy front, the subject of concern is doing likewise, possibly causing the interviewer to get a "false read" from the interviewee. Studies have
shown this to be especially true of those subjects who have been raised in
an abusive environment, as they have spent an important formative lifetime
developing this affect-modulating skill in order to better ascertain how to
survive in a situation or risk. Thus another excellent reason to remember that
a good background done before conducting interviews can prove to be very
helpful, as the history of abuse could alert the interviewer to be attentive to
image management by the interviewee.

Other "Reading" Techniques

There are many other techniques that go well beyond these authors' levels of
expertise, although they all have their share of relative usefulness and success and have been utilized by us to a certain extent at one time or another in
our careers. The bad news — it takes a lot of practice — to the level of a seasoned athlete who is constantly trying to hone his skills. Rather than take the
reader through myriad articles and research on these and many other "body
language" study systems or remembering which words said in which fashion
suggest the more honest, trustworthy or straightforward subject, the reader
is challenged to explore and decide which of these are useful for him or her. It
is as personal as finding the right kind of exercise that will be something you
will do and at the same time is the most beneficial — hence the task is yours
to decide which of these other types of potential revealing behaviors may be
the most valuable.

NLP

Neuro-linguistic programming (NLP) covers a lot of ground and a single
comprehensive definition is impossible to state. Added to that is the fact that
the kind of training varies, the depth of the training can differ and often
there is a great deal of difference in training standards. However, there are
some common principles shared by all NLP proponents. For those looking at
utilizing NLP in the interview process, NLP can be an insightful tool to look
past the verbiage and determine the meaning or perception of the interviewee based on the structure of the responses and the non-verbal cues.

Through the more "Miltonized" versions of NLP, for example, a skilled
interviewer can, through a metaphoric principle, allow the interviewee to fill
in gaps of his stories in his own words so that the meaning is more intentionally owned or identified with the true beliefs of the subject. The "Mil-
ton Model" allows for a better system of rapport building with a subject.
It attempts to distract the conscious mind sufficiently so that unconscious

thoughts and perceptions can be revealed and discussed. It is therefore often considered to be a very comfortable way to achieve insights into the subconscious motivations of the interviewee, but it requires a lot of flexibility on the part of the interviewer who has to be extremely aware of the non-verbal feedback the interviewee is giving and then respond in kind as opposed to judging or analyzing.

A part of this process, accessing non-verbal cues (the more commonly known aspect of NLP for interviewers) allows the interviewer to understand the method by which a person is thinking or processing his thoughts so that an appropriate response can be made and increased rapport or influence can be exerted onto the interviewee. For example, the person whose eyes move in a level line to the right or left as he responds to a question and who answers, "That sounds right to me," may be more likely to process information in an auditory sense as opposed to a visual or kinesthetic process. This alerts the interviewer that he will obtain better results by formulating questions of the interviewee directed to the sense of hearing as opposed to the visual senses. Better to ask, "So what have you heard about this matter?" than, "So what have you seen?" NLP in totality is much more involved than just this short explanation, but it is a viable resource that may be considered by some interviewers to give them better insight of their interviewees.

Micro-Expressions

Micro-expressions can serve as another useful tool. They are basically the facial expressions projected by another for less than a second that are believed to be more revealing of true emotions not being exposed that often occur involuntarily. This ability then to detect facial micro-expressions allows the interviewer to sense someone's true intentions or motivations. It can also afford the interviewer an opportunity to demonstrate a more emphatic role that can serve to better develop rapport. Many find that while they are able to sense a "feeling" of a person's emotions, they are rarely able to define exactly why. Thus, reviewing the literature on this technique may further assist the interviewer in understanding what it is he or she is looking at when involved in a face-to-face interview.

Body Language or Nonverbal Communications

Reading body language is yet another technique that many feel is very revealing. This is the process of examining a person's movement of his body, his head and his gestures. Coupled with the subject's verbal language the interviewer can often detect differing emotions that raise questions as to exactly what the interviewee is actually feeling. Generally the individual is not even aware of the body movements he is making. Another useful advantage of this technique often not utilized is that the interviewer may "mirror" back the interviewee's body language — and thus increase the level of rapport.

Hence, body language is often referred to as the subtext of verbal communication — the body positioning, the space between you and the other person, the gestures given by the subject — do all of these match what is being said? Just as the way your voice can be used in many different ways to vary the meaning of the communications (from boring to intense, from slow to rapid, etc.), so too does the delivery of those words in viewing someone's eye movements, hand gestures, leg crossing, etc. make a difference — or maybe not! If I cross my arms in front of my body am I telling you that you are getting too close, that I am not going to answer that question and I feel a need to protect myself, that I am angry with you or that I am just plain cold? It's up to the reader if this then seems like the method for use — and there may just be parts of it that are right. More reading on the topic (and there is a plethora of material on the topic) should be done by all.

Verbal Judo

Usually thought of as utilized more by those who engage in conflict management, verbal judo is considered the *gentle art of persuasion* and therefore may be considered an effective technique for these kinds of interviews. The reason it can be so effective is that through this communication process it can seem to offer solutions to those who are under pressure. It teaches you to respond to communications — not react — which is a paramount difference.

While often thought of to be used primarily to deescalate stressful communications, verbal judo is also a technique that teaches you to praise someone without sounding like you are trying to control them. This method will also teach you how to be a better listener and thus indirectly makes you a better communicator. It is not a difficult technique to learn and may prove to be an effective strategy for many interviewers.

Other Verbal Communication Techniques

There are myriad differing styles, protocols and methods to interpret verbal communications — all with a certain amount of usefulness and varying degrees of difficulty to learn as well as remember. It would be impossible to list them all here as well as address all of the research for and against such systems. However, a few examples may help readers decide if they wish to explore some of these to determine their potential value in such an interview setting.

Most are familiar with the importance one can place on the use of certain words. For example, saying, "I saw the gun" is certainly more definitive than saying, "I saw a gun." But what of the person who answers, "I may have seen a gun"? Is he lying? Is he trying to manipulate the conversation for personal reasons? In the violence risk assessment interview, trying to obtain the most direct and objective information is the principal goal. Understanding what to be listening for can go a long way to ensure this objective.

As a general rule most people do a lousy job at detecting deception. We want to believe what we are being told, we want to believe that most people are good and that they will be honest with us. You cannot stop someone from being dishonest with you, but you can learn to hear the changes in a voice and pick up on the subtle nuances of the rate of speech; the pitch and volume can give you clues. Learning about all of these things will give you a better understanding of the validity and probable legitimacy of the information received.

Putting It All Together

Although each of the techniques touched on represents useful tools for managing the interview, it is more important to remember your role as the negotiator. You are trying to sell the notion to the subject that he gains a benefit by being cooperative. Thus, sensing and providing what the subject needs in order to feel this way is more important than trying to read all his reactions. Again, the importance of trying to know as much about the subject as possible before the interview to better understand his possible needs cannot be overemphasized.

For example, a witness in a company who is considered a good company person has a need to be perceived as just that and thus appealing to his or her sense of helping the company may satisfy that need. Alternatively, a victim may have a need to feel important and demonstrates that through always seeming to want to be the center of attention. Appealing to his or her sense of value may satisfy that need. A potential perpetrator may feel he is right and often belittles others to attain that feeling. Appealing to his perception of how he may feel he was justified in his behavior or how others were not right in their behavior, while careful not to acknowledge or validate the actual behavior, may satisfy that need.

The Interview Protocol

After one has prepared properly for the interview, has taken the time and effort to provide for the best interview environment and has established rapport with the interviewee, the next step is letting the individual know what is happening. Let's face it, the interviewee is still looking for guidance — he does not know what is expected of him nor the process of this discussion. Hence, the interviewer must discuss in general terms what the interview is all about, why they are there, why the interviewee is in attendance and what the object of the discussion is. This is not to say that all your cards are put out on the table, since every situation is different and some issues may be somewhat unclear at the time of the interview, or you need to not disclose all of the facts.

It is important, however, to be as frank and as descriptive as possible in order to establish a transparent framework for the discussion. In addition, and we believe most importantly from a psychological perspective, the interviewee must be told that since he is the one with the pertinent information, he is the one who is actually in control of this discussion. Your job is to facilitate the process so that the maximum amount of information is obtained. The process may start something like this:

> I want to thank you for speaking with me today. As you know, there has been a concern over the statement overheard by one of your co-workers yesterday concerning the use of a firearm in the workplace. Since I was not in the break room when this occurred and you were, you are the one with the information of just exactly what occurred. Tell me what happened.

At this point it is important to allow the individual to tell you in his own words exactly what he remembers. *Do not interrupt* — allow him to state everything he can about the event. Sometimes the interviewee indicates he is not sure where to start or how detailed he should be. Assure him that is not as important as telling you everything he can remember surrounding the specific incident. *"I was not present when the statement by your co-worker was made about using a firearm in the workplace so please tell me everything you think is important, no matter how small. Then I'll clarify things if I have any questions."* This helps the interviewee to feel more at ease, it helps him to feel free to tell you everything in his own words and style — that you will facilitate a more detailed or elaborate recount as necessary.

During the interviewee's narration, it is important that the interviewer show encouragement and approval so that the interviewee knows he is doing the right thing and so that he feels comfortable in continuing. This may be accomplished by a simple nod of the head on occasion or by uttering such astute comments as, "I see, and then what happened?" or "I understand, please continue." Not only is this considered active listening that shows the subject you are paying attention, but it helps maintain rapport with the subject.

It is also during this process where the interviewer can ply his trade of trying to "read" the subject. Paying attention to the behaviors, gestures, facial expressions and wording utilized by the subject during this time can develop a "snapshot" of the subject's behaviors for the interviewer to compare to the time when rapport was being built, and for use when future questions, possibly more sensitive questions, are asked. All of this information will go to determining the overall belief in the truthfulness of the information and therefore what can be trusted to use in the assessment of the potential risk or threat of violence. For there is no better time during this whole discussion process, where the interviewee can feel most in control, than when he is told to talk away — tell everything — in any manner and style he wishes. It is also the best time to listen attentively in order to pick-up on any prejudices, bias or hidden motives that could lead to false or misguided information.

Therefore it is one of the most critical times where the interviewer should be doing nothing more than listening. He or she should not be writing, thinking of other things or allowing distraction to creep into his or her mind. Some may believe this is the perfect time to be contemplating the next set of questions. They believe that the subject is giving just the right information to steer the direction of the next set of questions to confirm or contradict the supplied information. While this is a factor, most of the questions that need to be asked in a violence risk assessment case are fairly consistent; hence unless the information received is obviously questionable, the focus should be more on the manner and content of the story shared.

After the complete uninterrupted rendition of detail by the subject, the interviewer should now tell the interviewee what he can expect. *"Thank you, I just have a few questions so I can make sure I understand what you told me. If you are uncomfortable with answering the question or simply do not know the answer, that's okay."*

Many interviewers like to add, "Is that alright?" at the end of the above statement. It does allow the interviewee to perceive he or she has more control and in some cases it may be appropriate. However, it is better not to ask such a question, lest the answer, "No, it's not alright." For then the interviewer is stuck with either abiding by the interviewee's demand or overriding the request and causing immediate tension.

The types of specific questions to ask are contained at the end of Chapter 4, "Formula for Assessment." Notice a very important line after many of the questions: give an example, explain the answer or describe the behavior. This is a very important component of the answers one receives when conducting a violence risk assessment. A simple yes or no answer to a question leaves a lot to the imagination, perception and beliefs of the interviewer, and that is not the interviewer's role. As much as possible the interviewer must extrapolate as much information as possible from the subject in as objective a means as possible. Therefore, since we all process events and occurrences differently, it is important to try to recapture as much of that memory in as many different ways as possible, so we can understand the exact behavior that occurred in the incident. We assess perceptions of this through the physical acts.

The idea is to stimulate the entire senses one may have utilized at the time of the event in order to better enhance the total memory of the incident.

By asking the interviewee to explain a certain behavior that an individual exhibited, such as the question asking if the subject is experiencing any known stressors, the interviewee must draw upon his total recollection of the subject and specifically when and how he came to the conclusion that the person is in fact experiencing known stressors. At the very least this activates different spheres of the interviewee's mental imaging of an event that has often been shown to increase the reporting of correct information. If the answer does not seem sufficient or it is believed that more can be obtained, it is important that this probing continue on this image prior to going to another. Research has shown that if this image is left and another is brought up, going back to the original image will usually result in a lessening of the total recall of that original memory.

The "Saving-Face" Component

There are many reasons some may leave out information or supply erroneous information instead of the truth, and it is often not because they are trying to be deceitful but rather because they are embarrassed, feel guilty or fear they may get into trouble. Hence the "saving-face" technique is often utilized to solicit more and pertinent information. Sometimes it is an easy gap to bridge as they have said one thing one time and something different the next. When this happens, suggesting to the subject that he may have forgotten the information before, may allow him to feel better about rationalizing why there is this difference. In more serious cases, it may be necessary to go through a whole cluster of rationalizations for the subject before he finds one that he feels most comfortable with and can finally use as an explanation as to why he forgot to tell you something, misstated the information or flat out intentionally lied.

Death of a Story

Termed the "Death of a Story," it is important to realize that especially when interviewing potential perpetrators, they often have never been evaluated to the extent or level the assessment expert achieves. Hence, the procedure of how this occurs explains the process of obtaining necessary information as in the following example:

A 57-year-old male worked for a large construction company for the last 8 years and had actually been in the construction business for over 30 years. Prior to that he had served in the Marines for 2 years and had actually owned and operated his own karate studio. While rising to a supervisory level this subject was always seen as kind of a braggart, but nothing unusual for the culture in which he worked.

Several of his co-workers finally complained of his "stories" one day to the human resources division of the company as they felt this individual had simply gone too far. They reported that while it was not unusual for him to yell at them for no apparent reason, to show signs of moodiness and aloofness at times, and to blame others for most of his problems, his recent stories at lunch were completely inappropriate and had actually scared these co-workers. It was alleged that this individual would not only demean and belittle minorities as he described antics and actions that he observed of others, but he would brag about how he was often used by the government to kill people. He stated that he had over 100 kills and that he did it by slicing their throats. The final straw was when this individual stated, as the company was going through several layoffs, that if he ever were let go he would find the person responsible, go to that person's home, slice his throat, slice his wife's throat, and then would slice his dog's throat — but he would leave that person's cats alone as he loved cats.

The company wisely reached out for their attorney, who reached out for this author. After a comprehensive background check was completed and collateral interviews conducted, a decision was reached to place the subject on suspension with pay while the investigation continued. The subject was told by the company that some serious allegations had been made concerning his behavior that were of concern to the company and they had to conduct an immediate investigation. To be fair to all concerned, they could not reveal the exact nature of the allegations, but he was to go home with pay and he would be contacted by a professional experienced in handling these kinds of situations. The subject said he did not have any idea what it could be about, but had no problem with the suspension and left peacefully.

All background checks came up negative; there were no criminal or civil records on the subject anywhere. All indications of his military experience substantiated he was in the military, served his obligatory 2 years and had no special assignments or special forces training. Even inquiry through the martial arts industry met with no additional information. The interviews of all parties involved confirmed the allegations, as stated, as well as the genuine fear of the individuals. So an assessment phone call was made to this subject of concern and over the next few days the following five-step "Death of a Story" protocol was observed:

1. *Denial* — "I did not make any such statements." "I have no idea what they heard or how they could have heard such statements." "I do not recall making any such statements."
2. *Anger* — This is the "fight" in the "fight or flight" response to stress. "Well if the company is going to believe these statements and slit my throat over it (a revealing slip), then maybe I should just quit." "They put me into a position I never wanted anyway, maybe I should just get me an attorney." "We all did a lot of bullshit talking at lunch time and I told them a lot of my bullshit stories when I was in the military. But I'm not a violent guy. Hell, I once held a litter of kittens in my hands when they were being born (more revealing slips)."

3. *Bargaining* — An attempt to mask the reality of the situation. "Well, if the company will pay me what it owes me and lets me collect all my stuff, I'll just move on and we can forget the whole matter. I've had six heart attacks in the last 3 years and I don't need this stress."

4. *Depression* — Actually demonstrating some remorse. "Those guys should know better than to believe all my bullshit — I would never hurt anyone and I sure didn't mean for anyone to feel afraid of me."

5. *Acceptance* — Usually reached when the first four don't work. "I know I can't have my job back but I would like to get my stuff, collect my final paycheck and just move on down the road."

It is not unusual that at any time after step 1 (steps 2 to 5), if the company is looking for or willing to accept a person's resignation, the subject is often ready to negotiate such terms. Otherwise, this protocol generally holds fairly true to form, but cannot and should not be relied upon unless the background and collateral interviews reveal a low level of the potential toward violence of the individual (as with most cases). Further, the interviewer has to be in complete control of the interviews — such as in this case where the subject was told that an outside consultant would be contacting him in regard to this matter and that he would be his sole source of contact during this investigation.

The "Hope" Barrier

Last, it is important to address the "hope" barrier. This is especially significant for the potential perpetrator. It is his hope he will not lose his job. It is his hope that the truth of what was said or done does not come out (such as in the case of the above-described 57-year-old subject). It is his hope that he will not be embarrassed, especially when he sees any of his co-workers.

These issues should be handled as any good negotiator handles any other emotional issue. The most common one is the suicidal person where most people are afraid to come right out and ask the question, "Are you thinking of ending your life?" Generally it is believed by most people that this question will cause the person to think of doing such an act where he may not have been thinking of it before, whereas in truth, he has been thinking about it for a long period of time. Someone who is on top of a building threatening to jump has probably had the idea of ending his life enter his mind at one point or another in the last few hours. In fact, asking this question tells the person that you are willing to talk about it and that perhaps it is not something he has to keep bottled up inside.

Likewise then, asking the potential perpetrator what his "fear is" can often be extremely helpful in overcoming that last hurdle that prevents him from admitting to the issue and moving onto acceptance of his consequence. He has the "hope" that it might just go away. This obstacle might have to be couched in the third person, but nonetheless it is a legitimate question that can often, subconsciously at least, let the subject know that his hopes for an easy "out" are not going to materialize. The interviewer may say something like, I've seen this a lot and I know a lot of people think that if they just deny they ever did something like this, others might start questioning whether the incident occurred or not and then everything can get back to the way it was. Unfortunately, this is too important, it won't go away, and the longer it takes to resolve, the more people get involved and the worse it becomes for everyone.

The Telephone Interview

Some readers may have noted in the 57-year-old subject example above that it was mentioned how the violence risk assessment with the subject was conducted via telephone as opposed to face-to-face. Both have their place depending on case circumstances. Yet the debate continues as to which is more revealing and beneficial. This section will explore a few of those principles.

It would be easy to suggest that for the sake of convenience and speed the phone interview is the best way to go. It is often apparent that if the potential perpetrator is caught while his or her emotions are still elevated, an admission to the event and a speedy resolution to the problem can be obtained. While these are important issues, if there is one axiom that every good negotiator lives by it is that "Time is on your side." Remember we have consistently stressed the importance of conducting backgrounds and collateral interviews whenever possible prior to interviewing the subject of concern. However, changing times, expectations from those hiring the violence risk assessment expert due to the fear instilled by the subject's actions, and the cost involved all enter into this equation of deciding if the phone call makes better sense than the face-to-face interview.

There seems to be no denial that the ability to read someone's body language is statistically more significant and revealing than relying on his or her voice inflections, tone and wording. This makes for a strong case of the personal interview. Additionally, if you cannot see the person, how can you control the interview? While it has been stated that the intent of the interview process is to have the interviewee believe he is in control, as he is doing the majority of the talking, the reality is that the interviewer wants to have the ultimate control of the interview for there are specific facts and information that must be collected. Additionally, phone calls are often made where the subject feels the most comfortable and safe, like to the subject's home or personal office. This too then detracts from the ability to control the dialog environment. The subject could be playing with something, handling something or even looking a certain way that could be very revealing — yet none of this can be seen via phone.

There is still the potential for better controls when making a phone call, however. Arrangements can be made with the client to arrange for the subject to be in a certain office or small room, set up much like that for an interview, and the call is made into that. Sometimes this is actually a less invasive and easier situation to get the subject to talk to someone, as the initial thought of not having to see an assessor personally may be more appealing to a certain type of instigator.

Another thought is the considerable amount of previous discussion about mirroring and the fact that the interviewee is going to be looking for those important body clues from the interviewer so he knows how to respond or what is expected of him. The telephone prevents that from occurring and while it provides a slower start to rapport building due to the natural tendency to believe the phone is impersonal, that obstacle can be overcome because of the subconscious belief of a certain intimacy developed with the interviewer's voice in the ear of the interviewee when listening on the phone. This is the same principle as phone sex.

Additionally, because the object is not to scare people through this process, the suggestion that someone is going to call you for information is certainly less intimidating than learning that someone wants to talk to you in person. Subconsciously, it puts the interview process on a lower level of seriousness, which can always be escalated by the words and tone of the interviewer on the phone if necessary. It also subconsciously suggests to the subject that he has more freedom and that the likely consequences for his actions will be less. All of these feelings may and have helped make the process of suggesting rationalizations to the subject easier, so that he can more quickly come to an acceptance of his situation and the incident can be resolved.

Another by-product of the phone interview is when the concern is the legal issue of constructive restraint. It is often argued by those in the interview process that they believed they were not allowed their freedom — that the very nature of the face-to-face interview made them feel they were in custody, even though the interview was conducted by a non-law-enforcement person. The phone interview clearly eliminates that argument completely.

An additional advantage of the telephone interview is the lack of knowledge by the interviewee of the movements or actual physical actions being taken by the interviewer as compared to what is seen in the personal interview. For example, the interviewer may want to suggest to the interviewee that he has a paper in front of him that indicates certain facts of the case; this could not be shown to the subject. Subconsciously this makes the subject feel the evidence may be stronger than it really is for there is no way to see it and so human nature convinces the subject to think the worst. The interviewer may want to follow a script more distinctly and the phone allows such an action. Questions that are important to ask can now be put out in front of the interviewer with no fear that reading them will reveal his concerns or prejudices or that the subject will feel he is being disrespected. And, of course, the manner of dress or the appearance of the interviewer is of no concern during the phone interview as he cannot be seen.

The final factor that might be considered in this debate is the one of trying to "read" the subject. Words spoken, how they are used, the speed of the delivery, the tone and inflection of the voice are all important "reads" of another by one who is attempting to determine where a person is really coming from. And just as the blind person will tell you his blindness has improved his ability to hear, so too are these voice characteristics much more pronounced when concentration on the other physical characteristics is taken out of the equation. There is no denial that it still takes a great deal of time and practice to perfect the techniques of "listening" so that an effective "read" can be accomplished. But so too must the body language expert admit that subtleties and movements may mean one thing or something else — unless put in context with a lot of other things. That takes practice and it is up to the reader to decide which element he or she is most comfortable with and which interview format will work best for him or her in any given case.

The most important thing in the interview process on the phone is still the same as the person-to-person one: LISTEN! Some would argue that it is easier to get distracted or allow other thoughts to creep in while on the phone. This may be true, but experience and practice, and the willingness to concentrate on the conversation should prevent all but the novice from experiencing these problems. It is well known that we can listen many times faster than we can talk, hence internal conversations while others are talking is not unusual. The key is what those conversations are about. They should be directed at listening to what the subject is saying, taking good notes so that appropriate and complete questions can be asked later and constantly assessing the potential of risk of the individual being interviewed. This forced cognitive process of thinking about the potential of violence will mitigate unnecessary emotional clutters. It also serves to limit biases, as cognitively processing thoughts enhances comprehension while at the same time diminishes emotional distractions.

One of the greatest tools crisis negotiators use (and certainly you would be hard pressed to find any crisis negotiators at least in North America who do their job in any other manner than on the telephone) is silence. There is the old saying that silence can be deafening, but more importantly, psychologically it suggests to the other person that more needs to be said. This technique can be used effectively in person as well, but on the phone it can be devastating for the interviewee. The subject is already unsure of what he is supposed to do or say, so he wants to be sure and say the right thing. Saying nothing for even just 5 seconds can cause significant personal discomfort on the phone, whereas in person at least he can look at the interviewer's facial expressions, his body movements, his gestures, etc.

Subject Interview Form

As additional assistance for the reader, co-author Dr. Corcoran has put together a questionnaire that can be used as a guide when gathering information from a subject of concern. Patterned after the original questionnaire developed and shared at the end of Chapter 4, "Formula for Assessment," — "Witness Interview Form," this form, "Subject Interview Form," takes all of the issues that were mentioned as important to address in Chapter 4 and, together with this chapter, compiled a user-friendly set of questions one can use to interview a potential instigator. It is included at the end of this chapter.

While it is suggested that the questions be asked in the manner and order presented, it is also understood that circumstances may cause a variance of that plan. Please note that the questions are almost always compound in nature — to require at least two different answers within the same context from the subject and sometimes three or four. The reason for this is to determine the potential of the subject to be able to develop and carry out a plan — a critical component in any violence risk assessment. A subject who continually has difficulty answering these questions without asking for them to be repeated or explained is unlikely to have sufficient capability of planning an "attack" over the requisite period of time necessary to carry out a threat.

The positioning of the questions may also seem to be somewhat out of order, at least often jumping from one area of concern to another and/or asking a very similar question more than once. However, a careful review of the questions will confirm that each question does ask for a very specific answer and often in an attempt to have the subject thinking one way and then catch him a bit off guard to answer another question. For example, while the inquiry concerning if the subject has access to any weapons may sound similar to the question of the subject's immediate circle of family or friends owning weapons, it truly addresses two important and separate concerns. It is one thing for the subject to have access to a weapon, and he may very truthfully answer he does not. But the determination as to whether or not any family or friend owns a weapon, especially asked several questions removed from the question concerning the subject having access to any weapon, presents a different set of criteria for how a subject may very well end up having access to a weapon.

Last, it is admitted that the questionnaire on its face does appear quite lengthy — 16 pages of actual questions, 82 questions in all. At the same time it is important that anyone conducting a violence risk assessment understand from the beginning that this process of collecting the necessary data should not be shortened unless there just is no other alternative. The interview with the subject of concern should proceed in a cautious and calculating structure to ensure acquiring sufficient data to formulate an opinion. Anything less is not only detrimental to the assessment, but also unfair to the client you serve. It is also somewhat lengthy as this questionnaire was designed to be utilized in almost any arena — company, medical facility, school, college or university setting, etc.

Conclusion

Just as there are many different ways of asking questions to get answers, and many different ways of listening to obtain information, so too there are many different ways of gathering the data necessary for a successful violence risk assessment. But the most important criteria of all — make sure you are comfortable with your technique and that you can articulate why you did it the way you did. For if you haven't experienced it before you will eventually find that others will judge your actions somewhere down the road and you must be prepared for their interview.

APPENDIX 3.1

SUBJECT INTERVIEW FORM

All material contained within this questionnaire is protected by copyright law and may not be reproduced without the express written consent of The Workthreat Group, LLC. Additionally, all answers are to be considered privileged and confidential.

Name of Client: _____

Address of Client: _____
_____

Location of Interview: _____
_____

Date of Interview: _____

Length of Time with Organization: _____

Subject Interview Form

NAME: _____ TITLE/DUTIES: _____

Rapport: Notes during this process — look for hooks that may be missing from their lives involving elements of feeling loved, feeling valued, feeling good about themselves, feeling needed and/or feeling in control:

_____

_____

_____

_____

Introduction: Explain the reason for the interview — what are the expectations. Explain who you are and the relationship you have with the organization:

Narrative: Here the subject is asked to explain in his own words everything he can about the incident — do not interrupt except for encouragement or clarification:

_____

_____

_____

_____

_____

_____

_____

_____

_____

1. Tell me about your current position/title/job within the organization and how long have you been here: _____

   _____

   _____

2. Tell me about your current relationship with others in the organization:

   A. Co-workers _____

   _____

   B. Supervisors _____

   _____

   C. Managers/Administration _____

   _____

   D. Subordinates _____

   _____

   E. Clients/Students/Patients _____

   _____

   F. Others (vendors, delivery, etc.) _____

   _____

3. Tell me how any of these relationships have changed recently: _____

   _____

   _____

   _____

   _____

   _____

4. Tell me how you immediately handle conflict or a disagreement with any of the following:

   A. Co-workers _____

   _____

   B. Supervisors _____

   _____

C. Managers/Administration _____

_____

D. Subordinates _____

_____

E. Clients/Students/Patients _____

_____

F. Others (vendors, delivery, etc.) _____

_____

5. Tell me how you felt after the conflict or disagreement, say within an hour or so of the event, and how you felt approximately 24 hours later:

_____

_____

_____

_____

6. Please describe any grievance or complaint you filed or thought about filing over an incident or an individual within the organization: _____

_____

_____

7. Please describe any suspension you have experienced — the events surrounding the issue and how you handled it: _____

_____

_____

_____

8. Tell me about a time when you were frustrated or upset in the organization because you were unable to do what you wanted to do (eat at a certain time or location, consistently leave at a specific time, take a break at a specific time, etc.): _____

_____

_____

9. Tell me those of whom you associate within the organization that you would consider friends and describe for me why you feel they are your friends and/or why you now consider them to not be your friends: _____

_____

_____

_____

10. Is there anyone in the organization you feel is similar to you in nature or beliefs and please tell me why you feel that way: _____

_____

_____

11. Who in the organization do you feel knows you the best and why is that: _____

_____

_____

12. Please describe for me your role within the organization — what is expected of you and what are your responsibilities: _____

_____

_____

_____

13. What are your personal goals within the organization — what do you expect to accomplish or get out of this association: _____

_____

_____

14. Who or what may prevent you from accomplishing your goals and why is that: _____

_____

_____

15. If you had no obstacles or concerns of any kind, what would be your ultimate hope for your future within this organization: _____

_____

16. What is the worst thing that could happen if you did not realize your goals within this organization: _____

_____

17. Concerning the situation that occurred that we are discussing here today, have you ever experienced this or a similar kind of situation in the past and please describe that: _____

_____

18. Have you ever thought about committing a violent act in the past, and please describe that for me (someone cut you off on the freeway, a friend or relative really hurt you, etc.): _____

_____

_____

19. Please take a moment to put yourself back into the situation that you described in the last question and describe for me how you processed it — what went through your mind, how did you handle it initially, how did you continue to handle it and how long did it take you to get over it — if at all __:

_____

_____

_____

_____

_____

20. Are you aware of anything or anyone in this organization that has caused or contributed to your behavior (stress, unfair treatment, recent events, etc.) and please tell me about it: _____

_____

_____

21. Please describe anything or anyone in this organization that may have caused and/or contributed to the stress or problems of anyone else involved in this inquiry: _____

_____

_____

22. What "pet peeves" or actions of others tend to irritate you the most, especially of anyone in this organization: _____

_____

_____

23. What "traits" do you value most in those you associate with in this organization: _____

_____

_____

24. Tell me why you want to be with this organization: _____

_____

_____

25. How does your family feel about you being in this organization (if no family, then "significant other" or close friend): _____

_____

26. Please describe for me a couple of times in the last few months when you decided to do something you like to do instead of coming to this organization: _____

_____

_____

_____

27. Tell me about your childhood — where did you grow up and did you have any difficulties: _____

_____

28. Tell me about your siblings, did they experience any problems with you and did you experience any problems with them as you were growing up: _____

_____

_____

_____

29. Tell me about your parents, how they treated you and others and if they were always around as you were growing up: _____

_____

_____

_____

30. Please describe any abuse going on in the home to anyone, including yourself: _____

_____

_____

31. What is your current relationship with your family (parents and siblings):

_____

_____

32. Tell me about a time you felt like you wanted to get even with someone, how that made you feel and how you eventually handled the situation (if any such events are described, ask for additional ones): _____

_____

_____

_____

33. Tell me about your hobbies, special interests, special vacations, etc.: _____

_____

_____

_____

34. Tell me about your education — what grade did you complete, how did you like school and your instructors, etc.: _____

_____

35. Please describe the weapons you have access to such as guns or knives and where they are now: _____

_____

_____

36. Do you have any history of experience with weapons (military, law enforcement, security, personal — gone hunting, gone to a range, etc.): _____

_____

_____

37. Who in your immediate circle of family and friends owns weapons (relatives, friends, etc.): _____

_____

_____

38. Do you have any history of drug and/or alcohol use — please describe:

_____

_____

39. Have you ever experienced any injuries, especially to the head: _____

_____

_____

40. Do you have any medical problems: _____

_____

_____

_____

41. What are your favorite books, magazines or newspapers: _____

_____

_____

42. What kind of television programs, movies or videos do you enjoy (please list some titles): _____

_____

43. Please describe any recent dreams or fantasies you have had: _____

_____

_____

44. Tell me about any organizations, clubs or groups you have joined or want to join: _____

_____

_____

_____

45. Have you ever sought any mental health assistance (clinic, marriage counseling, EAP, psychologist/psychiatrist, institution, other): _____

_____

_____

46. Tell me about any volatile event that you were involved in outside of this organization (domestic, friends, random, animals, etc.): _____

_____

_____

_____

47. How many serious relationships have you had in your life and please explain why the last several ended: _____

_____

_____

_____

48. Have you ever had any problem with another person over your desire or preference of having some form of consensual sex and please describe that for me: _____

_____

_____

49. Please describe your current living conditions (living alone, with others, in an apartment, home, etc.): _____

_____

50. How is your current financial condition: _____

51. Please describe any additional stressors you have been experiencing in the last few months: _____

_____

52. Please describe for me any changes you have had in your life in the last 6 months and how has this affected you: _____

_____

_____

_____

53. Please tell me about a time you made a fatalistic statement (something like, "I don't care if I live or die." Or "I have nothing to live for."):

_____

_____

_____

54. Tell me about a time you thought about or attempted suicide and when it happened: _____

_____

_____

_____

55. Please describe any court orders that have been taken out on you, including anything current (restraining, child support, etc.): _____

_____

56. Please describe for me when you felt the following emotions, when these emotions were felt or are usually felt, and how you handle them:

    A. Depression _____

    _____

    _____

    B. Moodiness _____

    _____

    _____

C. Frustration _____

_____

_____

D. Outbursts _____

_____

_____

E. Throwing or slamming things _____

_____

_____

57. How do you handle stress — what do you do when you feel stress: _____

_____

58. Who do you talk to when you have a problem or concern, can you be completely open with them and how do you communicate with them (phone, in person, email, etc.): _____

_____

_____

59. Describe for me how you respond to any changes in your life (relationships, rules you have to follow, new supervisor/instructor, etc.):_____

_____

60. Have you ever been in trouble with the law, including juvenile problems:

_____

_____

61. Please describe for me the times you were misunderstood, especially in recent times, and what steps did you take to correct this: _____

_____

_____

_____

62. Describe for me a recent time when you could not accomplish something because of someone else — either what they did, did not do, or may have said to you or others: _____

_____

_____

63. Do you consider yourself responsible and please describe for me events or circumstances that would show that: _____

_____

64. Do you consider yourself impulsive and please describe for me events or circumstances that would show that: _____

_____

_____

65. Describe for me a time when you thought about or actually threatened someone — what and when were the circumstances and how was it handled:

_____

_____

_____

66. Describe a time you thought about or actually did follow someone or continue to call or write that person and describe the circumstances surrounding that person: _____

_____

_____

_____

67. Have you ever heard voices: _____

68. Please describe for me a time when you had to act secretive — when and why: _____

_____

_____

69. How would you describe your outlook on the world: _____

_____

70. How would you describe your own self-esteem: _____

_____

71. Please explain any changes in your beliefs or religion in the last 6–12 months: _____

_____

72. What are your long-term goals and how have you planned to obtain them: _____

_____

73. Please describe for me times when you are feeling bored and in need of stimulation: _____

_____

_____

74. Please describe for me a time you felt you lost control and may have over-reacted. When did this occur, to whom and how was it eventually handled (if one given, ask for more details): _____

_____

_____

_____

75. When is it alright not to tell the truth — and please give me some examples:

_____

_____

_____

_____

76. When is it alright to be angry or upset: _____

_____

_____

77. When is it alright to trick or to try and manipulate someone: _____

_____

_____

78. Describe for me a time you felt guilt or remorse about something you said and about something you did: _____

_____

_____

_____

79. What accomplishments in life are you most proud of: _____

_____

_____

80. What have you done in the past that you most regret: _____

_____

_____

81. If you could start your life all over again, what would you change: _____

_____

_____

82. Is there anything else you think is important or significant that I have not asked or we have not talked about: _____

_____

_____

_____

_____

_____

Others to interview or things to do (although you may have already determined whom you should interview or you have actually interviewed them, has this interview triggered others who should be interviewed or other things you should look into):

_____

_____

_____

_____

Records reviewed (list all records reviewed of this subject, as well as the dates of the review so that there is a history for your documentation):

_____

_____

_____

_____

_____

_____

To Always Be Read to Subject at End of Interview

Thank you for talking with me today, your cooperation and candor are appreciated. As I know you are aware, this is very serious as well as sensitive matter. Therefore, I would appreciate you keeping this interview confidential and not discussing it with co-workers, students or friends. Additionally, anything that may come to you later about this matter, I would appreciate you notifying me about it, regardless how minor an issue you may think it is.

Name of interviewer (*please print*) _____

Best way to contact interviewer: _____

_____

Formula for Assessment

4

Introduction

The subject of this chapter is one of great ongoing discussion among all practitioners of violence assessment or violence risk assessment — and probably always will be. It incorporates many of the topics discussed throughout this book, such as what behaviors we should be looking for to provide accurate prognostications of future violent behavior. What other factors, such as mental illness, family support, organizational anxiety or dynamics, head injuries, employment, family history, etc., should be considered? If we consider these behaviors and factors, how should they be weighed to provide an assessment that heightens victim safety, while balancing the effect that a false-positive finding might have on potential offender rights with the correct use of limited resources?

In this chapter, we will briefly cover a number of the various vehicles that have been designed in an attempt to address these considerations, and in Chapter 5 we look at two tools in greater depth as well. All have attempted to take knowledge from the empirical literature and structure a process that helps assessors gather information and sort it in some way for the purpose of clarifying the elements of an individual case, therefore providing them with a more transparent way to reach a conclusion of risk level, communicate that assessment, and, in some cases, also suggest interventions or other future activities to reduce that risk (e.g., conditions for probation or parole, training, counseling, etc.). One tool we will focus on in particular, the Assessment and Response Grids designed by the co-author of this book, Jim Cawood, and Dr. Stephen White of Work Trauma Services, has never been discussed in the literature before the first edition of this book was published. This particular tool, which was originally developed in 1993 and subsequently revised, provides a quick way to quantify risk and practical suggested responses for various components of the risk management team at different levels of assessed risk. This product has been used in federal and state agencies and public and

103

private corporations for about 15 years and has allowed both new and experienced assessment practitioners a way to both initially assess and manage cases and to monitor changes as the case continues to unfold.

In conducting a review of the literature regarding assessment instruments and tools and the research supporting their individual characteristics and validity, some valuable material was located, particularly from the late 1990s forward. An article in the *British Journal of Psychiatry* entitled Violence Risk Prediction: Clinical and Actuarial Measures and the role of the Psychopathy Checklist[1] is particularly useful for anyone interested in understanding, in a quick read, the early history of violence prediction and how various instruments have been developed to aid in the process. Table 1 of that article compares the "content lists" for the Psychopathy Checklist–Revised (PCLR) (Hare, 1991), Psychopathy Checklist–Short Version (PCL-SV) (Hart et al., 1995), Historical/Clinical/Risk/Risk Management 20 item scale version 2 (HCR-20 V.2) (Webster et al., 1997), Violence Risk Appraisal Guide (VRAG) (Harris et al., 1993) and the MacArthur Violence Risk Assessment Study (VRAS) (Monahan et al., 2000).[2] With the exception of the MacArthur VRAS, authors Dolan and Doyle compare the content of the most used instruments in the area of violence prediction and then go on to discuss their strengths and limitations according to various studies that were available up to the date of submission of that article.

It has been proven by a plethora of studies that actuarial-based violence risk assessment instruments are more accurate than clinical judgment alone. Several of the above-named instruments incorporate the "scores" of other instruments into their own instruments to enhance their decisions. Those in that article that did so use the scores of one of the Psychopathy CheckList (PCL) products. The HCR-20v.2 incorporates the score of the PCL-R or PCL:SV. The VRAG incorporates the PCL:SV score, as does the MacArthur VRAS. This product family is used because it has been widely tested and found to be the best predictive family of instruments for future violent behavior currently available. Dolan and Doyle's conclusion is the same as the authors of this book for the use of these types of instruments or tools: use caution and understand the limitations of the various products. At the present time, there has not been enough research concerning the validity of any single instrument or tool in a wide enough range of populations (adults, youths, penal settings, open society, different ethnicities, different intelligence levels, etc.) to trust any of these products to make significantly accurate stand-alone predictions in any individual case, across all populations and, in fact, there may never be. At the present time, the real value of these products for the practitioner is that they can serve as a method of tracking the collection of relevant case information, providing a framework for assessment and a secondary way to view the assessment, all of which serves to make the assessment more complete and less subjective. In other words, these instruments and tools can help stop lazy analysis by encouraging assessors to do all their homework and serve as a possible hedge against allowing personal feelings, in any given case, to significantly skew their professional opinion.[3]

The assessment products mentioned above and any that we would consider for use, now or in the future, have two common elements. They have been grounded in the professional literature for the historical and behavioral elements they identify as important for use in the assessment and, if they provide a numeric "scoring system," they do so in a transparent way that allows the user to understand the numerical weighting of the elements. Some assessment tools on the market do not match these criteria and, although one family of tools, the MOSAIC series, is touted as being used across a wide spectrum of criminal justice and law enforcement agencies, it has never produced any information that allows for an understanding of the numerical values that its computer program generates for levels of concern or risk.[4] Given the sophistication of current practitioners and the need for moving toward a transparent system of assessment that demystifies decisions that affect the freedom and safety of both victims and instigators, it is our hope that practitioners will vote with their time and resources to support tools that provide transparency, not mysticism.

It is unfortunate that these products are not used more uniformly for the purpose suggested above. In an article titled "Offender Risk Assessment: Guidelines for Selection and Use,"[5] author James Bonta cites one study by correctional psychologists[6] that involved the use of actuarial risk scales to predict recidivism, in which they are asked about their use of three instruments specifically developed for criminal offenders. Only 11% reported using the PCL-R and 1% reported using the Level of Service Inventory-Revised (LSI-R) or the VRAG. This study implies that the responding correctional psychologists were either using less specific instruments, such as the Minnesota Multiphasic Personality Inventory (MMPI), or just clinical judgment, thereby making less valid assessments that can affect community safety.

Most of the discussion concerning the use of these products in the assessment process revolves around a cluster of issues including cost, ease of use and to what degree they enhance accuracy of the assessment. Most research, at this point, clearly shows that enhancing accuracy of assessment is strongly supported; however, the cost and ease-of-use issues are valid concerns that still need to be addressed.

Costs can be broken down into two areas, hard and soft. The hard cost, that of the instrument or tool itself, score sheets, etc., is very minimal, less than $100 U.S. in most cases. The greater cost is the soft cost, compiled from the costs for training that enables use of the instrument and the ongoing cost of time to do the necessary information gathering to provide sufficient data to use the instrument. Based on the studies available concerning the cost of injuries due to violence, the question becomes which is more costly, the expense of using these instruments or the cost to society of not identifying and successfully intervening to prevent violence from occurring? It is recognized that readers of this book are probably "the choir" on this issue, but that also means fighting to get the ability to spend the time necessary to do information-intensive, objective assessments. A favorite cliché is appropriate here: "You pay now or you pay later, but you always pay more later."

Regarding the ease-of-use issue, the most direct practical concern we have encountered revolves around the fact that some of these products require the collection of information that is not readily accessible during different types of assessments, particularly when time is a critical factor. Extensive access to family history (e.g., particularly collateral interviews with family members), medical history (e.g., particularly copies of actual medical records) and even criminal records (e.g., hard copies of police reports, investigative notes, etc.) may not be accessible for a substantial number of assessments because there is no ability to legally obtain the records (e.g., an assessor working for an employer or victim may not have the legal authority to even request the records); the time frame to identify the source of the records, request them and obtain them is prohibitively long; or, in the case of interviews, assessors may not have access to investigative resources to track down the necessary family members and witnesses for interview. Again, these obstacles should not, in our minds, devalue the use of appropriate instruments and tools. The assessor should manage any given case using an ongoing assessment model.

In the case of the materials not being legally available, the assessors have done what they can at that point in time and can document what material their assessment is based on and what material was legally unavailable. Some assessment tools have procedures for their use when the information is incomplete and some do not. Depending on the product of choice, the assessors may not be able to include the "score" of the instrument or tool in their assessment, but could still use it as a reference for gathering the information that is available.

If time constraints are an obstacle to the use of a tool or instrument, the assessor could provide an initial qualified opinion of current risk and make recommendations concerning further information gathering, identifying sources and making suggestions concerning the speed at which the information should be gathered. A dramatic case might involve a report of the subject's going to his car or home to get a gun. This leads to a practical assessment of high risk and triggers a protective response, which could include evacuation, lock down, law enforcement notification and other responses. However, once those interventions are in motion and the situation stabilizes (e.g., the subject is in custody, is found without a gun, etc.), the assessment process continues, more information is gathered and reassessment occurs.

This cyclical process of assessment continues until all the required information is gathered and processed, which may be days, weeks or even months later. Even if the instigator is incarcerated in a penal environment or mental health institution, the assessment should ideally continue until the steps are completed and a monitoring mechanism is established for ongoing assessment as necessary. Therefore, the use of assessment products as a part of the assessment process is a practical achievable course of action, even in a crisis-driven situation.

As practitioners ourselves, we understand that, in situations where instigators appear to be incapable of continuing their violent trajectory at that moment due to incarceration or incapacitation, there may be a push by supervisors, managers and clients to stop the assessment process, due to time and fiscal concerns. However, it is rare that the instigators will not regain the ability to continue their behavior in the future and completing the assessment and implementing an intervention strategy while the case is still fresh is the best practice to effect long-term safety. In line with that philosophy of best practice, we believe that completing assessments that include appropriate instruments or tools is a level of practice that assessors should strive to achieve. This not only helps protect the assessor from making errors that can lead to claims of negligence or incompetence, but also enhances the protection of the victims, clients and institutions that rely on the assessors to maintain their safety. The more objective the information in the assessment, the higher the accuracy of the cumulative subjective opinion.

Behaviors to Be Explored for Violence Risk Assessment

In reviewing the literature of violence risk assessment and conducting an analysis of our practice, several categories of information have been identified as being of use for the assessment of future risk of violence. These categories are generally referred to in the professional literature as historical or actuarial information, which are static risk factors; clinical factors, which are dynamic risk factors; and other risk factors that are also dynamic risk factors. Many of the behavioral factors found in each of these categories are similar to those that identify antisocial personality disorder and psychopathy, which should be no surprise to anyone. In Chapter 2 we identified many of these behaviors as we reviewed the process of information gathering, including the threat assessment outline that was published by the California District Attorney's Association (CDAA) from work conducted by a group of assessment professionals brought together for a project under the auspices of the CDAA. However, here we have summarized behaviors many assessors and creators of assessment instruments or tools have found to be important to identify. They can be grouped into several major categories, each with several detail areas. These categories and areas of interest include:

- Mental Health History
  - Any diagnosis, treatment and outcomes: particularly depression, paranoia, bipolar, schizophrenia, borderline personality disorder (BPD), narcissistic personality disorder (NPD), antisocial personality disorder (ASPD). These can be more or less important in any given case depending on who the target population is and the degree of substance abuse experienced by the instigator (Monahan & Steadman, 2001).
  - Hostile or aggressive attitude toward others
  - Violent thoughts or fantasies
  - Suicidal or homicidal ideation
  - Hallucinations, particularly command-type
  - Psychotic thoughts, particularly with violent content
  - Lack of compliance with treatment(s)
- Medical History
  - Loss of consciousness
  - Major head trauma
  - Brain lesions or tumors
  - History of extended pain (chronic or due to other illnesses)
  - Lack of compliance with treatment(s)
- Family History
  - History of violence or abuse, physical or sexual
  - Parent ever arrested/used drugs
  - Unstable family relationships
  - Lived with both parents to age 16
- Relationship History
  - Promiscuous sexual behavior
  - Many short-term relationships
  - Verbal or physical abuse, either as instigator or victim
  - Parasitic lifestyle (e.g., living off others)
- Employment History
  - Short periods of employment (under a year)
  - Reasons for leaving usually involuntary or related to negative perception of personal treatment
  - Pattern of declining compensation
  - Consistently choosing a level of employment significantly lower than the intellectual ability
- History of Violence or Conflict
  - Young age of first violent or criminal offense

- Hostile or aggressive attitude
- Bullying or victim of bullying
- Initiating physical violence toward others
- Subject of protective or restraining orders
- Arrested or convicted of violence toward others
- Violated terms or conditions of legal orders, probation or parole
- Substance Use (abuse) History
  - Use of substances causes aggressive or violent behavior
  - Use of alcohol, methamphetamine or cocaine
  - Use of any substance with resulting job loss, memory loss or loss of consciousness
- Relationship with or Use of Weapons
  - Unauthorized carrying of firearms on person or in vehicles
  - Inappropriate display of weapons
  - Use of weapons to intimidate or frighten
  - Offensive use of weapons to injure or kill
  - Inappropriate emotional stimulation when a weapon is thought of or used
  - Intense preoccupation with violent use of weapons
  - Acquisition or modification of a weapon, particularly linked to an emotional event
- Recent or Current Events and Conditions
  - Impulsivity
  - Loss of significant family member(s)
  - General relationship problems
  - Lack of personal support
  - Stress
  - Primary relationship disruption (separation, divorce, etc.)
  - Substance abuse (particularly alcohol, methamphetamine/cocaine)
  - Employment problems
  - Legal problems, including commission of crimes
  - Health problems

Obviously, the presence or absence of any of these historical facts or behaviors, or factors similar to these, does not mean the actual instigator in any given case is either going to act violently or not. However, the more destabilizing factors currently present, coupled with a history of instability and inappropriate thoughts and actions, should lead an assessor to become increasingly attentive to the case and concerned for the safety of the potential victims. Minimization, rationalization and denial (cognitive distortion) are powerful forces that work against case facts and obvious behavioral cues, even for experienced and well-meaning assessors.

Witness Interview Form

As mentioned above, much of the information we have learned to acquire
has come from the studies of violent behavior by individuals who have antisocial personality disorder (ASPD) or are judged to be psychopaths. For
example, a study of released inmates[7] clearly showed that, on release from
custody, psychopaths were four times more likely to commit a violent offense
than their nonpsychopathic counterparts. Thus, instruments such as Hare's
Psychopathy Checklist Revised, mentioned above, can prove very helpful to
the assessor. In fact, another study[8] substantiated that violent offenders generally score higher on this instrument.

One of the difficulties, however, with this and other "instruments" is the
manner in which they are presented and the presumed necessary qualification of the assessor to properly check off the right observation. It is one of the
reasons co-author Dr. Corcoran put together a question-and-answer format
for many of these indicators, plus specifying the necessity for the assessor
to write a specific example given by the interviewee to further clarify the
observation, as well as help the assessor accumulate as much objective data as
possible. It is simply called the Witness Interview Form and is contained in
its full format in Appendix 4.1 at the end of this chapter. Also see the Subject
Interview Form in Appendix 3.1.

The 78 questions of this questionnaire can hardly be considered original,
as they are simply a compilation of numerous researched concepts, assessment tools and the experience obtained from handling thousands of cases
since 1970. Starting about 20 years ago (with only about 45 questions), the
intent was to put together a "user-friendly" tool for assessors in the field that
recognized or addressed the common potential for violent character traits
(some psychopathic traits, from conning and manipulating others to lack of
remorse or guilt in areas where most people would feel remorse or guilt) as
well as familiar, often-discussed customs (from history of alcohol or drug use
to familiarity or discussing firearms). Further, by requiring the assessor to
complete the area that asks for a specific example to substantiate the answer,
the assessor would have a permanent record of the interviewee's statements
related to the concept. This would allow the assessor to review the information later to better determine the veracity or motivation of the person interviewed, as well as corroborate these answers with other data. It also gives
assessors a record of how they reached their conclusions so they can verify
that they were as objective as possible. And finally, the questions serve as a
valuable resource to demonstrate the consistency of the interviews, much as
law enforcement personnel, even those who have more than 20 years in the
game, will still rely on the Miranda warning card to read to suspects.

From the information derived from this questionnaire, which can actually
be used with victims as well as witnesses, an outline of the general personality

of the subject can be formed. Many assessors utilize this form in the field and then consult with Dr. Corcoran concerning possible character traits to better design an approach to the instigator. They also request information concerning likely responses and behaviors they can expect from an instigator, so they can plan to address them. Additionally, with a few modifications, these same questions can then often be used when interviewing an instigator.

But even this questionnaire or any format of information gathering cannot be expected to be a complete indicator of someone's total potential for violence. Many other resources, as discussed in this text, must be added to this tool. One such instrument that helps assessors determine where they are in the assessment process, and where they need to go, is the Assessment and Response Grids discussed in the following section.

Assessment and Response Grids (Version 2)

This assessment and response tool set was originally designed in 1993 by Cawood and White for use in training their corporate clients and providing a common "language" to use for assessments with them. It was designed to be a simple tool set, based on the professional literature[9] and the practical knowledge learned through managing hundreds of cases. It is used when incidents are referred to an assessor or incident management team (IMT) within an organization. Instigator behaviors are compared with those categorized by levels of risk for physical harm. Response options are then suggested by designated component of expertise (e.g., assessment, security, legal, etc.). It should be noted that, even though the professional literature was used as a basis for the grids, certain behaviors have been arbitrarily assigned levels of risk by the authors of this tool, based on their education, training and experience coupled with how they saw the tools being used by clients.

This tool set was designed to assess and manage risk of physical harm to an identified victim or group of victims; it was not designed to make a general assessment of risk for behaviors less than physical violence, or for undefined victims such as society in general. It was also not designed to be used without some level of professional consultation, a suggestion that was incorporated into the Response Grid so it would not be forgotten. However, as client IMTs have become more knowledgeable through case work and consultation, the grids have provided a degree of independence in low- and moderate-risk cases that the teams consider to be of great benefit to them. These tools have been used to train elements of several federal agencies, including agents of the U.S. Postal Service, Department of Homeland Security, U.S. Marshals Service, and Internal Revenue Service; members of the Royal Canadian Mounted Police; both state-level law enforcement and general service agencies such as the California Highway Patrol, California Department of Motor Vehicles, State Compensation Insurance Fund and California Department of Corrections; and dozens of corporate IMTs, including Hewlett-Packard, Wells Fargo Bank, Nordstrom and The First American Title Company. In all of these different environments, this tool set has proven to be an accessible, practical and useful guide for assessment and response (intervention).

The assessment tool separates behaviors and case information into three risk levels: Low, Moderate and High. In the Assessment Grid, the information elements fall under the following categories:

- Escalating aggression
- Weapons involvement
- Negative mental status
- Negative employment status
- Personal stressors
- History of violence and conflict
- Buffers
- Organizational impact
- Organizational influences

Under the Response Grid, the suggested responses correspond to the three risk levels and fall under the categories:

- Assessment
- Security
- Legal
- Employee relations actions
- Treatment

We will go through each of these categories and provide an understanding of the type of behaviors in each section of the Assessment Grid and the type of response options delineated in the Response Grid. The discussion of each category will be accompanied by an illustration of that category in the appropriate grid for reference.

The Assessment Grid

Escalating Aggression

This category (see Figure 4.1) captures physical behavior that the subject of the assessment has so far manifested toward the identified victim(s). This includes intimidating actions, repeated bullying, verbal threats, unwanted physical contact, stalking, etc. In general, as the actions become more frequent, more intense or more specifically aggressive or violent in nature, the risk of physical harm goes up. If physical harm has already taken place, or other types of acts like firing a firearm in the direction of victims, attempted

Low Risk	Moderate Risk	High Risk
• One or two indirect threats or intimidating actions • Intimidating style, at least occasionally • One or two angry outbursts or hostile style • One or two incidents of perceived harassment • Unacceptable physical actions short of body contact or property damage (e.g., door slamming, throwing small objects)	• Two or more threats with increasing specificity • Conscious intimidation or repeated bullying; impulsive • Repeated angry outbursts or overt angry style, inappropriate to context • Repeated pattern of harassment • Intentional bumping or restricting movement of another person	• Clear, direct, multiple threats; ultimatums — especially to authority; evidence of a violent plan • Intense undissipated anger • Repeated fear-inducing boundary crossing or seeking direct contact; stalking; violating physical security protocols with malicious intent • Grabbing, grappling, striking, hitting, slapping or clearly using harmful force

Figure 4.1 Escalating aggression.

murder, exploding a bomb near victims, burning the victim(s)' domicile or vehicle, etc., it should be obvious that the victims are at great risk and assessors and assessment teams should immediately take all available steps to protect the victim(s) from harm.

Weapons Involvement

This category (see Figure 4.2) involves the behaviors of the instigator around weapons, particularly related to emotional attachments or displays. The first item mentioned in each category of risk is the location of a firearm, but this location information can apply to any weapon. The location of the weapon, like all assessment information, is particularly interesting when case information can show a change over time. It could be a behavior pattern that brings the weapon under more constant physical control of the instigator or into greater physical proximity to the victim(s). Either of these patterns could increase the risk of harm to the victim(s) by having the weapon more accessible for use against the victim(s) at any given moment. In the Low Risk box, the mention of "Long-term sanctioned use" is actually a buffer of sorts, but, because of the importance of weapons in the violence risk assessment, this buffer was placed in that box for immediate accessibility. In the Moderate Risk box, one behavior noted is "Acquire new weapons or improve weapon(s)." This is significant when it has occurred in a time frame around an emotional or other significant event for the instigator, particularly when it involves the victim(s), because it shows a possible attempt to prepare for an action involving the weapon.

Low Risk	Moderate Risk	High Risk
• Firearm in home • Long-term sanctioned use (e.g., hunting, target shooting, etc.)	• Firearm in vehicle • Increased training without known reason (e.g., not hunting season, competition approaching, etc.) • Emotionally stimulated by the use of a weapon for any purpose • Acquires new weapons or improved weapon(s) • Inappropriate display not directed toward others	• Carries firearm on person outside of home • Escalated practice or training in association with emotional release or issue preoccupation • Intense preoccupation with or repeated comments on violent use of weapons • Use or display of any weapon to intimidate or harm

Figure 4.2 Weapons involvement.

Negative Mental Status

This category (see Figure 4.3) involves behaviors that reflect mood or thought changes or disorders and the use of substances that can affect mood and possibly cognition. In the language of this category, many different terms are used to describe certain behaviors and thoughts that might appear to be subject to interpretation. Certain terms such as "felt entitlement," "mental preoccupation," "paranoid thinking" and others could be misinterpreted by some users of the tools; however, during the training in the use of this tool, examples are provided for clarity. Also, in the High Risk box, neither hallucinations nor delusions are specifically mentioned, but, during the training in the use of this tool, both of these items are explained and added to the language of this box. It is also explained that, should instigators have communicated their thoughts in such a way as to indicate the possible existence of hallucinations, delusions or psychotic violent thoughts, the assessor(s) should initially assign a High Risk assessment level, until the instigator has been evaluated by the assessor or another trained assessment professional in a face-to-face assessment interview (Monahan & Steadman, 2001).

Negative Employment Status

This category (see Figure 4.4) involves employment-related actions that have occurred or might occur and incorporates this information into the assessment. This category is important whether the instigator is an employee of the client or not because of the effect that employment can have on emotional balance and situational stability. If the instigator is an employee of the client, this is also a factor that can be controlled to a certain degree; however, if the instigator is not an employee, it is an uncontrolled, but important element in assessment, such as when an instigator is threatening a wife or significant

Low Risk	Moderate Risk	High Risk
• Tendencies toward depression, agitation or "hyper" behavior • Tendencies toward suspiciousness, blaming others, jealousy or defensiveness • Low or moderate substance use without links to violence-related behaviors • Anger, some felt entitlement or humiliation over any negative employment action or relationship setback	• Depressed, mood swings, "hyper" or agitated • Paranoid thinking, bizarre views, defensiveness, blaming others, hostile attitude, hostile jealousy • Substance abuse, especially amphetamine, cocaine or alcohol • Unremorseful but compliant to avoid punishment (e.g., jail) • Mental preoccupation, persistent anger, entitlement or humiliation over any negative employment action or relationship setback	• Depression unrelenting or with notable anger, high agitation or wide mood swings • High paranoia, homicidal or suicidal thoughts, psychotic violent thoughts • Substance abuse drives or exacerbates aggression or violence; verified amphetamine or cocaine dependence • Obsession and strong feelings of anger, injustice or humiliation over any negative employment action or relationship setback; feels desperate, trapped

Figure 4.3 Negative mental status.

Low Risk	Moderate Risk	High Risk
• Possible discipline, negative performance review or termination, nonviolence-related • Bypassed for raise, promotion, recognition or opportunity	• Recent or pending disciplinary action or negative review • Probable or pending termination or demotion, reinstatement unlikely • Unstable employment in last year	• Separation or termination inevitable • Terminated and all legal and other recourses for reinstatement or compensation exhausted and ruled against subject

Figure 4.4 Negative employment status.

other who is an employee of the client. No one needs to be reminded of the high number of violence cases that have appeared to revolve around employment-related issues.

Personal Stressors

This category (see Figure 4.5) deals with other stressors in the instigator's life that may elevate the level of risk of physical harm. These stressors include intimate relationship disruption; health, financial or legal problems; lack of a support system and a negative or destructive coping style. One issue that is noted in the High Risk box is being a target of high provocation

Low Risk	Moderate Risk	High Risk
• Mild disruption in primary intimate relationship • Mild financial problems • Minor legal issues • Minor health problems • Inconsistent support system	• Primary relationship disruption (birth, separation, betrayal) • Significant financial pressures — to increase with job loss • Legal problems • Demoralizing health problems • No or marginal support system • Negative coping style	• Recent relationship loss (death, divorce, betrayal, abandonment) • Serious financial crisis • Serious legal problems • Serious health problems • No support system • Destructive coping style • Target of high provocation by associates or intimates

Figure 4.5 Personal stressors.

by associates or intimates. This item is noted because of the situations in schools and the workplace in which individuals are the target of a bully or bullies and eventually respond with violence to stop the destruction of their sense of self. This is not as uncommon as some might believe and, like other individual behaviors, is not a stand-alone sign of immediate risk for physical violence, but it can be significant when linked with other risk factors. In most, if not all, documented cases of workplace mass murders or school mass murders, the perpetrators have perceived themselves as being victims, if not of bullying, then of mistreatment, even though, many times, they have been perceived by others to be the more aggressive individual or bully.

History of Violence and Conflict

This category (see Figure 4.6), which is self-evident, charts some historical information that has shown a connection to later acts of physical violence. Those who are familiar with the professional literature will see some types of historical behavior that have been linked to antisocial personalities. In the High Risk box, one of the items is "Highly isolated; loner style." This item is not only referencing people who appear physically isolated from others or have physically isolated themselves from others, but also those who have communicated that they feel isolated and alone. This sense of isolation, whether involuntary, voluntary or perceived, is often quoted as part of a "profile" of a person who commits physical violence. We do not feel that "profiles" are accurate in this way, but perception of isolation and not wanting to feel alone can easily be linked to depression and the rage that can surround it and, for that reason, it can be something to note as a part of the assessment process.

Low Risk	Moderate Risk	High Risk
• Early life problems at home or school • Pattern of mildly conflictual work relationships in past • Behavior-related job turnovers	• Victim or witness to family violence as child or adolescent • History or pattern of litigiousness • Arrests or convictions, nonviolence • History of serious work conflicts	• Has violated protective orders • Arrests or convictions for violence • Credible evidence of violent history • Failed parole or probation programs • Highly isolated; "loner" style

Figure 4.6 History of violence and conflict.

Buffers

This category (see Figure 4.7), like the History of Violence and Conflict category, is something that was added to Version 2 of the Grids. Often, the behaviors associated with risk are evaluated in an organized way, but the behaviors that might decrease the assessed level of immediate risk of physical violence are not as systematically considered. Some of these buffers are drawn from their opposite risk factors, such as "Adequate coping responses," while others are behaviors that might not be thought of if only risk factors were considered. Each of these buffers illustrates an instigator behavior that shows some form of appropriate behavioral control, emotional response or lack of additional stressors. Identifying buffers can generally lower the assessment of the immediate level of risk and can provide suggestions for ways the incident can be stabilized by strengthening the buffer during the intervention. Obviously, in any given case, the strength of the behaviors in other categories may outweigh the mitigating effects behaviors in the category could have on the overall assessment of risk level.

Organizational Impact and Organizational Influences

These two categories (see Figure 4.8) are meant to track environmental influences that could serve as situational destabilizers in those cases where the potential victim is part of an organization. The inclusion of any of these items in the situation will influence the level of assessed risk by generally elevating it, in the same way that buffers can generally lower it.

The first category, Organizational Impact, reflects how the people in the organization perceive their risk and how it may be affecting their behavior. Any of these perceptions, when elevated to certain levels, can cause individuals to be less functional at work, can impact their willingness to provide information, or, counterintuitively, can impact their follow-through on tasks that will help preserve safety, such as remaining aware of surroundings and

- Evidence of respect or restraint shown
- Responded favorably to limit-setting, especially recently
- Wants to avoid negative consequences for threatening behavior (e.g., jail, legal actions)
- Genuine remorse for scaring people
- Genuine understanding that violence or threats are not an acceptable course of action
- Absence of inappropriate emotional associations or attachment to weapons
- Appropriate seeking of legal help or other guidance with issue
- Wants to genuinely negotiate or appropriately resolve differences
- Job or relationship not essential to self-worth or survival strategy
- Engages in planning for future
- Adequate coping responses
- Positive family or personal relationships; good support system
- Religious beliefs prohibit violence, provide solace
- No financial, health or legal problems

Figure 4.7 Buffers.

Organizational Impact	• Employee(s) fear of violence • Supervisory/management personnel fear of violence • Highly vulnerable specific target(s) of serious harassment/stalking/predatory searching • Fear-induced employee(s) performance disruption, job avoidance/absenteeism
Organizational Influences	• Heavy workload, high stress environment • Generally adversarial, conflictual or mistrustful work environment • Counterproductive employee attempts to intervene or prevent violence • Co-worker or supervisor provocation of subject • Co-worker (or others) support of or encouragement of violent course of action • Management lack of knowledge of workplace violence dynamics or warning signs • Management denial or minimization of potential seriousness of situation • Management lack of crisis management experience, skills or tolerance level • Management active negative case management responses • Management resistance to accepting appropriate or specialized assistance • Management unavailability or remoteness from location of situation/key individuals

Figure 4.8 Organizational impact and influences.

reporting changes in behavior. Fear can be debilitating. This type of fear can "feed" certain instigators, empowering them to take further action to torment or control the victim(s).

The second category, Organizational Influences, is meant to determine whether any organizational or managerial factors are exacerbating the situation, either by commission or omission. Certainly, the more adversarial and actively hostile management is to workers in general and the instigator in particular, the greater the possible escalation.

Both of these categories, like buffers, offer areas for the assessor to work on during the intervention phase to stabilize and improve the situation going forward. Management education and training, appropriate discipline of managerial misconduct, reengineering of work processes and improving communication within the organization can all have a positive influence on reducing the risk of violence, for the immediate situation and for the organization in general.

The Response Grid

The suggestions for action in the Response Grid are meant to provide an orderly way to respond to the given levels of assessed risk where there is no immediate concern for physical harm. As mentioned before, if physical harm is imminent, call 911 and leave the area; do not reach for the Grids. The steps in each of these categories, with the exception of the post-assessment or action items under the Employee Relations Actions category and the entire Treatment category, are meant to be taken in parallel with each other, up to a certain point. In other words, steps in Assessment should be taken at the same time that appropriate Security and Legal steps are being taken by personnel assigned to implement those responses. Certain options in the Assessment category, specifically items 5 to 7, should be done only after appropriate Security and Legal actions have been completed because those later items need the information or structure provided by the completion of Security and Legal assignments. The options in the Employee Relations Actions Treatment categories should be considered only after the assessment process has been completed to the point that decisions can be made concerning what actions, if any, would be appropriate to strengthen the stability of the situation. Obviously, if the person is assessed to be an immediate danger to self or to others from a mental health perspective, then involuntary commitment, though listed as a High Risk treatment option, really becomes an intervention and assessment response.

If an initial assessment of risk is a "wobbler," such as a Low/Moderate or Moderate/High (these do happen in assessment, even though it is discouraged for logistical reasons), the response should always correspond to the higher category of risk. In this way, although the assessor and the IMT could be slightly over-responding, being conservative is always the more prudent course, as the time to conduct certain activities, like background checks, may not be available to allow redoing them in greater depth if the continuing assessment should lead to a higher classification later on. Assessors should be leading a response that is ahead of the velocity or trajectory curve of a situation, so if a sudden escalation occurs, the preparations are in place to manage the situation to maintain safety.

Assessment

This category (see Figure 4.9) outlines what steps an assessor or IMT should take to gather more information to enhance the assessment. It reminds the user to gather the initial data of the incident report, conduct informant interviews, review employment-related files and consult with a threat (violence) assessment specialist, as appropriate.

In the Low and Moderate Risk boxes, item 5 is listed as a "management 'reality check' meeting with (the) subject of concern." This means that, in cases that have been assessed as Low or Moderate risk, if the organization has appropriate personnel available (e.g., appropriately trained, psychologically prepared, emotionally solid), they might conduct a highly scripted interview with the subject that will provide information about the subject's current level of emotion, impulsivity, internal boundaries, ability and willingness to cooperate in resolving the situation and to take direction, coaching and limit setting, etc. As stated, the purpose is to check the subject's current reality. If appropriate personnel are not available, then the assessor or other

Low Risk	Moderate Risk	High Risk
1. Employer representative initial data intake	1. Employer representative initial data intake	1. Employer representative initial data intake
2. Employer informant interviews	2. Employer informant interviews	2. Employer informant interviews
3. Employment-related file review, if applicable	3. Employment-related file review, if applicable	3. Employment-related file review, if applicable
4. Consider threat assessment specialist phone review with Core IMT	4. Threat assessment specialist phone or on-site consultation with Core or Full IMT	4. Threat assessment specialist phone and on-site consultation with Full IMT
5. Management "reality check" meeting with subject of concern	5. Management "reality check" meeting with subject of concern	5. Threat assessment specialist on-site interviews with target(s) and informant(s)
	6. Threat assessment specialist on-site interviews with target(s) and informant(s)	6. On-site evaluation by psychological assessment team
	7. Fitness-for-duty or formal risk evaluation (off-site) or on-site evaluation by psychological assessment team	7. Post on-site evaluation for involuntary hospitalization

Figure 4.9 Assessment.

appropriately trained personnel would conduct this interview. In the High Risk box, this option is not available because, at this level of perceived risk, a professional assessor or a psychological assessment team is required to conduct an appropriate assessment interview.

Security

This category (see Figure 4.10) outlines the investigative and security steps that need to be considered for each level of perceived risk. A "cursory" background investigation will encompass 7 to 10 years of the instigator's (and possibly the victim's) life. As mentioned in Chapter 2, this will include checks of legally available criminal, civil, financial and other records for use in understanding the subject's past behavior. A "full" background investigation encompasses the subject's adult life from age 18 to the present. Any records prior to age 18 are usually considered juvenile records and not available for review by many assessors. If these records are available to the assessor, they should be located and reviewed as well.

In the Moderate and High Risk boxes, "law enforcement liaison" means contacting the appropriate law enforcement agencies for information-gathering purposes, as well as establishing communication channels for use in security or tactical operations. If there is to be an interview with the instigator inside a particular law enforcement jurisdiction and armed security or law enforcement personnel will be on site who are not connected to the jurisdiction, then a liaison should be established to speed assistance and minimize the possibility of an injury if law enforcement were to arrive on the scene and begin to engage the wrong personnel.

Low Risk	Moderate Risk	High Risk
1. Cursory background investigation — recent local, criminal and civil history	1. Full background investigation 2. Law enforcement liaison 3. Security plan for interviews with management, informants and subject 4. Security plan for "knock and talk" with nonemployee subject	1. Full background investigation 2. Law enforcement liaison 3. Full security plan for interviews, perimeter protection and reaction team 4. Consider target relocation 5. Security plan for termination or "knock and talk" 6. Security for TRO service 7. Target education on personal security and possible legal actions

Figure 4.10 Security.

The "security plan for interviews" encompasses the possibility that at any stage of the assessment process it could be determined that a risk of disruption or harm may be present for the interviews. When interviewing the instigator, this may be obvious, but, in some cases, the instigator might learn of the interview process and attempt to disrupt it by barging in, intimidating witnesses or actually attacking the people involved. In those situations assessed to involve the potential for this type of action, a security plan should be developed and implemented to protect the process from disruption and the participants from harassment, intimidation and harm.

The security plan for "knock and talk" involves those times when instigators are not readily available to the assessor, either because they are not employees or because they are not available at a work site. A security plan then needs to be developed for protection of the assessment personnel when they physically contact the subjects at home, work or other uncontrolled venues. This normally requires detailed law enforcement liaison, a movement and tactical plan for various contingencies and preparing the assessor(s) in what and what not to do to maintain safety. Some of this process can be truncated if local law enforcement can be appropriately involved and they have behaviorally trained officers, such as hostage negotiators or psychological technicians, who would be willing to participate in or conduct the assessment. Participant safety in these types of assessments is always difficult and requires careful planning and execution.

The "security for TRO service" means service of a temporary restraining order. It would also encompass the security planning and execution of any contact of a nonassessment nature with the subject, such as the service of any court order including a protective order or permanent restraining order, cease-and-desist letter, termination letter, return of personal belongings, etc., that may be a part of case management.

Legal

This category (see Figure 4.11) outlines the legal oversight that should be exercised when a violence risk assessment is being conducted. Issues of invasion of privacy, harassment, discrimination and others can be raised regardless of whether employment status is involved. Certainly, reviewing public communications will limit any exposure to claims of defamation.

Employee Relations Actions

This category (see Figure 4.12) outlines the actions to be taken by Employee Relations or Human Resources professionals after the initial assessment and response process has been completed. The exception to the post-assessment items is management's meeting with the subjects to inform them of their status and the requirement for evaluation (assessment). Also, the personnel

Low Risk	Moderate Risk	High Risk
1. Legal audit of employment-related issues and actions, including Title VII, privacy, harassment, etc. 2. Legal consultation on incident management strategies, including communications strategy to maintain privilege and control and direction of cursory background investigation	1. Legal audit of employment-related issues and actions, including Title VII, privacy, harassment, etc. 2. Legal consultation on incident management strategies, including communications strategy to maintain privilege and control and direction of full background investigation 3. Termination action review 4. Management of restraining order process 5. Consider civil or criminal legal action	1. Legal audit of employment-related issues and actions, including Title VII, privacy, harassment, etc. 2. Legal consultation on incident management strategies, including communications strategy to maintain privilege and control and direction of full background investigation 3. Termination action review 4. Management of restraining order process 5. Consider civil or criminal legal action

Figure 4.11 Legal.

Low Risk	Moderate Risk	High Risk
1. Post-assessment employment action or counseling 2. Referral for treatment (suggested versus required) 3. Post-action constituency communication	1. Management meeting with subject to inform of status and requirement for evaluation 2. Possible post-fitness for duty referral for treatment 3. Post-action constituency communication and debrief as necessary 4. Post-evaluation employment action or counseling	1. Management notification to subject of required meeting (for on-site evaluation) 2. Possible post-assessment treatment referral and liaison 3. Post-action constituency communication and debrief as necessary 4. Post-evaluation termination

Figure 4.12 Employee relations actions.

assigned to this category will be responsible for providing personnel files and use of benefits information and participating with Legal in discussions of communications and prospective personnel actions. If this is not an employee-related assessment, then this category is not relevant.

The term "post-action constituency communication" refers to communication with appropriate co-workers related to "Duty to Warn." For further information on this concept, refer to Chapter 10.

Treatment

This category (see Figure 4.13) refers to those treatment options primarily available to employers at different levels of assessed risk. However, some of these options, like involuntary treatment for substance use, marital problems or mental conditions, may be available to courts, while involuntary commitment based on dangerousness to self or others is available to law enforcement personnel, the courts and mental health providers.

Methodology for Use of the Grids for Case Management

The user receives an initial report of an incident and begins the basic information accumulation necessary to make the initial assessment as to whether 911 should be called. This assessment is not based on the Grids, but on the immediacy of the initial case information. As mentioned before, a 911 call could be made in the belief that a person is in proximity to a target group and is actively seeking a readily available firearm, or for a variety of other reasons, including that the current understood circumstances meet a predetermined criterion for seeking emergency assistance, such as a very specific threat related to explosives, or the belief that an instigator is currently hunting for a particular target and the time for location of that target is unknown, but possibly short.

However, if the case, as initially presented, does not require emergency assistance by public resources, then the assessor does an initial review of

Low Risk	Moderate Risk	High Risk
1. Voluntary or required inpatient or outpatient (possibly EAP-administered) treatment for identified problems — family, marital, substance abuse or mental conditions	1. Voluntary or required inpatient or outpatient (possibly EAP-administered) treatment for identified problems — family, marital, substance abuse or mental conditions 2. Possible treatment in conjunction with continuous fitness-for-duty requirement	1. Voluntary or required inpatient or outpatient (possibly EAP-administered) treatment for identified problems — family, marital, substance abuse or mental conditions 2. Possible treatment in conjunction with continuous fitness-for-duty requirement 3. Possible involuntary commitment with possible involuntary medication, for 72 hours or longer

Figure 4.13 Treatment.

information and begins the process of gathering enough information to make a threshold assessment for risk. As outlined in Chapter 2, this would include interviewing the initial report providers and any immediately available witnesses to the current event of concern. It would also include a review of *immediately available* records (e.g., incident reports, personnel files, witness statements, etc.). Once the initial burst of information gathering is accomplished, then the behavioral information that is learned is matched to the similar entries across the behavioral categories of the Assessment Grid. As previously mentioned, the Assessment Grid category boxes are ranked from left (Low Risk) to right (High Risk), with Moderate Risk listed in the middle column box. The behaviors in the categories are not ordered within each risk box by importance (e.g., the listing is not from top to bottom by seriousness of behavior), but are grouped by similar types of risk behavior.

Once all the currently known case information is matched to the Assessment Grid categories, two types of analyses are possible. The first is whether any categories of information contain no case-related information. If this occurs, the most likely reason is that the information-gathering process, so far, has not touched on all the relevant areas of behavioral interest. This should cause the assessor to note the information areas that still need to be explored in the information-gathering process. If several of these categories have missing information, then no *formal* initial (threshold) assessment should be made at that time and more information gathering should take place immediately.

Assuming that all the categories have some data present, those data for any missing categories have been explored and are not present, or there is already a significant amount of data in the High Risk areas of the Assessment Grid, the second analysis, that of initial risk, can be made. The grids provide for some flexibility in assessment related to the judgment and experience of the assessor(s). In IMT settings, assessment is best done by consensus among all the team members participating. In other cases, it may be the assessors by themselves or with other knowledgeable or experienced colleagues. The initial assessment is an average of the information found across the Assessment Grid, except in those cases where certain elements are present (e.g., psychotic violent thoughts, active hallucinations, homicidal or suicidal ideation or intentional use of a weapon to harm someone), which will immediately skew the analysis to an initial assessment of High Risk.

Once the initial risk assessment has been made, the assessor or IMT then turns to the Response Grid and follows the appropriate steps to gather more information, continuing to reassess the case with each new piece of information provided and taking appropriate steps to protect the potential victim(s). These protective actions may involve either direct or indirect interaction with the instigator, or both.

Illustrating Use of This Tool with a Case History

The use of this tool might be best illustrated with a case, e.g., "Daniel," in Appendix 4.2. Read the account of the situation and then use the Assessment Grid to make an initial assessment of risk and the Response Grid to make a decision about the initial steps you would take to continue to assess and manage the case. You might want to duplicate this practice exercise out of the book and use a marker to highlight the different elements in the chapter that you find to be of interest in your assessment.

This case example is not uncommon for most assessors. It has elements of both workplace violence and domestic violence; the potential for multiple victims; seems to be escalating; and has psychological, emotional, organizational, political and legal elements and an unclear time frame. One visualization of analysis is the Ed Sullivan[10] "spinning plates" analogy. Mr. Sullivan had a performer on his variety show who would spin plates at the end of long flexible poles. The act was built around how many plates he could get up and keep spinning without having any of them fall to the stage. The performer would end up running up and down the stage, keeping track of the spinning of each plate, while adding new poles and new plates until the process seemed impossible. Analysis is like that in the sense that each piece of data in the analysis needs to be identified and "kept spinning" or active in the analysis until an appropriate place is found for it. "Dropping" any piece of data, by losing that element through forgetfulness or inattention, prior to the conclusion of the case leads to poor, if not catastrophic, results.

Our analysis of this case breaks down as follows:

First Level: Assuming All Information Presented Is Found to Be True

Time Frame:	Friday morning discovery — escalation last 3 weeks
Instigator:	Daniel
Potential Victims:	Jerry, Susan and Robert
Behavior:	
Escalating Aggression:	Repeated angry outbursts (but under breath, unknown whether he knew he was overheard or wanted to be) (Moderate Risk)
	Evidence of a violent plan? Possible, if so, High Risk
Weapons Involvement:	Ownership of firearms with escalated practice in association with emotional release (High Risk)
Negative Mental Status:	Possible paranoid thinking, hostile jealousy (Moderate Risk)
	Apparent mental preoccupation, persistent anger (Moderate Risk)
Negative Employment Status:	Recent disciplinary action from Jerry (Moderate Risk)
	Probable termination (Moderate Risk)

Personal Stressors:	Significant financial pressure — to increase with job loss (Moderate Risk)
	Primary relationship disruption (perceived betrayal) (Moderate Risk)
History of Violence or Conflict:	History of litigiousness (Moderate Risk)
	Pattern of mildly conflictual work relationships (Low Risk)
Buffers:	Appropriate seeking of legal help (so far)
Organizational Impact:	Employees fear potential of violence
	Management has personal fear of violence
	Stated possible fear-induced employee job avoidance
Organizational Influences:	None known to date
Threshold Assessment:	Moderate Risk, unknown time frame
Response Level:	Moderate Risk

Initial Response Actions: (see Chapter 2 for more details)

1. Contact (at a minimum) Core IMT and threat assessment specialist and do initial data dump.
2. Reclassify or confirm Threshold Assessment.
3. Identify initial Response actions and responsibilities for each team member.
   - Interview: James, Jerome and Jerry immediately to get first-hand information in more contextual and behavioral depth.
   - Initiate: full background investigation of Daniel, even though results will not be fully known until Tuesday or Wednesday of next week.
   - Initiate: law enforcement liaison, looking for wants, warrants, "calls for service to the residence"; other contacts with law enforcement that may involve drugs, violence or weapons; connect with patrol division to understand who to contact for site response planning if necessary.
   - Initiate: review of legal audit of employment-related issues, need for duty to warn communication and drafting of potential language.
   - Discuss: pros and cons of approaching Susan or Robert and interviewing them; make initial decision concerning who, when and what approach.
   - Discuss: pros and cons of approaching Daniel on Friday evening versus Monday or Tuesday for a "management reality check meeting" by team members or threat (violence) assessment specialist or assessment team; make initial decision concerning who, when and what approach to use.
   - Decide: when, where and how to reconvene for next assessment, response plan extension and implementation.

How did you assess the case? What were your initial response considerations and actions? One of the most effective ways to train is to develop practical exercises from real cases and then use them at periodic IMT training sessions to refine process, clarify assessment insights and plan for future response options. If the responsibility of developing and delivering practical exercises is shared by all team members, it is a cost- and time-effective, value-proven way to enhance both individual and team member assessment and response knowledge and skill level.

Control

This chapter has been about methodology of assessment; seeking different ways to view and analyze behavioral data so that we have the most well-rounded assessment of the instigator, which maximizes the possibility of a successful intervention. Another quick analysis that can be done is a "control vector" analysis. This analysis is based on the concept that all human behavior, including violence, is exclusively centered around the need to establish or re-establish control. Therefore, in any violence risk assessment, after we have developed a comprehensive set of behavioral data, we ask the following three questions: How desperately is the person seeking control? What has the person done in the past to achieve a sense of control? What might he or she be willing to do now? The answers to these three questions can quickly allow the formation of a sense of velocity and trajectory of the case that will cut through the "chatter" and give us a powerful, practical perspective about what level of risk the case might pose and what steps might be taken to disrupt the path to inappropriate action. If we can provide the instigator with a sense of control, without giving up real situational control, this will lower the instigator's need to use violence. An extended explanation of this concept and use in case analysis is provided in the Control Addendum at the end of this chapter.

Summary

The use of a structured methodology or "formula" for assessment improves the quality of assessment by providing the assessor a framework to guide the gathering of information and a more objective way to view the case facts. This methodology is substantially enhanced by using an assessment instrument or tool based on understandings of behaviors and thoughts relevant to the prediction of violent behaviors in the type of potential violence being assessed. The use of an appropriate instrument or tool provides a more objective and accurate assessment than the use of clinical or subjective judgment alone. The reality of case assessment is that time and money are always limited, but, given the responsibilities of the assessor both to the victims and the instigator, neither of these factors should stop the assessor from providing an assessment that is information intensive and as objective as possible each and every time. For the protection of everyone's rights and for the freedom and the safety of all concerned, the standard of assessment practice should be raised by making it more objective and transparent.

Endnotes

1. Dolan, M., and Doyle, M. (2000). Violence risk prediction, *British Journal of Psychiatry*, 177, pp. 303–311.
2. Discussed in Developing a clinically useful actuarial tool for assessing violence risk, *British Journal of Psychiatry*, *176*, pp. 312–320.
3. For a more detailed discussion of current instruments and their uses, the entire issue of *Criminal Justice and Behavior*, Vol. 29, August 2002, is devoted to the topic of contemporary risk assessment. Each author is well known and tackles a particular area of interest to readers of this book.
4. J. Reid Meloy also addresses this concern in his book, *Violence Risk and Threat Assessment: A Practical Guide for Mental Health and Criminal Justice Professionals,* Specialized Training Services, 2000, pp. 158–159. Chapters 9 (Psychopathy) and 10 (Other Risk Assessment Instruments) in his book are also sources of information on risk assessment instruments that could be valuable to the reader.
5. *Criminal Justice and Behavior*, Vol. 29, August 2002, pp. 355–379.
6. Boothby, J.L., and Clements, C.B. (2000). A national survey of correctional psychologists, *Criminal Justice and Behavior*, *27*, pp. 715–731.
7. Cornell, D.G., Warren, J., Hawk, G., and Stafford, E. (1996). Psychopathy in instrumental and reactive violent offenders, *Journal of Consulting and Clinical Psychology*, 64(4), pp. 783–790.
8. Harris, G.T., Rice, M.E., and Cormier, C.A. (1991). Psychopathy and violent recidivism, *Law and Human Behavior*, *15*, pp. 625–637.
9. For those readers who are interested, most of the literature references for each category of the Grids are listed in the reference list for this book. Those who are interested in specific references for any given category can contact Jim Cawood for discussion.
10. Ed Sullivan hosted a television variety show called *The Ed Sullivan Show* in the 1960s. He hosted the first television appearance of the Beatles, Elvis Presley and many other artists and acts.

Appendix 4.1

WITNESS INTERVIEW FORM

All material contained within this questionnaire is protected by copyright law and may not be reproduced without the express written consent of The Workthreat Group, LLC. Additionally, all answers are to be considered privileged and confidential.

Name of Client: _____

Address of Client: _____

_____

Location of Interview: _____

_____

Date of Interview: _____

WITNESS INTERVIEW FORM

NAME: _____ TITLE/DUTIES: _____
LENGTH OF TIME WITH ORGANIZATION: _____
KNOWN SUBJECT FOR: _____
RELATIONSHIP TO SUBJECT: _____
(*Use the back of the page to write more information when there is not enough room in front.*)

QUESTIONS/EXPLANATIONS	*YES*	*NO*	*UNK*
1. Has the subject ever talked about weapons? (Guns, knives, etc.)	☐	☐	☐
2. Has the subject ever used any weapons? If yes, explain how it is known: _____ _____	☐	☐	☐
3. Has the subject ever been known to own or carry any weapons? If yes, explain: _____ _____	☐	☐	☐
4. Is there any known history of drug and/or alcohol use? If yes, explain: _____ _____	☐	☐	☐
5. Has the subject mentioned any movies, TV shows, and/or videos? If yes, describe: _____ _____	☐	☐	☐
6. What kinds of books, magazines and/or newspapers has the subject talked about or mentioned reading? _____ _____			
7. Has the subject ever talked about any dreams or fantasies? If yes, please describe: _____ _____	☐	☐	☐

QUESTIONS/EXPLANATIONS	YES	NO	UNK

8. Has the subject ever mentioned he belonged to or wanted to belong to any club, group, organization and/or association?
   If yes, please describe:_____
   _____

9. Are you aware of the subject seeking mental health assistance?
   Circle: Psychologist/Psychiatrist   Marriage Counselor
   EAP   Mental Institution   Other: _____

10. Is the subject considered weird, eccentric or strange by anyone?
    Examples:_____
    _____

11. Is there any known history of violence by this subject specifically toward any women, children or animals?
    Examples:_____
    _____

12. Is there any known history of domestic violence this subject has been associated with?
    Examples: _____
    _____

13. Is there any known history of sexual harassment this subject has been associated with?
    Examples:_____
    _____

14. Are you aware of any promiscuous and/or unusual sexual behavior on the part of this subject?
    Examples: _____
    _____

15. Are you aware if this subject has had many short-term marital and/or serious relationships?
    Examples: _____
    _____

QUESTIONS/EXPLANATIONS	YES	NO	UNK

16. Are you aware of subject's current living
arrangements?
Explain: _____

☐ ☐ ☐

17. Is there any indication this subject is
living off others?
Explain: _____

☐ ☐ ☐

18. Are you aware of this subject's financial
condition?
Explain: _____

☐ ☐ ☐

19. Are you aware of any stressors subject
is dealing with?
Explain: _____

_____

☐ ☐ ☐

20. Are you aware of any criminal activity
this subject may have been involved with
or may currently be doing?
Explain: _____

_____

If so, are these crimes repetitive, consistent
or varied? (Circle)

☐ ☐ ☐

21. Are you aware of any court orders
against this subject?
Restraining   Child Support   Other _____

☐ ☐ ☐

22. Are you aware of any threats this subject
has ever made?
Explain: _____

_____

☐ ☐ ☐

23. Are you aware of this subject following or
stalking anyone?
Explain: _____

_____

☐ ☐ ☐

24. Has the subject ever talked about or
attempted suicide?
Explain: _____

_____

☐ ☐ ☐

QUESTIONS/EXPLANATIONS	*YES*	*NO*	*UNK*

25. Has the subject ever talked about
    starting fires?
    Explain: _____

26. Any known physical injury in the past,
    especially head trauma?

27. Has the subject ever made any fatalistic
    statements?
    ("I don't care if I live or die." "I have nothing
    to live for.")
    Explain: _____

28. Are you aware of the relationship the
    subject had with his parents as a child
    growing up?
    Explain: _____

29. Has the subject ever described any family
    history of violence, i.e., between parents
    and/or siblings?
    Explain: _____
    _____

30. Are you aware if the subject had any
    juvenile problems?
    Explain: _____
    _____

31. Any known history of immediate family
    criminality, i.e., father arrested, sibling
    juvenile problems, etc.?
    Explain: _____
    _____

32. Any known history of being abused
    as a child?
    Explain: _____
    _____

33. Have you ever seen this subject depressed?

34. Has the subject ever said he hears voices?
    Example: _____

QUESTIONS/EXPLANATIONS   *YES*   *NO*   *UNK*

35. Does the subject seem to get frustrated,   ☐   ☐   ☐
    especially lately?
    Example: _____

36. Does the subject ever act secretive?   ☐   ☐   ☐
    Example: _____

37. Would you say this subject usually displays   ☐   ☐   ☐
    a glibness, superficial charm or phony
    behavior?
    Example: _____

38. Does the subject seem to have a grandiose   ☐   ☐   ☐
    sense of self-worth, acting pompous or
    egotistical most of the time?
    Example: _____

39. Would you consider this subject not to tell   ☐   ☐   ☐
    the truth?
    a. Circle best descriptive degree:
       Occasionally; Sometimes; Frequently;
       Almost always; Always; Pathological.
    b. Circle best descriptive reason:
       Exaggeration; Intimidation; To purposely
       blame others; To get out of trouble
       (by shifting blame).

40. Would you consider this subject conning or   ☐   ☐   ☐
    manipulative?
    Examples: _____
    _____

41. Does the subject generally portray a   ☐   ☐   ☐
    callous self or one with little empathy?
    Examples: _____
    _____

42. Does the subject demonstrate a lack of   ☐   ☐   ☐
    remorse or guilt over things he/she has
    done in which most others would feel remorse
    or guilt?
    Examples: _____
    _____

QUESTIONS/EXPLANATIONS	*YES*	*NO*	*UNK*

43. Have you ever noted any romantic involvement this subject has ever been involved in?
   Has it ever appeared obsessional? _____

44. Do you consider this subject impulsive?
   Examples: _____

45. Do you consider this subject responsible?
   Explain: _____

46. Does the subject generally fail to take responsibility for his own actions?
   Explain: _____

47. Does the subject always seem to blame other people and/or events for his problems?

48. Would you say this subject seems to need a lot of stimulation in his life or he may indicate he is bored?

49. Does the subject generally exhibit poor behavioral controls?
   Example: _____

50. Describe the subject's temperament, especially any recent changes.
   a. Mood swings: _____
   b. Tantrums: _____
   c. Outbursts: _____
   d. Throwing things: _____
   e. Slamming things: _____

51. How does the subject usually respond to direction or corrections from:
   a. Administration: _____
   b. Supervision/Instructor: _____
   c. Co-workers/Students: _____
   d. Others (list): _____

52. How does the subject usually seem to resolve conflict? _____
   _____
   _____

53. How does this subject usually respond to changes, such as rules, expectations, etc.?

_____

_____

54. How would you describe the relationship between this subject and co-workers/students?

_____

55. Has this relationship changed in the last several weeks/months, and if so, how? _____

_____

56. What do you feel are this subject's expectations of this organization?

_____

_____

QUESTIONS/EXPLANATIONS	YES	NO	UNK
57. Are you aware of any complaints this subject has filed? If so, did they seem reasonable? _____	☐	☐	☐
58. Does this subject seem obsessed with his job?	☐	☐	☐
59. Does the subject have any known suspensions from work? If so, how did he respond to these? _____	☐	☐	☐
60. Is the subject considered a troublemaker? a. If so, give example(s): _____	☐	☐	☐
b. Does he/she associate with other known troublemakers?			
61. Does the subject demonstrate any personality conflicts? (Just doesn't seem to get along with most people.) Example: _____	☐	☐	☐

QUESTIONS/EXPLANATIONS   YES   NO   UNK

62. Would you consider this subject to be a loner?   ☐   ☐   ☐

63. Are you aware of any changes in this subject's   ☐   ☐   ☐
    belief toward any religion or cause?
    a. Explain: _____

    _____

    b. Any others share this belief or
       enthusiasm? _____

    _____

64. How would you describe this subject's outlook on the world?

    _____

    _____

    _____

65. How would this subject describe his own self-esteem?

    _____

QUESTIONS/EXPLANATIONS   YES   NO   UNK

66. Would you say this subject lacks realistic,   ☐   ☐   ☐
    long-term goals?

67. Have you witnessed a confrontation this   ☐   ☐   ☐
    subject has had?
    a. If so, describe incident, body language,
       voice tone, etc.:

    _____

    _____

    _____

    _____

    _____

    b. What did this subject do immediately after the confrontation?

    _____

    _____

    c. How did this subject act 24 hours after the confrontation?

    _____

    _____

    _____

QUESTIONS/EXPLANATIONS   YES   NO   UNK

68. Has the subject ever indicated by words,   ☐   ☐   ☐
    actions or suggestions that he/she wanted
    to get even with anyone?
    Describe: _____
    _____

69. Are you aware of any specific tactics   ☐   ☐   ☐
    employed at work or school to control or
    manage this subject's conduct?
    Example: _____
    _____

    The results: _____
    _____

70. Describe a typical day at this organization for this subject:

    _____
    _____
    _____
    _____
    _____
    _____
    _____
    _____
    _____

QUESTIONS/EXPLANATIONS   YES   NO   UNK

71. Do you feel this subject has the potential for   ☐   ☐   ☐
    violence?
    If so, why? _____
    _____

72. Are you afraid for your safety because of   ☐   ☐   ☐
    this subject?

73. Are you afraid of this subject because of his: a. intimidations; b. retaliation
    potential; c. bullying behavior; and/or d. other _____

74. Are you aware of anything or anyone in this environment that may have caused and/or contributed to this subject's behavior (stress; unfair treatment; recent events; etc.)? _____

_____

_____

_____

75. Are you aware of anything or anyone in this environment that may have caused and/or contributed to the stress or problems of anyone involved in this inquiry?_____

_____

_____

_____

76. Are there any known hobbies, special interests, special vacations and/or outings that this subject likes to do? _____

_____

_____

77. Are there any activities that this subject seems obsessional about? (Has to be in at an exact time; has to wash the car every weekend; has to eat lunch in a certain area.) _____

_____

_____

78. Is there anything else you think is important or significant that has not been asked or talked about?_____

_____

_____

_____

_____

TO ALWAYS BE READ TO INTERVIEWEE AT END OF INTERVIEW:

Thank you for talking with me today. Your insight and candor are very appreciated. As I know you are aware, this is a very serious as well as sensitive matter. Therefore, I would appreciate you keeping this interview confidential and not discussing it with co-workers or friends. Additionally, anything that may occur to you later about this matter, I would appreciate you notifying me about it, regardless how minor an issue you may think it is.

Name of interviewer (*please print*)_____

Best way to contact interviewer: _____

Appendix 4.2

Case History: Daniel

Imagine you are a human resources director at a local manufacturing company in the Northwest. It is a Friday morning and you have just arrived at work, having already participated in several conference calls involving some issues with your sales force on the East Coast. As you walk into your office, your assistant hands you a series of messages from the operations manager asking you to call immediately. You dial her intercom line and you can tell immediately she is stressed about something. She asks to come to your office and speak to you concerning a confidential matter that is time critical.

She arrives about 5 minutes later and states she has just received a report concerning one of her manufacturing employees, Daniel, who works the swing shift in the plant. Daniel is married to another production employee, Susan, who works the day shift. Claudia, the operations manager, states she's just been informed by Daniel's supervisor, Jerry, that several workers on the swing shift have come to him over the last week concerned about several comments that Daniel has made. Jerry told Claudia the swing shift workers reported that, in the last 3 weeks, Daniel has been acting in an "agitated" way. They stated he had always been somewhat of a complainer, but lately, he has been openly muttering under his breath on the line. The comments initially were about whether Susan was having an affair with one of her co-workers, Robert, but then they began to involve Jerry and whether Jerry was laughing at Daniel because his wife was having an affair and he did not know.

One of the workers, James, had reported that, at the beginning, Daniel was just generally talking to himself about Susan and the idea she might be having a relationship with someone, but over the last week or so he had begun mentioning Robert. When he started mentioning Robert, he began speculating underneath his breath about whether he should attack Robert and how he might do it. In the last several days, this had progressed to his being overheard talking to himself and saying such things as, "I wonder if I should confront him at his home or at the plant?" and "I wonder if I could get away with it if I shot him or whether I should make it look more like an accident?"

In the last several weeks, another worker, Jerome, had overheard Daniel talking to himself about Jerry, originally stating things like, "I'd think Jerry knows what's going on, he knows everything that goes on in the plant." Then he had been overheard saying, "Jerry must know and he must really be enjoying himself knowing my wife is stepping out on me and thinking I don't know."

Claudia stated she was very concerned about this situation because it seemed to be becoming more volatile and, if something happened in the plant, innocent people could be hurt. She stated the workers who had come forward to talk to Jerry had also mentioned they thought Daniel and Susan were experiencing some relationship problems based on some financial difficulties they had due to the illness of one of their children. Daniel had mentioned a month or so ago that creditors were calling at the home trying to collect on the debts they owed and they just didn't have the money to pay. She also had heard that Daniel had several firearms in his possession and had talked about how much he enjoyed going down to the range and shooting the weapons as a method of stress reduction. Daniel had talked about how, when he was at the range, he could control what the gun would do, unlike other parts of his life. Jerry had also mentioned that, in the past, Daniel had a running argument with one of his neighbors concerning their property line and an easement and there was talk of several lawsuits to try to resolve that issue. The co-workers had mentioned they were concerned about their safety and felt that if this situation didn't get resolved, they might have to take some time off just to stay out of the way until it calmed down.

Claudia stated Daniel was scheduled to come into work today at 2 P.M., and management was not planning to run a weekend shift. She asked that this matter be taken care of as quickly as possible, so people could get back to focusing on their jobs. She stated if the solution was to fire Daniel because he was in violation of their harassment or violence policy, so be it.

A quick review of Daniel's employment file showed he had been with the company for 3 years and had been on the swing shift for his entire employment. He was seen as an above-average worker, but had a series of disciplinary issues focused around challenging his supervisor, Jerry, concerning work rules and, lately, some issues around being late to work. There was a note in his file from the payroll department that, about 2 months ago, someone had filed a garnishment on his wages for $3500, to be paid off at the rate of $150 per pay period.

A review of Susan's employment file showed that she had been employed with the company for 5 years and was considered an excellent worker. She had no disciplinary issues on file and her attendance and timeliness were perfect.

A review of Robert's employment file showed that he had been employed by the company for 1 year and had one complaint registered against him for sexual harassment. The investigation of that complaint had been completed and not enough information had been confirmed to sustain the complaint.

What is your initial assessment?
What is your initial response?

APPENDIX 4.3

Control Addendum

In this addendum we are departing slightly from our normal approach in this book of providing concrete, grounded, practical information, to explore the concept of control. Ultimately, we believe that this exploration will provide a basis for concrete assessment and intervention steps in a variety of conflict situations, including violence. However, first we believe a more general exploration of the concept is in order.

The idea of unifying concepts or principles has fascinated people throughout the ages. Whether you look at the cosmology of Anaximander, the philosophy of Plato or Ken Wilbur, the scientific thought of Galileo, Einstein or Fritjof Capra, or the religious thought of Lao Tzu or the Dalai Lama, their visions were and are an attempt to develop and deliver a holistic explanation of how the universe, and all the elements in it, function as a whole. I (co-author Cawood) have also been fascinated with this idea of a unifying concept, particularly as it applies to human behavior. About 15 years ago, a thought began to gel in my mind about the concept of control, and the more I explored it, the more I came to view it as the foundational construct for all human behavior. In this chapter, we touched on it as the central motivation for all violence-related behavior and the core assessment vector for all successful interventions. We will continue to explore that more fully in this addendum, but I also want to explore and anchor a wide range of human experiences and endeavors, so that the quest for control can be understood as the core drive of all human existence. If we understand this concept and truly embrace it, we could use this understanding to unlock a wide range of vexing problems, both personal and those that the human species seems to revisit on a regular basis across the expanse of human history.

Science

Science could be defined as the systematic study of the physical universe: its properties, forces, the interaction of all its parts, both seen and unseen. First, the human species studied the immediate world around them — plants, animals, weather, fire, water, air and earth. Next, we moved on to the heavens, at least all that we could see with the human eye. Then, we began speculating about what was unseen — the very small, the very far away and the "hidden" forces that seemed to influence the things we could see, from a falling apple to the movement of a planet. If we could understand these things and how they worked, then maybe we could control them, and if we could control them, then we could survive longer and have a more prosperous life. The knowledge that comes out of scientific inquiry provides us a greater perception of control. This perception of greater control reduces our anxiety, while increasing the actual ability to more effectively control the workings of our own bodies and the world around us, allowing us to live longer. The resulting control over our world that scientific knowledge has provided the human species is seen in everything from the great diminishment of widespread disease, to the increase in food production, to the increase in human population, to the increase in the average life expectancy for the majority of the human species currently living. Paradoxically, our greater control has also changed, as the ecology of the planet is changing, currently to our detriment, and has allowed some diseases to spread more quickly between continents.

Psychology

This discipline is built on the study of human cognition, emotion and behavior, and the study of the interplay between these elements. As with the other branches of systematic study (science), this discipline strives to understand, so it can provide tools to better control the development of human beings and help them make adjustments that will enhance their quality of life. Whether sports psychology, forensic psychology, violence risk assessment, clinical psychology, counseling psychology, organizational psychology or the plethora of blended or other psychological disciplines, the more we understand about human perception, thinking and action, the more we can control interaction with ourselves and others to provide specific outcomes that reduce internal and external conflict, speed learning and increase productivity.

Religion and Philosophy

The world is a scary and, seemingly, chaotic place. Life seems capricious. Nature is constantly doing things that change the world around us. Life is hard and short, and time to think raises questions about the reason why we are born at all, our purpose for being on this planet, and what happens to us after we die. If we could just understand these things, control these forces, influence the outcomes or at least learn to accept the reality of our circumstances so that we can continue to function with less angst and doubt, that would be good.

So a man or woman begins to explain about nature, its forces and the structure and working of the universe and we feel less at risk. We understand more about why things happen (even though it may be just superstition) and this understanding gives us the perception of how we need to act to maintain greater control. If we just provide offerings to that man or woman, his or her church, his or her religion, the Gods; if we just turn the other cheek; if we just pray, as taught, to these deities, each day or several times a day or meditate on these "truths"; if we understand and act in a way that is in harmony with the force that created the universe; if we sacrifice ourselves against the infidels or give our lives as a substitute for our family or friends, then we will avoid more bad events and, in the afterlife, will reach nirvana, or heaven, or Asgard.

Another man or woman tells us that to live a "true" and meaningful life and avoid bad events, it just takes an understanding of human nature and how humans really are. There are no divine forces, there are no deities, no afterlife. Wasting time on how we got here, and why, is not important; what is important is the "now" and understanding how we view the world and how our vision is skewed by our physical and mental limitations. To gain this understanding we must have Socratic dialogue, take an existential perspective and be skeptical. Only then will we truly be able to transcend our limitations and discover and embrace the knowledge that will keep us safer and, therefore, make us healthier and happier. Then, and only then, we will be in control.

Families, Societies, Politics and the Law

One of my favorite phrases when doing violence risk assessment work and behavioral analysis in organizations is "Everything is family dynamics." It is astonishing that so many people seem to lose sight of this basic premise. If you embrace this concept and use the same intervention techniques that might apply to dysfunctional families, the problems that are presented regarding group behavior become clear very rapidly and can largely be solved. Family structure, communities, societies, politics and the law are all groupings and systems that grew out of a survival need to establish and maintain control. The more people lived together and shared the burden of survival, the more likely the majority of the species and, then, particular groups of the species, were to survive long enough to pass on their genetic traits. However, you put people together and friction arises between individual wants and needs and what is good for the group. In the beginning, families were the only unit; then families clustered together in communities; then communities banded together into societies. Kingdoms arose, empires were created and then the battle for world domination began. It is all about control — wanting it, getting it, having it, maintaining it, losing it, working to get it again. The law, a relatively new construct in human history, is a socially acceptable means to "battle" with others to get what you want or defend what you have. This socially acceptable means of confrontation can replace the need to physically hurt or kill others. But when the rule of law does not provide the result needed, or is not fairly administered, physical violence is always available as a means to establish or re-establish the perception of control.

Emotion

If everything is about control, then what about the interior world of the human species? Many researchers now believe that emotions are perceptional states, triggered by chemical reactions in our nerves and synapses. The purpose of emotion is to provide additional context to our incoming sensory data, so that we can enhance our understanding of what is happening around us and to us. This enhanced understanding furthers our survival by providing a variety of warnings against acts that could diminish our survival, as well as incentives to act in ways that enhance our survival. Understanding increases our ability to control our surroundings or involvement in what is happening and, therefore, our survival, both individually and collectively. The warnings include anxiety, fear, anger and, possibly, disgust and shame. The incentives include pleasure, happiness, contentment, love and peace.

Taking two of these emotions, anger and love, we can illustrate a direct vector back to control. Every human being on the planet gets angry for only one of two reasons: either someone or something did something the person didn't want to happen, or that something or someone didn't do something the person did want to happen. This includes being angry at oneself. Whether alone, in the family, in traffic, at work or in the community, we get that rush of anger when something happens that we cannot control. Some would postulate that actually fear happens first, the fear that comes from the immediate impression that control has been lost, and then anger quickly kicks in and overcomes the feelings of fear so we can act, such as in fight or flight. Whether that is true or not, anger is about losing a sense of control. Therefore, as mentioned in this chapter, we can control our anger and the anger of others if we can quickly understand how we or they have sensed control has been lost and then give back a sense of control. In the case of potential violence, we give them back the sense of control without giving up long-term situational control.

Love is also linked to control, both the feeling of it and the proof of it. When we are in the state of "being in love" we feel euphoric, outside of time, filled with joy. Control of our thoughts and feelings has been lost to this larger force, this state of being, and the release from the need to have control is marvelous and uplifting. How do you prove you love God or someone? You can't just say it, because we say things we don't mean. Just saying it does not make it so. The only way to prove love is to act in ways that prove that the deity or person is more important than you are. We prove this by giving up control to them. We prove love to a deity, to our spouse or family, and to communities or our nations, by giving up some, or all, of the control over our resources, including our time and attention, to them. In some cases, this means giving up our very existence for their benefit. In exchange for giving up this control, we believe we can, or actually do, experience a euphoria greater than can be experienced in other ways. This intensely pleasurable sensation can help carry us through future times in which these same commitments cause us pain, hardship and death, making those sacrifices for the "greater good" noble, acceptable and possible to accomplish.

The other emotions mentioned can be connected quite quickly. Anxiety alerts us to the possibility of harm, when we are not yet afraid or angry. Shame and disgust alert us that some thought or behavior has crossed a line of appropriateness that could jeopardize our ability to accept ourselves or be accepted by others, thereby risking our ability to survive. Pleasurable feelings come from doing that which enhances our sense of well-being, as does contentment. The experience of positive feelings creates the desire to experience more positive feelings, thereby reinforcing certain behaviors that give those feelings, which, when naturally occurring, usually enhance our survival, such as eating, resting, maintaining a normal body temperature and having sex. This is where drug use becomes interesting, because certain drugs, including alcohol, methamphetamine and cocaine, can create artificial positive feelings that can reinforce behavior that actually diminishes control over oneself and that can be life-threatening.

Violence Risk Assessment and Intervention

"The control vector" analysis is one method of analyzing an individual's behavior to quickly help determine what level of violence risk he or she may pose and also what possible interventions could be used, both immediately and over time, to diminish the likelihood of a violent act. Violence is a means to establish or re-establish a perception of control over the object or person it is directed against, even oneself. Therefore, when analyzing someone's behavior to determine potential violence risk, we can ask ourselves three questions to determine the control vector: How does this person perceive he is losing control? What has he physically done in the past to obtain a perception of control? What might he be willing to do now? The answer to the "how" question can provide a quick insight that leads to an intervention strategy. The answers to the "what" questions provide some quick information concerning the current level of risk and possible path of escalation. An additional benefit of this analysis is that it keeps the practitioner in a cognitively engaged mode, which diminishes his immediate emotional escalation and allows him to think more clearly to control the situation. No one can be highly cognitive and emotional at the same time; the neurotransmitters of "fight or flight" actually disrupt the electrical signals to the neocortex, diminishing cognitive reasoning. So by engaging the mind in reasoning, the practitioner "keeps his head," while those around him might be losing their ability to process clearly, and therefore the practitioner is in a better state to actually control the situation.

Let us first illustrate this control vector concept with the simple example of a child having a tantrum. Every parent of more than a year has gone through a situation where the child becomes angry and frustrated and starts lashing out, maybe slamming objects or screaming. If we just tell the child to "stop" that does not work. So we have to figure out what he or she wants, or wants to happen, and then provide the child alternatives that are acceptable to us. This allows the child to experience having us respond to him, which immediately strengthens his sense of control and diminishes his need to act out, but because we only provide him alternatives we are comfortable with, we are actually controlling the overall situation.

Another example could involve a domestic abuser. The individual has called his or her spouse's office and threatened to kill the spouse because the spouse did not do what the abuser wanted the person to do. The abuser has a history of destroying furniture and punching the spouse, in the privacy of their home, when the spouse has not done what the abuser wanted. This is the first time that the abuser has called the spouse at work to threaten him or her. Regarding the "how" question, it is simple to understand that the spouse not performing the act requested caused the abuser to perceive he or she had lost control of the spouse because the spouse did not comply with the abuser's wishes. The answers to the "what" questions reveal that the abuser has destroyed property and physically assaulted the spouse to re-establish control, and the new behavior of calling the worksite raises the question of whether that behavior will escalate now by moving out of the home and migrating to the work property. So the short-term intervention options might include a response plan for the possibility that the abuser will show up at the worksite and also a discussion with the spouse about how and when he or she plans to go back to the residence and what might be done when he or she gets there to deescalate the situation if the abuser is still angry.

Finally, what if you have a paranoid, delusional threatener who claims that people are spraying his cubicle with chemicals to try to force him out of the company? He has stormed into the Human Resource office and said that if they don't stop the spraying, he will have to take "other measures." He has no known history of violence, but his storming into the HR office is a significant escalation from previous behavior. In this case, the "how" question would be fully understood by sitting down with the threatener and exploring, in depth, his entire belief system and how this chemical spraying fits into his perception of reality. The level of immediate risk is fairly moderate, as the person has no known history of physical acting out, but his actions are an escalation and that leads to concerns about the time frame the threatener believes has to be met before he takes "other measures" and what those measures might be. Interviewing the threatener causes him to perceive that he is regaining a measure of control because he has your attention, and your understanding of his belief system may lead to information that provides alternatives to inappropriate actions to mitigate this concern about chemicals. Alternatives might include a brief leave of absence while the workplace is tested, consultation with medical providers to help alleviate the perceived effects of the exposure to the chemicals, a fitness-for-duty examination that leads to treatment for the threatener for what is diagnosed as "delusional disorder with paranoid features," etc. Any of these possible alternatives could provide a deescalation of the immediate concern of his acting out violently. He perceives he has re-established control over his environment by getting us to work with him to solve the problem, but we are actually controlling the outcome by providing him alternative solutions that solve the actual underlying problem (his delusional belief system), thereby reducing the long-term risk of an escalation to violence.

This same control vector analysis could be used in political confrontations, legal confrontations and any other situation where humans, as individuals or in groups, are having confrontations. Can we assess exactly how they perceive they are losing control, or why they feel the need to establish control, and interact with them to give them a perception of control, while actually only giving them concessions we are willing to make, thereby actually being in control of the outcome? Every human thought, emotion, and action involve the concept of control.

Assessment Tools

5

One of the biggest changes in the field of violence risk assessment that has occurred since the writing of the first edition of this book is the substantial increase in discussions and study of violence risk assessment protocols and tools. Since the mid-1990s the research and studies have continued to accelerate exponentially in number[1] and specificity. Traditionally, violence risk assessment process and tools were divided into the actuarial group and the clinical judgment group. Then a group of researchers in British Columbia (Hart, Kropp, Webster, Burgess, et al.) began to discuss a blended approach that they labeled Structured Professional Judgment (SPJ). The argument for this new approach was that purely clinical judgment is inconsistent and its use does not allow for replication and testing of processes and results, while the actuarial methods, illustrated by the structure of the Violence Risk Assessment Guide (VRAG), are very rigid and do not allow the incorporation of low base rate, but important risk elements, in any specific case, while also not contributing to case management analysis and intervention strategies. SPJ, on the other hand, incorporates both static and dynamic risk factors, based on empirical research criteria, while also building in some flexibility in case analysis, with the goal of understanding not only the level of risk that might be present in any given case, but also the dynamic factors that could be influenced in the case intervention and management phases, to maximize positive outcomes, meaning reducing the number of future incidences of violence. This new approach was incorporated into the design of many tools, including the Historical/Clinical/Risk Management 20-item scale (HCR-20), Spousal Assault Risk Assessment Guide (SARA), Structured Assessment of Violence Risk in Youth (SAVRY), The Risk for Sexual Violence Protocol (RSVP), Sexual Violence Risk-20 (SVR-20), Jail Screening Assessment Tool (JSAT) and the Brief Spousal Assault Form for Evaluation of Risk (B-SAFER), to name a few. These tools, by their structure and, in some cases, content, show that they come out of the "Psychopathy School" of tools, in that they currently use, or have used, a similar structure for coding (0,1,2) and/or have

other methodological or risk factor similarities. There are numerous studies that have shown the validity of the SPJ approach when the HCR-20, the
SARA and other SPJ-based tools have been tested.[2] These types of tools have
also been compared to their progenitor, the Psychopathy Checklist Revised
(PCL-R), and have been found to have similar validity, while adding a risk
management component.[3] Since the authors of this book conduct the vast
majority of their assessments outside of controlled environments and do
not have clients who allow for unlimited time to do assessments or unlimited budgets to use assessment tools, we have pared down our process to the
minimum we believe is appropriate, including the use of one tool per case
if possible. Obviously, a concern that has been explored extensively in the
assessment literature in the last 5 years is whether the tool that the assessor is currently using in his case has already been tested on that same case
population of individuals (e.g., youth, adult, inpatient, outpatient, prisoners,
mentally ill, etc.). This degree of tool testing, in a wide range of populations,
is in the beginning stages even now. Depending on your normal caseload,
we would encourage you to identify and research the validity of tools for
the majority of case populations that you work with and use those tools
that have proven to be the most effective. However, if there is an absence of
specific tools, or testing of tools, in a particular population you work with,
then, based on our experience and training, we believe that a general tool
that reflects on the SPJ methodology, such as the Assessment and Response
Grids or the HCR-20, is currently the most effective way to conduct violence
risk assessments and interventions, as long as you acknowledge in your
assessment documentation the possible limitations of the tool. Frankly, any
tool you are using, as mentioned in Chapter 4, will not stand on its own to
defend you should a case turn violent and negligence is litigated. Therefore,
all practitioners should develop their case management and documentation
practices so that they can articulate what they knew, when they knew it and
what they did about it, and why. Remember, you do not have to be ultimately
right in what you did to be able to defend yourself. If we all had to be right
every time, then every practitioner in a field with risk (e.g., law enforcement, medicine, psychology, the law, the military, etc.) would never be able
to practice. You have to be able to show that the recommendation(s) you
made, or actions that you initiated, were reasonable and in good faith at the
time the actions were undertaken, given accepted guidelines and standards
of your profession and/or practice area. These tools can help us accomplish
the goal of better assessments and interventions, while also providing better
documentation to explain and defend our choices.

The SPJ methodology has also been endorsed by the Association of
Threat Assessment Professionals (ATAP) in the development of its Risk
Assessment Guideline Elements for Violence (RAGE-V), which was released
in September 2006. This guideline was developed over a 4-year period of

time by a multi-disciplinary team of violence risk assessors because of the inconsistent violence risk assessment methodologies being used to determine levels of violence risk. It has been introduced in North America and in the European Union and is gaining momentum as a tool that can be used by both assessors and consumers of assessment reports (e.g., judges, prosecutors, law enforcement officers, probation and parole departments, human resources professionals, security professionals, etc.) to guide their analyses of cases and assessment reports. It provides the minimum level of factors that should be considered in any case to provide valid foundation for a violence risk assessment to be made. It also acknowledges that in any given case, certain information will not be available or applicable to that case, but by working through the risk factors, triggers, inhibitors, etc. the assessors will be able to document that they considered those factors, including being able to articulate why they were or were not considered in any given case. In the case of consumers of assessment reports, they can use the RAGE-V to actually question assessors about their methodology and determine if the assessment is adequately supported. We have included a copy of the RAGE-V as an appendix to this chapter. We encourage you to read it and use it in your work. It can also be found online at www.atapworldwide.org if you would like it in electronic form. To conclude this general discussion of methodology and tools, we want to be perfectly clear that *the days of the 1- to 3-hour clinical interview and administering an MMPI-2 to provide a violence risk assessment are over.* That is not an adequate, valid or defensible process.

Next we will discuss the HCR-20 and SARA in violence risk assessments, as we did with the Grids in Chapter 4, and discuss how they might be used. The HCR-20, current version 2,[4] is one of the most practical and versatile of the SPJ tools we have found. It has been tested with a variety of populations and found to provide valid results in those populations.[5] The name of the tool derives from the 20 Historical, Clinical, and Risk Management factors that comprise the tool. The 10 historical factors (previous violence, young age at first violent incident, relationship instability, employment problems, substance abuse problems, major mental illness, psychopathy, early maladjustment, personality disorder and prior supervision failure) are obviously static risk factors in that they are historical information that cannot be altered. The 5 clinical factors (lack of insight, negative attitudes, active symptoms of major mental illness, impulsivity and unresponsive to treatment) are dynamic risk factors that can be altered during the intervention phase and could help manage the case. Finally, the 5 risk management factors (plans lack feasibility, exposure to destabilizers, lack of personal support, noncompliance with remediation attempts and stress) are also dynamic risk factors that can be altered during the course of the intervention to help deescalate the level of violence risk. In the published tool, the coding for each element uses the 0,1,2 structure that was cloned from the PCL-R. As stated in the tool, the coding of each item is generally defined as 0 (No — The item is definitely absent or does not apply), 1 (Maybe — The item possibly is present, or is present only to a limited extent) or 2 (Yes — The item is definitely present).[6] There also is a coding for "Omit" (Don't know — There is insufficient valid information to permit decision concerning the presence or absence of the item). In addition to this general understanding of the coding scheme, coding of any particular item has been further delineated depending on that particular item. For example, coding for the H1 factor (previous violence) is 0 for no previous violence, 1 for possible/less serious violence (one or two acts of moderately severe violence), 2 for definite/serious violence (three or more acts of violence, or any acts of severe violence).[7] Unlike the PCL-R, which has cutoff scores for psychopathy (≥30), the HCR-20 does not use cutoff scores. It recognizes that the presence of one item, such as psychopathy or a major mental illness, could be a single factor that skews the assessment of any case into the high risk category; therefore, the provided coding sheet allows for the summary of numbers associated with the various factors, but then asks the assessor to decide if the case should be categorized as a Low, Moderate or High risk, much the same as the Grids do, as explained in Chapter 4. Interestingly, the HCR-20 version 2 does not provide for any development of risk intervention strategies, though it does suggest that changes in the dynamic risk factors will change the level of risk. Therefore, intervention strategies that act on changing the dynamic risk factors to lower levels of concern would tend to reduce the risk for future violence. The *HCR-20 Violence Risk Management Companion Guide,*[8] published in 2001, addresses this issue. This guide not only looks at each factor and explains what it means but also addresses each dynamic risk factor and the types of intervention that could be used to mitigate this factor as a concern. In addition, this guide adds two interesting supplementary items, a "Management Planner" and a "Tracking Chart." The management planner takes the five clinical and five risk factors, which are all dynamic risk factors, and provides a means to document the specific "action items" that are to be followed up to address management of each of the factors. The tracking chart provides a way to reassess the person and show, over six assessments, the changes in the coding of each dynamic risk item, thereby allowing changes in the coding of the clinical and risk items to be seen at a glance. This concept of a tracking chart was used recently in the creation of the WAVR-21, a tool developed by Dr. J. Reid Meloy and Dr. Stephen White for the assessment of potential workplace violence cases.

The addition of these supplemental materials moved the HCR-20 away from being only an assessment tool to providing a practical way to extend its use to encapsulate the intervention strategies that derived from the assessment and to track the efficacy of the intervention strategy over time. In 2006, author Cawood attended an 8-day training session in Vancouver,

British Columbia hosted by the Vancouver Police Department and the Mental Health, Law, and Policy Institute of Simon Fraser University, which was taught primarily by Dr. Stephen (Steve) D. Hart and Dr. P. Randall (Randy) Kropp. During the course of this training program, the use of the HCR-20, SARA, B-SAFER, Stalking Assessment and Management (SAM), SVR-20, Child Abuse Risk Evaluation (CARE) and RSVP was taught to the participants and guided practical exercises were worked for most of the tools to illustrate and reinforce the correct use of the tools. During this training program, the participants were provided with new worksheets for both the HCR-20 and the SARA. The new worksheet for the HCR-20 further enhanced the value of the HCR-20 by not only allowing for documentation of the risk factors but also incorporating into the worksheet other useful information. Specifically, it allowed for capture of patient-identifying information, referral information, reason for referral, sources of information reviewed, information not reviewed, psychosocial history, recent and past violent behavior, recent and past violent ideation, the development and documentation of three levels of risk scenarios, the development and documentation of case management strategies for the articulated risk scenarios and a sheet for the documentation of summary case judgments. In the documentation of the risk factors, this worksheet not only provided space for the documentation of the specific behaviors or information that fell under that risk factor for the individual case, it changed the coding of the risk factors to Yes, Maybe, No and had two levels of coding, one set for presence of the factor and one set for relevance of the factor. This new coding of the risk factors for the HCR-20 and SARA moved away from a numerical code that could provide the false appearance of numerical certainty when none was truly intended to the more general understanding of what the coding originally meant, as mentioned above.

This worksheet provides categories of risk level that help the assessor develop and document the three levels of risk scenarios (low, moderate and high). These categories are Nature, Severity, Imminence, Frequency/Duration and Likelihood. The Nature category asks questions like, "What kind of violence is the perpetrator likely to commit?" and "Who are the likely victims?" Under the Severity category are questions like, "What would be the psychological or physical harm to the victims?" The Imminence category includes questions like, "Are there warning signs that the risk is increasing or imminent?" Under the Frequency/Duration category are questions like, "How often might the violence occur — once, several times, frequently?" Under the Likelihood category are questions like, "Based on this perpetrator's history, how likely is it that this type of violence will occur?" As you can see, going through the exercise of actually having to consider these categories and provide specific answers not only helps to clarify the assessor's thoughts and document what he has considered, but also provides a quick summary that can be communicated to the recipients of the risk analysis of what types of future risk scenarios are most likely and why that is believed to be so.

The Case Management portion of the worksheet is broken down into Monitoring, Treatment, Supervision, Victim Safety Planning and Other Considerations. Taking the information from Scenarios 1, 2 and 3, as developed on the Risk Scenarios page, questions are then asked in each of these categories to draw out appropriate management options. Under Monitoring, questions are asked like, "What events, occurrences, or circumstances should trigger a re-assessment of risk?" Under the Treatment category questions are asked like, "What treatment or rehabilitation strategies could be implemented to manage the risks posed by the perpetrator?" Under the Supervision category are questions like, "What restrictions on activity, movement, association or communication are indicated?" Under the Victim Safety Planning category are questions like, "What steps could be taken to enhance the security of the victim?" Under the Other Considerations category are questions like, "What events, occurrences or circumstances might increase or decrease risk?" Again, working through these questions prods the assessor to articulate and document his thinking for how to manage the case for each of the risk scenarios that has been developed based on the case material. This speeds communication with the consumers of the assessments and also helps protect the assessor should he have to defend his assessment and intervention strategy.

Finally, this worksheet provides a "Summary Judgments" page that captures five "issues" and allows for both coding and comments. The five issues that are captured are Case Prioritization, Serious Physical Harm, Immediate Action Required, Other Risks Indicated and Case Review. Under the Case Prioritization heading, questions are asked like, "What level of effort or intervention will be required to prevent the person from committing violence?" The coding of this heading is delineated as High/Urgent, Moderate/ Elevated or Low/Routine. Under the Serious Physical Harm heading, questions are asked like, "To what extent is this opinion limited in light of information that is unclear, unavailable or missing?" The coding of this heading is labeled High, Moderate or Low. Under the Immediate Action Required heading, questions are asked like, "What preventative steps were or should be taken immediately?" The coding for this heading is labeled Yes, Possibly or No. Under the Other Risks Indicated heading, questions are asked like, "Should the person be evaluated for other risks?" The coding for this heading is labeled Yes, Possibly and No. Under the Case Review heading, questions are asked like, "What circumstances should trigger a special review (re-assessment)?" The coding for this heading is just Date for Review. In summary, the HCR-20, with the addition of this new worksheet, is a robust tool, not only for conducting defensible violence risk assessments in a variety of contexts and involving a variety of populations, but also for deciding on case priori-tization, case management strategies and communicating the assessments and other information to the consumers of the work. We would encourage you to become familiar with it and determine if it will be of value in your assessments.

The SARA[9] is an example of an SPJ tool that is designed for a specific type of violence risk assessment, in this case spousal assault or domestic vio-lence. This tool has not been tested nearly as much as the HCR-20 regard-ing its validity, but several studies have been made, including a validation study by two of the authors, Kropp and Hart, that was published in 2000.[10] In general, in the studies we reviewed, the SARA showed the ability to dis-criminate between offenders with and without a history of spousal assault, between spousal assaulters who would recidivate and those who did not, and a better than chance predictive validity using the actuarial scores. Like the HCR-20, it uses a coding system of 0,1,2. In the SARA, the coding variables are defined as: 0 = absent, 1 = subthreshold, 2 = present.[11] Like the HCR-20, there are also individual definitions of the coding for each of the 20 items that are being rated. The 20 items are organized into four general categories, Criminal History, Psychosocial Adjustment, Spousal Assault History and Alleged (Current) Offense.

The three items listed under the Criminal History category are: past assault of family members, past assault of strangers and acquaintances, and past violation of conditional release or community supervision. Under the Psychosocial Adjustment category are 10 items: recent relationship problems, recent employment problems, victim of and/or witness to family violence as a child or adolescent, recent substance abuse/dependence, recent suicidal or homicidal ideation/intent, recent psychotic and/or manic symptoms, and per-sonality disorder with anger, impulsivity or behavioral instability. Under the Spousal Assault History category are seven items: past physical assault, past sexual assault/sexual jealousy, past use of weapons and/or credible threats of death, recent escalation in frequency or severity of assault, past violations of "no contact" orders, extreme minimization or denial of spousal assault his-tory and attitudes that support or condone spousal assault. In the last cate-gory, Alleged (Current) Offense, are three items: severe and/or sexual assault, use of weapons and/or credible threats of death and violation of "no contact" order. The worksheet located in Appendix A of the SARA manual concludes with an area to record "Other Considerations" and then provides a space for Summary Risk Ratings, using the Low/Moderate/High scale. Appendix B of the SARA manual provides a "Checklist of Information Sources" that creates a tracking sheet to document sources used for the assessment, included under the general categories of Interviews, Collateral Information, Questionnaires and Psychological Tests, which is broken down into two subcategories, "With offender" and "With victim."

The new SARA Worksheet is similar to the HCR-20 worksheet, as described in detail above, with the exception of substituting the SARA categories for information collection and the word "spousal assault" for the word "violence" in those questions used to help the assessor develop the risk scenarios. The fact that this worksheet format can be so easily translated from a more general violence assessment tool to use on a specific subtype of violence seems to indicate that the authors, Kroop and Hart, given their extensive experience in building assessment tools and conducting assessments and interventions, believe that the worksheet covers all the major areas of any appropriate violence risk assessment and those areas that should be addressed for any intervention. Given our experience, we agree. These worksheets would serve as a useful tool to any practitioner conducting any violence risk assessment, regardless of the type of potential victim or violence dynamic. That being the case, we would suggest that you obtain a copy of the new HCR-20 worksheet from Dr. Hart or Dr. Kropp and start using it as a general tool for documenting your violence risk assessments. It will only enhance the quality of your case work.

Practically, you might decide to use the Assessment Grid for initial assessment of cases because it allows a practitioner to quickly "grid" early information and make some quick, valid determinations of risk levels, which then flow quickly into initial response steps, laid out in the Response Grid, including the gathering of a greater depth of information, legal considerations and initial protective steps. Then using the HCR-20 Worksheet, one might document the information learned during the course of the case, including from interviews and the other sources, and develop risk scenarios and more specific case management strategies. As the case progresses, the Assessment Grid would provide a quick way to continue to reassess the case and the Response Grid could provide concrete actions to be considered, while the Worksheet (adding new pages for reassessed areas, scenarios and strategies) would document the evolution of the case, including its escalation or deescalation and the outcome.

In summary, SPJ is emerging as the most valid and practical standard methodology for violence risk assessment. Increasingly, it has been shown to provide a significant increase in assessment validity over actuarial and clinical assessment methodologies, while moving beyond assessment into the areas of guided case intervention and management. It is a proactive methodology, rather than static, and this provides a greater opportunity for practitioners to intervene and divert instigators who are on a path from violent thought to violent action.

Endnotes

1. A literature search on the American Psychological Association's PsycNet for the term "violence risk" yielded a total result of 83 articles, books, dissertations, etc. from 1980–1995. The same search conducted for the years 1996–2008, a significantly shorter span of time, located 927 publications, of which 557 were dated from 2003 (the year of publication for the first edition of this book) through early May of 2008. There was a tenfold increase in mentions over the last 12 years compared to the prior 15 years, and 66% of the increase in the last 12 years was dated in the last 5 years.

2. See Douglas, K. S., Yeomans, M., & Boer, D. (2005). Comparative validity analysis of multiple measures of violence risk in a sample of criminal offenders. *Criminal Justice and Behavior, 32*(5), 479–510.

3. Ibid.

4. HCR-20 v.2, Webster, C. D., Douglas, K. D., Eaves, D., & Hart, S. D. Mental Health, Law and Policy Institute, Simon Fraser University, 1997.

5. For more information on this, look up the annotated bibliography for the HCR-20, which has been posted at www.violence-risk.com/hcr20annotated.pdf. This site also has links to other, primarily SPJ, assessment tools for different populations and some general violence risk assessment information that could be of value to you.

6. HCR-20 v. 2, p. 20.

7. Ibid., p. 29.

8. HCR-20 Violence Risk Management Companion Guide, Douglas, K. D., Webster, C. D., Hart, S. D., Eaves, D., Ogloff, J. R. P., Mental Health, Law, and Policy Institute, Simon Fraser University, 2001.

9. *Spousal assault risk assessment guide*, 2nd Ed., P. R. Kropp, S. D. Hart, C. D. Webster, & D. Eaves, The British Columbia Institute Against Family Violence, 1995. Another version of this tool, published in 1999 and called the MHS version, is available from Multi-Health Systems, Inc., one of the largest purveyors of psychometric instruments. You can review its selection of tools and instruments at www.mhs.com.

10. Kropp, P. R., & Hart, S. D. (2000). The spousal assault risk assessment (SARA) guide: Reliability and validity in adult male offenders. *Law and Human Behavior, 24*(1), 101–118.

11. SARA, 1995, p. 19.

APPENDIX 5.1

Risk Assessment Guideline Elements for Violence*

**Considerations for Assessing the Risk
of Future Violent Behavior**

ASSOCIATION OF THREAT ASSESSMENT PROFESSIONALS

ATAP Risk Assessment Guideline Elements for Violence Committee:

The Committee was established in October 2002 by the Association of Threat Assessment Professionals (ATAP) in response to a perceived need for a multidisciplinary group to consider how future violence risk was being assessed in a wide variety of settings, both in the public and private sectors. As the preeminent organization for violence risk assessment and threat assessment professionals worldwide, ATAP has an important role to play in helping both the public and private sectors assess, manage and understand situations involving potential violence risk whether from stalkers, school children, domestic abusers, co-workers, criminals, domestic and foreign extremists or emotionally and mentally destabilized individuals.

This is the first time that ATAP has made the decision, as an organization, to become involved in providing considerations and guidelines for these

* Reprinted with permission from the Association of Threat Assessment Professionals, Anaheim, CA.

types of threat assessment* and risk assessment undertakings. ATAP felt that publishing guidelines was a necessary step in moving this field of endeavor toward a common framework that could be used to provide a contextual and methodological understanding for the opinions that are formulated in this arena. Further, guidelines provide a means to evaluate the foundation and the robustness of these opinions.

We, ATAP and the Committee, do not consider this document to be the end of the discussion, but the beginning. It is our hope that through dialogue and use, this guideline will continue to evolve in order to improve opinions concerning the risk of future violence. This is essential, as these opinions are used to incarcerate and release people from custody, restrict freedom of movement and association, regulate possession and use of property, and determine the use of limited resources to monitor and intervene in individuals' lives.†

---

* ATAP recognizes that the term "threat assessment" has been utilized to describe a variety of activities across a range of contexts (e.g., generalized assessment of terrorism risk, vulnerability assessment). For the purposes of this document, threat assessment is defined as the determination of the level of targeted violence risk posed by an individual or group toward a specific target.

† ATAP recognizes that threat assessment activities are either performed by or involve a range of professionals from different backgrounds (e.g., mental health, law enforcement, security) who are obligated to meet different standards of practice appropriate to their respective professions. This document and all its parts are not intended to serve as an ethical standard or dismiss the applicability of other empirically supported factors or procedures appropriate to the situation at hand. The nature of the questions asked; time, setting, and situational factors; and applicable laws should be taken into consideration when performing risk assessments. As this document evolves, different scenarios and potential conflicts may arise and will be considered. These guidelines do not replace the need for judgment, thorough training, and consultation with colleagues when appropriate.

Risk Assessment Guideline Elements for Violence:

Considerations for Assessing the Risk of Future Violent Behavior

1.0   Title
2.0   Revision History
3.0   Committee Members
4.0   Scope
5.0   Summary
6.0   Purpose
7.0   Keywords
8.0   Terminology
9.0   Practice Advisory: Psychology
10.0   Practice Advisory: Law
11.0   Practice Advisory: Information Gathering
12.0   Bibliography
13.0   Appendix A: ATAP Model Violence Risk Assessment Process

1.0   Title

The title of this document is Risk Assessment Guideline Elements for Violence: Considerations for Assessing the Risk of Future Violent Behavior.

2.0   Revision History

Baseline Document

3.0   Committee Members

Chairman:
James S. Cawood, CPP
President
Factor One

Members: Gary S. Reynolds
Michael A. Crane, Esq.   Senior Vice-President, Director
Vice President, General Counsel   Financial and Electronic Crime
IPC International Corporation   Investigations
                                       Wells Fargo Bank

Kate Killeen, Esq.
Deputy Executive Director
California District Attorneys
    Association

Glenn S. Lipson, Ph.D., ABPP
Diplomate in Forensic Psychology
American Board of Professional
    Psychology

Kris Mohandie, Ph.D.
Forensic Psychologist
Operational Consulting
    International, Inc.

Michael Prodan
Sr. Special Agent/Criminal Profiler
South Carolina State
    Law Enforcement Division

Jodi B. Rafkin, Esq.
Former Assistant U.S. Attorney
U.S. Attorney's Office

Mario J. Scalora, Ph.D.
Assistant Professor of Psychology
Clinical Psychology & Law/
    Psychology
Training Program
University of Nebraska, Lincoln

Stephen W. Weston Esq.
Lieutenant. (Retired)
Office of Dignitary Protection
California Highway Patrol

William J. Zimmerman
Detective
Protective Intelligence Division/
    Threat Assessment
United States Capitol Police

4.0 Scope

The Association of Threat Assessment Professionals' Risk Assessment Guideline Elements for Violence (RAGE-V) has applicability for both the private and public sectors. The RAGE-V is an exploration and explanation of interrelated processes and activities that will assist in evaluating the potential risk of future physical violence from a known individual, including those inspired or motivated by group philosophy or beliefs.

5.0 Summary

The RAGE-V is an approach to assist individuals and organizations to consider the factors and steps necessary to provide for thorough, well-considered opinions concerning the potential risk of future physical violence from a known individual. It is based on a wide review of relevant literature, as well as the practical processes developed and implemented for this purpose by a wide range of professionals and organizations that make up the violence risk assessment community. The applicability of these considerations, in any specific case, may depend on the situation, context, discipline of the individual assessor (e.g., education, licensing), and the particular circumstances and questions for the evaluation.

6.0 Purpose

At the present time, many assessments of future violence risk assessments are conducted in an eclectic manner, without an agreed-upon approach or process, either on the part of the requestors of these assessments, or the assessors that provide them. This often leaves the individual being assessed and the venues that use these assessments without an adequate understanding of what elements might be considered, if not acted on, for arriving at valid assessment conclusions. It also means there are end users of these assessments who are at a loss about how to determine whether the underlying assessment methodology used in any individual assessment was based on a solid foundation that allows for that assessment to be trusted. Ideally, a solidly based and trusted assessment would be the basis for taking actions that would significantly affect the safety and liberty of individual citizens and society as a whole.

The purpose of this document is to provide well-grounded considerations and practical suggestions, based upon a cohesive, multidimensional understanding of appropriate violence risk assessment process elements and informational resources. It also provides a stepwise process to be considered during each assessment of potential violence risk. This document was designed to be used by all providers and end users of these assessments to provide a quick reference for suggesting essential considerations and resources that could be used in specific cases, or as a guideline for questioning assessors about their methodology and decision making in a specific scenario. This document has been developed by a multidisciplinary team of assessors and reviewed by a wide array of assessors, academics, and end users, and represents the currently perceived best practices for consideration in a wide range of assessment cases. It is an important step toward the development of practice standards for violence risk assessment.*

7.0 Keywords

Mitigation Strategies, Violence Risk Assessment

8.0 Terminology

Approach-Behavior: Actions toward a target of interest that is escalating with a particular goal in mind.

Assessor: The person using this document to aid in the formation of an opinion of violence risk.

---

* While thorough and detailed assessments are desired, situations may arise that challenge the ability to obtain relevant information or address factors included within these practice advisories due to emergency/time constraints. As a result, the assessor is advised to practice within relevant professional standards and advise his client of the relevant limitations of the violence risk assessment conclusions presented.

Commitments: In this context it refers to involuntary or less than voluntary hospitalizations for psychological problems. Hospitalizations occur when someone poses a danger to himself or others.

Inevitability: The belief that no matter what actions one takes the course of events will not change.

Mitigation Strategies: Implementation of measures to lessen or eliminate the occurrence or impact of an incident of potential violence.

Process Variables: Examines the interplay between one's own beliefs and how that fuels or prevents actions and behaviors.

Protective Inhibitors: Beliefs, relationships, injuries, lack of resources, or abilities that can limit whether a person is likely to follow through with dangerous conduct.

Violence Risk Assessment: The process of identifying behaviors that may signal an individual's preparation to commit a violent act, assessing those behaviors in the context of that person's past history of behavior and other known incidents of violence that have demonstrated those behaviors, quantifying the level of risk from this behavioral information by using professional judgment and objective, appropriate tools to provide a balanced assessment, and presentation of that assessment to the requestor of the assessment, in such a way as to qualify the opinion and its limitations appropriately.

9.0   Practice Advisory: Psychology

Behavioral Information of Interest Could Include:

Process Variables

- Approach behavior
- Evidence of escalation — threats, proximity seeking
- Fantasy rehearsal
- Evidence of deterioration — deteriorating mental state, psychosis
- Actively violent state of mind — suicidal or homicidal thoughts
- Command hallucinations, thought insertion/withdrawal, paranoia of imminent threat
- Diminishing inhibitions
- Diminishing or impaired coping
- Inability or limited view or ability to pursue other options
- Obsession
- Evaporating protective inhibitors
- Sense of inevitability (tunnel vision, foregone conclusion)
- Pre-attack or ritualistic preparatory actions (writing of suicide note, suicide video, religious rituals, purchase of camouflage clothing)

- Recent acquisition or preparation of weapons, escalation of practice with no sanctioned reason
- Subject's response to assessment and inquiries.

Risk Factors

- Weapons-use connected to emotional release, fascination with destructive power
- Motivational factors (What is driving the individual?) — delusion, fanatical beliefs, revenge, entitlement, grandiosity, need to force closure
- Drug use — methamphetamine, cocaine, alcohol, steroids
- Head trauma
- Criminal history, including history of violence, homicide, stalking, threats, assaultive behavior, violation of conditional release
- Prior voluntary or involuntary commitments
- Past suicide attempts, or suicide ideation, to include suicidal thoughts, statements, gestures, and attempts
- Adverse responses to authority and limit setting
- Reference groups, heroes, affiliations, and community attachments
- History of mental problems that compromise coping, or enhance appeal of violence — may include:
  - Depression
  - Paranoia
  - Psychopathy
  - Bipolar
  - Personality disorders (narcissistic, paranoid, borderline, antisocial)
- Perceptions of injustice or insoluble problems.

Inhibitors/Stabilizers — consideration of available inhibitors and the person's access and utilization of them

- Treatment availability, utilization, and past receptivity
- Family
- Other social support
- Spiritual or religious beliefs opposing violence
- Connectedness and healthy affectional bonds.

Triggers — identification of potentially stabilizing or destabilizing triggers

- Pending perceived negative job event
- Rejection and abandonment
- Increased psychosis
- Civil (family court, child custody, etc.) or criminal justice system event(s)
- Disruption of support system
- Financial problems.

Analysis Guidelines:
Consideration of multiple behavioral and risk factors

- Consideration of contextual factors
- Consideration of deterrent factors, mitigating factors, or inhibitors to risk, as well as risk factors
- Consideration of potential stressors as well as resiliency factors
- Access sufficient credible, first-hand collateral data sources
- Avoidance of over-reliance on single factors in most cases
- Factors considered must be scientifically relevant or those typically considered within the field based upon empirical and published literature
- Must assess the impact of gathering information and investigative/threat assessment process itself upon risk.

Objective Instruments and Tools:
When appropriate, utilize objective instrument(s) or tool(s) appropriate for the context (e.g., psychopathy-related instruments (PCL-R, PCL-R SV; etc.; HCR-20; Spousal Risk Assessment Guide (SARA); Violence Risk Assessment Guide (VRAG); Level of Service Inventory — Revised; Cawood/White Assessment Grid; MOSAIC-DV; The Classification of Violence Risk (COVR); and others).*

- Assessor must avoid sole reliance on checklist/instrument/tool.
- Assessor must be trained and qualified on relevant instrument or tool.
- Instrumentation utilized must be reliable and valid as well as appropriate for the issue at hand.
- Assessor must be aware of the limitations of any instrumentation utilized.
- Assessor must stay current with new developments and outdated versions.

Additional Considerations:
When conceptualizing risk level, assessor must recognize professional limitations pertinent to the threat assessment.

---

* We are encouraging the use of Structured Professional Judgement (SPJ) which is aided by the use of tools and other appropriate practice parameters. Issues of reliability, validity for certain types of assessments or subjects, peer review acceptance, and training in the technique or method should be considered before relying on any protocol or tool. The listing of the above instruments and tools should not be considered an endorsement of said instruments or tools. The user can decide on whether they are appropriate. The above-listed instruments and tools are known more widely in the mental health and law enforcement assessment communities. Being known does not mean that they are defensible in a court or other venue.

- Seek out relevant consultation or expertise when necessary.
- Qualify assessment when necessary (e.g., availability of information, recognize assumptions, potential changes in relevant context, time limited nature of assessment).
- Be aware of the complex contextual, legal, ethical, and regulatory issues that impact the violence risk assessment process.

10.0   Practice Advisory: Law

The legal system often views psychological testimony with distrust and disbelief. There is the perception that either side to a legal case or controversy can, for enough money, find an "expert" who will say what they want to hear. One of the goals of this assessment guideline is to foster consensus and bolster credibility in the area of violence risk assessment. The laws governing what must be disclosed to different parties and what might be considered admissible are contextual, issue sensitive, and jurisdictional.

For civil testimony on the risk of future violent behavior to be admissible in court in the United States, taking into account the jurisdiction, the expert might have to comply with the standards set forth in *Daubert v. Merrell Dow Pharmaceuticals Inc.*, 509 U.S. 579 (1993), and *Kumho Tire Co. v. Carmichael*, 526 U.S. 137 (1999). Criminal courts may have different standards, as do some state courts. The trial judge, when relying on *Daubert*, must be satisfied that the evidence is based on scientific knowledge, or is reliable, and ensure that the evidence will assist the trier of fact, or is relevant. The *Daubert* court decision provided four factors that could be used in this evaluation: 1) whether the theory has been tested or is testable; 2) whether the theory or study has been subject to peer review; 3) whether there is a known or potential error rate; and 4) whether the technique is generally accepted in the relevant field (*Daubert*, 509 U.S. at 594).

Each discipline or field of investigation imposes upon its members sets of different legal controls and expectations. For example, a law enforcement officer may have additional obligations pertaining to searching law enforcement databases not accessible to other individuals in the private sector. Mental health assessors may have Duties to Protect and Warn in different jurisdictions. Psychologists, in particular, may have the burden of selecting appropriate measures relying upon testing and ethical standards. Warnings regarding protections against self-incrimination differ for different disciplines and, thus, the burden shifts accordingly based upon these expectations. This document cannot address practice and professional standards for all the disciplines involved in violence risk assessment or dangerousness appraisal. It does not take the place of any individual assessor's need to know what standards and procedures are in their area of expertise. *Nonetheless, there is a shared foundation and approach that all professionals in this area can be held accountable to when performing an assessment and arriving at their opinions.*

For civil cases in the United States, it is becoming standard, based on Rule 26 of the Federal Rules of Civil Procedure, for expert witnesses offering an opinion on the risk of future violent behavior to provide a written report prior to testifying. This report sets forth their opinions and the reasons for their conclusions, information relied upon, qualifications of the expert witness, and compensation being exchanged for the assessment and testimony. Any assessor offering an opinion on the risk of future violent behavior should have an appropriate basis for his opinion and documentation in a form suitable for its intended purpose, which may include the production of written reports.

Attorneys for all parties to the litigation should review that report carefully before the assessor/expert witness takes the stand. The assessor/expert witness should be questioned on the methodology he used. The assessor/expert witness's background and experience in the field of threat assessment should also be questioned. How many assessments has he done? Has he qualified as an expert in a court of law? If so, how many times? What materials havs he reviewed and relied on in forming his opinion? To whom has he spoken, and for how long? Section 9.0 of this guideline provides a good checklist of issues to explore with an assessor/expert witness.

11.0   Practice Advisory: Information Gathering

In general, the more behavioral information available about the subject of an assessment, the greater the ability to provide an accurate assessment. The ability to gather information in any specific case, and at any particular stage of an assessment, will depend on the immediacy of the issues, and the civil rights and employment context of the person being assessed. Different assessors have different access to information and some of this information may be protected by law. The list below includes the types of information that has been found to be helpful in assessments; however, depending on the circumstances of each individual case, this information might not be available in a timely manner, could be protected from disclosure, or not legally attainable.

Obtain Information on Victim/Target/Reporting Subject:

- Past history of reports
- Motivation for reports
- Possibility of unintentional or intentional misinformation

Focus of Information on Victim/Target/Reporting Subject:

- Is the subject/target of the threats a chronic victim? Or is the individual in a position or situation that typically receives threats or inappropriate contacts?
- Is the victim connected to a controversial situation or has he or she been in the media recently?

- Is the report being made out of fear, desperation, retaliation, safety or the want of attention?
- Is there a possibility that the information reported was skewed, misunderstood, or fabricated?

Information on the Subject of Assessment:

- Current location
- Ability to access subject/victim
- Research behavior(s)
- Motivation: both positive and negative
- Past history of threatening or violent behavior, including stalking
- Criminal history: local, county, state, federal: person of interest — arrest, conviction; reporting party of incident, victim
- History of behavior in a jail or correctional institution, if applicable
- Probation or parole history, if applicable
- Civil court history: federal, state, local level
- Vehicle operation history
- Mental history (when available)
- Substance abuse
- Military history/training
- Support structure in area
- Weapons seeking, possession, recent acquisition, or recent modification
- Changes in behavior

Focus of Information on Subject:

- Is the subject in a location or does the subject have the ability to approach or attack the victim or not? (e.g., in jail, indigent, incapacitated)
- Does the subject have immediate access to the victim? (e.g., family, co-worker)
- Positive motivation of the subject to get to victim? (i.e., love, hate, wronged, personal issue)
- Negative motivation of the subject? (i.e., embarrassment, loss of employment, financial, incarceration)
- Does the subject have a history of violent or threatening behavior? Typically, this may be in a criminal history report; however, this trait may have never been reported and may have never resulted in a criminal arrest or prosecution. Interviews with neighbors, family members, or co-workers should be conducted. Other sources for this information include restraining orders or divorce documents. Determine the provocation, circumstances, and extent of any reported past violence (e.g., involving weapons, type and extent of injury).

- Does the subject have a history of criminal actions? Specifically crimes that indicate the subject is non-compliant to the standard rules of society (e.g., trespass, disorderly conduct, fail to obey a lawful order).

Other Sources of Information for Past Violent Behavior:

- Premises history: law enforcement records of response to an address. Check all past addresses of a subject.
- Contact history: check all jurisdictions where the subject has lived or worked for field interviews, listed as suspect, witness or victim.
- Obtain copies of police reports where the subject was involved as a suspect, witness, or victim. Good source of past conduct.
- Court records supporting a restraining order, divorce proceedings, civil case, or child custody.
- Interview neighbors of past addresses including apartment managers. Can be an excellent source for information on disturbances, police responses, and past boy- or girlfriends.
- Does the subject's vehicle operating history record disclose a recent trend of violation?
- Does the subject have a history of mental health treatment or non-compliance with treatment/medication?
- Does the suspect display signs of some form of obvious mental illness? (e.g., delusions, hallucinations, grandiose ideations, paranoia, homicidal/suicidal thoughts)
- Does the subject have a history of substance abuse? Criminally documented, self disclosed, or confirmed by witnesses.
- Does the subject have training in weapons tactical operation, or knowledge of the tactical or commercial use of explosives? This training is not limited to military service. The suspect could belong to a gun club, militia, or be self-taught.
- Is there any information indicating the subject may be seeking or preparing a weapon or destructive device?
- Is there evidence of "final act" behaviors (e.g., last will, destroying own property, giving property away, ritualistic acts)?
- Is there evidence of research, planning, or stalking-type behaviors? This type of evidence could include visits to libraries, use of the internet to research potential victims, diaries, equipment lists, "hit lists," target information files, etc.
- If safe and appropriate, take advantage of opportunities to establish communication with the subject to determine future intentions. Also make a thoughtful analysis into whether the situation would allow safely seeking additional sources of insight into the subject's future intentions, such as family members, friends, co-workers, neighbors or utilizing these additional sources to monitor the subject's future behavior.

APPENDIX A

ATAP Model Violence Risk Assessment Process

Notification of Concerning Behavior/Incident:

Assess source quality and capture quality (e.g., first-hand information?; direct or indirect contact with reporting party)

"Three C's" — Content, Context, Circumstances — What is new/changed?

Initial assessment of immediacy of violence and accessibility of target

Initial consideration of protective actions including appropriate initial notifications and explanations (e.g., less savvy recipients = more detail vs. more savvy recipients = less detail)

Initiate Fact Finding:

Information could be obtained from any or all of the below listed sources:

Victim(s)
Witnesses
Family members including lovers, intimate partners, spouses
Friends/co-workers
Law enforcement personnel
Instigator
Records — Restricted/Private/Public
Examination of forensic evidence
Contact information — direct (verbal or physical contact) or indirect (mail, e-mail, letters, packages, pages, IM messages, faxes, etc.)
Wiretap and surveillance
Money transfers
Other informants

Behavioral information of interest could include information from direct or indirect sources:

Process Variables:

- Approach behavior
- Evidence of escalation — threats, etc.
- Fantasy rehearsal
- Evidence of deterioration — deteriorating mental state, psychosis
- Actively violent state of mind — suicidal or homicidal thoughts
- Command hallucinations, thought insertion/ withdrawal, paranoia of imminent threat
- Diminishing inhibitions
- Diminishing or impaired coping
- Inability or limited view or ability to pursue other options

Risk Factors:

- Weapons — use connected to emotional release, fascination with destructive power
- Motivational factors — what is driving the individual — delusion, fanatical beliefs, revenge, entitlement, grandiosity; need to force closure
- Drug use — methamphetamines, cocaine, alcohol, steroids
- Head trauma
- History of criminal, violent, homicidal, stalking, threats, or assaultive behavior, violation of conditional release
- Prior involuntary or voluntary mental health commitments

Inhibitors/Stabilizers:

Consideration of available inhibitors and the persons' access and utilization of them

- Treatment availability, utilization and past receptivity
- Family
- Other social support
- Spiritual beliefs opposing violence
- Connectedness and healthy affectional bonds

Triggers: (Past, Present, and Future)

- Pending perceived negative job event
- Rejection and abandonment
- Increased psychosis
- Disruption of support system
- Financial problems
- Civil and criminal justice system events

- Obsession
- Evaporating protective inhibitors
- Sense of inevitability (tunnel vision, foregone conclusion)
- Pre-attack or ritualistic preparatory actions (writing of suicide note, suicide video, religious rituals, purchase of camouflage clothing)
- Recent acquisition or preparation of weapons, escalation of practice with no sanctioned reason
- Subject's response to assessment and inquiries

- Documented homicidal or suicidal thoughts, psychotic violent thoughts
- Past suicide attempt
- Ordinary response to authority and limit setting
- Reference groups, heroes, affiliations, and community attachments
- Perception of injustice or insoluble problems
- History of mental problems that compromise coping, or enhance appeal of violence — may include:
  - □ Depression
  - □ Paranoia
  - □ Psychopathy
  - □ Bipolarity
  - □ Personality disorder (narcissistic, paranoid, borderline, antisocial)

Analysis Guidelines

Consideration of multiple behavioral and risk factors:

- Must involve consideration of contextual factors, mitigation factors or inhibitors to risk — as well as risk factors, potential stressors — and as resiliency factors
- Access to sufficient credible, first-hand collateral data sources
- Must assess the impact of gathering information and investigative/threat assessment process itself upon risk
- Avoid over-reliance on single factors (factors considered must be scientifically relevant or those considered within the field based upon empirical and published literature
- When conceptualizing risk level, must recognize professional limitations pertinent to the threat assessment — seek out relevant consultation or expertise when necessary
- Qualify assessment when necessary (e.g., availability of information, recognize assumptions, potential changes in relevant context, time limited nature of assessment)
- Assessor must be aware of the complex contextual, legal, ethical and regulatory issues that impact the violence risk assessment process

Categorize the Level of Risk
(e.g., Low, Moderate or High, 1–5)

Provide Assessment Results to Appropriate Parties:
(e.g., Individual Victim, Employer, Incident Management Team, Law Enforcement, Court Correctional System, Probation, Parole)

The Victim's Role

6

Introduction

While most of the focus of the assessment process often appears to be dealing with instigators, their backgrounds and processes, it is equally important
to understand the active involvement of the victims. In law enforcement, for
example, the importance of this concept is brought to bear when victims
who report a crime and wish to remain anonymous are told nothing can be
done in their case because no victim — no crime. In the assessment process,
unless there is an understanding of the relationship of victims to instigators,
a critical component for understanding the threat potential as well as possible
resolutions will be overlooked. It is the forensic model of understanding the
victims' physical, emotional and psychological components and then cor-
relating them to the instigators' physical, emotional and psychological elements as they relate to victims within a specific environment that allows the
assessor a narrower range of material for consideration to better determine
a threat's true potential for violence. Progression through this chapter may
demonstrate how this understanding often develops and, by assessing each
element, a more focused and complete picture can be achieved.

First, there is the obvious relationship (direct, indirect, none at all or only
imagined) between victims and instigators and how this interaction (or lack
of it) can either raise or lower the element of risk. It is also important for an
assessor to develop an understanding of the perception of this relationship
on the part of both instigators and victims, for their perception is the reality
that is the motivation behind their behavior. It is important for the assessor to clarify the integral dynamics of the connection between instigators
and victims because, in general terms, the more personal the association, the
stronger the potential for violence.

Next there is the relationship of the organization or environment to
the victims, as this can motivate responses from an individual that would

not otherwise be exhibited or revealed in any other context. How do victims perceive their role within the organization or environment and how are they expected to interact with co-workers, peers, subordinates, etc., and thus instigators? Are there components among these observations that might enable a necessary change on either the part of the organization or environment or the victims?

The role of the assessor is to clearly define the methodology or motivational factors of victims by recognizing character traits, behaviors and nuances that make up the personality of a specific victim. This might be considered the victim's own internal organizational structure, which is discussed in more detail in Chapter 7. An assessor who is aware of this internal structure can then determine whether there is the possibility of change when change is indicated, the possibility of agreement and performing recommendations or suggestions where adjustment is indicated, and whether victims can be trusted not only to carry out these "changes" but whether they may circumvent the system for their own reasons or motivations and thus create an even bigger or more convoluted problem to deal with.

Physical Concepts

The first step is exploring the relationship between victims and instigators. Allowing victims to explain the facts they feel are notable in their case is generally the most revealing and, by first exploring this relationship, victims are allowed to explain those issues that are uppermost in their minds before they get lost or muddled in other information. This also develops insight for the assessor into what victims perceive or fail to be aware of that could be a central focus of the problem. Is there a more intimate bond between them than was perhaps otherwise known? Are victims completely unaware of how their association with instigators can produce an adversarial connection or that particular instigators view certain victims' behavior and methods as attractive or difficult, loving or unsympathetic, beneficial or harmful?

Depending on the physical closeness of victims and instigators and on the level of intimacy they may be experiencing or have experienced, differing expectations of behavior are more likely. One expects a spouse not to have an affair with someone else as there is the ultimate intimate bond between married people. That same expectation does not hold true for someone you have just met, unless your own misperception of the meeting causes you to believe you should be able to expect this level of commitment — even if the "meeting" was nothing more than a visual observation of the victim at some distance (which is illuminated in great detail in much of the current literature on stalking). The assessment process leads to determining these differing levels of assessed risk based on the manifested physical relationship as well as the perceived relationship. Through the careful interview and background-accumulation process, the assessor's task is to make these determinations not only to ascertain the level of the violence potential but also to make reasonable yet effective recommendations on how to proceed in handling these cases.

Such recommendations may include suggestions for contacting and dealing with the instigator, or, conversely, why it is not a good idea to do so. They might consist of suggestions for steps to mitigate or prevent future potential problems. Or they may involve the careful planning for continual monitoring, as well as bringing in additional consultants, experts or support personnel (attorney, psychologist, law enforcement, private protection, etc.). This then requires the assessor to ask the necessary questions of the victim to gain this insight and follow that up with other information (interviews, record checks, etc.) for confirmation before designing methodologies of approaching and dealing with the instigator. Care must be exercised, as some of the information provided may be distorted (intentionally or not), embellished or simply untrue. Of utmost importance to the assessment process is the best first-hand information. It then becomes the job of the assessor to dissect and determine what is germane and helpful in the overall process of determining actual violence potential and ways of lessening or preventing it.

For example, it is often reported by victims that they started in their company at the same level as the instigator and, at that time, considered the instigator a friend. The victims indicate they have had the occasion to socialize with the instigator away from the job site, possibly to have a friendly drink at the local pub after work. But then, when victims became supervisors, the relationship between them and instigators began to change as they spent less personal time together and more time where the victims felt they had to delineate problems or expectations of the job to the instigators. The victims now state that they categorize the relationship as purely professional and feel there is little or no friendship left with instigators. The questions should then focus on understanding the process of how the victims believe they now interact with instigators.

If they reveal there was previously a "friendship" but now there is only this business relationship and the instigators seem to have a problem with discipline or correction issues, has this transition been understood or accepted by the instigators? The victims may indicate they feel they have a "corporate" responsibility to expect a certain level of working together between supervisory and line personnel or they may express their own level of expectations or "esteem" from instigators because of their position. But if the instigators still believe in a preestablished relationship, many of the victims' current actions are only going to frustrate and confuse the instigators. Thus, the assessor must probe this dynamic very thoroughly with the victims to pick up not only real relationship issues, but also perceived connections with the victims by the instigators that may be evident initially or discovered later, for these are just as real to the instigators.

The collection of this information begins with the first interview with victims. While cursory data can prove useful for comparison and determining possible intervention processes with the victims prior to this interview (e.g., asking those who have brought you into this process what they know about the victims and their relationship with the instigators), the actual assessment of the potential for violence by the instigators will best be realized through this meeting as the victims seek to explain their situation. Allowing the victims the opportunity of characterizing their relationship with the instigators, of explaining how they interact from their perspective and how they handle this interaction or lack of same will not only outline potential risks involved in the association but will also allow for dynamic explanations of the process as seen from the victims' perspectives. Thus, the first interview holds the key to developing mitigating components to lessen the potential for violence by the instigator.

Case History

To elaborate on our example and demonstrate this process, let's look at Jane, who actually started at ABC Company 2 weeks after Fred. Both were in their late 20s, had some prior general work experience and were high school graduates. Jane was a single mother and 6 months away from finishing her junior college degree, while Fred had never been married and was a devout "I hate school" kind of guy. As was the traditional practice of this organization, they were both assigned to the mail room, to allow them to become acquainted with the total workings of the organization. This also allowed others to see how they "fit in" with this environment. Jane and Fred did socialize about once a month for the next year, dropping by the local pub after work for "one for the road." There was never any intimate relationship between the two, they always got along well together, but there were no other contacts between them during this year.

Jane was soon elevated to an assistant facilities position that required her to supervise, among other things, the mail room. Soon, she began to see an opportunity to implement some of her efficiency ideas, but it always seemed Fred was resistant. Eventually, it became obvious to everyone there was real tension between these two. Jane, not having had the time to "socialize" with Fred since her promotion 6 months ago, decided to invite Fred out for a beer after work one evening to try and "work things out." A disruption occurred at the bar between them and Fred was overheard by several co-workers who were also at this tavern to say to Jane, "You'd better watch your back, sweetheart," as he stormed out. Jane was visibly shaken.

Over the next month, tensions increased at the work site between Jane and Fred. Fred was overheard by some other co-workers mumbling about

Jane's being a "bitch" and that she simply doesn't realize how if it weren't for him her safety would be in jeopardy. This comment brings in a request for a violence assessor's services, as the company is concerned and not sure what might be brewing here. The assessor's interview with Jane reveals corroboration of all this and, when asked about her current interaction with Fred, she says it's fine. "I guess you would say it's a bit tenser than it used to be, but I only need to talk to him about his problems with poor performance and lack of cooperation when working with others." Your questioning should now focus on the chronology and nature of their interactions to determine whether there are any clearer indications of why Fred appears so angry toward Jane.

This questioning has now confirmed that her way of handling this matter appears to be one of avoidance, except for necessary disciplinary matters. The assessor also discovers that, when Fred and Jane last went out, Jane had revealed some personal family issues to Fred. She says this was her attempt at trying to win Fred over by trying to play on his sympathies in the hopes he would become a more responsive employee. But, when Fred reached for her hand at the bar, she quickly pulled away and eventually the conversation became more heated as Fred finally became upset and left.

The assessor also learns Jane has no romantic feelings for Fred, does not think that Fred might have any feelings for her, is not afraid for her safety and just wants Fred to straighten up or she will terminate him. Jane has no idea what Fred means by the comment that "if it weren't for me her safety would be in jeopardy," but she does recall running into him a couple of times in the last few months at a supermarket she frequents. She thought this was a little strange, as she knew Fred lived at least 10 miles away from this location, but she never bothered to ask him because he volunteered, "Oh, they have the best cuts of meat here."

A competent assessor has, by now, explored the victim's perceptions of the relationship with the instigator. He has also probed the process of their interaction and, because of this, has probably uncovered the crux of the problem, which is that, in his mind, the instigator has developed more than a working relationship with the victim and may be stalking her. Now there exists a much better assessment of the possible violence potential and a lot more information than seen by anyone else on the surface. There is also tremendous information to help determine how to proceed in this matter and what recommendations might mollify the potential for violence. Thus, the important goal for the assessor is getting past the obvious relationship questions and delving deeper into the dynamic of the relationship, at least as it is perceived by the victim.

But what if there is no direct contact? There are the high-profile people who are "admired" from afar and, whenever they are seen by instigators on television or at a public function, the instigators believe that certain words or looks from the victims are directed to them. Letters are then sent to the VIPs and, when there is no immediate response, the letters become more threatening. On a smaller scale, there are the employees who are "lusted" after by co-workers who happen to see them in the lunch room and have sent several "suggestive" e-mails to the victims telling them how to acknowledge the same feelings. When the directions are not followed, harassment, such as finding the victims' car tires slashed at their residences or dead mice left on their cars when they are parked in the company parking lot, can occur.

The assessor should first try to narrow the focus of the victims, for they generally are trying to think of everyone or simply feel that almost anyone could be the instigators. While this may be true, the goal is to try to understand the dynamics of the relationship between the victims and the instigators to determine a probable course of behavior as well as the potential for violence. Hence, all attempts at identifying instigators should be exhausted before going to the realm of hypothesis and theories. Certainly, the victims will explain they have gone over and over this in their minds and with others, but to no avail. But the assessor's experience in dealing with these types of issues as well as bringing a fresh, objective mindset into the equation may prove the deciding factor.

Alas, most of these issues result in a true unknown and the only information is what is in the letter, the e-mails, the telephones calls and the accompanying behaviors (malicious acts, annoying or intimidating activities, etc.). While an understanding of the psychological underpinnings of this information assists dramatically in the assessment process (the letters present an organizational process suggesting an obsessive-compulsive personality disorder, thus emphasizing the need for control; the e-mails clearly demonstrate a breakdown in the perceptions of the boundaries between the instigator and the victim, etc.) and should always be considered for a more integral and valid evaluation (hence the usefulness of a mental health professional trained in this field), the assessor can only consider what is presented. Thus, the content of the material should be painstakingly reviewed.

Look for the passion involved in the writings, as this is the driving force behind higher potentials of violence. Certainly, unrequited love as a stimulus of hostility is as old as mankind. But instigators of greater concern are those who believe their victims are seriously in love with them — and the victim doesn't even know who they are. Such instigators may express little if any sexual enticement, but articulation of some form of a spiritual union or even an idealized romance should be a red flag (Hinckley writing to Jodie Foster, for example, indicating he would not kill Ronald Reagan if she would merely spend the rest of her life with him).

On the other hand, the good news is that these individuals generally have transitory fixations. In other words, they are just as likely as not to move on to another victim. This is why the "passion" of their writing becomes important, because, as the "need" for getting together begins to wane and diminish in intensity, the likelihood is that the instigators have found another target. And, while most of these individuals are not violent, those who represent a hindrance toward their targets are at a higher risk.

Case History

Take the case of Mary, who had a loving, passionately sexual live-in relationship with Ronnie for about 2 years. After it became clearly evident that Ronnie had a physical abuse problem, Mary moved out over one weekend. Unfortunately, Mary had met Ronnie at work and, while Ronnie no longer works for the same company, Mary does. Mary has been receiving annoying phone calls at her cubicle at work from Ronnie for the last few days and was recently overheard by her good friend and co-worker to say, "Leave me alone, or I'm calling the police," as she hung up and immediately began sobbing. Confiding in her co-worker, Mary has now told her story to the supervisor, who immediately calls Human Resources, who immediately calls you.

The assessor should first determine the level of safety and security for the victim as well as the organization before moving forward with any assessment. Is there an immediate threat that needs to be neutralized? (Mary says she moved out over the weekend and feels confident Ronnie has no idea where she has moved as it is not with any friend or relative.) Regardless of the personal safety Mary may feel, the fact that Ronnie was a prior employee of this company must be taken into account. For, even if he has not mentioned he would see Mary at work, there is no reason to believe he would not consider this. After all, he would be familiar with the environment and thus not feel that intimidated or uncomfortable at the work site. And, since it is likely he does not know where Mary is now living, he's sure he can always find her between the hours of 9 A.M. and 5 P.M. — at work. Hence, initial security precautions should be addressed at the job site before proceeding with the assessment process, which may run the gamut from nothing more than awareness discussed with appropriate personnel to hiring armed security personnel.

Now the assessor should determine the true level of physical contact between the victim and the instigator. This is necessary to re-evaluate the initial security concerns as well as to determine the perceived dynamics in order to recognize the violence potential. Again, the assessor's role is to focus primarily on behaviors and facts the victim can describe about the instigator so a better personality model is interpreted. Most of these concepts are brought to the forefront by following the assessment grid and the witness interview form supplied in Chapter 4. Then, by applying the response grid contained in that same chapter, the best subsequent steps can be determined.

Additionally, ascertaining the exact nature of their current relationship (married, legally separated, divorced, etc.), whether there are children involved, any common property they still share or any other reason Ronnie may have to contact Mary or be involved with her should be delved into. These questions help decide the strength of Ronnie's need to contact Mary. While issues of control are the usual underlying concerns and the highest likelihood of violence occurs where the instigator has been divorced or separated from the victim (Bureau of Justice Statistics, 1992), clarifying peripheral interest may greatly enhance the negotiation of future behaviors with the instigator and, at the same time, point to issues that will allow the victims to feel reassured that there is the possibility of resolving this matter.

Many times, assessors ask questions of others that may seem highly personal and revealing. Humans being what they are, these feelings have a tendency to cause the interviewer to be less than candid or to be hesitant to probe as deeply as necessary. If an assessor finds himself unable to utilize these tools or unable to go into or open up topics that appear to bring discomfort or even embarrassment to either himself or the interviewee, then it may be necessary to realistically determine one's level of effectiveness as well as reliability. The assessor's responsibility is to collect all the information as objectively as possible, as it all possibly influences the assessment process. An assessor cannot worry about "feelings." We have had numerous situations where difficult and even painful interviews have led to initial "concerns" as to what was actually trying to be obtained or determined. Perseverance, in as professional a manner as possible, is essential in these cases, because the liability taken on by the assessor once involved in this practice is ultimately decided by the end result. Without all the facts, without all the information, the end result may finish tragically.

Back to our case with Mary and Ronnie, as it is important to also consider whether there is a violation of law that could require police assistance or intervention. While it is not uncommon for the victim to be reluctant to get law enforcement involved, insistence for reasons of safety and long-term management of the issue should be reinforced. At the same time, it is important to remember that, in certain cases, many law enforcement agencies are now mandated to take immediate steps that may go beyond what is preferable in this case. For example, if Mary tells the police Ronnie hit her, as he has done in the past, and if there is any evidence of this act (Mary still has a welt on her arm), in many jurisdictions, the local police must arrest the suspect, regardless of what the other person may say. In other jurisdictions, this process must go through an "investigative" procedure whereby a detective may first obtain a warrant for the arrest of Ronnie. In either case, the end result is basically the same — a fairly short time between the interview of the victim and the arrest of the suspect. Hence, these issues must also be explored and ultimate decisions must be based on safety for Mary as well as others who may be secondary in this (co-workers, friends, etc.). The assessor must therefore feel very comfortable in understanding these ramifications so that suggestions are not given that detract from possible alternatives that may be the best avenue to take, despite initial uncomfortable feelings of dealing with outsiders or the wishes of the victim.

Part of this consideration also involves the contemplation of a restraining order. Should the restraining order be just on the victim or should it also encompass others in the workplace (a corporate restraining order)? The assessor must be familiar with these issues, which are explored in Chapter 7, as it is critical for all parties involved to be aware of and comprehend the possible ramifications such an order may involve. Again, the assessor must feel very comfortable in explaining the diversity of these effects so suggestions are not given that detract from possible alternatives that may be the best solution.

Physical relationships are, at times, convoluted, yet they play a pivotal role in the assessment. Intelligent and thorough interviewing techniques will help clarify them, but they are only one part of the issue. Obtain these data carefully, then connect them to the rest of the assessment process.

Emotional Concepts

This area is more easily defined within the boundaries of the relationship victims have with their organization or environment and how this corre lates to the association with instigators. The affective sentiment the victims bring with them or develop in this setting sets the tone for their interaction with others in that environment. The assessor's responsibility is therefore to determine what the motivational passions of these victims are because their actions are determined by these and they are consequently reflected in their daily actions. Certain passions may drive victims to interact with others in such a manner as to antagonize possible instigators.

One of our first major international clients requested we conduct a threat assessment on an employee who had threatened to kill a plant manager. The instigator was currently out on medical leave and did not seem to pose an immediate threat, so we responded to the site and began our interviews with co-workers, supervisors, etc. Upon completion of our questioning, we found the subject of concern had indeed threatened the life of the plant manager. In addition, due to numerous other documented behaviors over the years, it did appear he posed an actual risk to this person. However, we also discovered one additional fact. Almost without exception, every worker we interviewed held similar opinions about the plant manager and all felt, in the right place at the right time, they too would want to harm this man.

This manager's passion was to achieve results, while his motivation was to achieve recognition. What mattered more than any personal problems of any of the workers who answered to him was the ultimate achievement of specific goals. These accomplishments were realized through manipulation of supervisors and unsympathetic handling of personnel difficulties. In this case, the emotions of this victim were tied directly into the performance of his job and the subsequent rewards, which substantiated his self-worth. Thus, assessors should realize their function in conducting an assessment is not only to determine the potential of violence as it may pertain to the victim, but also to clarify the contributing factors toward the total risk potential, especially within a specific environment or organization.

Other contributing emotional concepts include the family's support or lack of it and how this may be reflected by either victims or instigators in their need to feel a sense of worth. While the primary focus of the assessor should be that of the influence of a specific environment and how two people interact within that environment, additional influences must be considered in determining how outside influences can affect the environmental stimulus. Family environment, therefore, must be considered, because the culture we live in suggests this is an important aspect that can indeed have a profound effect on a family member's character.

Obtaining information regarding family support or involvement in either victims' or instigators' lives may not always be easy. The answer to these inquiries by the assessor is often guarded, or it may be information that is unknown to outside witnesses. However, sometimes even the lack of such information can prove useful. "Gee, I never hear him mention anything about his family, but I think he is still married with a couple of kids," can suggest a lack of emotional ties or compartmentalizing. It may further be reinforced if the person interviewed adds almost nothing more to the picture by responding with, "My family life is just fine." This suggests the necessity for a follow-up question such as, "That's great, can you explain what that really means?" to obtain any valid or significant information. This may liberate notable data to substantiate strong family ties. On the other hand, your questions may develop a sense of despondency or dejection over the issue of family that might open the door to further exploratory understanding of this relationship and thus provide insight into emotional problems that might contribute to the overall dynamic between the victim and the instigator.

Case History

An exemplary employee for more than 23 years was working at his position in a manufacturing plant when his work was stalled because his machine broke down. The protocol for this organization was for the operator of the machine to request maintenance to come and repair the machine and to wait until the repairs were completed before continuing with his work. This employee was very conscientious and had a passion for trying to turn out the best product within the confines of his time allotment. Every time he operated his machine, he was motivated to meet or even beat his expected quota. This breakdown caused him to demonstrate extremely agitated behavior and frustration. He finally went to his supervisor and said he had called maintenance four times in the last 4 hours, was consistently told they were busy and would respond when they could. He declared he was ready to "bring his gun in to show maintenance he meant business." This long-time employee was fired on the spot for his comment.

The company was concerned over the threat of violence and asked for a threat assessment in this case. None of the usual red flags was evident in background checks, interviews with others and review of work history. A personal interview with this now ex-employee did reveal he had recently been served divorce papers by his wife and had just found out the day before he made this "threatening" comment at work that his only son had an incurable form of cancer with a prognosis of less than 6 weeks to live. He was reinstated with behavioral guidelines, but this example clearly points to the emotional power of family as a contributing factor in considering potentials of violence.

Status plays a role in this consideration as well. If victims who are in positions of management believe their roles within the organization demand they receive a certain amount of respect and appreciation automatically, and their previous relationships with instigators have been as equals, this could present levels of animosity and antagonism between the two. If the victims need to feel the power of control through their position, instigators may find this frustrating or develop resentment, especially if there was a prior friendly relationship. If there was no prior relationship between them, this role may cause irritation and dissatisfaction on the part of the instigator that may develop into a dislike or even a professed hatred.

Thus, the emotional attachment to victims' status should be considered through interviewing them and asking directly what their roles are and what their expectations of those roles within the organization are. It should be asked of others, also, "How do these victims present themselves in their current positions and have there been any changes noted in the last few months?"

Psychological Concepts

There are copious sources of psychological explanations and theories that can greatly enhance the assessor's understanding of these traits. Therefore, only a general grouping of the more common characteristics based upon these authors' experiences is presented.

The Domineering Victim

This includes those who intimidate, browbeat, bully, come across as officious or simply have a dominant personality. (It is certainly descriptive of the personality previously mentioned in the earlier example wherein everyone wished the manager ill will.) They may either suggest a possible threat of violence is way out of hand and the instigator should simply be removed or they present a state of denial, suggesting that they have no idea why this is occurring. They often have little time for interviewers and may demonstrate little concern when questioned. They may actually have little knowledge of any instigators or seem to be predisposed to cast a bad light on them in almost all aspects of their environment (work performance, co-worker interaction, etc.).

With this type of personality, the main task for the assessor is to allow victims to perceive they are "winning," as this is their primary stake in their behavior. Approaching most victims as if we were preparing to "dance" with them allows great latitude. Assessors wish to lead, yet they must have the cooperation of interviewees to allow the dance to flow, to have it appear effortless and to conclude with their experiencing a satisfied, harmonious interaction. But domineering victims have their own ideas. Your skill in adapting your interview to facilitate fluidity can make the difference between having a positive experience versus getting everyone's toes stepped on. Thus, the first trick is getting these victims to engage with you, as they are more accustomed to giving orders than interacting with peers.

After you have explained your mission and who you are, open the dialogue by suggesting that you have already established that the victim is somebody or has achieved something (everyone appreciates compliments and, once heard, the listener has a tendency to listen for more). Tell him you heard from others that he is a remarkable supervisor and that you know this situation must be terribly stressful. Or, if you are aware of a certain reward he has recently obtained, congratulate him on this and ask something about it, such as how he worked toward that goal.

Next, it is important the victim understand your objectives and the specific role they play in this assessment. This is not the time to suggest that this victim may be a contributing factor, although this is highly likely with these types of victims. Rather, the victim should be made to feel it is his very ability to deal with others that will assist you in compiling valuable insights to piece together the necessary portrayal of the instigator to better understand the true potential level of risk, especially as it relates to violence toward him.

Since you have already subconsciously suggested he is a wonderful person, thus tipping his senses toward paying attention for more praise, he is eager to hear more. Now is the time to carefully phrase your questions in this interview to push the victim to describe observed behaviors of the instigator he may not have paid close attention to before. Make your inquiries as positive as possible, while suggesting to victims that only their unique insight can result in a true picture of the instigators. Take a few moments to visualize your request of victims by making certain the explanations you give them are clear and thoughtful, yet solicitous.

For example, the interview may proceed as follows: "While disciplining subordinates is never a pleasant task, you have certainly observed many ways people handle your direction and correction."

This suggests understanding of what one is supposed to feel about discipline — never easy, but necessary — so victims will feel less challenged. It also builds up their level of expertise by suggesting they have experienced many responses to their authority and a positive spin has just been proposed regarding their authority style by suggesting discipline is merely correction or direction.

"Can you help me better understand how Pete reacted when you were faced with resolving his difficulties?"

Now we are soliciting the victims' help in understanding the instigators' behavior while at the same time suggesting they were only trying to help instigators, not punish or chastise, which may often be the case. These individuals are often searching for answers to problems even more vigorously than you may be looking for yours. Unfortunately, many of the psychological manifestations of these victims are results of perceived successful coping strategies (e.g., masking behaviors) they have developed and learned over the years because they actually lack insight and confidence or the ability to feel in control. Hence, this process may give them exactly what they need — a different perspective with a viable option for changing the dynamics.

"I am going to be asking you a few questions today to which you may not have the answers or you simply feel uncomfortable answering them. I know your responses will help me tremendously, but also remember there is no right or wrong answer. The questions are important, but a guess or an unsubstantiated answer can prove more detrimental than no answer. After all, our primary concern is for your safety (and, to immediately mitigate any attempt for them to respond with some type of 'I'm not afraid' answer) and the safety of those around you." This type of explanation has now given them alternatives and, at the same time, has told them what you expect so they won't have to deal with their own insecurities or feeling they may not be in control.

One last concern often at the forefront of dealing with such victims is their attempt to direct your questions, investigation or opinions about instigators. This is part of their makeup and, while at times it is annoying and even frustrating, using it to your advantage will prove more useful. "I appreciate that insight," or "You may be right about that," is a good beginning to your reply. Then finish with, "I just need to be sure I cover these issues with everyone so it appears I am being consistent," or "I just need to make sure I look into this matter this way, under direction of legal counsel."

Instigators, of course, may react to this type of victim in a number of ways, depending on their own psychological makeup. It is generally thought that victims like this tend to anger most subordinates and thus bring a lot of "threat" problems on themselves. Yet instigators may merely be frustrated with this type of behavior when it was directed toward a specific issue, thus giving the observant assessor the tools for a possible compromise. Or instigators may have a similarly domineering personality and simply feel they cannot back down lest they show others weakness and lose face. But, more likely than not, such instigators feel they have been wronged or treated unfairly and have taken the style of the victims as a personal affront. Thus, an important mitigating element here may prove to be allowing instigators to understand an action on the part of the victims was a personality flaw and not personally directed only at them.

Additionally, it may require clarifying for victims how some individuals require a bit more explanation or personal attention and allowances should be made as we are all different. (Of course this type of victim will not readily accept this as "his problem." Therefore, to be successful, careful construction of your explanation must include the valuable element of what's in it for the victim, e.g., increased productivity, improved performance, safety, etc.)

The end result of your interview and assessment when dealing with these types of victims may prove to be the most difficult part of the case, as it often depicts the victims as bringing a lot of this action on themselves. And, as discussed, your conclusion must be as objective and exacting as possible, which may mean recommending ways of dealing with victims as well as instigators. But remember your role. It is not one of human resources or of legal counsel, but of assessor. While it is imperative that you understand many of the same rules and guidelines that must be followed by Human Resources, security, legal counsel and others, it is also just as important to outline the behaviors and issues leading to your assessment findings, so anyone reading such a report would reach the same conclusions. This will allow your client to understand what is going on in order to determine what additional tools or resources are necessary to deal with this.

The Fantasy Victim

These are people who see themselves as very important, superior, have a sense of entitlement, are exploitive of others, lack empathy and are perceived as arrogant. They are ambitious and expect others to bow to their wishes as they believe they are obviously better qualified to make the decisions. They can be charming and persuasive in order to get what they want, and they expect to be treated with special regard as they are entitled to their goals because they are truly superior. They differ from domineering victims in that they take the time to manipulate others to achieve their goals, whereas domineering victims have no time for this cultivation and merely brush others aside. Fantasy victims welcome the opportunity of dealing with you to prove their superiority and, since you were brought in by others who may be important for these victims to influence, they want a crack at conning you on to their team.

The difficulty here is the inappropriate, false, tainted or embellished information the assessor is likely to receive from them. While domineering victims may simply state the people you are inquiring about are of no consequence or have been a constant thorn in their sides, fantasy victims may also make up a story for retaliatory reasons, attention-seeking needs, attempts at manipulating you or just because they need to feel special. Chapter 3 of this book makes suggestions about how to intervene and guard against this type of problem.

The primary focus of this type of victim's "story" is due to a variety of defense mechanisms such a personality is using to avoid having to deal with reality. Hence, rationalization, grandiosity and fantasy play crucial roles in the daily activity of these individuals. Pointing this out will only be met with denials, as these victims have already repressed the reality so sufficiently they now genuinely believe their own fantasy.

Therefore, it is important for the assessor to understand, when initially addressing these victims, that normal courtesies may be considered insulting. These individuals feel they are very important and they have already explained their situation and just need it rectified immediately. And, unlike the domineering victim, it is not a question of "winning" because, in their fantasy world, they always win. For example, it is immaterial that they might have been accused of sexual harassment by instigators, because they are above the normal rules and policies that are for the "common" person.

Approach these people by admiring their accomplishments and the control they have over their environment or organization. But remember, they are "special," so trying to compare them to someone else or trying to bond by stating you can relate to some aspects of their success would only be perceived as an insult. Thus, building them up, as the assessor might try with domineering victims, will not be as effective. However, these types of persons welcome the opportunity to hear themselves boast and see others respond in an admiring manner as a golden opportunity to expand upon their grandiosity. So "dancing" the active listener dance with this type of person will prove the most beneficial.

Attempting to appeal to their concepts of what is best for their future or the future of the organization can prove futile as well. These individuals have already projected a fantasy future of high achievement and tremendous success and wealth. Hence, any reference to the actual mechanics of making this happen ("Since Mr. Jones [the instigator] has always shown a high level of success in your department, perhaps reassigning his reporting procedures may prove to lessen the problem while, at the same time, assure you of maintaining a successful sales force.") in order to try and mitigate the violence potential will fall on deaf ears. Besides, Mr. Jones was not a part of his fantasy, so why should he care what happens to Mr. Jones?

Instigators are generally feeling overly controlled and pressured by this type of victim. These victims have already fantasized the end results and that just leaves the grunt work to accomplish it. So they simply tell their subordinates where they are going (the goals to be achieved) and, as soon as this is expressed, they believe it is accomplished. If someone has a way of achieving the goal more quickly and easily, they receive little if any credit for this accomplishment. But, if something goes wrong, it is fully the incompetence of the subordinates that is to blame. Hence, there is a lot of resentment and frustration on the part of instigators who are in a subordinate position.

The Ineffectual Victim

This includes those who may come across as delicate, fragile, inadequate, vulnerable, helpless, powerless, easily led, vacillating, soft, unconvincing or uncertain. They often seem like someone just asking to be picked on. Their character may be such that it becomes so frustrating or annoying that one would almost expect some form of negative response to their directions. Or they simply add to the confusion and misunderstanding of the organization or the department as they cannot establish consistent guidelines or boundaries. These victims usually represent the larger challenge to interviews by assessors as they are generally noncommittal, wavering and indecisive.

The key to the successful assessment with this type of personality is allowing them to perceive that you understand their difficulties and want them to lean on you. The immediate warning that must be expressed here, however, is the care that must be taken not to allow these people to become so dependent or reliant on your guidance and suggestions that any future inquiry that develops (perhaps an administrative hearing, a restraining order deposition, etc.) makes them sound as if everything they say has come from you — in one fashion or another. ("Well, the assessor asked me if I ever saw John hit his desk or clench his fists and I thought I had to give him one or the other" or "The investigator told me others mentioned seeing this behavior of John so I thought I was supposed to agree with him.") Chapter 3 gives the reader more information concerning this issue.

While many investigators often begin their interviews by asking a victim to give them an overview of what has happened, it is even more important with this type of victim that an assessor make this his starting point. Generally, these victims are checking you out, trying to see if they can figure out what you're looking for. When they "understand" you, it gives them a feeling of safety and protection and a sense of direction, ironically often the very traits that cause uneasiness or anxiety in their environment or organization.

It is during this "overview" explanation that much of your work with this type of victim begins and successful results can be established. Remember, they are looking for clues from you as to what will be the most pleasing or "right" response. Hence, allowing them to explain everything with minimal interruptions and giving them looks of absorbed interest will go a long way toward gaining an understanding of their true perspective, untainted by modeling to fit their belief of what you want.

Their first run at this will never be complete or final, as they are too busy looking for clues from you. Be careful not to interrupt, even where there are facts you may need clarified or issues you may need expanded. This is a time where use of your active listening skills becomes important.

Taking notes is always important, but you must realize this type of victim will be noting every time you pick up the pen to write and deciding if what he has just said is more important to you than other statements. This is a distraction you cannot afford. You run the risk of forgetting something, but, on the other hand, you have not given any more weight to one thing he has said over another. By not taking notes, or taking as few as possible, you are demonstrating your attention, which feeds the victim's "need to please."

After these victims' dissertations, your response should be one of thanks and interest. If there still seems to be some uncertainty on the part of these victims, have them go through their story once more, only this time lead them, but in general terms. "So on Monday morning, you arrived at 8:00 A.M. and what was it you observed?" You would not want to say, "Did you say you saw John hit his desk or just shout?" Again, if possible, you may not want to be writing anything ... just listen. Acknowledgment words such as, "Ah yes, now I understand" or "I hear you" are also helpful as they reinforce in the minds of these victims that you are listening to what they have to say and what they say has meaning to you.

Now you can go into your predetermined questions. Let them know you are not trying to put words into their mouths. You are conducting an assessment that requires the consistency of asking specific questions, many of which you do not expect them to necessarily have the answer to and many of which have already been answered by the initial story. (This helps subconsciously reinforce in the victims' minds that they have pretty much committed to a certain answer if you can refer to that answer when you come to that specific question. This is important later and should not be brought up on the initial discovery.) Further, it is important that they can supply specific examples of each of the reported observed behaviors asked about, since a pattern of behavior by the instigator is crucial to the determination of the potential risk of violence.

The last bit of advice on this part of the interview is to try to ask your questions in as close to the reverse of the story as possible. Many investigators have long ago learned the value of asking a suspect to recount his story in the reverse sequence of his initial account. By so doing, the events that have been explained several times in an orderly sequence become more difficult to delineate if they are not genuine. We can all read a story when it is placed in front of us and, after reading it several times, can generally recount the story to someone else, albeit probably not exactly as written. Asking someone to then recount the facts of that same story in reverse order becomes somewhat difficult, unless they really know the story and have recounted it numerous times.

The object, then, of asking ineffectual victims to recount their story in reverse after they have given it to you in a chronological sequence is to determine whether the story they have relayed to you is complete or only something they told you just to please you. It is true that recounting their story numerous times in a normal manner may enable them to express the facts in reverse order more easily. On the other hand, if the story is not really the truth, those areas that were untrue will probably be recounted incorrectly, out of sequence, or completely forgotten about. The intent is not to trip up the victims so much as it is to ensure they are consistent with their accounts. They have gone forward in their minds with a specific sequence of events — perhaps even two or three times — hence the brain "computer" has been programmed to respond with a particular retort when proceeding this same way. But, if you reverse the order it requires the brain to "put on the brakes" a bit and that can prove quite revealing by illuminating information that was left out or uncovering attempts at eliminating uncomfortable details.

Another character trait not uncommon for these types of victims is to hesitate a little longer than usual before answering your question. Alternatively, they may have uncharacteristically long pauses during the actual answer they are giving. While they may truly be trying to determine the correct answer to your question, the likelihood is that they are probably trying to determine how to answer in a way that will most please you. If this occurs, to avoid misunderstandings while obtaining the best information possible, ask them to describe a definite act or behavior presented by the instigator that addresses the problem or concern raised by the question. If their account is more incorrect or fabricated than true, they will have difficulty supplying such an example — if they are capable of providing one at all.

Remember, they want to please you. So, continual retorts of "no such behavior" cause them to feel anxious or frustrated, since their perception is that they are not able to give you what you want. Hence, it would be wise for the inverviewer to occasionally remind the victim that the design of these questions is to reveal patterns of behavior. Because one question may not produce a notable behavior example does not mean other questions will not yield sufficient information to make these deductions.

Finally, going over the whole story once more can prove very beneficial with such victims, making sure it is they who are doing the talking and you who are doing the listening. Now it is appropriate to refer to your notes, if you have taken any as they explain their account. Be cautious of the style in which the questions are asked. Tell them it is for clarification, as you want to be sure you understood the answer. This is also the time to clear up any discrepancies, making sure you preface your comments acknowledging this is something *you* were not clear about.

Of course, there will always be that time when you become aware of a discrepancy and you really need to confirm what they just said — now, instead of later. It is still wise to go to at least several other questions first and then return to the inconsistent point. It's as if you were the famous television sleuth, Lt. Colombo. "I have to apologize. I thought I recall you saying you saw John hit his fist against his desk." (The way the victim first reported it.) "I don't remember when I heard that but didn't you just say you never saw John hit anything?" (The last thing the victim said.) "I want to make sure I have this right, can you explain this to me once again?" A soft inquiry and tone for this type of question, especially for this type of victim, will reduce the likelihood of the person feeling "caught" and reacting defensively.

The "Nice Guy" Victim

This is the person who may appear orderly, organized, on top of things and friendly upon the initial meeting. Unfortunately, not wanting to "offend" anyone, his or her style lends itself to an independent or self-governing style within an environment or organization. Some people can handle this, as it can allow for more individual creative freedoms. Others find it difficult to operate under this leadership, as there are few boundaries and inconsistent levels of accountability.

When considering this in the specifics of a work environment, this is often further complicated when it's actually a "peer" of the victim who presents this style, not the actual primary victim, and this peer is supposed to be supervising the instigator. While this peer may easily end up a secondary victim, frustrations are easily mounted on the part of the victim when the "nice guy" gives no response or reaction to the instigator's bothersome or inappropriate behavior. This position makes it difficult for victims to intercede and allows instigators to feel they can continue with their threats.

For this section, let's concentrate on the assessor's trying to deal with these psychological concepts belonging to the actual victim. This is probably the easiest type of interview as these people want to be thought of as very helpful and likeable. It is not so important that they please you as it is for the ineffective victim, but they do want you to know they are aware of what is going on, that they are in charge and they can give you whatever you want. The key to dealing with this type of victim is to start out by making small talk to find the common elements with which you and they can bond (both enjoy fly fishing, bowling, etc.). Then you allow them to feel as if they have truly scored some points with you ("Well, Jack, you certainly know how to tie those flies. You'll have to give me some pointers later.") and then solicit their assistance ("I can sure use your insight into this."). Unlike ineffective victims who are still going to be carefully muddling through their thoughts to tell you what they think you want to hear, the "nice guy" victim has now been reassured you see him as a nice guy, that he has the ability to get you something and that he knows what is going on (both on a personal level with the flies and a professional level with his insight into this problem).

The same general rules still apply with this victim as other interviewees. Ask behaviorally oriented questions and ask for behaviorally explained answers with examples. The same cautions need to be explained; there is no right or wrong answer and, because of other interviews, a pattern of behavior will unfold that should be consistent, i.e., they should report only what they have actually seen.

The most difficult aspect of dealing with this type of victim is generally convincing them to explain all they are aware of, as they often feel they should hold something back. This is because they think people they interact with will think less of them if they reveal certain information so they will not be thought of as the "nice guy." They also fear they may reveal to you that they are not as organized or on top of things as they want you to perceive. Hence, developing an alliance with these victims is very important. Similar to the ineffective victim, you must guard against their believing you're trying to become their next best friend. But, with "nice guy" victims, because you have let them know you share some common interests, they can often move past their concerns. This can be even more emphasized by telling them you share their concern over the welfare of all others in the environment — including instigators. By discussing this matter to its fullest, you can assure them others will be appreciative in the long run (validate that they are "nice guys") and instigators will get the proper help or assistance they need (another "nice guy" thing to do).

The psychological aspect of the instigator toward this type of victim is generally one of frustration over not having clearly defined limits and boundaries within the organization. We all like to feel we have a certain amount of control in our lives and understanding of what is expected as well as the consequences for straying outside those margins can bring a certain amount of tolerance to the table, even if personalities do not see eye to eye. Looking for ways the instigator can gain back some of these "controls" while at the same time providing understanding of these concepts to the victim may prove useful in dealing with this aspect of elevated risk.

The "Romantically Involved" Victim

Oftentimes, these victims may actually be catalysts for instigators. It is not unusual to find that they have been psychologically (put-downs, name-calling, etc.) or physically (hitting, slapping, etc.) abusing instigators prior to instigators taking any action. In fact, this was a common belief shared by many ("She probably brought this on herself.") until research and common sense clarified the actual issues. But it is important to enter into the assessment process understanding this element — not that it should in any way diminish the act of violence potential of the instigator, but victims may have originally placed themselves in this position, albeit unconsciously.

These individuals are often seen by many as warm and affectionate. Frequently, however, they are actually quite fearful of the outside world and insecure, preferring to be taken care of by someone else. It is important to realize that the connection in such a relationship — the association of this type of victim and an instigator — is most often independent of sexuality. That is not to say sex never plays a role in the association between instigators and victims, as it is often stated initially that it was a driving passion that brought them together in the first place. However, there are plenty of examples of what could best be termed "nonsexual love" in the stalking literature. Our role is to consider the process; hence the passion may be sex, but the motivation may be one of control, or of needing to be controlled — or both.

Perhaps even more simply, the relationship may be based on needs, each fulfilling the other's ("I have what you need and you have what I need.") by exploiting and/or taking over or attempting to confine the other — thus the passion. However, the ultimate satisfaction requires the achievement of the underlying driving force — the motivation — and, in this case, it is one of pleasure or control. Therefore, the issue of sex does not have to be involved.

This is important to the assessment process, as the problem develops when these needs are not met. While often clinically shown how lack of a parental role or character may have contributed to this difficulty, the main issue for the assessor is breaking down these motivational factors in order to best categorize the potential for violence. For example, if Mary from our earlier example (Mary and Ronnie who lived together until Ronnie got too physical and Mary then moved out) is indicating she and Ronnie initially hit it off, had some similar interests and the sex was so phenomenal it was the deciding factor in their decision to move in together, the assessor should visit this concept to determine the strength of this bond. While sex can be an extremely compelling physical as well as psychological component to any relationship, this basic animalistic need can be resolved in a less potentially problematic setting than a relationship gone bad. But concern should be felt if Mary outlines that she felt comfortable with allowing Ronnie to "take charge" of their everyday activities; that she felt it was "cute" as well as reassuring to forget her cell phone at her desk and return 10 minutes later to find 15 messages from Ronnie asking her where she was; and that the reason she left without telling Ronnie where she was going was the fear she had for her safety as he becomes extremely volatile when he thinks she is not readily available. "He told me his mother had left their family when he was very young and his father didn't handle it very well, so I just thought it was some old issues … but not a big deal." Unfortunately, for the assessment process, this can be a "big deal," not only for the victim, who the instigator may now decide has abandoned him as well, but also for anyone he believes may be standing between him and the victim and his "needs" to take back this control.

There can be a similar predicament involving "romantically involved" victims in the case where they do not even know the instigator. Unfortunately, pictures of the victims and stalking behavior to watch them both reinforce passions of instigators. If there is no actual contact, the assessor must then attempt to determine the motivation of instigators by reviewing the literature (e-mails, letters, etc.) left for the victims. Where there appears to be a strong sense of entitlement by the instigators, and the victims present an even stronger sense of putting distance between themselves and the instigators, the instigators may interpret this as abandonment. The level of violence depends now more on the psychological makeup of the instigators, but, in some cases, this so-called rejection can be a precursor to violent anger.

A more common example occurs with couples who date a few times and eventually one of them decides the other is just not for him or her. Have the people who have made this decision caused the other people to feel put down or rejected? Or have the people who were asked not to call anymore taken an angry approach, blaming the others for all their problems and now leaving them harassing voicemails at home and at work? This is important in the assessment process, as there are concerns if the focal point of the anger is the other person.

Here, the assessor should try to determine how the victims perceived their relationship. Was there a feeling of equality or did the victims resent the instigators? If so, these instigators may have begun having similar feelings toward the victims, which would be a good follow-up direction for questions such as, "Did you ever get the feeling they were frustrated or irritated with you?" to determine whether the instigators had been showing any signs of anger. Or did the victims feel bored on their dates or just found the instigators uninteresting, again suggesting the need for further review of the instigators' behavior as observed by the victims. If instigators were seemingly oblivious to this lack of interest by the victims, they may feel that such a dramatic closure of this relationship was uncalled for, and hence, harbor a great deal of animosity toward the victims.

And what if victims indicate they felt the instigators were just real down-ers? The victims describe their "dates" as disasters because, whenever they would try to do something, it seemed that the instigators were never very good at whatever it was they were trying to do (play miniature golf, go-cart racing, etc.) and the victims would tell the instigators this. The victims also report that the instigators would often belittle themselves, or put themselves down over their inadequacies. The concern here is, if such instigators are prone to feeling shame, as this example seems to indicate, the action by the victims may now have confirmed these feelings of shame, and the instigators now feel worthless. Trying to avoid this terrible feeling, the instigators can transfer blame to the victim, and thereby avoid feeling ashamed.

Again, the importance of trying to determine the mindset of instigators becomes equally as important as delving into that of the victims in these cases. However, often the only data available to the assessor are what the victims can supply. Thus, the assessor must carefully interview the victims to try to piece together the dynamics of the relationship in question to better ascertain the potential for violence.

The Criminal Victim

There are those who fan the fires of violence. Just as there are victims who enter into a scheme to make money that is not necessarily legal and find them-selves at an unplanned deeper level of criminal intent, there are those who purposely oppose individuals demonstrating aggressive tendencies with the intention of further irritating them, thus triggering the violent act. Certainly, these victims must be held accountable for their inappropriate deed. But, just as degrees of negligence determine the amount of liability a person may be subject to, so too should the degree of involvement a person has in the pro-cess of violence be an integral consideration in the assessment process. The assessor should therefore be mindful of this style of personality.

These victims generally present an irritable and aggressive style of per-sonality. They seem to always be looking for a fight, verbal or otherwise. They have a constant problem at work getting along with others and challenge supervision every time any change is implemented, discipline is enacted or correction is suggested. They seem to care nothing for others and are always indifferent toward the possibility of other people getting hurt or mistreated.

The assessor should first determine at what level these victims can be approached because part of the difficulty is their belief that lies and deceit are completely acceptable behavior. Questions concerning their perception of their status in life can thus prove extremely useful. If they feel they have not been treated fairly, that the instigators have received more than their fair share in some situation, then an additional label of jealousy can be applied to this personality. Once this is understood, the assessor should realize the primary driving force — their passion — behind their reports is desire for retribution. Their motivation, or ultimate goal, is to receive compensation for the anger and resentment they feel — they want to feel in control. And what better way of achieving this feeling than causing the instigators to lose control and commit an inappropriate act.

These people could also be motivated by the need to be noticed, the need to be feared and thus the need to have everyone show them the proper respect, whether deserved or not. These individuals will do whatever it takes to make sure others back down and will demonstrate very aggressive forms of antagonism and belligerence. The assessor should be mindful with this style of personality that these individuals are actually acting this way as a defense, hence, the assessor should not challenge their self-made reputation. It is likely the victims did challenge this perceived status, and therefore the instigators will declare that the victims are out to get them with untrue stories of inappropriate actions.

Although understanding some of the common criminal victim types, the assessor is still left with approaching this personality with the same objective intent as with any other interview because a determination of the potential for violence is still in question — although, in this case, it may more likely be by the victims than by the instigators. The assessor should also understand that this personality, although disrespectful and challenging in nature to authority, does appreciate the constraints those in authority can enforce. The assessor should operate from this realization, re-affirm the level of deference these characters feel they are owed, yet remind them of the necessity for facts and behaviors that can be consistently substantiated, lest disciplinary procedures be initiated against those reporting false information.

Summary

Are there other "victim" profiles? Of course, there is always the "perfect" victim who seems capable of telling you everything you need to know in an extremely objective and descriptive style. There is also the extreme of the ineffective victims, previously described, who, because of a lifetime of low self-esteem due to social failure and "victimization" among their peers, begin to identify with the instigators until these victims believe whatever treatment they are receiving from the instigators is appropriate.

It is also important to note that all the victim types discussed in this chapter can easily be found in the workplace. But this text is about looking at a process, applying that process to the dynamics of the interactions concerned and deciding how best to approach and assess those dynamics to determine violence potential. We want to try to correlate our experiences into some form of valid research or method and then ask the reader to help us improve what we have discovered and shared. Only through the sharing of what is being done with those who develop the theories and explain the causes, then comparing their experiences, research and studies with ours, can we ever hope to better understand this thing called violence.

Remember the "golden rules" until you have comfortably figured out a particular victim's style and then try some of these ideas:

- *Listen* — Sometimes they feel no one else has.
- *Don't strive for the power* — You're there to collect data.
- *Be a mirror* — If you reflect sincerity and concern, generally so will they.
- *Ask behaviorally oriented questions* — And get examples.
- *Be yourself* — Someone who is emotional (that includes most victims, even those who are lying) is very aware of someone else who is uncomfortable around him. You achieve more results being yourself in the long run than trying to be just like either of us.

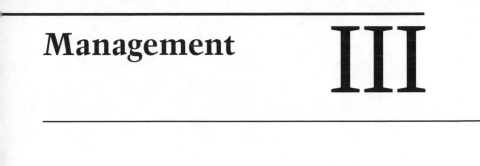

Management III

Organizational Influences — Personal and Professional

7

Introduction

Organizational influence can have a powerful and sometimes surprising impact on the assessment process. This sphere of influence is especially revealing as it affects individuals' daily patterns. It affects how they behave toward others and, of course, the persons of concern. It affects how they communicate or fail to do so. It is possible to ascertain their "rituals" and routines. The assessor can establish the patterning of the community within which he interacts. You can determine core values, as well as symbolic gestures and falsehoods. Added to this is the degree these are shared by those within the environment and obviously the persons of concern. Age, gender, social status and perceived role play a part in the evaluation of this setting, but it is this scene, this situation, this specific environment that is an important application of consideration in a violence assessment, because it is often one of the largest contributing motivational factors in the violent act.

Reviewing the organizational area in the Assessment Grid in Chapter 4 points to many of the commonly understood problems and influences within the organization, their impact on the instigator, victim and others and why they are a necessary component in the total assessment process. Not only does this grid point to obvious issues such as stress and heavy workload as potential situational stressors that can escalate a violence problem, but the lack of understanding, responses and training on what to do on the part of management personnel in an organization are all too common maladies in today's workplace. The grids then point to how the biggest reaction to what is lacking in an organization can cause fear. Can there be a more motivating argument to substantiate the need to consider this category in any and all assessments of violence? But why is this so often overlooked and can anything really be done within an organization to mitigate the violence? The short answer is, for an organization to change, it needs to be motivated.

The opportunity of "working the street" as a police officer, both for a large metropolitan city (about 750,000 people) and a medium-sized one (about 200,000) afforded me (Corcoran) some tremendous insights into these concepts. Between what was present in the cities worked and what showed up in neighboring towns, dealing with juvenile gangs was nothing unusual. What was surprising when one could confront those young gang members to talk face to face was the discovery that they really weren't bad kids. Yet, no matter how much time they spent in custody away from their "bro's," a few minutes with me or many years in a juvenile facility, when they got back to their "hood" they went right back to their "gang-bangin'" ways, including talking about and committing violent acts. Thus, the lesson was learned early on, that the cry for police intervention to break up gangs made about as much sense as telling the police to go break up families. Just as one's family offers certain feelings and expectations, so does a gang — and so does the organizational environment. After all, as defined by *Webster's Dictionary*, a gang can be nothing more than "a group of persons working together." This is why it is important for the assessor to tie in the organizational influences affecting the potentials of violence in order to point to necessary change and clearly demonstrate what motivational factors can induce that change, without overstepping the boundaries of the organizational structure (family).

What is also necessary to realize is how the internal organizational matrix of the individual contributes to the final behavior. Each reaction, perception or belief that makes up individuals influences their external reaction, perception or belief, changing its meaning and modifying its impact. For example, if employees are normally outgoing, but they discover that their behavior is frowned upon by their immediate supervisor, they may lessen the level of their demonstration while working in the same environment with this person. This may not affect some employees appreciably, but similarly outgoing people who are oversensitive begin to be depressed by such restraints. These are two types of people with similar personalities but different reactions due to their internal organizations, which produce differing effects (one type is able to adjust while the others may resent the supervisor for "making" them act this way).

This is noteworthy because the concepts of "normal," that an act is either within the boundaries of acceptable behavior or not, may not be as important when assessing a situation as when evaluating accumulated information. This applies directly to making a determination of the potential toward violence as well. How many times have you been cut off by an inconsiderate driver in traffic, and find yourself making a threatening statement or signifying your displeasure via a gesture? This may be considered a fairly "normal" reaction within our society, hence, for assessing that one situation, the potential toward violence may appear to be at the low end of the scale.

However, take someone like Joe, who has been out of work for more than 6 months and has recently lost his only remaining family member, his mother, to a drunk driver incident. Joe is now currently driving to the unemployment office with a gun he has decided he is going to threaten the employees with, as they just informed him they were stopping his unemployment compensation. If Joe is the recipient of the inconsiderate driver incident during this time, the "norm" of the potential of violence takes on another meaning. His internal organization is going to react to this differently from most of us who simply are annoyed by some driver who is not paying attention. The assessment of accumulated information would allow the assessor to make the more accurate determination of the potential for violence in this case, as the situation that has brought this to the forefront may take on an entirely different effect from "normal."

So the assessor, in the violence potential assessment process, is dealing with concepts of what is a threat and, to that end, the organization can have surprising influence. We often say people are normal when they function as individuals capable of achieving their own sense of accomplishment or fulfillment. But doesn't the "norm" depend more upon the environment? When we are young, we try to fit in with our peers by acting, talking and even dressing like the rest of the group. We say we want to be "different," yet in reality we become the same as the others. This is because any behavior exists on a continuum, or a broad range. The "normal" behavior you brought into the group changes, perhaps even to a pathological component, but the broad range of behavior (dressing like one person, talking like another, etc.) is now the norm.

This continuum is also present in an organizational environment where "normal" is influenced by the practice of that environment and those who interact within it. And if, in fact, the organization has a maladaptive or even a pathological component to it, then the continuum of behavior may modify a person's "norm." The difficulty with this is when an individual's internal organization permits, modifies or even accepts this new norm, but other individuals may not, which thus increases the potential for conflict.

Organizational Structure

Numerous organizations are, in essence, building the same thing, manufacturing the same component or delivering the same service, yet each goes about accomplishing its feat in different ways. It makes sense then, that how the organization is structured and how the people are organized have significant impact on how the work is done and how the people behave. The differences in industries dictate differences in their organizational structures out of necessity. But, in the same industry, there are also different behavior relationships within companies. This is primarily due to the environments they serve. Just as youngsters try to fit into their group in high school, so too must an organization try to fit in with its surroundings.

Difficulties can begin when management makes decisions that are not accommodating to the environment, causing the effectiveness of the organization to falter. Individuals within an organization must work toward a common goal to make the company successful, which, in turn, requires fairly consistent behavior. This allows for a sense of predictability (we should be able to produce 100 widgets a day) and a sense of enduring activities (thus we will always be needed for this market) regardless of surrounding events such as workers coming in or leaving, mergers and reorganization or streamlining.

The problem with this depends upon several factors that lead back to management, as the power structure, or who has the control, heads the list of influences. Is this a command organization dictated to by a few decision makers at the top and reinforced at the worker level by specific policies and procedures? Does a specific manager have the need to feel in control, believing subordinates are not capable of making decisions that will lead to the desired success? Or is the authority decentralized? Are subordinates allowed to take control over their own work, as long as it gets done in the manner or style that leads to success of the organization?

The assessor should attempt to decipher these elements to better understand the compelling reasons instigators may perceive there is a problem and victims may perceive they need to perpetuate the action, although the victims' or instigators' perceptions may be that they are merely acquiescing to the expected norm of their organization. For example, the command structure may prove useful in some organizations (a police agency, for example, where the paramilitary hierarchy is maintained) but in today's world, for most businesses, there are so many changes and competitors to keep ahead of, the inspirations of co-workers often outweigh the apparent control of a hierarchical company. In an establishment where this is the format, are the employees satisfied with this (it gives them structure and all they have to do is show up for work) or does it cause them anxiety and tension as they are not allowed to vary from the established policies and procedures? Perhaps it is merely the instigator, who, as a more free-thinking spirit, simply does not fit into this environment. Hence, such individuals would feel their discounted "suggestions" are a personal affront and might view this one supervisor (the Fantasy Individual, as discussed in Chapter 6) who has "stolen" their ideas and never given them credit for their accomplishments.

The opposite setup from this is the organization where control is decentralized to the point where instigators might be unsure of whose directives or influence carry the most weight and, therefore, what the best path is to accomplish their tasks. Some character types need structure, a clear delineation of what is expected of them. In a less structured organization, all they get from supervision (for example, they may report to two different supervisors) is, "This is the goal. Do what you think is best." Unfortunately, since each supervisor is overseeing different aspects of the work, this complicates the instigators' process of deciding what to do. One element of the task is dependent on the other and, if neither has a definitive course, the instigator may feel lost. Because these supervisors offer no real guidance or support, such personalities might feel that supervision (and thus the organization) is obviously against them and is trying to set them up for failure. Thus, frustration takes over their entire work experience.

The other factor to consider is the intricacy of the organization. For example, I was raised on a farm and was very comfortable in the rural environment, where the biggest stress was worrying about the weather. There was not much complexity in the day's activities (feeding the animals, picking fruit, watering plants, building a fence), since none of these tasks was a primary source of family income. But, when I first became a Secret Service agent and was assigned to the Los Angeles Field Office, not only was there a complicated hierarchy and numerous differing tasks, many of them life threatening, but it also took 6 months just to learn the Los Angeles downtown freeway system well enough to prevent the embarrassment of getting lost just going to the office.

To add to the daily stress, I had to learn what was expected in each of the different Secret Service units. What were the different rules when conducting one type of investigation versus another? What were the different protocols for different protectees? Every supervisor had different values and attitudes, yet who was right? An agent could wake up in Los Angeles in the morning and be in Washington, D.C. by evening, looking one way because of an "undercover" role in Los Angeles, yet expected to look entirely different for the protection role in D.C. Control problems existing in such an organization would seem easily discernible. However, whether it was dedication, wise employment screening, good management or just plain luck, control problems were not evident there — but many other organizations are not so fortunate. The assessor is therefore tasked with determining how these levels of intricacies affect the interaction of those who must operate within these organizations and whether such nuances are part of the causal relationship, or, at the very least, perceived as part of the problem, even if not cognitively recognized by the victim or the instigator.

Part of the answer to the issue of complexity, as well as an additional problem touched on by the previous example of employees with two supervisors, is how jobs are assigned within the organization. Some duties or products require a multitude of tasks. They can be approached by having many people do a few simple tasks that are coordinated by another person. This often leads to the concept of specialization (one person puts the widget in the boxes all day long) but it can also lead to low enthusiasm and low self-esteem. Alternatively, one person can be given the responsibility of handling it all, thereby giving that employee a sense of control and autonomy and generally contributing to ability and job satisfaction. A certain degree of specialization can be reached here as well; however, it is generally recognized that the specialization is the individual, not the work (this person handles all the electrical work for the project). Assessor awareness of these fine complexities can illuminate a host of possible contributing factors that then suggest numerous different ways of resolving the issues of potential violence.

Case History

Helen worked for an assembly plant where she was required to pick out large bolts that had damaged threads. Once she allowed the "good" bolts to proceed down the line, other workers then placed them into various parts of a large machine. She had been there for about a year before deciding to tell her supervisor that, if they would broaden the belt in her one area, they could greatly increase their volume. This was uncharacteristic of Helen as she was normally very shy, kept to herself and rarely did anything more than go to work or to the library. The supervisor looked into the matter, found Helen to be right, broadened the belt area and then hired Mabel who now worked with Helen and had the same task as Helen.

Mabel was a few years younger than Helen and would often pass the time on the line explaining to Helen her weekend escapades in Tijuana, which always included graphic detail of her sexual experiences. Helen, while not considered prudish by her peers, nevertheless took offense at these stories and told Mabel to stop telling them to her, as they made her feel uncomfortable. Helen even went to her supervisor and told him that she was fearful for her safety, as Mabel's stories were not only offensive, but they caused her to not pay as close attention to her job as she should.

Mabel continued to relate her antics anyway and one day, Helen picked up a bolt, threw it across the belt into the middle of the room (no one was ever in this location) and yelled, "It seems some people only hear what they see. Do you see how easily these bolts can fly off the belt?" Mabel was visibly shaken, went into the office of the supervisor, who then told Helen to go home for the rest of the day. After conferring with Human Resources, the organization decided to conduct an assessment, as they were concerned for the potential of future violence by Helen.

Looking at the organizational influences as opposed to the numerous other issues that make up the assessment process, an assessor can quickly see that Helen is doing a simple job that is coordinated by another. As discussed, this often leads to the concept of specialization, thus allowing Helen to feel good about herself (she even uncharacteristically made a suggestion that improved the company's production). But the assessor must also remember this type of job can lead to low enthusiasm and low self-esteem and, in this case, perhaps is part of the problem.

In fact, the interview process in this case substantiated that Helen had begun to feel the company did not think much of her because, after they implemented her idea, they hired another person to work with her. She had not asked for help and she felt the company was telling her she was not capable of doing the job when they hired Mabel. Hence, this simple act, which the company did to increase production and to assist Helen, was misinterpreted and probably contributed to a potentially violent scenario. The assessor would be able to make numerous recommendations to rectify this problem (employee rewards for suggestions; employee-of-the-month recognition programs; moving Helen or Mabel, or perhaps having them work different shifts; etc.) and, when the suggestions are combined with other considerations, the assessor may be able to verify a low level of violence potential. This illustrates how important assessor awareness of these complexities is, as they can illuminate many contributing factors that then suggest numerous different ways of resolving the issues of potential violence.

Organizational Culture

It was a simpler time 30 years ago. The organizational culture was mostly hierarchical in nature — a clear delineation between levels of workers, supervisors and management, reinforced through breaking down tasks to their simplest levels that required little skill. Control was thus centralized and powerful. Elevation to the decision-making level required acceptance of this level's values. That continuity of behavior referred to earlier was at its peak. Those who learned to adapt survived — but at what cost? Some believed that their job success was due to their own personal identity, others that only those who could become "company men" would succeed. Regardless, assessments to determine the potential of violence were being conducted even then and from our experience, at about the same rate as it is today. The only real noted difference was that there did not seem to be as many convoluted issues to deal with.

Clients and customers began to change; the organization's culture had to do likewise to fit in and be accepted. We began to see downsizing, rightsizing, layoffs, mergers, outsourcing and restructuring, which led to numerous emotional and, at times, physical demonstrations of displeasure by employees. Organizations sought more and more information to make decisions, but found the markets were shifting more rapidly and unpredictably than ever before. Thus, the new horizontal organizational structure began to emerge, and, with it, a whole new culture. Employees and supervisors began making decisions together. Depending on the level of control necessitated by the nature of the product or service, employee competence and, of course, the final decision-maker's attitude, the degree of this change in structure was determined. Now the continuity of behavior becomes more muddled. Loyalty and long-term commitment to the organization are not as important as gaining respect for each other's values and sharing information or skills that lead to common goals.

Just a few years ago, while I was sitting at the front desk of a police department, a young man (approximately 27–28 years old) came in, identified himself as an FBI agent and asked if there were any openings, especially dealing with computer crimes. He stated he had been with the Bureau for about 5 years now, had been assigned to the computer fraud division and wanted to branch out for more general experience in dealing with computer crimes before putting himself out into the private sector, where he knew he could make a fortune. Although the request seemed surprising (at least, from my perspective, as getting into such a specialty was generally considered quite notable), it was reflective of the new culture within organizations, apparently even in some of the more traditional types.

So how does this new culture affect the assessment process? One of the first cultural concerns in the organization an assessor should consider is the company's attitude toward employees. The organization must now look to ability and skill and then negotiate to acquire and keep qualified individuals, while at the same time eliminating those who don't contribute. Twenty or more years ago, the mindset of those entering the workplace was that hard work would mean that rewards would naturally follow. But, with those old expectations of longevity and loyalty by "older" employees equating to job security, increased expectations from the organization can cause clashes to develop.

The example is, of course, the 40-something employee who has worked for a specific company for more than 20 years. His actions, while perhaps reflective of other elements, may very well be influenced by the effects of the changes in the organizational culture, and the assessor must be cognizant of this concern when conducting an assessment where the instigator may very well be of this "old guard." Additionally, the assessor must be aware of the dynamics of how the organization handles this new culture, if it even acknowledges the changes — and how are those who are not "fitting in" managed? These are important first questions the assessor should consider when determining issues generating potential violence.

The assessor must also consider the economic realities of those they evaluate. Are they demonstrating or have they talked about financial difficulties? Are they living a parasitic lifestyle? Both of these questions are automatically asked in the Witness Interview Form in the appendix to Chapter 4 and have been found by these authors often to be overlooked by some assessors. Hopefully, this section of this chapter clarifies why these questions should be asked as well as explaining how important it is for assessors to have no problem with delving into such "personal" issues. For, if there are any indications that these difficulties exist, then further explanation should be sought to confirm the problem is not just something unique or temporary. Some personalities, especially those who have a continual problem with finances, would automatically blame the organization for putting them into this financial difficulty.

It is also foolish to believe a comparable level of racism and bias does not exist in the organizational culture on a par with what is present in the environment, thus producing a comparable level of stress. While the adept manager may look for the opportunities that diversity creates, others bring with them the baggage of their environment. These problems are not limited to simple hostility between workers, as it also affects competition for positions or ideas and permeates the perception of unfair bias. Both authors have been exposed to "toxic workplace" syndromes permeated by such behavior. Unfortunately, the amount of time and energy spent in dealing with the mitigating curative resolves of these issues is often greater than what is expended in dealing with an "instigator," because you are addressing a cultural influence larger than just the organization or any one individual.

The case of the demanding plant manager for whom almost everyone felt ill will (referred to in Chapter 6) serves as a prime example. From observation, it was apparent this one manager, although in charge of a large manufacturing plant with several hundred employees, was virtually unknown to corporate administration. When inquiries were made about him, the response was, since his production was good and the plant was heading in the direction the corporation desired, there was no apparent problem. In fact, those few responsible for his initial hiring (he had been hired away from another national firm) reported they found him to present an intelligent, professional and even charming personality during his interviews and his references all reported positively.

However, what was found through interviewing numerous employees in this plant was that this manager (we'll call him George for this example) was not trusted by anyone at the employee level and there were obvious manipulations at the supervisory level. For example, the employees told of situations where they had an emergency family medical situation and, unless they had accumulated time on the books to take off, they were not allowed to do so, even after speaking to George directly to plead their case. George always appeared to be cool and unresponsive to the employees and would often refer to "company policy" in order to justify his rulings.

On the other hand, George seemed very friendly toward a certain group of supervisors. It was interesting to interview the supervisors he was friendly toward and to compare their data with the information obtained from those he acted more distant toward. It seems the supervisors George was friendly toward were those on the apparent "fast-track" within the organization.

They reported having a very close and comfortable relationship with George. George told these "fast-track" supervisors they were doing a great job but they had to be more observant and cautious of the other supervisors, least production fall and their advancement slow. Those supervisors who were not a part of the "fast-track" group (they were mostly the older, more experienced ones who had worked their way up in the organization) reported that George had little time for them, had little information, if any, on how things should be done and would often chastise them when there was a mistake or performance was not up to par.

The personal interview with George revealed he had little concern about employee personal problems such as family illnesses, indicating he was hired to perform a job and was going to get it done. Even explaining the consequences of such an act (lower morale, lower productivity, etc.) seemed to have little influence on George as he even quoted the "policy" during this assessment process to justify his position. It became apparent George was manipulative, unemotional, self-serving and loyal only to himself. This is why, in this case, while it was true the instigator was a threat to George, George's actions precipitated similar feelings from many others in this plant. The situation was only going to get worse, an important realization for any assessor.

Unfortunately, as indicated in Chapter 2, the organization elected not to address this issue. Hence the "culture" of the organization seemed bent on shifting toward such behavior, as it was not only tolerated, but a follow-up on this case revealed that George had joined the corporate administration team within 1 year of the assessment. George clearly demonstrated his own bias by his manipulation of specific supervisory personnel. But, if the assessor understands this about a case, there is the opportunity to address such a problem and possibly obtain measurable results, thereby reducing the level of stress within the workplace and mitigating the level of risk by the instigator.

The key to success in modifying the culture in an organization relies on getting the top of the organization to buy into the changes, changes that must not be so radical that they seem impractical or "just not right for us." This is especially difficult when the changes are suggested or brought in from an outside assessor (consultant). It is therefore necessary to first establish a link between the deeper values and beliefs of administration, which may mean compromising on some of the personal beliefs and values of the assessor. It has to do with finding the right motivational factors. If ABC company's primary objective is to produce 10 million widgets by the end of the year, then you can be assured the company culture is geared to this. Thus, the presentation of the proper changes in internal behaviors of those who are dysfunctional must clearly demonstrate how this goal is better obtained through the appropriate changes. This is not always easy and not always within the expertise of the assessor. Hence, a lot of thought and careful consideration of all that is presented must be taken into consideration.

Organizational Conflict

Whenever two or more persons or groups assume an attitude or stance toward one another, *Webster's Dictionary* says you have a relationship. Hence, any organization should be considered the sum of its relationships. And the most common and misleading temperament in any relationship is conflict. Yet conflict, as well as agreement, should be considered a norm when reviewing a situation.

I recall one of the first couples I ever counseled: They began by saying they were coming to me after 5 years of marriage on the advice of a friend as they wanted to learn how to better communicate. Being the wise (novice) therapist, naturally my first response was, "So your conflicts seem unfair?" (After all, I knew simple miscommunications often gave rise to conflict.)

"Oh no," was the reply. "We never have conflict."

"Never?" was my response.

"Oh no. We're very much in love and we never quarrel or fight."

Surprised, I then asked, "What happens when you disagree or have different opinions?"

"That never happens," they stated. "We would just like to learn how to communicate more effectively."

Still wanting to force my perception of the problem on this "loving" couple, my retort was, "Well, how do you discuss differences?"

"Oh, we pretty much agree on everything," was their reply.

My perception made me very uncomfortable with these two. But it exemplifies how they did not understand the total involvement or responsibility of a relationship ... conflict as well as agreement is critical. It is the process of working through differences that improves understanding and helps the relationship to grow.

When one is the brunt of the conflict, it is not easy to believe the rhetoric that all conflict can be enriching, especially since we traditionally view conflict as a win or lose proposition. We are caught up in the dilemma of not wanting to lose the issue and so we puff up our chests, kick our adrenaline into gear and dig our heels in, prepared to go toe to toe until the other person understands our point (that is, agrees with it). Or, not wanting to hurt the other person's feelings, we say nothing. What we fail to consider is what the cost will be to us or the organization if we don't resolve the conflict. Certainly, there is the tremendous waste of time involved, for we always spend more time on unresolved conflict than on working out a solution. And as any good business person knows, time translates into money.

Unfortunately, most organizations, much like the first couple just described, tend to ignore the conflict in the hope that it will simply go away. Obviously this gives the unresolved conflict even more power than if it had been settled, as it is always an underlying theme gnawing at everyone involved and thereby causing lower morale, decreased productivity, increased absenteeism, etc. Settling an issue may not be sufficient either, as this often does not reach the heart of the conflict but merely accommodates those involved. What often happens when a situation gets elevated to the level of concern, requiring an assessment of the violence potential, is that one or both of the parties involved have become aggressive. Aggression may be used to express a strong emotional belief about an issue and instigators have no intention of giving in to someone else's opinion or it may simply be the only way they have learned to be heard. It is not necessarily a clear signal of violence.

We are not going to go into the numerous benefits of conflict or how best to approach conflict to achieve a successful resolution; there are plenty of books to avail yourself of. And, when considering the approach to resolving the conflict, all the issues previously discussed play just as integral a role in how to approach and resolve the conflict as does the consideration of the actual "problem." What we will address is the responsibility an assessor has for defining the conflict or aggression in order to truly determine the degree of risk involved for potential violence.

Any kind of direct or physical form of aggression or conflict is unacceptable in the organization and should not be tolerated. There are always mitigating circumstances, but once an action has occurred, there is little room for negotiation. However, we must understand aggression occurs at every level of our society. Hence, the question to consider is whether the hidden, diffused, chronic or deviant form of conflict should be considered as volatile or improper as the physical or direct.

Both authors have been the recipient of a phone call from the client who says, "We have a problem. After Joe was reprimanded by Pete, his supervisor, he was overheard saying to a co-worker that, 'Pete better watch his back.'" Even more daunting is the call that says, "Bill was having problems on the line getting his supervisor to respond to approve his work so he said, 'What do I have to do to get a response? Go home and get my AK-47?'" The response by management to these cases has run the gamut from doing nothing to firing the employee immediately, which is always interesting to try to correct after someone who is already stressed has been terminated. Where do we draw the line between what is tolerable and what is not? That debate will go on for a long time and will not be decided in this text because there are too many variables to consider. What we want is for the reader to consider the linear aspect of the conflict within the organization when approaching the assessment process.

First rule of thumb: conflict and thus aggression, from a behavioral perspective only, is a preconditioned response to a stimulus. If the organization has an expectation of a certain amount of aggression (and it may be subtly suggested through the format of competition, the way a supervisor corrects a subordinate, etc.) or it simply chooses not to immediately punish an antagonistic act, then the behavior is being taught to all who observe and the line of demarcation becomes even more complex when looking at the many causal issues of conflict. Conflict becomes a way of interacting with others and thus solving problems. The "norm" of the organization dictates employees' expectations and responses. Thus, the risk of a violent act becomes more difficult to determine on the basis of only one component (Bill threatened to go home and get his AK-47) and points once again to the critical necessity of having the assessor look at all the factors involved before determining the level of violence potential.

Bill's comment about going home to get his gun would surely be viewed as an aggressive act. But the assessor, by asking the necessary questions, should be determining whether this organization might have had a contributing hand in this. The first question could be something as simple as, "Why did you make this comment?" And the reply might be something as nonrevealing as, "I wanted to get my supervisor's attention," or, "No one seemed to care so I wanted them to know I was serious." Either way, the next question should be more probing, "Why is this important to you?" The answer may prove very revealing or additional inquiry may be necessary. In this case, the reply was, "I have 4 hours to get out my four pipes for this project. I knew I could do it in 3 hours and that would have given me an extra hour to get started on these new tubes they want." "Sounds like you're very dedicated," was the response. "Dedicated! We're talking bonuses here, son. The more I do in the time I have the more I make. And the more I get done at the end of the quarter compared with Harold and Jim gives me even more. These guys were screwin' with my livelihood and I've got too much depending on this." The assessor must understand this "statement" by Bill might actually have a basis of normalcy within the organization. There are always other issues that can be pointed to as well to complete the assessment picture, but an assessor must give this type of disclosure its proper place in the process.

The Internal Organization of the Individual

Just to add complication to difficulty, the character and personality of an individual, as suggested briefly before, should be considered in the assessment process as well. The overlap of specific traits and the understanding of these differences have made for constant confusion and challenge in the world of psychology so will do the same for the assessor. And this is often not as easy to determine from simply talking to others, thus supplying one more argument for the importance of interviewing the instigator versus not.

It is important for the assessor to try to comprehend these character differences. Even though people may act in a certain way based on their personalities, there may be other traits they are drawing upon that cause a certain behavior in a given environment. Thus, the motivation for the "questioned" behavior may be completely different from what is usually perceived. This motivation may be external or may come from the perceptions of the environment by the individual.

It is the purpose of an assessment to try to discover these traits, which may mean first discovering the individual's motivation, or internal organization. And rather than getting into the psychodynamic nuances of the antisocial personality versus the narcissistic personality, and the psychopathology or sociopathology that exists between these and others we see predominantly in these violence assessment processes, it is basically the job of the assessor to develop a comprehension of the function of each of these traits within the personality. If this is accomplished, better insights toward the potential for violence these individuals possess can be determined. The determination of these characteristics will also assist in developing ways of handling, approaching and dealing with the individual. Thus, the assessor must probe for internal causes as well as external.

For example, Joe and Bill from the previous example may both be considered by their co-workers to be very thin skinned. Both may be known in the organization as simply not being able to tolerate much before they get upset and let others know their feelings. Yet Joe reacts because he needs to feel more in control of the situation and Bill reacts because he wants others to help him. They demonstrate the same trait — anger — yet the motivations are exactly the opposite. One pushes to achieve his goal (Joe — constantly bickering and mumbling about his circumstances and muttering, "He better watch his back.") while the other pulls (Bill — doesn't know how in a competitive environment to get others to help him, so he makes an out-of-character "shocking" statement). Which is more prone to violence?

The answer cannot rest on one simple issue (again, we emphasize that assessments must be a consideration of the totality and not just one segment) but pushing generally angers others more quickly than pulling. Yet, in our previously mentioned example, Joe made the seemingly less violent comment ("He better watch his back.") and Bill said he was thinking about getting a gun. So Joe, who is pushing, needs to be looked at from a control standpoint; the assessor should look to determine why Joe feels out of control and what might help him to feel back in control. Bill, on the other hand, needs to understand that there are better ways of asking for help.

Once this insight is obtained, the assessor should add to it the sense individuals have in choosing their "victims." It becomes somewhat more complicated, as much of what may depend on how the individual perceives his status or personality is played to by another, especially in a specific environment. Thus, a Bill or a Joe may actively place himself in certain situations with specific individuals because he knows, in that environment with this person, achieving his goal is possible. Joe knows who he can "push" into compliance and Bill knows who he can best "pull" into agreement. Unfortunately, their goal may not be achieved and, thus, an inappropriate trait is manifested. They may come upon unknown victims and try their technique, but it doesn't seem to work on them. Or the potential victims have developed their own internal organizational dexterity and are now just not going to take it anymore from Joe or Bill.

Once again, it becomes evident that, by addressing the motivational factors of these individuals, the organization can experience changes in their behavior. Since the organization should not be expected to be their therapists, the incentives should be based on job performance and goals. While this course of action is not always successful, it can prove beneficial. To ensure as complete and accurate a picture of the potential for violence as possible, assessors are charged with determining these delineations and should educate themselves in defining them for their clients.

Summary

1. It is as important to profile the environment and the actions of those involved in the environment as part of the assessment process as it is to look at the "profile" of the instigator and the victim. Only then can one outline the interaction of the individuals of interest within the organization and the dynamics involved among all concerned. This is accomplished through the process of eliciting past behaviors, conduct and modifications, especially as they relate to activities within the environment.
2. By examining the organizational structure, culture and how it addresses conflict, a better determination of the actions can give valuable insight into the overall potential of future violence. The dynamics of the environment may prove to be strong precursors or contributing factors to an already predisposed individual.
3. Determining the process individuals go through to arrive at their behavior, looking at the motivational factors that cause them to strive for their goals and comparing them to the environment will prove more valuable than assessing the specific action of an individual.

Post-Secondary
School Violence

8

The Problem

Recent post-secondary school violence incidents have sparked a major rush to psychologists, other mental health professionals and law enforcement experts, as well as educators to address the issues and develop programs and strategies to identify and handle potentially violent events. Much has been written on school violence, but the data collected by and large cover grades K–12. Those prevention tactics and techniques are often inappropriate or simply not practical at the post-secondary school level. The very nature of the post-secondary school culture suggests a need for a different approach to deal with potential acts of violence and their prevention.

The professional literature and studies are voluminous as everyone is concerned for the safety of our youth. Hence, every school, school district, governmental organization and private person dealing with this topic have jumped to analyze the problem and propose ways of dealing with it. Yet still the emphasis is on the youth violence ... does dealing with violence at the post-secondary level result in a different approach and understanding of how to identify, handle and ultimately prevent violence at this level?

Let us start by being clear what group we are addressing in this chapter — post-secondary educational groups. As explained in the currently popular online encyclopedia of our times, *Wikipedia*:

> *Post-secondary* or *tertiary education*, also referred to as *third-stage, third-level education*, or *higher education*, is the non-compulsory educational level following the completion of a school providing a secondary education, such as a high school, secondary school, or gymnasium. Tertiary education is normally taken to include undergraduate and postgraduate education, as well as vocational education and training. Colleges and universities are the main institutions that provide tertiary education (sometimes known collectively as

219

tertiary institutions). Examples of institutions that provide post-secondary education are vocational schools, community colleges and universities in the United States, the TAFEs in Australia, CEGEPs in Quebec, and the IEKs in Greece. They are sometimes known collectively as tertiary institutions. Tertiary education generally results in the receipt of certificates, diplomas, or academic degrees.

We are not suggesting that the literature is void concerning violence at this level of education — there are several studies and scholarly works that address violence at the post-secondary level of education as well as how suicide and alcohol/drugs come into play. Searching the data of professional journals revealed a plethora of material (*Journal of Interpersonal Violence, Journal of the New York State Nurses Association, Journal of American College Health, College Student Journal, Journal of Counseling Psychology, American Behavioral Scientist,* and the *Journal of Mental Health* to name just a few) and all of these have informative articles that were written in 2000 or later. Where the literature is nominal at best, however, is in the realm of what this entire text is devoted to assessing … the potential of a violent act of another that may harm or even kill another. Not to diminish the importance of interpersonal relationships, suicide, alcohol and drug abuse contributing to this problem, but the concern that is expressed more today than any other in this environment is how do we recognize someone who has the potential for violence before the act occurs so that appropriate preventative measures can be implemented?

Other concerns include what the National Center for Education Statistics notes, that "it is difficult to gauge the scope of crime and violence in schools without collecting data, given the large amount of attention devoted to isolated incidents of extreme school violence." With all of the conflicting conclusions concerning the overall situation of crime in schools, colleges and university environments as well as the ability to collect meaningful data and trying to add outcome assessments to those facts, it becomes extremely difficult for anyone to assess the effectiveness of policies and procedures and what impact they actually have on these incidents. Even the FBI's National Incident-Based Reporting System Data on Crime in Schools and Colleges acknowledges it cannot separate the information it receives from colleges versus other educational levels the way the current program is set up ("… crimes committed at school, college, and university locations are all combined into a single NIBRS location code. Separating elementary and secondary schools from colleges is difficult, if not impossible, in the NIBRS format.").

However, even with all of these statistics identified and the psychosocial difficulties acknowledged, what are the current tactics most often recommended repeatedly by all the experts? Look to CPTED for answers (crime prevention through environmental design), provide for better access controls, develop better visitor management solutions, implement advanced technology into the emergency planning and response processes (cameras, automatic notification systems through pagers, cell phones and intercom systems, etc.), and/or increase the physical security through the addition of security officers. Unfortunately, most of these measures just contribute to a completely new industry of security.

None of these responses is wrong and they all have a place when we consider how to deal with this issue. Every school in the world must be prepared to handle these emergencies, from terrorists and criminal activities to natural disasters and accidents. But the reality of cost, availability and just common sense often precludes the use of the latest and greatest materials. Therefore, other professionals suggest turning more to understanding the different cultures of those within our schools.

Instructors and mental health practitioners are suggesting more and more ideas and programs that present climates of safety, respect and nurturing for their students. The general population at large encourages faculty and other staff members not only to pay attention to the academic needs of the students, but the social and emotional needs as well. Yet the carnage continues; so what can be done?

Assessing the Real Issues

This chapter focuses on what we have been driving home repeatedly throughout this text — identification and prevention of the planned attacks of violence rather than the more common and recurring forms of violence such as fights, assaults, rapes, etc. Planned attacks are just that — someone has developed a plan to attack another — which in the world of violence and the threat assessments process is always a larger concern than the more common recurring forms of violence. This planned attack is directed at a specific target and thus the threat assessment is directed to the potential perpetrator, the potential victim(s) and any relationship that exists between the two, as well as the environment in which this incident may occur. We do this because of the consistent recurring demonstration of three key components of this kind of violence. First, violence is not a spontaneous act. Second, violence occurs due to a relationship that is built up (or is torn down) over a period of time and thus the "target" is selected by the perpetrator. Third — because of the other two components — if sufficient attention is paid to the indicators of this "plan," the violent act can be mitigated and in many cases completely avoided.

We willingly admit there may be initial difficulty in identifying the target. It may be a site or facility instead of a person; it may be several persons such as a class instead of one person; and the target may not be the end victim as the perpetrator misses or simply goes to the wrong location and the victim is not there. However, the universally recurring theme in the acting out of violent acts in the post-secondary educational arena points to the fact that these individuals have had some difficult periods over time and it has been noted by others within the educational community in which they attend. They feel hurt, misunderstood, find school difficult or they feel alone and often are depressed and in despair. Thus, there is the need for the aforementioned "programs" of trying to create those climates of respect and safety ... but there is more.

Studies conducted by the U.S. Secret Service in its 2002 report in conjunction with the U.S. Department of Education showed that in all of the school shootings considered for this study, almost all of the shooters shared their lethal plans with other students. Unfortunately, these concerns were not shared with the faculty. Yet other studies confirmed that students are willing to turn to trusted adults when they know of such information, but only in an environment that has been fostered over time as one conducive to concern and safety. This also clearly demonstrates that the students themselves should be part of this process of looking for and identifying potentially troubled individuals. This may require a systematic process to insure fair and confidential reporting systems; nonetheless, they can be very helpful. Information shared by students may be useful for not only preventing an action, but also for sharing valuable resources in the collection of necessary information for an effective assessment.

The Secret Service study also found that, in almost all cases, the attacker never threatened his victim directly and some made no threats at all. Clearly then the school must rely on other behaviors and/or communications before it becomes too late. Often the college setting emphasizes the "rights" of the individual to the exclusion of the safety of the masses over concerns of "privacy issues." While idealistically this notion should be supported, in today's world even those who pose a threat must be considered real and careful prevention planning should incorporate how to work through concerns such as "privacy."

More and more we hear of how we need to become aware of the person who puts his affairs in order, visits friends and relatives not visited in quite a while just to say hello and seems to present a certain "calm" that he has never exhibited before. Experts tell us these may be the signs of a person preparing to commit suicide. No one waits for this person to get on the bridge before asking the simple question, "Are you okay?" Yet we still feel we cannot ask the same of someone we suspect is having some difficulties in school until they say the magic words, "I'm getting my gun and shooting you."

Of course, everyone is looking for the perfect character check-off list — let us see how many indicators this person has and the more red flags the more likely they will commit the act. There is no such thing — there is no profile — it is just that simple. Hence, the necessity to focus on what we can measure is critical — behavior and communications. The behavior indicates the person is upset, perhaps has demonstrated acts of aggression in the past to resolve his or her issues or is in need of help. Their communications, especially to others, may also be very revealing. However, the problem is getting to that next step — doing something about it once discovered or noted as well as knowing what to do and who to contact.

Finally, planning on the quick and effective response by those trained to handle the potentially violent act such as local law enforcement is completely wrong. Make no mistake, law enforcement has become better prepared today to handle these events than ever before. This co-author has personally trained with other police officers in making immediate entry upon arrival at a school to neutralize any violent act. Nevertheless, think about it – how many minutes will it take for your local police or sheriff to arrive once the call is made. How many minutes will pass from the time someone comes on campus and commits a violent act before police force is even considered and the call is made? These are valuable minutes.

The Violence Risk Assessment Plan

There are just two main concerns, albeit they are somewhat convoluted in their entirety, that those in the post-secondary educational arena should address for a successful violence prevention/threat assessment plan. First, the student of concern is not just the one who has made a threat — that is an easy one to pick up on. The larger concern is the student who poses a threat as explained previously because he has, or is in the process of, developing a plan and has the potential of being able to carry out that plan.

Second, and perhaps even more important, the potential for violence does not escalate because the student has more "traits" of a potentially violent individual (he is a loner, he is depressed, he blames others for his problems, etc.). You cannot profile — period! The potential for violence escalates as you are able to determine the relationship between the potential attacker, the victim and the environment in which the incident may occur (Pete seems shy in Mr. Wilson's class and when he makes a mistake, Pam will often snicker. Today when it happened, Pete slammed his book shut and there was an awkward silence in the class for a few seconds.).

First Concern

The Secret Service study that spanned over 25 years of shootings discovered that school shooters did not threaten their targets directly over 80% of the time. However, that study also confirmed that these same 80% did communicate their intent and/or their plans to others before the attack. How many times have you said something in anger that could be interpreted as an angry gesture suggesting a potentially violent act — like the last time someone cut you off on the freeway — yet you really didn't mean it? But someone who is upset enough to plan an attack, who thinks about how it will make them feel and relieve their pain, who contemplates how he or she will approach the victims and wait to see the look in their eye — this portrays a more definitive problem and actually paints a more frightening picture.

We are not saying that threats of violence should be dismissed — that would be like dismissing the person who says he feels like shooting himself and we have all been taught these threats must be taken seriously. While these kinds of threats demand immediate and important consideration, it should not be the primary consideration in the determination of the potential for a violent act. When one makes a verbal threat, direct or indirect, he should be taken seriously, he should be followed up on, and he should be dealt with appropriately. But it is the plan, the build-up, the course of behavior over a past period of time — these are the clearer guides for determining the individual's capacity for committing the violent act.

Second Concern

There are actually three main components that must be considered when assessing this part of the puzzle. First, the attacker — What is known about this person? How has this person acted or reacted to stressful events in the past? How has he responded to suggestions or directions from others at both the peer level and the instructor-to-student level? Is he someone who seems to be able to reach out to others or is he more withdrawn? Looking for these key behaviors and noting these elements help define the individual of concern and his potential for violence.

Second, the concern is in identifying the potential victim. Again, from past behaviors, does the student of concern have a continual problem with a particular student, teacher, class (I hate chemistry) or group of students (I hate "jocks")? Has there been any recent trouble between the student of concern and any particular person(s)? Awareness of this behavior can be revealing and important when trying to put together the total picture of a potentially violent act.

Third, the concern is being aware of the environment — the circumstances of the potential attacker's situation. Is this environment conducive to fostering nurturing and caring behavior? Is the environment open to hostilities, perhaps displays of teasing and/or bullying behaviors? Has the particular subject experienced a recent loss of face or failure in his endeavors/projects/grades within this environment? Are the other students supportive and respective, or do they ignore this person or, worse yet, communicate directly or indirectly messages that violence is an acceptable behavior?

It is the addition of all three of these concerns that helps determine if the possible attacker has a higher or lower potential toward violence.

It is the relationship among all three of these factors that escalates the concern of the potential toward violence. The assessment plan must consider the relationship of the attacker to the potential victim(s) within the specific environment — and all of this must be done with a critical mindset, looking for credible facts, not just suppositions or rumors.

Further Criteria to Conduct a Successful Violence Prevention Program

Not all threat assessments in a post-secondary educational environment discover substantial information about a subject. There are always concerns of student privacy and confidentiality issues. The nature of such concerns is well beyond the scope of this chapter, especially since it is subject to change. However, we can share a few recommendations and observations.

The first recommendation is to be familiar with your local and state laws and regulations as you need to know the limitations they can place on interviewing, collecting data and sharing information about subjects with others. Because of school shootings, many of these laws have been modified, making the retrieval and sharing of important information more reasonable. Yet one should always know the boundaries and expectations of the field in which they engage themselves so that proper procedures and protocols can be adopted and applied not only to attempt resolve situations, but also to be sure what information you can share (or cannot share) with others.

Federal law governing students is generally contained in the Family Educational Rights and Privacy Act (FERPA). However, the primary intent of these laws is to protect students' "records" that are maintained by the educational facility, and identifying information from these records cannot be shared without prior written permission from the student at the post-secondary level. As in most cases, there are a few exceptions: health and safety issues, for example — a student's records can be shared with identified authorities if it can be shown that this information is necessary for the protection of the student or others. It should also be noted that FERPA does not govern information that might be shared that is not included in the student records. Please review Chapter 10, "The Laws of Violence Risk Assessment and Intervention," for more information on this and other notable laws to understand when conducting an assessment.

Additionally, who has the capacity and the ability to conduct the threat assessment? Who knows how to make the necessary inquiries to produce a sufficient outcome? Who knows how to conduct an objective and concise investigation? At what point does the post-secondary educational organization need to bring in outside experts? Thus there is a need in post-secondary educational facilities to organize a threat assessment team — a group who meets on a regular basis to review problems that may be presented by those within the institution as well as those who set the policies, procedures and training necessary for everyone to deal with potentially violent acts. This team would also know how to conduct threat assessments as well as who to call in — from inside as well as outside of the organization — to assist with the threat assessment process. And last, this team, or at least a designee from the team, should be available 24 hours a day, 7 days a week, with clear directions and explanations to everyone within the entire post-secondary institution of how to contact them.

The Actual Assessment Process

It is our belief that in the post-secondary school climate, it is even more important that the assessment process be initiated by any behavior or communications of concern. The focus of the assessment should be based on the facts immediately presented — what did the subject actually say or what did he actually do — and then look at the progression of factors that led to the actual event (what is the plan and what is the relationship between the potential perpetrator, victim and environment). It is not the time to rely on prior events to make suppositions about likely facts and or behaviors. It is not the time to compare this individual's behavior to a series of factors shared by other perpetrators. It is a time to look objectively and critically at this specific person's progression of ideas and behaviors toward the specific act — and those should be corroborated with as much information as possible gathered from appropriate investigations and interviews.

This kind of information is necessary to make the assessment and includes several key factors. First, what evidence is there that supports the fact that the potential perpetrator has been formulating ideas or developing plans to attack a specific target or targets? Even the student who one day blurts out that he is going to "get even" with another student has not necessarily met this level of confirmation that he or she is going to commit a violent act. What other behaviors has he exhibited that suggest he is planning such an event or who else has he told he is going to do this?

What is often overlooked in this aspect is that it should be corroborated that it is believed this individual can carry out the plan. Have others confirmed that this person has the ability to do what he says? Have others confirmed that this individual is acting consistently with what he has been saying to further substantiate his planning? For example, the statement was made by a potential attacker that he'd like to shoot someone, yet it is known he has no weapon, has no immediate way of obtaining a weapon and has made no attempts to obtain a weapon or learn how to use a weapon. This would be less suspect than the person who goes to the local range and begins target practicing and who tells a friend that he uses this pastime as a way to vent his frustration over his history professor. These questions need to be asked of other students, teachers and staff.

Second, usually the first question asked by law enforcement is what are the real motives of the potential perpetrator? Anger is not always a necessary motivator to a violent attack. In the post-secondary educational arena, a perceived wrong and retaliation to end their "pain" is a more common motivational factor with students. A perceived loss in status due to a failing grade or a terse comment in regard to the student's response to a question in class is also a more common motivational factor causing students to be provoked into a violent act. So what is the real intention of the exhibited behavior or inappropriate communication?

Third, the threat assessor must determine the true target. Especially in the post-secondary school arena, it is not always as simple as one person. Sometimes the potential attacker believes the whole class has caused his pain or an entire group has belittled him (the jocks in history class, the chess club that meets in the cafeteria, etc.). Other times the potential perpetrator may be looking at multiple targets as a more symbolic gesture of retaliation for the perceived wrong (it's the entire school's fault he is failing his chemistry class and everyone on campus is to blame) — thus prompting an important first question to be answered — why is this person considering this action?

Fourth, has the subject of interest shown any recent signs or interest in targeted violence? In the school setting, potential perpetrators will often mention past school shooters and how they accomplished their acts or how they could have done it better. Sometimes it is found these individuals begin hanging out with or developing a real interest in those kinds of people or groups who directly or indirectly give their permission for violent acts. Additionally, has the subject begun to exhibit more attack-related behaviors or activities? Have they been going to a range to learn to shoot a weapon or asking around for someone who knows where they can buy a certain kind of weapon or ammunition?

Fifth, what is the mental health status of the subject? We are not looking for a psychological diagnosis here nor are we saying that those who have a mental health problem are more likely to commit a violent act — although one may argue that any shooter in a school setting must have some mental issues. This category has more to do with how the potential perpetrator's lifestyle may be affecting his ability to be completely mentally healthy, which could be due to drug use, alcohol abuse and, yes, a mental health issue. So what is known about the subject's drug or alcohol use? What is known about his current level of stress? These are answers that can help the assessor determine the greater potential of violence.

Last, what other events in this person's life right now could possibly have any effect on causing this person to want to commit a violent act? Are there other destabilizing events going on in this person's life? It may be issues at home, personal problems on campus, health issues, etc., and many of these are difficult to discover. However, they can play an important role in assessing the subject's true potential toward violence.

Case Studies

While it is not the intent to cover every post-secondary school shooting in this chapter, certainly the majority of those that have occurred in the United States are described. There will be no discussions added by the authors to these case histories, no indications of what could have been done, should have been done or other avenues or alternatives that might have been explored — just what is known through research of commonly available public records.

The intent of this information is to allow the reader to have widespread information in a single location for review of what has happened to date so that appropriate decisions of how to mitigate such behavior or actions may be considered for the institution of concern. We are all excellent "armchair quarterbacks," but the successful violence risk assessor realizes there is always more to learn and there is never enough information. Therefore, the event is only described briefly, the facts known of the subject of concern before the event are described, and the facts discovered about the subject of concern after the event are described — albeit some more briefly than the others.

07/12/76: Fullerton, CA — Cal State Fullerton — Custodian

On July 12, 1976, Edward Charles Allaway walked into the library at CSUF and shot nine people, killing seven. Though several other library employees looked out from their offices during this shooting spree, Mr. Allaway walked right past them and went toward a man and a woman before him, two of his co-workers, thought by most to be his only real friends at work. Some say Mr. Allaway had dated the woman, although her brother states they were just friends. The woman apparently refused his advances — she was the only woman shot that day. The others shot were employees of the university, not co-workers of Mr. Allaway. His remarks during the shootings indicated that he felt his victims were responsible for his failed marriage in some way.

Facts Known prior to the Event

Mr. Allaway was a library custodian. He was 37 years of age. Other custodians on the job said Mr. Allaway was upset that the university hired a Mexican-American from the outside as lead custodian. They also said he seemed to be distraught over his recent separation from his wife.

Mr. Allaway had a sister who was a secretary in the sociology department at Cal State Fullerton. She actually helped him get this job and Mr. Allaway stayed with her for a few months when he originally moved out to Southern California.

Mr. Allaway had reportedly filed a grievance with a union representative of the California State Employees Association. Speculations persist as to what was in the grievance. Mr. Allaway was scheduled to meet with his supervisor the morning of the shootings to draw up an internal grievance with other union representatives. Some say the grievance was over Mr. Allaway's request to transfer to a different building on campus, while others say the grievance was in regard to the pornography that disturbed Mr. Allaway that he claimed was being shown at the library.

Mr. Allaway came to Fullerton with a chip on his shoulder, other custodians in the library have said. Most the time he was a quiet man who kept to himself, but on occasion he would lash out against his co-workers. Some accused Mr. Allaway of being overtly racist. Black custodians complained that Mr. Allaway would become quite surly if they tried to show him a certain way to do something. Mr. Allaway claimed to others that he was upset over the pornographic movies that were being shown in the library and that he felt his wife had been made to participate in them.

Facts Discovered after the Event

Mr. Allaway was later diagnosed as a paranoid schizophrenic, and he claimed to the psychiatrist conducting the evaluation that certain co-workers had driven him to kill. They taunted him about his wife, he said, and they forced her to appear in pornographic films.

Mr. Allaway did spend at least 36 hours immediately before the shooting locked in his apartment with the loaded rifle he had just purchased at a K-Mart in Buena Park, according to a psychiatric evaluation prepared after Mr. Allaway's arrest. He had the presence of mind when he bought the weapon to ask the sales associate about the rifle's jamming mechanism and to reload the rifle in the stairwell after he'd already fatally shot six people.

Mr. Allaway's parents live in an apartment built just above a grocery store in a "not high-class" suburb of Detroit. When interviewed about the shooting they didn't seem surprised about the shootings. They didn't doubt that Mr. Allaway could have done such a thing, although there was a look of devastation on Mr. Allaway's mother's face when she spoke about seeing her son in the courtroom on the day of his arraignment. They confirmed they believed their son had a history of mental illness long before he moved to California.

Mr. Allaway moved from Michigan to Southern California in early 1973, days before his first wife divorced him. In Michigan, Mr. Allaway experienced many of the same symptoms that would lead to the library shootings. He received shock therapy treatments during a month-long stay in a mental institution.

Mr. Allaway met his second wife a few months after moving to Orange County. Shortly after, the couple embarked on a cross-country camping trip, looking for jobs wherever they could find them when their money ran out. Eventually they returned to Orange County. At home though, Mr. Allaway's life began to unravel. He accused his second wife, too, of sleeping around with other men and appearing in pornographic films that employees at the library were producing.

During the criminal trial, Mr. Allaway's second wife attested to his prejudiced behavior against blacks and Mexican-Americans. She also attested to Mr. Allaway's jealous streak, which led him to threaten his wife with a penknife, saying he'd cut her face if she ever cheated on him. Mr. Allaway and his second wife divorced shortly after the shootings. A later police investigation confirmed that four employees of the University were discussing making a pornographic film at the library. The police also confiscated 20 commercially produced pornographic films from the library but were never able to confirm that Mr. Allaway's wife was in any way involved in this.

08/18/78: Palo Alto, CA — Stanford University — Math Department Doctoral Student

On August 18, 1978, Theodore Streleski, a graduate student in mathematics at Stanford University, murdered his former faculty adviser with a ball peen hammer. Shortly after the murder, Mr. Streleski turned himself in to the authorities, claiming he felt the murder was justifiable homicide because his advisor had withheld departmental awards from him and demeaned Mr. Streleski by belittling his 19 years of trying to earn a doctorate and by insulting his shoes in front of his peers.

Facts Known prior to the Event
Mr. Streleski had been pursuing his doctorate in mathematics for 19 years. He told all that would listen that he felt the Stanford faculty was withholding his advancement within this program for no good reason.

Facts Discovered after the Event
Mr. Streleski had a "hit list" of others he had intended to kill as well — all of them colleagues of his academic advisor. Mr. Streleski was subsequently convicted of second-degree murder and he served only 7 years in prison due to good behavior. His defense was one of diminished capacity and at trial he told the court that he felt the murder was "logically and morally correct" due to how he was treated.

Mr. Streleski had the opportunity to apply for parole three times while incarcerated. He turned all three opportunities down, citing that he was unwilling not to set foot again on the Stanford campus as a condition of his parole. When he was finally released in 1985 he made a statement that still bothers people as it indicates he has no remorse for his crime: "I have no intention of killing again. On the other hand, I cannot predict the future."

1987: Boston, MA — Harvard — Math Department Doctoral Student

Felix Chau, a third-year doctoral student, committed suicide. Chau was supervised by Elias Corey. Professor Corey was the supervisor of three Harvard doctoral students who committed suicide. The other two suicidal students were:

Fung Lam (died 1997), in his sixth month at Harvard
Jason Altom (died 1998), Ph.D. student supervised by Corey

Facts Known prior to the Event
It has never been determined if Professor Cory was a factor in Chau's suicide.

Facts Discovered after the Event
The suicides of Harvard graduate students have caused the University to revamp its supervisory procedures.

1989: University of Florida School of Medicine — Graduate Student

In 1989, Jens Peter Hansen, a graduate student at the University of Florida's School of Medicine, went to the home of his 41-year-old professor of pathology and shot him. The professor's body was found in his home soon after deputies received a call that a burglar alarm had gone off there. Mr. Hansen, also 41, was taken into custody from a car seen leaving the home.

Facts Known prior to the Event
The professor whom Mr. Hansen shot was the chairman of a committee that had just voted to terminate Mr. Hansen's graduate study with a master's degree. Mr. Hansen had been in the program for 7 years.

Facts Discovered after the Event
Mr. Hansen is serving a life sentence, according to a notice in *The Florida Independent Alligator*, a student newspaper.

11/01/91: Ames, IA — University of Iowa — Graduate Student

Gang Lu was a 28-year-old doctorate student of physics from China. He shot six people, killing five of them before killing himself. Four people were killed in Van Allen Hall, the physics department's building, including his academic advisor, the chairman of the physics and astronomy department; an assistant professor; and Mr. Shan, a fellow physics graduate student, also from China. At one point Mr. Lu left Van Allen Hall, then returned and shot one of the victims a second time. Then Mr. Lu walked several blocks to the administration building. At this location he asked for the associate vice president of academic affairs, whom he shot. He then shot her 23-year-old receptionist — the bullet entered her spine, permanently paralyzing her arms and legs. Mr. Lu then went upstairs and shot himself.

Facts Known prior to the Event

Mr. Lu was considered to be temperamental by those who knew him. In fact, many said that he frightened some people because of his abusive tantrums. He often told others that he was angered by what he saw as unfair treatment by some faculty members and administrators. He also told people he was angry at the university's failure to award him its prestigious $2,500 Spriesterbach Dissertation Prize. In fact, he wrote several letters to university officials appealing their decision to award the prize to Linhua Shan, another promising graduate student from a small town in China and Mr. Lu's roommate.

Mr. Shan and Mr. Lu shared an apartment near the university. Mr. Chi, another doctoral candidate from China who also lived in the apartment, said that he warned Mr. Shan to move out because of Mr. Lu's temperament. When Mr. Chi heard what happened at Van Allen Hall he guessed that it was Mr. Lu before he even got the word of who it really was. Mr. Chi is quoted as saying, "He had a very bad temper and saw himself as Number One. He had a psychological problem with being challenged."

Facts Discovered after the Event

Mr. Lu had applied for a permit to buy a firearm, a requirement in Iowa, on May 21, almost 6 months before this event occurred. It only took 3 days before he was granted the permit. He was required to produce identifying documents, including his visa and Chinese passport. Police also found a loaded .22-caliber handgun on Mr. Lu that had not been used in the incident.

A later investigation turned up four neatly typed three-page letters that Mr. Lu had apparently intended to send to news organizations. In the letters, all but one of his victims were named. Others named in the letters, but not victims that day, included the university's president. Mr. Lu had also outlined in these letters his grievances (which were no different from the facts known before this event) and his plans to exact deadly revenge (which was to shoot all of these people).

12/14/92: Great Barrington, MA — Simon's Rock College of Bard — Student

Wayne Lo began shooting rampage at around 10:30 P.M. at Simon's Rock College of Bard. There is no public record information of the relationship between Mr. Lo and those he shot. The victims included a 37-year-old professor and an 18-year-old student, who were both shot dead. Wounded in the shootings were a 42-year-old security guard, a 19-year-old student, a 15-year-old student, and an 18-year-old student. Lo dialed 911 after his rifle jammed, informed the operator he was the shooter and surrendered to the police when they showed up. He was taken into custody without incident.

Facts Known prior to the Event

Wayne Lo was born in Taiwan but his family immigrated to the United States in 1987. They settled in Billings, MT and his parents ran a restaurant business. Mr. Lo attended Lewis and Clark Jr. High School and then Billings Central Catholic High School. He was a violinist and played in the Billings Symphony beginning his freshman year of high school. Mr. Lo also attended the Aspen Music Festival where he studied under Dorothy Delay.

In 1991, Mr. Lo was accepted by Simon's Rock College of Bard in Great Barrington, MA. He was awarded the W.E.B. DuBois minority scholarship to help with the tuition. Fellow students report that Mr. Lo did not adjust well to the liberal college environment of Simon's Rock. They said he held views that were racist, homophobic and anti-Semitic by almost all at the college. This resulted in Mr. Lo becoming more and more excluded by his fellow students.

On the morning of the day of the shootings, a package arrived at the college for Mr.Lo from a company called Classic Arms. The dean of the college was aware of this and several other obvious signs that Lo was keeping a weapon on campus in violation of the law. When, more than 3 hours before the shooting, a friend of Lo's became convinced that he was about to use the gun, he called campus security (getting an answering machine) and then a residence advisor at Mr. Lo's dorm. The advisor called the dean of the college and then the college provost. Both the dean and the provost knew all of these facts at least 45 minutes before the shootings. They also knew that Mr. Lo was in his dorm. The police were not called at this point and there was no alert made to any students as both men decided they wanted to wait for another residence director to arrive so they could all question Mr. Lo together.

Facts Discovered after the Event

The package Mr. Lo received at the college on the morning of the shooting from Classic Arms was an ammunition order that he had placed 2 days earlier. Mr. Lo then went to Pittsfield, MA, about a half-hour drive from the college, and purchased an SKS semiautomatic rifle at a gun shop that afternoon.

Mr. Lo's attorneys argued that he had diminished capacity at the time of the shootings and they entered a plea of not guilty by reason of insanity. Mr. Lo's psychiatrists testified he was suffering from schizophrenia while the prosecution expert psychiatrist attributed Mr. Lo's actions to a narcissistic personality disorder. The jury went with the prosecution and Mr. Lo was found guilty and sentenced to two consecutive life sentences without possibility of parole terms plus 19–20 years.

01/26/95: Chapel Hill, NC — University of NC — Student

Wendell Williamson, a 26-year-old, was a third-year law student at the University of North Carolina. On 1/26/95, he opened fire on the campus with a semiautomatic M-1 rifle. He killed a university sophomore and lacrosse player as well as a Chapel Hill resident who was visiting the campus. He also wounded two others, a police officer and a student who escaped unharmed when the bullet ricocheted off his keys. Williamson was eventually shot in the legs by officers, and then tackled by a bystander who was shot in the struggle with Williamson.

Facts Known prior to the Event

Wendell Williamson was a student at the University of North Carolina. About a year and a half prior to the incident, Williamson, hearing voices and experiencing delusions, availed himself of the campus mental health system. He saw a psychiatrist who worked for the student health service and was treated for his delusional behavior. Williamson had shown up for all six free treatment sessions the health service allowed and was compliant with his medication regimen. Williamson had said that once he began taking his medication, the voices he was hearing stopped and his delusions of being telepathic also faded away. The killings took place in 1995, nearly a year after treatment ended.

Facts Discovered after the Event

Williamson was found not guilty by reason of insanity, diagnosed as a paranoid schizophrenic and committed to a mental institution. Williamson sued his former psychiatrist at the health center for not properly referring Williamson to another mental health practitioner as the psychiatrist retired before Williamson shot his victims. Williamson also accused the psychiatrist of not being vehement enough in telling Williamson how important it was to stay on his medication.

08/15/96: San Diego, CA — San Diego State — Graduate Student

Frederick Davidson, a 36-year-old graduate engineering student, shot to death his three academic advisors at San Diego State while apparently defending his master's thesis.

Facts Known prior to the Event

Mr. Davidson was an Army veteran. He enrolled at San Diego State in 1987 and got his bachelor's degree in aerospace engineering in 1991. He then spent the next 3 years in further study without declaring a major. Mr. Davidson then entered the master's program in mechanical engineering in 1994.

A retired professor of English rented a room to Mr. Davidson for 2 years prior to this event. He experienced Mr. Davidson snapping at him for "prying into his personal business" a few months prior to this event when he had asked Mr. Davidson if he would be graduating. He also said that Mr. Davidson had revealed his ambivalence toward his faculty advisor. He would sometimes refer to him as a close colleague and friend, but at other times as an "enemy."

Mr. Davidson's academic advisor had collaborated with him on research, and they published two articles together. These articles were funded by McDonnell Douglas, and much of Mr. Davidson's research involved "shape memory alloy," a metal that can be twisted and will hold its shape until heated.

According to the landlord, Mr. Davidson was extremely neat. He often saw him nervously straightening papers that were out of alignment on his desk. He also said that Mr. Davidson's room was very bare with only a framed undergraduate diploma and a nature calendar on the wall and minimal furniture.

Mr. Davidson had few close friends and no romantic attachments. It was reported he would sometimes go to Las Vegas for gambling and shows. Others said that his parents had divorced when he was young and they described him as a loner, who spent most of his time working hard in a research lab.

Facts Discovered after the Event

Mr. Davidson had made very careful plans prior to the shooting. Knowing he was going to be defending his master's thesis in a specific third-floor classroom in the Engineering Building, he decided to hide a 9mm semiautomatic Taurus handgun and five spare clips in the metal first-aid kit box on the wall of this classroom. Mr. Davidson apparently slipped into the room about 10:00 A.M. and hid the gun and ammunition about 4 hours prior to the incident. When he returned to the room about 2:00 P.M., the three professors were seated at a table and three student monitors were standing behind them. His faculty advisor stood up, walked over, greeted Mr. Davidson and stated the purpose of the meeting was to query Mr. Davidson about his thesis. Without saying a word,

Mr. Davidson turned around, walked a few steps to the first-aid box, retrieved the gun and opened fire, killing his advisor. Everyone else in the room ran for cover. Mr. Davidson hunted them down, and ignoring the students, fired 23 rounds during the 4 minutes that followed his initial shooting. When the campus police responded to the Engineering Building, they found Mr. Davidson pacing back and forth in the hall, holding a gun to his side. He told the police to shoot him at least twice as they had their guns drawn and pointed at him. Mr. Davidson then just dropped his gun, and was led away sobbing by police.

08/28/00: Fayetteville, AK — University of AK — Graduate Student

James Easton Kelley, a 36-year-old, was a University of Arkansas graduate student who had recently been dropped from a doctoral program after more than 10 years of study. On 8/28/00, he went to his English professor's office, the person who was overseeing his coursework, and shot him to death. He then committed suicide by shooting himself in the heart.

Facts Known prior to the Event

Kelley's dismissal followed several semesters during which Kelley enrolled in and then dropped English department classes several times according to university official statements. A letter to Kelley from the university noted that Kelley had pledged to take three comprehensive exams by the end of the 1999 spring semester, but had not done so. For the year's fall 2000 semester, Kelley had signed up for seven credit hours as a non-degree student.

Facts Discovered after the Event

August 28, 2000, at approximately 11:30 A.M., Mr. Kelley went to a Wal-Mart 10 miles from the Fayetteville campus. There he purchased 50 rounds of .38 caliber bullets and returned to school. Mr. Kelley then went to Locke's office, and shortly after noon shot his advisor three times, killing him instantly. Kelley then killed himself with the same gun.

The investigation after this incident concluded that Mr. Kelley killed his professor because he blamed him for his dismissal from the school's comparative literature program. That conclusion was reached in part due to letters that were sent to Mr. Kelley by his advisor that were found in the briefcase Mr. Kelley carried to his advisor's office on the day of the shooting. Angry handwritten notes were found in the margins of the letters that were believed to have been written by Mr. Kelley. "Another lie!" was a note written in the margin of one of the letters. It went on to say, "Just plain fabricated Aryan lies." The letter was written in early 1999.

Then in May 1999, the advisor sent a letter to Kelley telling him he had been dismissed from the comparative literature program. "You have our best wishes for the future," the letter concluded. In the margin of this letter Mr. Kelley wrote "You'll need best wishes." In this letter, Mr. Kelley's academic advisor had written that the comparative literature committee "remains convinced that you are a talented person; however, these talents have not been sufficiently directed toward completing the requirements of your Ph.D. in a timely fashion." Mr. Kelley's handwritten notes to the side of this paragraph said, "You hateful son of a bitch," and, "The grounds for my termination were baseless."

01/16/02: Grundy, VA — Appalachian Law School — Student

Peter Odighizuwa was a former student at Appalachian when he arrived on campus on the morning of 1/16/02. It is uncertain if he had his .380 ACP semiautomatic handgun with him at this time, but he went to talk to one of his former professors about his academic problems. As they finished their discussion, with no real resolve, Mr. Odighizuwa told his professor to pray for him and then he left the campus.

At about 1 P.M. that same day, Mr. Odighizuwa returned to the school waving his gun in the air, yelling to all, "Come and get me." The students did exactly the opposite and ran away. Mr. Odighizuwa then decided to go to the office of another dean and a professor. Mr. Odighizuwa shot and killed them both at close range. He then went throughout the building, shooting and killing a 33-year-old student and shooting three others.

Mr. Odighizuwa then left the building in which he had done all this shooting. He was approached by two other students who were off-duty law enforcement officers. Both individuals had retrieved their weapons from their cars and had then pointed at Mr. Odighizuwa who eventually dropped his weapon. Upon doing so, several other unarmed students tackled Mr. Odighizuwa to the ground where he was subsequently held until the police arrived.

Facts Known prior to the Event

Mr. Odighizuwa was from Nigeria. Mr. Odighizuwa had withdrawn from school voluntarily due to poor academic performance according to University officials. Mr. Odighizuwa stated he felt he had a C average and shouldn't have had to withdraw. This was Mr. Odighizuwa's second attempt at law school. He had actually flunked out the previous year, but in an unusual move the university allowed him to try again. Mr. Odighizuwa had also been treated for stress by a physician just 6 months before the incident. When questioned about his treatment with Mr. Odighizuwa, the physician said, "I had no idea that it would affect him this way. However, he was a time bomb waiting to go off."

Facts Discovered after the Event

Mr. Odighizuwa was found incompetent to stand trial in 2002 and was institutionalized under psychiatric care. However, in 2005, he was found mentally competent after 3 years of treatment. He pled guilty to the murders to avoid the death penalty and is currently serving multiple life terms in prison plus 28 additional years.

10/28/02: Tucson, AZ — University of Arizona College of Nursing — Student

Robert S. Flores was a 41-year-old student at the Arizona College of Nursing. Somewhere around 8:30 in the morning, Flores entered the college with two guns and went to the second-floor office where he shot and killed one of his clinical associate professors. A few minutes later, he went into the fourth-floor lecture room where several students had been taking an exam for about the last half hour. He went up to the professor, talked to her for a few minutes and then shot her dead. He then walked to the back of the lecture room and fatally shot one more professor before telling all the students to leave. Within minutes of the last student leaving the lecture hall, Flores shot and killed himself.

During these shootings, Flores had threatened to blow up the buildings and was wearing a backpack. Police found no explosives in the backpack and after evacuating all the buildings, used a bomb-sniffing dog with no results. The dog did have a reaction to Flores' car, but again, no explosive devices were discovered in either his car or his residence.

Facts Known prior to the Event

Flores was apparently disgruntled over being barred from taking a midterm examination and, in fact, witnesses to the shooting indicated he was still talking about it as he went on his rampage. College officials said that there was no indication in the school records that he was in danger of being expelled or dropped from the program. However, he had recently failed his pediatrics class and was currently struggling in his critical-care class.

The classes he failed and was having difficulty with were taught by the people he shot. Some students said they had heard him indicate he was going to get some kind of revenge on these professors. Some of the quotes from witnesses at the shooting included other known information:

> "I know he was very stressed in a lot of different things and had a difficult time adjusting" (fellow student). "He came across as very aggressive and mean and seemed to have a lot of issues with being angry" (fellow student). This same student also claimed that Flores would call attention to himself by asking inappropriate questions and challenging instructors; "most of the people in the class didn't like him ... he was very obnoxious and rude."

He often talked of "ending it all" and said he "might put something under the college" (an instructor). "Mr. Flores ... conveyed to staff that he was depressed, that he was thinking of ending it all and that he might take some actions against the College of Medicine" (the university police chief).

It was also known that Flores was divorced with two children, was a Gulf War Veteran and that he was having financial problems trying to make his child support payments. He also worked at the Veterans Affairs Hospital in Tucson.

Facts Discovered after the Event

Flores mailed a 22-page typewritten suicide letter to the *Arizona Star* the same day as the shootings and it was delivered to the *Star* the following day. The letter was apparently written in two stages over a period of several weeks before the shootings. Contents of the entire letter: http://cgi3.azstarnet.com/specialreport/.

The letter stated, "Greetings from the dead. You have received this letter after a rather horrendous event. I understand that I have committed homicide and that I have broken the laws of our society. I will save the taxpayers money and take care of the problem."

"You have vandalized my heart, raped my soul, and torched my conscience." (This has been highlighted as it is an exact quote used by perpetrator Cho at Virginia Tech in the video he sent to NBC — see that information below.)

Mr. Flores went on to say such things as, "I didn't have to do it. I could have left. I could have fled, but now I am no longer running. If not for me, for my children and my brothers and sisters that you [expletive]. I did it for them." The letter described his failed marriage, poor health, depression, and perceived slights from the nursing school that he attended.

Other notable quotes from this letter include:

"To the sociologist, it wasn't the Maryland sniper. I have been thinking about this for awhile."
"To the psychiatrist it's not about unresolved childhood issues. It is not about anger because I don't feel anything right now."
"The University is filled with too many people who are filled with hubris. They feel untouchable. Students are not given respect nor regard."

He ended the letter with, "Tonight is my last night on this planet so I guess I will finish this letter."

Other information discovered after the incident made authorities believe Flores had initially planned on shooting more people but for some unknown reason changed his mind and did not. Flores actually had five handguns on his person when police checked his body, and approximately 250 rounds of ammunition with him. He left no suicide note and reportedly had no problems with any of his student peers — just the professors whom he shot and killed.

Flores reportedly had a concealed weapons permit.

05/09/03: Cleveland, OH — Case Western
Reserve University — Former Student

Biswanath Halder, a 52-year-old former student of Case Western, was dressed in camouflage shirt and pants when he entered the University's Peter B. Lewis Building. He then began shooting at students and professors with apparently no discrimination, firing hundreds of rounds from his two handguns. He killed a 30-year-old graduate student and injured a professor and a Ph.D. candidate student.

Police were called and SWAT entered into a 7-hour standoff with Mr. Halder, chasing him throughout the building and engaging in several firefights with him. Altogether there were 93 people trapped in various class-rooms, offices and closets, trying to hide from Mr. Halder, while this rampage went on. Finally, in a fifth-floor classroom closet, they cornered Mr. Halder who gave up without incident. He had been shot twice during the altercation.

Facts Known prior to the Event

Mr. Halder had sued the school over the last couple of years, and was apparently angry that his lawsuit had been dismissed after he recently lost an appeal on his case. One of the individuals in the Peter B. Lewis Building during this time was an employee of the university that Mr. Halder believed had added and deleted things from his own personal web site, which was the basis for his lawsuit.

Mr. Halder had actually earned his MBA from Case Western in 1999. He had moved to the United States from India about 30 years previously with the intent of making millions. After obtaining his degree he continued to take classes at the university, although he had not declared his major at this time.

Mr. Halder was known around the university as being somewhat of a loner. It was said that he lived alone in an attic apartment and was never seen to socialize. He was considered weird and eccentric because he wore odd clothing, acted strange and wore an obvious toupee.

The real problems started in 2000 when Mr. Halder discovered that someone had hacked into his computer and deleted thousands of files. The hacker not only deleted these files, but he left behind numerous offensive messages on his computer. According to Halder, these files were the critical infrastructure of his multi-million dollar business. Mr. Halder accused an employee of the university of this hacking as this person was the computer lab supervisor.

Mr. Halder and this computer lab supervisor had a history of not getting along. Apparently the supervisor had to discipline Mr. Halder several times as he kept breaking the computer lab rules. The supervisor said that Mr. Halder seemed to just simply ignore any of his disciplines or warnings and would pretty much just do what he wanted.

Despite numerous denials by the computer lab supervisor to Mr. Halder that he never hacked into his computer, Mr. Halder did not believe him. Mr. Halder continuously and persistently complained to the university of this action by this supervisor and demanded that the university dismiss the supervisor. Since the university did nothing according to Mr. Halder, he actually took his accusations to the local police. The police could find no evidence of what Mr. Halder claimed had occurred, would not pursue the matter and thus Mr. Halder decided to sue the university and the supervisor.

Mr. Halder had a history of litigious actions. He filed numerous lawsuits against several computer companies all during the 1970s and 1980s after they refused to hire him, claiming discrimination in each case. In late April 2003, Mr. Halder's lawsuit against the university and the supervisor was thrown out of court.

Facts Discovered after the Event

Mr. Halder was sentenced to life in prison, even after his attorneys argued that, while he did what everyone claimed he did, everyone knew he was mentally ill and thus he should be given a lesser sentence. His attorneys said that Mr. Halder would even bark orders at them to do things that had nothing to do with this case. He once told them to go get him a roll of 2-cent stamps, for example.

09/17/03: Dyersburg, TN — Dyersburg State Community College — Local Resident

On September 17, 2003, Harold Kilpatrick, Jr. walked into the second-floor classroom in the Eller Building of Dyersburg State Community College at about 12:45 P.M. and barricaded the door. Mr. Kilpatrick had a 9mm semi-automatic and a hunting knife. He took 15 students and a teacher in a pre-algebra class hostage at about 12:50 P.M. Mr. Kilpatrick then told the students and teacher that he wanted to talk to them about personal problems. Mr. Kilpatrick later released four of the hostages, one of whom was pregnant.

The Dyersburg Police Special Operations Response Team and Hostage Negotiation Team had to talk to Mr. Kilpatrick through the classroom wall. Mr. Kilpatrick told them he wanted to commit suicide and that he had left a suicide note. Earlier, however, Mr. Kilpatrick was refusing to even talk to the police directly, using his hostages as intermediaries on cell phones. But later in the evening he began talking with police and even ordered pizzas and sodas to share with his hostages.

After 9 hours of holding the remaining 11 hostages, Mr. Kilpatrick opened fire in the classroom, prompting police to move in immediately and having no option but to fatally shoot him. During this shooting between the police and Mr. Kilpatrick, one student was shot in the abdomen and leg and another student was shot in the chest. Both were transported via ambulance, along with a female student with heart complications, to the Dyersburg Regional Medical Center by ambulance.

To date it remains unsure whether the gun wounds sustained by the hostages were from Mr. Kilpatrick or police gunfire. One student who was held hostage fled from the building immediately before Mr. Kilpatrick began shooting. Police believe that action may have actually spurred Mr. Kilpatrick to begin shooting.

Facts Known prior to the Event

Mr. Kilpatrick was known by his relatives and friends to have a history of mental illness. Those closest to him reported he could not afford the proper medication for his illness and thus was not taking any medication at the time of the shooting. One family member reports that she knew his diagnosis was that of a manic-depressive and that he had not been able to take his medication for nearly 2 years before the incident.

Mr. Kilpatrick was from Memphis but had recently been staying with his sister in Dyersburg. In fact, Police confirmed that Mr. Kilpatrick was facing charges of assault and kidnapping in Memphis involving a former girlfriend — a case completely unrelated to this shooting. He was neither a student at the community college nor was he an employee. Another of Mr. Kilpatrick's relatives confirmed that he had applied for admission to the college. Shortly before the shooting incident Mr. Kilpatrick was rejected for financial aid at the institution, and therefore could not attend.

Facts Discovered after the Event

The suicide note Mr. Kilpatrick had said he wrote was eventually discovered at his sister's home. In this note he also said he "wanted to kill some people and die today." Mr. Kilpatrick also said in the note that he was a member of the terrorist group al-Qaida and claimed to have talked with Osama bin Laden.

09/02/06: Shepherdstown, WV — Shepherd University — Father Shoots Sons

On September 2, 2006, Douglas W. Pennington shot his sons Logan and Benjamin, then himself, with a .38 caliber revolver during a visit to the Shepherd University campus. The shootings occurred at about 2 p.m. in the parking lot. The Penningtons were all pronounced dead at local medical facilities.

Douglas Pennington traveled to the campus in the Eastern Panhandle to visit his sons, but investigators could not determine why Pennington shot his sons and whether he intended to kill them when he came to the campus. Witnesses said Pennington had not been arguing with his children before the shootings occurred.

Facts Known prior to the Event

Logan Pennington and Benjamin Pennington were seniors at Shepherd University.

Facts Discovered after the Event

The police said that Douglas Pennington went to the campus from the Grant County, WV area to visit his sons and that the motive for the shooting was probably a family issue of some type. Officials said the motive in the shootings will probably never be known.

04/02/07: Seattle, WA — University of Washington — Ex-Boyfriend of Staff Researcher

On April 2, 2007, Jonathan Rowan, 41, entered his ex-girlfriend's office at the university where he shot and killed her before killing himself. Campus police responded to shots fired and found the two bodies in an office on the fourth floor of Gould Hall, the university's architecture building. A total of six shots were fired and a handgun was found on the scene. There were no witnesses and no one else was harmed. Mr. Rowan's ex-girlfriend was 26 years old. In the weeks previous to her murder she was seeking a restraining order against Rowan. Rowan, a British citizen, had no ties to the school.

Facts Known prior to the Event

Mr. Rowan's ex-girlfriend filed for and was granted a temporary restraining order against Mr. Rowan on March 6, 2007, after he called her office and threatened her. The conditions of the order required Rowan to stay 500 feet away from his ex, her residence, workplace and dog.

Mr. Rowan robbed his current roommates at that time and was on the run. Mr. Rowan called his ex-girlfriend's office again on March 7 and 14 with threatening phone calls. The restraining order papers were on hand at the office to be served, in case Mr. Rowan showed up. Photos of Mr. Rowan were passed around to friends and co-workers, and they were warned of his threatening behavior.

The ex-girlfriend had changed her cell phone number and moved. She told her new landlord about her problem ex-boyfriend and that he had no idea where she moved. The ex told police that she had no way of getting in contact with Mr. Rowan or where he was but he knew where she worked.

One of the earlier events that had occurred between Mr. Rowan and his ex was on January 5, 2007. When she returned home Mr. Rowan began throwing candlestick holders at her, tackled her to the floor and punched her. They both lived at this residence at this time. The ex wrote in the report she filed with the police that she forgave Mr. Rowan for this act because he was drunk at the time.

Another indication of Mr. Rowan's demeanor occurred in February 2007. He called his ex and threatened suicide because he couldn't see her anymore.

Facts Known after the Event

Not much is known about Jonathan Rowan. He entered the United States from the United Kingdom in 1996 on a green card that expired after 90 days. It is not known for sure if this was his real identity. He also went by the names of "Robert Richardson" and "Nathan Rowan."

Mr. Rowan supported himself by designing web sites and selling cars. He was known to like to tell stories. He said he was a professional ice skater, owned an international chain of hotels, was jailed in France for smuggling champagne, was threatened by the IRA, built an iron fence at one of the Queen's castles and that he left the United Kingdom because he was involved in a mail-order scam.

Mr. Rowan was described as "likeable but strange." He charmed people with his British accent but was also known to be very erratic because of heavy drinking and drug use.

04/16/07: Blacksburg, VA — Virginia Tech — Student

On April 16, 2007, Seung-Hui Cho, 23, a senior English major at Virginia Tech, shot and killed a man and a woman at point blank range in the Amble Johnston Hall Dormitory. Two and a half hours later Cho traveled across campus where he chained closed the doors at Norris Hall and worked his way through four classrooms, shooting people at will. Cho wounded 17 people and killed 31 people, including himself; most of the people were shot multiple times. The only connection between Cho and any of the people he shot was the fact that they were students at the same school.

Facts Known prior to the Event

Mr. Cho was born in Korea on January 18, 1984. Since the age of 3, his family noticed that he did not like to be touched (he experienced "emotional trauma" related to a medical procedure on his heart). Throughout high school and growing up, he spoke very little to his parents and avoided eye contact. Mr. Cho was designated as a "special needs" child in elementary school with poor communication skills; he had "emotional issues."

Sometime in middle school, Cho was diagnosed with "Severe Social Anxiety Disorder" (he would cry on the spot if anyone talked to him or tried to make eye contact with him). He expressed mental and emotional symptoms of shame and guilt. In high school, Cho was enrolled by his school in the Special Education Program for Emotional Disabilities and Speech and Language. In July 1997, Mr. Cho was taken by his parents to the Center for Multicultural Human Services (CMHS), a mental health clinic, where his parents took him to weekly appointments.

Shorty after the Columbine shooting in April 1999, Mr. Cho wrote a paper about suicide and homicide; thereafter, he was diagnosed by another psychiatrist at the same aforementioned mental health clinic with "Selective Mutism" and "Major Depression." He was prescribed antidepressants, which he took for a year.

By the time Mr. Cho left high school and went to Virginia Tech, he had stopped taking all medication and was no longer receiving any type of mental health counseling or therapy. No one at Virginia Tech was aware of his past emotional and mental problems, or his "special needs" status throughout elementary and secondary education.

Mr. Cho exhibited bizarre behavior at Virginia Tech as reported by classmates and roommates who lived with him at the dorm. He posted lyrics of dark, heavy metal music on Facebook. He scribbled heavy metal lyrics on the walls of his dorm room and hall way. He often said he had a twin brother (which he did not have) named "Question Mark." He wrote poetry about his classmates eating babies and burning in hell.

He once wrote, "You low-life barbarians make me sick to the stomach that I wanna barf over my new shoes. If you despicable human beings who are all disgraces to [the] human race keep this up, before you know it you will turn into cannibals — eating little babies, your friends. I hope y'all burn in hell for mass murdering and eating all those little animals."

Mr. Cho sought mental help, on his own, twice in November 2005, but these were reportedly "telephone triage" sessions with a counselor who kept no written record of the conversations and does not remember the content of those conversations. Mr. Cho was reprimanded by campus police in December 2005 for harassing a young woman by writing to her on Facebook, sending cell phone text messages, and scribbling weird notes on her dorm room door. After the incident, Mr. Cho made a comment about suicide and was assessed by a clinical social worker for New River Valley Community Services Board, which found Mr. Cho to be "mentally ill."

Mr. Cho was admitted to St. Albans Behavioral Health Center of the Carilion New River Valley Medical Center for "Mood Disorder: Non-Specific," whereupon he was prescribed medication for anxiety (Ativan). He was deemed, however, not a threat to anyone or himself on the basis that Mr. Cho had "not received any previous mental health treatment" — which, of course, was wrong.

The Circuit Court of Montgomery County presided over hearings about Mr. Cho's commitment to the aforementioned hospital and the "special justice" ruled that Mr. Cho "presents an imminent danger to himself as a result of mental illness." He then went to Cook Counseling Center (where he earlier received "phone triage") but received no diagnosis.

In the Spring of 2006, Mr. Cho wrote a fictional essay for a creative writing class in which he portrayed a character named "Bud" who was contemplating the following: "I was going to kill every god damn person in this damn school, swear to god I was, but I … couldn't. I just couldn't. Damn it I hate myself!"

Mr. Cho was considered a loner and did not have many friends at Virginia Tech. Students and teachers said that they felt unnerved when he was around. He lived in a dormitory on campus and his roommates described him as a shy guy who did not talk much.

A year and a half before, a former chairwoman of Virginia Tech's English Department pulled Mr. Cho out of another teacher's creative writing class because of his anger, and taught him one-on-one. This chairwoman stated that Cho's writings never talked of guns or killing but were disturbing enough that she did seek help from police and university officials. There was no explicit threat so authorities could do nothing. The chairwoman encouraged Mr. Cho to seek counseling. Mr. Cho did write two screenplays that dealt with death and revenge.

Facts Known after the Event

Mr. Cho sent NBC News headquarters in New York a package from his apparent alter ego, "Ismail Ax" (which was also written in red marker on his forearm as discovered by police when they found his body). The package was mailed by overnight delivery from a Virginia post office at 9:01 A.M. on Monday, about an hour and a half AFTER Mr. Cho first opened fire. The package did not arrive at NBC until Wednesday.

The package contained a 23-page written statement, 28 video clips and 43 photos. The videos and letter enshrined the acts of Eric Harris and Dylan Klebold from Columbine and stated that their "violent acts would bear 'children.'"

"You had a hundred billion chances and ways to have avoided today," Mr. Cho says in the video, "but you decided to spill my blood. You forced me into a corner and gave me only one option. The decision was yours. Now you have blood on your hands that will never wash off."

"You have vandalized my heart, raped my soul, and torched my conscience" (in video and an exact quote from Robert Flores — please see "10/28/02 — Tucson, AZ — University of Arizona College of Nursing" above).

Mr. Cho went on to say, "You thought it was one pathetic boy's life you were extinguishing. Thanks to you, I die like Jesus Christ, to inspire generations of the weak and the defenseless people." Your Mercedes wasn't enough, you brats. Your golden necklaces weren't enough, you snobs. Your trust fund wasn't enough. Your vodka and cognac wasn't enough. All your debaucheries weren't enough. Those weren't enough to fulfill your hedonistic needs. You had everything."

After the shooting, Mr. Cho was found with no identification (save for the words "Ismail Ax" written with red marker on his forearm. They traced the purchase of the two guns he had through paperwork found in his backpack.

A note with a bomb threat directed at engineering buildings on campus was found at Norris Hall. In the 3 weeks prior two bomb threats were received at Virginia Tech, now believed to probably have been made by Mr. Cho.

A search warrant of Mr. Cho's room discovered a note that stated, "You caused me to do this" and complained about "rich kids," debauchery" and "deceitful charlatans" on campus. Other than his run-in with the university police over his stalking issue Mr. Cho had no problems with law enforcement except for two speeding tickets received in the 3 weeks prior to the shooting.

In an interview by the Virginia Tech newspaper after the shooting, a student is quoted as saying that Mr. Cho, "was the kind of guy who might go on a rampage killing."

09/21/07: Dover, DE — Delaware State University — Student

On September 21, 2007, Loyer D. Braden, 18, a freshman at DSU, shot into a crowd of people, wounding a male and a female. Mr. Braden also fired at a second male student. The shots were fired at the group as they left a campus café. A month later the female student died from her wounds.

Facts Known prior to the Event
A few days before the event, Mr. Braden and one of the males fired upon were involved in a fight in a university parking lot. The police report did not state which male was involved in the fight. Thursday night Mr. Braden and one of the males he fired at later got into a verbal argument at the café. Later that night Mr. Braden returned and fired into the group where the three who were wounded were walking, which included the individual he had the argument with earlier.

Facts Known after the Event
Mr. Braden graduated in June from Immaculate Conception High School in Montclair, NJ, where he played basketball and football. He was from East Orange, NJ. In 1998, Mr. Braden was among a group of Boy Scouts and Cub Scouts who escorted jazz great Lionel Hampton to an East Orange elementary school that had named a concert hall in Hampton's honor.

His family and coaches were shocked to hear this news and stated that it was very unlike his character. Students on campus implied that the shooting could have stemmed from a Washington/New Jersey rivalry or a card game gone bad but nothing was confirmed.

02/08/08: Baton Rouge, LA — Louisiana Technical College — Nursing Student

On February 8, 2008, Latina Williams, 23, entered a second-floor classroom at Louisiana Technical College, spoke with the instructor and left.

Ms. Williams shortly returned through another door to the rear of the classroom and fired six rounds killing two female students, reloaded and shot herself in the head. There were about 20 students in the classroom at the time.

Facts Known before the Event

The only connection between the shooter and those who were shot was the school. There was no evidence of a disagreement or bullying between any of the females involved. She had recently displayed signs of paranoia and losing touch with reality.

Facts Known after the Event

Investigators discovered that Ms. Williams had not spoken to her family in Mississippi much in the past 2 years and it is believed that she was living in her car. She recently gave away or sold several possessions. She bought the .357 revolver and a box of ammunition at a pawn shop in New Orleans the day before the shootings. Investigators also believe she called a crisis counselor anonymously on the morning of the shootings indicating that she was planning to take her own life. No suicide note was found. The investigation never found a motive for the shooting.

02/14/08: DeKalb, IL — Northern Illinois University — Student

On February 14, 2008, Steven Kazmierczak walked out onto a stage and began firing into a crowd of students, killing 5 and wounding 16 before killing himself. Four of the deceased were women. He used four guns in the shooting (three handguns and a shotgun), two of which were bought 6 days prior to the incident, and he brought the weapons to the scene of the crime in a guitar case, as well as tucked under his coat. His Remington 48 shotgun and his Glock were the two bought 6 days before the incident on February 9, 2008. He also had a High Point .380 handgun (purchased in December 2007) and a Sig Sauer 9mm (purchased in August 2007). All of these guns were purchased from the same gun dealer in Champagne, IL.

Facts Known before the Event

Mr. Kazmierczak grew up in the Chicago suburb of Elk Grove Village, not far from O'Hare Airport. His family lived most recently in a middle-class neighborhood of mostly one-story tract homes before moving away early in this decade. His mother died in Florida in 2006 at age 58. He was a B student at Elk Grove High School, where school district spokeswoman Venetia Miles said he was active in band and took Japanese before graduating in 1998. He was also in the chess club.

Mr. Kazmierczak had been honored in 2006 by Northern Illinois University with a dean's award for his work in sociology, the *Chicago Tribune* reported. According to the newspaper, Mr. Kazmierczak "had established himself as an authority on prison systems, having co-authored a manuscript on self-injury in prison and the role of religion in the formation of early prisons in the United States." The *Tribune* said Mr. Kazmierczak wrote both papers under the guidance of nationally renowned criminal-justice expert Jim Thomas, a professor emeritus at Northern. He had also served as a member of the NIU Academic Criminal Justice Association and was a teaching aide during his undergraduate years.

He was once a patient at a psychiatric clinic in Chicago (admitted there by his parents after high school). Apparently he used to cut himself. He was also reportedly discharged from the U.S. Army for a "psychological condition."

Mr. Kazmierczak had a State Police–issued FOID, or firearms owner identification card, which is required in Illinois to own a gun, authorities said. Such cards are rarely issued to those with recent mental health problems. The application asks: "In the past five years have you been a patient in any medical facility or part of any medical facility used primarily for the care or treatment of persons for mental illness?"

While searching for a motive for the Valentine's Day attack, authorities questioned family and friends and tried to determine whether he had recently broken up with his longtime girlfriend. Even though she said this was not like him and that he was the most wonderful man, his girlfriend said that in the weeks up to his rampage, Steven sent several disturbing packages to Jessica Baty (girlfriend) including:

Gun holster
Bullets
The book *The Antichrist* by Friedrich Nietzsche

Ms. Baty also knew her boyfriend had purchased at least two guns. He told her they were for home protection.

Authorities questioned family and friends and tried to determine whether he had any other problems that may have caused this incident. One person who knew Mr. Kazmierczak and Ms. Baty, who spoke to the Associated Press on the condition of anonymity, said the couple's relationship was on-again, off-again and "really rocky." Mr. Kazmierczak was controlling, she said. "He was abusive, had a temper," she said. "He didn't actually hit her; he would push her around."

Mr. Kazmierczak had also begun the long process of having his arms blanketed with disturbing tattoos. He had three tattoos on his arms: one was a tattoo of a sadistic serial killer, "the macabre doll" from the movie *Saw* riding a tricycle with a background of bleeding cut wounds (from when he slashed himself at a younger age). A second tattoo was of a skull with a dagger going through the middle of the head. And the third tattoo was of a satanic pentagram. Friends said that he was embarrassed to let people see them.

Facts Known after the Event

According to AP, he spent more than a year at the Thresholds-Maryhill House in the late 1990s, an alternative high school program for children suffering from mental illness. He graduated in 1998 and underwent a year of psychiatric hospitalization at the insistence of his parents because he refused to take his meds and was cutting himself.

In September 2001 he enlisted in the army but was "administratively discharged" in February 2002, 6 months later. After graduating he started at Social Work School at University of Illinois, Urbana-Champaign. According to the *New York Times*, he dropped out of his HBSE (Human Behavior in the Social Environment) class in the fall, a class required for all full-time students. He told his professor that he was taking a full-time job at a prison. He began training at the Rockville Correctional Facility, but after 2 weeks, according to the chief of staff, he just stopped coming, as reported in the *New York Times*.

No motive has ever been established for the shooting. There is no connection to the shooter or anyone in the class. Investigators are trying to find a missing SIM card from his cell phone and a missing hard drive from his computer to look for any clues.

Discussion

After the Virginia Tech massacre, the deadliest school shooting in U.S. history where 32 people lost their lives after one mentally disturbed man went on a killing spree across campus, many people began focusing on this issue with a renewed sense of urgency … especially as it pertains to the perpetrator having a mental illness. In fact, a total of 32 states nationwide now report mental health–related information to a federal database that gun store owners and dealers are required to check before selling guns. However, unlicensed dealers at gun shows around the country don't need to do background checks on potential buyers. What is perhaps even more relevant is the fact that not every school shooting incident has anything to do with mental illness, meaning that while keeping guns out of the hands of the mentally ill is a good idea, the mentally ill persons are not involved in the overwhelming percentage of all school shooting cases.

What seems to be painfully common about the perpetrators in many of these school shootings are expressed feelings of estrangement and rage; to call some of these youthful offenders "disturbed" is to understate the devastating phobia of the assailants considerably. Paranoia, deep depression and self-perceived isolation are all common symptoms reported by the various guilty parties. In almost every case there were elements of disassociation from their fellow students — typically blamed on some fear or anxiety later discovered or confessed by the perpetrators, eye witnesses or victims that survived the incidents.

Almost all of the perpetrators presented are males. While there are many risk factors that contribute to the likelihood that any one person presents a threat, Roger Depue, Ph.D., in Appendix M of the "Virginia Tech Review Report," notes that:

> When a cluster of indicators is present then the risk becomes more serious. Thus, a person who possesses firearms is a loner, shows an interest in past shooting situations, writes stories about homicide and suicide, exhibits aberrant behavior, has talked about retribution against others, and has a history of mental illness and refuses counseling would obviously be considered a significant risk of becoming dangerous to himself or others. (go to: http://www.vtreviewpanel.org/report/index.html for the full report)

Careful assessment of most of these cases, even without the benefit of a full case history, indicates one of the more prominent features is the fact that these shooters all developed a plan. They bought weapons, many of them wrote notes and/or told others of their concerns and plans. The question therefore becomes more of why wasn't something done before the act took place?

This is why we stress the importance of collecting as much information as possible, utilizing the assessment tools discussed and explained throughout this text (especially in Chapters 3, 4 and 5), and why we believe in the fundamental truth that, "If it's almost perfect, it's not. If it's not perfect, it's not right ... If it's not right, it's wrong!" Use the tools, use them as you re-read these cases and then notice how many "concerns" become evident very quickly.

Conclusion

There are some things we did not discuss in this particular process — such as the importance of conducting a background check on the subject, both criminal and civil, to look for past indicators of violence. It is believed that a true assessor skilled in the actual art of threat assessments would do that as a matter of course. However, it is also not a common thread in the post-secondary educational arena for the simple reason that the usual attackers have not had sufficient years of life to accumulate such revealing information. Further, it is believed that in the post-secondary educational setting, the time necessary to acquire these data may not always be available before an appropriate response is necessary. This and many of the elements discussed in this chapter on how to handle the potentially violent perpetrator need to be thrashed out and decided upon by the recommended threat assessment team created in this environment.

It is also important to remember that the use of profiles is ineffective and that inductive investigations (relying on prior events to guide inferences about current facts) are not helpful in post-secondary school-targeted violence. What is more revealing and productive to prevent violence in these settings is deductive investigations, where specific facts of the specific event leading to the concern are expanded to include what plans or ideas over time may have led to this event. Only then can an adequate assessment be made of the entire relationship of the perpetrator to the victim within a specific environment so that motives, ideas, communications and behavior can be weighed for a more accurate method of successful prevention instead of attempting to predict the potential toward violence.

Security

9

Introduction

This chapter is about the concept of security as it pertains to protecting individuals in the type of everyday caseload that most assessors will work. It is not a chapter on executive protection and all the different aspects of protecting individuals in a variety of settings using the most sophisticated methods available. To learn more about that type of process, there are numerous books (some of them good) and courses (again, some of them good) that you can pursue. If protectees have the resources to hire standing teams of protective personnel for weeks or months at a time, then they are extremely lucky. This rare victim does not make up even 5% of my caseload, the majority of which is in the private sector.

In the realm of violence assessment and intervention, security is the foundation of the overall process. Security from physical violence is what the process is meant to achieve; at the same time, it is a reality that can never be completely obtained. The joke in computer security is that to make a computer completely secure, you would need to encase it inside an impenetrable housing, with no connection to the outside world in any form, including any human connection. This, of course, would make the computer effectively useless.

The same is true with security of people. We can make them incredibly secure, but then their quality of life becomes nonexistent, making them almost dead to the world. So, in a real sense, security is another type of balance, this one between safety and quality of life. Many victims understand the essence of this dynamic and that is why they may make decisions and act in ways that seem to jeopardize their safety. Our job as assessors and assessment teams is to provide victims a well-informed model of projected risk and suggested mitigation methods involving monitoring, intervention and security. It is not a failure on our part if they are fully informed and choose a course of action different from our choice. That is their right. It is a failure for us when we have not provided them with the best possible understanding of our assessment and mitigation strategies and worked to help them implement any that we can, even if they are not our first choice. The phrase "to serve and protect" comes to mind, not "judge and dismiss."

As I have written before,[1] the basic concept of security is to divert someone from committing an unsafe or harmful act and, if diversion does not work, to delay perpetrators as long as possible so that someone can respond and stop them from completing or continuing the act. Professional security, even proactive security, can only create the perception of protection, create physical barriers to delay result, provide monitoring and notification systems and then refine response to minimize the time in stopping the harmful acts. It can never stop all loss from occurring. On a practical basis, this means that security in a violence intervention context is about altering perception, hardening sites, providing notification methods, preparing response plans and staging qualified security personnel — depending on the assessed level of projected risk of physical violence.

Perception

In the area of perception, we have to address two different issues, the perception of the victim and that of the instigator. We have to educate victims concerning the tools they can use to alter their own internal perception and the perception that others have of them. We need to alter how instigators view the likelihood that they would be successful in committing an act of violence against the victims.

Victim Perception

The first perception that has to be addressed with victims is their sense of the situation. Most victims facing a potential threat of physical harm end up falling into the two extreme ends of perception, either that there is no real risk (denial), or that there is nothing they can do to stop the risk (fatalism). Neither of these perceptions is helpful to the victim and, therefore, to safe resolution of the situation. Ironically, they both lead to the same result: no action on the part of the victim to take preparatory steps to address the risk. So the first step in a security plan is to alter the victim's perception away from either of these two poles. This involves discussing the process of violence assessment, educating victims concerning their role in the process and getting their commitment to work with you and the assessment team to keep themselves safe. In cases where either denial or fatalism is very strong, I attempt to change the perception and commitment of the victims by demonstrating a larger context for the process. I explain to them that they have the right to make a decision that will affect only their safety, but, in this particular context (e.g., home, office, community, etc.), their decision could impact the safety of others (e.g., children, family members, co-workers, innocent third parties, etc.) and they should recognize that they have a responsibility to help protect the safety of these other people, even though they do not feel personally that they want or need to participate. This tactic often gains their cooperation because it validates their sense of control and acknowledges the legitimacy of their choice, while providing them a face-saving way to comply with the requests of the assessment and intervention team. I have found this particularly helpful with self-directed high-functioning people who seem to be more scared of acknowledging a perceived loss of control than they are of the possibility of physical harm.

Once we have passed through this first step with the victims, the next step is to provide them increased awareness. Security professionals who protect people recognize that their primary job is to use a heightened sense of awareness to identify risks before they are manifested and then change the situational dynamic to preempt the possibility of an attack. If an attack occurs, even as they respond, in a larger sense they have already failed because they have not prevented the attack from starting. Since, in most cases that violence assessors will work, victims are going to be primarily responsible for their own safety for the majority of the time on any given day, we need to teach this heightened awareness to the victims. That means we need to teach them to monitor their environment for cues that show they are at potential risk (countersurveillance) and then teach them what to do when they are aware of these cues. This is actually a fairly simple process and one that many people, particularly women, have had to exercise, at some level, all their lives.

First, we have to give the victims permission to trust their instincts concerning when they may be at risk. Most adults can provide examples of situations where they have felt suddenly at risk, even though they may not be able to articulate why they felt this way. This is an ancient survival mechanism we all have built in, even though we make excuses for it and are usually too embarrassed to act on it. We address that directly by asking victims when they have felt a sudden risk in the past, what they did about it and how they felt afterward. Using that information, we apply each of those past incidents to a possible situation in the current case (e.g., exiting the home, office, store, etc., and seeing a suspicious person or the instigator at a distance when walking or driving; coming upon a situation or a person of concern while walking in the open or an enclosed space, like a hallway, or while driving; being confronted by someone while at home, office, store, church, etc.) and give them a new way to respond and get them to ask questions and then agree to think about this new response. By working through these examples with them, we, the "professionals," are giving them permission to act by removing the greatest barriers to action — rationalization and the fear of embarrassment. This works best when you can give them some actual physical actions they can use to remind themselves to exercise their new awareness skills. Some of these actual physical actions include:

- Suggesting that potential victims carry a pad of paper and a pen with them at all times to record information concerning what they see, rather than relying on memory. This includes putting a pad of paper and pen next to each of their phones at home, at work and in their car. I suggest that, if they see, hear or experience something unusual or spot the instigator in an unusual place, they write down the date, time and all the information they can capture. In the case of a domestic violence situation, where victims are still living with instigators, I suggest that they keep the information in a location where the instigators will not know they are doing this, such as a trusted friend's or relative's home, at their offices, etc.
- Teaching the victims how to exit their homes, offices and other locations in a manner that will allow them to scan and assess the environment before they get too far away from a protected space.
- Teaching the victims how to park, approach and start their vehicles to minimize the possibility of someone's successfully attacking them.
- Teaching them what to do if they find out they are being followed on foot or by car.
- Teaching them what to look for as they approach their homes, offices, churches, schools, workout facilities, etc., and what to do if they note something of concern.

Instigator Perception

Taking the aforementioned steps will enhance the ability of potential victims to spot a potential risk situation before it escalates into a real risk situation and will give them proven ways to respond that will minimize the immediate risk. This education will change how the victim acts, which will also change the situational perception of the instigator. Instigators who are targeting victims will note changes in their awareness, pattern of movement and response to particular interactions. They may even note an increase in confidence and poise when harassing or confronting the victim. This will cause instigators to make changes in their future behavior, either by discouraging them from continuing, since they are not getting the desired response, or increasing their level of engagement to reassert control over victims. Timing the change in their perception of the victim, with changes in the perception of security around the victim, can have the cumulative effect of ending the problem behavior(s). This ending of behavior can mean that instigators divert their attention to another target who will not be as much work to manipulate for their own ends.

This shift in perception leading to cessation of behavior is most often seen in victim–instigator dynamics involving nonintimate relationships. My hypothesis on why we see this in our caseload is that the level of emotional energy present in nonintimate relationships is much lower than that in intimate relationships, therefore the commitment to continue adverse behavior in light of increasing resistance, coupled with the availability of less-organized targets, enables the instigator to move on at lower thresholds of intervention. Intimate relationships, with their higher levels of emotional energy, require higher levels of intervention to divert instigators from continued action. Therefore, when dealing with the assessment of cases involving current or past intimate partners or family members, assessors should anticipate that enhancing the awareness and response capabilities of victims will lead to a perceptual shift of instigators that may cause an immediate escalation of their physical actions to reestablish their sense of control over their victims. This would be a corollary to the understanding that the most lethal time for domestic violence victims is the time immediately after they abandon the joint residence and their aggressors have lost physical control of them. Consequently, the assessor and intervention team should plan to implement a block of security changes at the same time, anticipating any initial escalation in the actions of the aggressor and putting security measures in place to address the anticipated course of escalation, rather than attempting to linearly address these issues. Playing "catch-up" (defensively or reactively) in response to an instigator's actions is a sure way to get people hurt. As learned in the martial arts, people who act always have an advantage over people who react.

Site Hardening

Site hardening is a term for encompassing all the physical security changes that can be done to make the target less vulnerable to attack at any given location. These changes can occur at any location, including the victim's job site or residence. It might also include the hardening of a vehicle by adding optional protective equipment. While all the options cost money in some way, a range of lower-cost options are available that, when implemented, can provide a significant increase in safety.

The first level of site hardening is establishment and enforcement of basic security procedures. The cost of these procedures is generally reflected in the cost of the time required to change the pattern of movement into and out of a given space and the time necessary to check that the procedures are continually being followed. Doors and windows (vehicle, office and residential) are kept shut and locked at all times. In the case of offices or office buildings, rear and side exits that can be locked down are kept locked and people are directed to enter the space by one door or set of doors, preferably being forced to pass by a receptionist or other person who can observe and potentially screen arrivals. These screening procedures might include the implementation of some form of identification to check and track (e.g., sign-in sheets, badge issuance, etc.). In the area of residential security, this process would entail not opening the door to anyone and being unwilling to admit them to the residence before verifying who they are. This would mean locating places that family members could physically observe the person at the door, before approaching and talking with the person. This would allow family members to hide the fact that anyone is home, if the person at the door turned out to be the instigator or was acting suspiciously. Also, family members should be trained to talk through the door to people (or in the case of vehicles, remaining locked inside and talking through closed windows), rather than opening the door a crack to talk. If the caller is wearing the uniform of a utility or law enforcement agency, family members should request a call-back number to an office or supervisor to confirm who the person is. The channeling of people into one avenue of entrance that is monitored and requires some form of identification to allow admission increases the perception of security and the likelihood that instigators can be identified and stopped before they are able to get into physical proximity to the victims.

The next procedure to address is answering questions in person or over the telephone about the current activities or location of the victims. Family members, co-workers, children and others (e.g., child-care workers, etc.) need to be taught or reminded about what to say if they are contacted by someone asking about the victims. This is a good practice in general, but clearly important in these types of situations. Children can be taught to say the person can't come to the door or phone and never to provide any information about themselves or their family members to anyone not approved by their parents. Receptionists and other co-workers can be taught to say they don't know where the person is or what they are doing, but they will take a message and forward it to the person of interest. Anyone who is asked to protect information on the activities and location of the victims should also be asked to notify a designated individual if someone requests this information. This notification system will be a good device to track attempts to gain information on the victims. This tracking can provide information that can help assess escalation of risk by revealing patterns of increased frequency of contact, changes in the type of information requested and emotional tone when requested. There would be a significant difference between someone calling in once a month and asking, "Is Jane in?" versus someone who called once an hour, called a variety of people in the building or company and became increasingly hostile in his or her inquiries over the course of a day.

The last general procedure that should be developed or enhanced is how to notify people in the protected building or site that there is an intruder, along with a special plan for verbal confrontations and another for someone with a weapon, including how to evacuate the premises to maximize safety. Remember, in an incident of dynamic violence involving weapons, there should be a plan for floorwide, buildingwide and sitewide notification and evacuation. The evacuation plan should have everyone fleeing the area of the weapon — by stairwells if multistory buildings are involved — and directing them to run and scatter away from the building until they are several blocks away and out of sight of the location. They should then enter the nearest public space (e.g., shopping center, office building, store, library, etc.) and dial 911 and then call a designated number at their company that can record who they are, what unit they are from and where they are. They should then make their way home and not return to the site until they have been able to contact a phone number or web site that will provide them with an all-clear, or wait until they have been contacted directly by the company and asked to return. Only if the armed person is between them and the stairwells should they seek shelter inside the office space. First, they should head for any office rooms that have been outfitted as "safe rooms."[2] If these are unavailable or also blocked, they should enter any office and barricade the door, staying out of sight of any glass that allows oversight of the office. If that option is unavailable, they should hide in cubicles, stack objects around themselves and remain very quiet until help arrives.

Having said that, let me emphasize that hiding should be the very last resort. The important lesson of the 101 California St. shooting in San Francisco in July 1993, the Columbine High School shooting in Colorado and other incidents of dynamic violence inside structures, is that *those who run live and those who hide die.* I disagree with the current strategy at schools to "shelter in place" during an internal incident and hope that help gets there quickly. Most school classrooms have glass in and around the doors or have windows that will allow a gunman to shoot into, if not enter, the classroom. That classroom now has a huddled mass of targets and hostages. If kids run out of the classrooms, down the halls, out the doors, through the fields and into the neighborhoods, they could be hurt or killed, but the gunman will quickly have fewer targets who are much more difficult to hit, rather than stationary pools of victims who can be shot or blown up. I also realize that this idea will make law enforcement response more difficult, because it creates more confusion that can aid in concealing the perpetrator, but the central issue should be increasing the safety of the victims in the opening 15 minutes, not trying to contain or arrest the instigator. In those cases where the incident is in the area of the school property, but not occurring within the school buildings or enclosed areas, seeking shelter in the building is an appropriate strategy because it draws the children and staff out of the open space into protected space where the incidents of collateral injury can be reduced. To summarize, when the threat is outside of the structure, lock the perimeter and shelter in place. The moment the threat is inside the structure, or is believed to be inside the structure, evacuate and move quickly out of the immediate area.

After the procedural options have been exercised, the next level of site hardening increases costs in the form of physical improvements to the sites of concern. These changes can take many forms, so I have grouped them, below, by type of site. This list of suggestions should not be considered comprehensive, but rather an attempt to remind assessors and their assessment teams of some options that can be considered appropriate.

Vehicles

- Never allow a vehicle to have less than half a tank of gas.
- Provide cell phone access, if not already maintained for personal security.
- Equip vehicles with "run flat" tires, which are commercially available and allow for driving dozens, if not hundreds of miles, when someone has attempted to disable the vehicle by slashing, stabbing or releasing air from tires.
- Install a locking gas cap.
- Install engine compartment (hood) locks with internal releases.
- Remove any door lock release parts that can be "hooked" to gain entry.
- Use a remote keyless entry with a panic function.
- Equip vehicles with burglar alarms with internal space sensor and pager or cell phone notification.
- In very extreme cases, strengthen glass and car panels if financially possible.

Residences

- Cut back or remove shrubs, plants and trees that block either the flow of light around the property, or sight lines when entering the property or, when inside the house, to approaches to the residence. This would include eliminating greenery where someone could hide either to ambush or to maintain surveillance of the residence and activity within.
- Increase lighting around the residence to maximize the possibility of seeing people approach the residence. Remember, when lighting is increased by adding light fixtures, a decision needs to be made concerning the purpose of the lighting and, therefore, its placement. If lighting is placed in a yard it will illuminate certain areas but leave dark places with shadows in other areas. If light is placed at a perimeter facing toward the residence, it will backlight and illuminate people in the yard and on the outside of the house for people looking

at the house from the street, but can make it difficult for occupants to see into the light and identify more than shapes (think about what the speaker sees when talking from a stage). If lighting is placed on the residence and illuminates the area, people in the house can see, but when approaching the house, they could be blinded. The best approach is to use a mixture of lighting to increase general illumination — maybe spot lighting for the driveway and approaches to the house and a mixture of house and perimeter lighting at the front, back and sides, depending on usage and exposure.

- Install locks on the windows, sliding glass doors and utility boxes for both power and telephone.
- Install deadbolt locks with 1.5-inch or longer deadbolts in all entry doors and make certain that the receiver for the deadbolt is anchored in the door jam by screws that go all the way into the framing timber around the door. These deadbolts, like the doorknobs, can be reinforced with a strengthening plate if there is fear of someone punching out the lock with a sledgehammer.
- Install a sign at the driveway or a sticker at other entrances to the residence that state that it is protected by an alarm and solicitors are not welcome. This type of signage gives the perception of protection, which may be enough to divert a less-committed instigator.
- In some cases, consider replacing main entry doors with steel doors and frames or solid hardwoods with no-glass panels.
- Install peepholes in all entry doors that will allow for wide-angle use and no direct means to reverse the peephole and look back into the room. An example of this type of peephole is the "Door Spy,"[4] which can be used in a variety of locations and provides not only a side-to-side view, but also a straight down view to see if something has been left on the doorstep.
- Consider installing an alarm system for all windows and doors. The system should provide for both local annunciation (horn and strobe light) and monitoring of all alarm functions by a monitoring service. If a system is to be installed, additional consideration could be given to panic buttons, pager or cellular notification of alarm and cellular backup if the phone lines are vulnerable to tampering and the assessed risk is high.
- Consider the installation of window film that will dramatically increase the tensile strength of the glass in windows and doors, and also because of the film's reflective properties, make it more difficult to track movement inside the house when it is lighter outside the residence (daylight hours). This will not make the glass bullet resistant, but it will make it much more difficult to smash and enter the

residence. An example of this type of glass film is 3M Scotchshield®
Ultra Safety and Security window films.

- In very high-risk situations, consider the strengthening and locking
  of a bedroom door or other location that will make an interior "safe
  room" or area for use if the intruder gets into the residence. This room
  should have one entrance, reinforced and locked, with a cellular phone
  inside (programmed with the local police dispatch number, not 911),
  some bottles of water, a fire extinguisher and possibly a large-caliber
  firearm, if the resident has been trained to use it properly. The purpose
  of the room is to shelter occupants for the 10–15 minutes it will take
  for law enforcement to arrive and stop the perpetrator.

Offices or Office Buildings

- Install signage at each entrance to the property, facility or office space
  that clearly states that the area is private property and contains whatever "trespass" language is required by state, county or local government law or regulation to enforce a charge of trespassing.
- Increase lighting in the parking areas, walkways, entrances and interior spaces so that individuals can enter and leave the area with a
  clear view during either day or night, to see who and what are going
  on around them.
- Limit access to each building or office space, as mentioned above, and
  monitor that access for individuals coming and going. Requiring all
  individuals to show some form of identification and visitors to identify themselves and sign in is a good practice.
- Consider whether it would be possible or helpful to program eleva-
  tors to lock off a particular floor without the use of an additional
  access card, code or key.
- Consider hardening the reception areas of the building or office
  space by constructing walls with access-controlled doors that will
  keep a person from walking past a receptionist into the general area
  of the building or office space. This may require constructing meeting rooms in the lobby or reception area, or bathrooms in a building
  lobby, so people cannot access the protected space by claiming they
  are going for a meeting or need to use the restroom. In some cases
  involving long-term exposure, the hardening of the reception desk
  and walls by the use of ballistic glass and armor plate might be necessary, though this would most likely occur in areas of ongoing terrorist action or offices or buildings trafficking in high-value products
  or strategic information.
- Consider the use of an alarm system or closed circuit television
  monitoring of locations that are less subject to ongoing observation,

including parking garages, site perimeters, remote doors and storage areas, etc.

- Consider adding panic alarms at access points, sensitive reception areas and parking areas for use in case of emergency. Obviously, for these systems to be useful, response plans would need to be developed.
- As mentioned above, install or expand public address or emergency notification systems and establish evacuation plans for incidents of dynamic violence. Remember that the plans for use in fires and earth-quakes will not be adequate because they rely on the ability to move people to holding areas around the buildings, which will only create a pool of potential victims in violence situations. This concern is fur-ther heightened when bombs or incendiary devices could be used.
- Consider the creation of "safe rooms" on each building floor.[3]
- In high-risk situations, consider the use of armed personnel, trained at local law enforcement level or above. They should be trained in both verbal, less-than-lethal and lethal confrontation methods. This is a very costly option and should be used only in very high-risk situations and only for the highest-risk times. The cost of a two-man team can run, in the United States, from $500 to $1500 per 8-hour shift, depending on geographic location and market conditions. In one job that lasted 5 days, when we had to cover a high rise in a major metropolitan area while a dangerous and aggressive former foreign military operator was located and arrested, the bill exceeded $70,000. See the security personnel staging section below for more tactical information on this option.

Monitoring and Notification Systems

Monitoring and notification of any behavior or activity are important because they allow for continued updating of the assessment, in real time, which can be essential for making response (intervention) decisions. These systems break down into two general categories: proactive behavioral moni-toring and notification systems and reactive incident-response notification systems. Both categories have a variety of different elements, any of which might be used, singularly or in various arrays, during any given case.

Proactive Behavioral Monitoring and Notification Systems

This system is the most important system for ongoing case management because it increases the flow of behavioral data to assessors, which improves the quality of their assessment and can shape the intervention plans. In any given case, the potential members of this system are victims, their family and

friends, residential sources, co-workers, employment sources, law enforcement, the courts and correctional facilities. The initial information available
from these sources was covered in Chapter 2 and touched on the issue of
ongoing information. It is further explored here.

To utilize any of these sources for ongoing information flow, assessors
must establish a rapport and connection with them, make it easy for the
sources to reach them and provide them some form of incentive to make the
effort. That does not mean that the assessor just waits passively for information (passive monitoring) because there will always be reasons that sources
of information will not follow through. Rather, it is recognized that assessors must first establish a willingness and commitment of sources to contact
them, often for reasons linked to feeling good about themselves — personally
or professionally, then actively follow up (active monitoring) on those cases
that have a high risk or are in a particularly volatile period.

As we have mentioned before, victims will make decisions about how
they will act based on their rapport with assessors and their own personal
insight as influenced by their upbringing, experience and current needs and
the ease of contact. Consequently, during the initial interview, the assessor
will be overcoming issues of denial through to hysteria, getting a commitment to work together and learning about the perception the victim has of
various possible support groups, including family, friends, neighbors, co-
workers and the criminal justice system (law enforcement, courts and correctional departments). Once the victim has identified positive or neutral
perceptions of these sources of ongoing information, the assessor begins to
make a list of them to create a proactive notification system. Some sources,
particularly criminal justice sources, will usually be employed as relevant
anyway, but the assessor must be careful in how and what he or she communicates to the victim from these sources, if there is an obvious prejudice
against them. Presenting information to victims from any suspected source
will only strain the rapport, particularly when this information changes the
assessment away from whatever direction the victims want it to go.

To ease the information flow and help verify and document contacts, I
suggest assessors establish toll-free numbers for information flow. Any established telephone number can be given such a number as a connecting vehicle.
The advantage of these numbers, particularly if established as nationwide
numbers, is that the assessor's company or agency pays for the call from anywhere in the United States and can have access to the originating call telephone numbers, including unlisted numbers, that are received through the
toll-free line. This provides confirmation, by date and time, of the originating number of any call and its duration. It also means that the source is not
paying for the call, which eliminates the excuse that they could not pay for
the call or did not have a phone they could call from (most public phones
have agreements to allow placement of toll-free number calls for no charge,

including a coin to start the process, though cell phones will still be charged for outgoing airtime). Certainly, in certain cases, you could also include other means to ease contact, depending on the source's desires, including an e-mail address, cell phone number (maybe with a toll-free covering number), pager, etc. If it is not easy, they may not call.

Once the sources of future information have been identified, they must be contacted and a relationship must be established. Cooperative victims should request the support of family and friends who are closest to them and introduce them to the assessor or assessment team member. If victims are not cooperative, I would still let them know what the plan is, so they are not surprised and perhaps begin to lose trust in the idea that they are working with the assessor in managing the process. This period of initial introduction to family members or close friends is a good time to use the same ECI interviewing style discussed in Chapter 2. This will allow the assessors to understand the personal perspective of sources on this matter, what type and depth of information they might be exposed to and the degree of cooperation they can anticipate from these sources. Just because victims trust these sources and believe they will help does not mean that the sources want to get involved or feel as if the victim might not actually be the problem. This is always an issue to be explored, particularly in cases involving domestic or co-worker violence, where the sources have had direct contact with the instigators and may have formed a positive perception or relationship. If assessors know that certain sources have had direct contact with the instigator, it is important that they explore that contact in a neutral way, assuming, for the sake of safety, that the content of the whole interview may be communicated back to the instigator. This will be an opportunity to use the interview for two additional purposes — intelligence gathering and situational modification by information perception management (spin).

For the intelligence-gathering part, provide a unique piece of information, not shared with others, to each source and see whether it is communicated back to the victim from the instigator. This will show that the source is in active contact with the instigator. My suggestion is that you do not tell the victim that you are doing this so that you can receive the information without an uncontrolled response by the victim. Specifically, I would be concerned that victims, having heard a piece of planted information from instigators, would either confront the instigator or the source with the fact they are communicating, thereby limiting the use of this connection for future indirect and uncensored input to the instigator to manipulate their perception.

For the "spin" piece, assume that everything said will be given to instigators, so spend time talking about the situation from their perspective and why they might feel it was appropriate to act this way. Not only does this establish the assessor's neutrality and objectivity, which can reassure reluctant family members or close friends who might know both victim and instigator that the assessor has not been "taken in" by the victim, but, if their confidence is communicated to the instigator, it will reinforce the idea that someone is trying to sort through the situation in a fair and even-handed way, which may provide a valuable return to assessors, if and when they have an opportunity to interview the instigator.

After learning what you can about peripheral sources' knowledge of the instigator, you ask them if they would be willing to help further. If they agree, give them your toll-free telephone number and ask them to call you if they see or hear anything, directly or indirectly, about the instigator and his actions. Let them know that, even though the victim might know these things, too, they, as sources who are not directly involved, might be in a position to let you know more quickly what is going on — speed can often make a critical difference. This action begins to build a network of sensor points that can feed the assessor information about the case development. Over time, assessors may get multiple reports of similar activity, but a great deal that has not been heard will surface as well. Each connected source, other than the victim, is a hedge against "victim fatigue" in which the victim becomes worn down by the situation and stops recording and communicating new behavior. Obviously, each source is also a potential means of continued validation of the authenticity of what the victim is reporting, especially in those cases where false victimization or process manipulation is suspected.

When contacting residential sources (e.g., neighbors, landlords, etc.) careful thought should be given to any negative consequences that could occur to victims or their families prior to contact. Neighbors have been known to ostracize victims or to limit play with their children because of their fear of being caught up in the violence. Landlords have even tried to evict victims for fear of future violence. Consequently, these sources may be of limited overall value. However, if the victim has a good relationship with these sources, they can be approached and can provide useful information, becoming a valuable source of future information based on their proximity to the victims' residence. As law enforcement officers have learned, often a "nosy neighbor" can be a wonderful source of information about what is going on in a neighborhood and can become a valuable resource to monitor activity in and around the residence in question.

Co-workers, who have a vested interest in maintaining a safe workplace, can be a good source of initial and ongoing information. Care must be taken to maintain the right level of confidentiality and privacy around an employed victim's circumstance, but co-workers often have information about what has happened in and around the victim and can provide ongoing information. In some cases, including them can also serve as a means to fulfill the enterprise's "duty to warn."[5] Receptionists and company operators can be a particularly good source to explore because they monitor the coming and going of the office staff and, in many cases, receive and transfer calls to the victim and others. If the instigators are an intimate partner, customer or vendor, they may already recognize their voices and be able to play a role, not just in information gathering, but, in some intervention strategies such as diverting the person or call to others who have been designated to manage contact from instigators.

The criminal justice system provides a variety of notification systems, informal and formal, both pre- and post-conviction, that can be used in assessment cases. The first and best source of ongoing criminal justice information is a good relationship with investigating officers of any criminal investigation involving victims and instigators. These officers make decisions about how to pursue their individual cases and assessors have to determine how they can engage the officers in making their particular cases those that will get continued attention. First, this means making the case a positive experience for the officers by providing information in depth and on time, facilitating access to the victim and keeping the officers fully apprised of any new information that is learned. In exchange, it would be appropriate under many "victim rights" laws that victims, or assessors as the victims' representatives, depending on the case and the relationship to victims, could be informed of the existence of any prior violent activities, weapons ownership, drug-related offenses or current restraining orders. As the case progresses, victims or assessors will attempt to maintain the relationship so that they can check in periodically to talk about the progress in the case and any new information or receive prior notification of any actions on the part of the officers that could cause a reaction in the instigators (e.g., interview, search warrant service, probation violation, parole violations, weapons confiscation and arrest).

Another good contact and source of information is investigators in the District Attorney's office. If a criminal case is forwarded to that office, investigators may get involved to help manage the case. Such people are usually seasoned investigators who have a little more time to manage their caseload than the average investigator. They can provide a wealth of information about the progress of a criminal case and some early warning if the person is to be released. Victim or witness advocates in the District Attorney's office are another source of information to be cultivated for ongoing help and information. They also can provide ongoing case information and support for victims if there are any hearings or a trial, as well as connections to county and state resources, including, in some cases, monetary help, to aid victims through the process.

Following arrest or conviction, many jurisdictions have a Victim Information and Notification Everyday system in place that can provide automated information on individuals who have been jailed. These systems are available 24 hours per day and, in many cases, can be set up to provide automated notification of pending or actual release or escape of a jailed individual.

Most state correctional systems and the Federal Bureau of Prisons have victim or witness notification systems for providing information on the release, escape, furlough, parole hearings and deaths of inmates. This information is often provided only by mail, so timeliness can be an issue; however, access to another means to monitor case information should always be of interest. We have used these formal systems and sometimes have learned about changes in the status of an instigator before law enforcement has been notified.

Other post-conviction or -incarceration notification and monitoring sources can be probation and parole officers who have been assigned to the individuals. However, care has to be taken in approaching these officers, as they may be limited in their ability to help and also in their interest, possibly due to a different agenda. In our experience, many probation and parole officers are focused on rehabilitation, which is an important goal, but sometimes clashes with the specific goal of the assessor, which is the safety of specific victims. Consequently, on top of the crushing case loads that the majority of probation and parole officers contend with that limit their ability to monitor any particular subject, there may be some protectiveness of their probationer or parolee that would limit their effectiveness as a resource for violence assessment and intervention cases. Like some psychiatrists who have treated instigators, we have had several probation and parole officers actually tell their charges that we had made inquiries and tell them what we were interested in knowing. This leakage of information was not helpful in managing the cases in question and reinforced the lesson for us that care should be taken in the initial contact to gauge the value of any contact versus the risk of having that person in the process, before the assessor discloses any sensitive information. Given the search and detention provisions of most probation and parole agreements, these officers can be a wonderful resource for tactical involvement in some types of interventions, particularly when there is need for a rapid search of a residence or person to locate weapons, collect evidence, or just place a person on an immediate hold to interrupt a particular course of action. Also, if the subject is normally difficult to locate, these officers can request a meeting with the subject that will provide a means to serve legal papers and establish interviews.

It should be noted that in this section I have not suggested using or relying on any mental health professionals who have, or are, treating the instigator. This is primarily because of the medical privacy and confidentiality laws and regulations that make it difficult for them to share information. I certainly would encourage consideration of initial contact in those cases where a release can be obtained or when the case is so serious that the potential benefit of contact outweighs the potential exposure of the contact or attempted contact to the instigator. If contact is made, the assessor should remind the provider of the confidentiality issues around the contact and that notifying the instigator of the contact could cause physical harm to the victim. Then, absent a release from the patient to talk to this provider, assessors can inform mental health professionals of information they have and ask if this is new information to them. Providing information is not against the laws or regulations for an assessor and giving currently treating mental health professionals more information to form their opinions can be very beneficial. Assessors can also ask whether this new information brings up any Tarasoff issues,[6] which may provoke an information response of value to the assessor. If nothing else, when contacting mental health professionals who are treating instigators, assessors are placing them on notice that a problem is being assessed and the mental health professionals may decide to seek more information on their own or take other intervention steps themselves that may not have been considered before. Thus, with the exception of a Tarasoff notification, mental health professionals may be of limited value as an element of monitoring or notification for case assessment and management.

Reactive Incident Response Notification Systems

These systems are used during an actual incident for the notification and direction of people during a dynamic incident of violence. This will usually be a segmented process, starting with smaller, private means of notification, like a hand-held radio or cellular phone and escalating to a building- or complexwide public address system. The general concept is a system of individuals charged with the responsibility to watch for particular people or individuals exhibiting certain behaviors, who notify others when such people show up or exhibit those behaviors. A response plan is then activated that may require a small team response or a buildingwide response, depending on the extent of the threat and how the incident escalates or deescalates. Response plans will be covered in the next section.

The use of cellular phones is limiting because they provide only point-to-point contact. This limits notification to one party at a time, slowing notification to everyone who might need to immediately know the information. The exception to this problem is the use of the NEXTEL network, which combines cellular phones and radios into one device and one network. However, like dedicated-frequency radios, the equipment is expensive, beginning with the monthly fee for cellular access, and the coverage is not always good.

Using dedicated-frequency radios can work for small campus settings and single-building issues, but there can be problems with reception in buildings with various construction materials and in high-rise buildings. In addition, if multiple teams are working the same problem with incompatible radios, communications between teams can become a significant problem (e.g., the controversy surrounding emergency communication problems at the World Trade Center during the early phases of the September 11th response). The first problem, interference issues, can usually be addressed by placing a "suitcase" repeater in the area to strengthen the radio signals. The second problem can be effectively addressed only by creating a central dispatching person or group to monitor all the different radio frequencies, or by expanding the number of hand-held units on one frequency to include all necessary individuals. Hand-held radios can usually be rented in most U.S. and European metropolitan areas for use, with contracts that will charge less for longer use (monthly or yearly) and more for week-long or single-day use.

In recent years, the use of Family Radio Service–frequency hand-held radios has greatly reduced the cost and portability of radio communication. Hand-held radios on these frequencies can be purchased for $30–$50 each, require AA batteries to run all day and do not require Federal Communications Commission licensing (unlike commercial-grade hand-held radios). Most come with the ability to work well on a combination of 14 frequencies with 38 different code options and in a variety of environments. Dropping one of these radios, which can be replaced at any Wal-Mart, is preferable to the hundreds of dollars and inconvenience of attempting to replace a dedicated-frequency radio. Their drawbacks are lack of power (optimum range 2 miles; real range can be as low as 100 feet in some concrete or steel environments that are rich in electromagnetic interference from computers) and the possibility that the communications will be overheard by others who have access to the same range of frequencies. The first drawback cannot be easily addressed, but the second can be handled by using short, not specific statements, such as "the subject has arrived," not "John Steinbeck is in the building," and using an unusual combination of frequency and coding for the radios being used.

Public address systems are necessary to communicate to everyone when there is a need to immediately lock down an area, or to start an evacuation process. In buildings where a public address system is not available, but companies have dedicated phone systems, the phone system can usually be configured for this purpose, by either programming the system to allow for an "all-call" function for each phone extension (assuming the handsets have speaker phone capability), or by adding overhead speakers to the space to be covered and having them wired into the key service unit or processing unit of the phone system for activation at any handset with a particular code. If neither a public address system nor a dedicated phone system is available, then the current generation of electronic bullhorn can be substituted as an alternative.

Finally, with the new technologies that are developing, eventually intervention teams might be able to use a blast message through a short messaging system or a blast e-mail to all cellular phones, Blackberry pagers or other e-mail–enabled devices, but the issue of coverage areas and "dead zones" would still need to be managed. Wi-Fi networks or other wireless networks might one day solve these problems, but hand-held radios may still be the most flexible and immediately deployable technology for the next 15 years. Time will tell.

The reality is that because of the various problems inherent in all these forms of notification, a blended approach that incorporates a backup system is usually the best option. The first decision to be made is who needs to have instant and direct communication; those people are usually assigned radios as their primary form of communication, possibly with cell phones as backup. Security team leaders, with a radio, cell phone and access to any public address system, usually assume the job of communication and response coordination. The next tier of team members is usually reachable by office extension number and cell phone. This blended approach allows for rapid response while balancing out the cost of establishing a network that may be needed for only a short time.

Response Plans

Response plans are essentially the same as intervention plans, but originate from a different professional vocabulary. The term "response plan" is military, law enforcement or security terminology, while "intervention plan" is medical or mental health terminology. In this section, we will use the term response plan to denote the security response in an overall intervention plan to divert or stop an act of violence.

Response plans in the area of violence intervention can generally be divided into several types of plans geared to the various types of problems that need to be addressed. These problems include security response for the interviewing process at a residence ("knock and talk") or in a commercial or work setting; security for a termination meeting; site security for the victims at their jobs but rarely at their residences; and dynamic security for those cases in which the victims may be exposed to a high degree of risk in a short-term environment, such as court hearings, board meeting or shareholder meetings, social gatherings, etc. We will address the basic approaches for each one of these situations; however, each case and each situation are unique and the response plans should be created in each case by a qualified security professional with that in mind.

The Interview and Termination Process

Response plans for both interviewing and termination processes are basically the same. The plan needs to address the issues of how to get the individual to an interview space, how to respond into that space to protect the participants, how to keep the situation in the space (containment) if a hostage situation should develop and how to have the person leave the space with minimum opportunities for disruption when the meeting is over.

The general security element for these plans is a two-man team that has been appropriately equipped and trained in interacting with emotionally and mentally destabilized persons, using verbal de-escalation techniques, nonlethal and lethal physical response, team tactics and room entry techniques. Both members of the team also should have the necessary physical conditioning to effectively use their training. The two-man team is used because, in a confrontational situation with a single responder, the instigator may decide he can overcome a single responder, whereas if there are two responders, the instigator may hesitate to act. In reality, a single instigator with the appropriate motivation and effort can overcome two or more responders on some occasions. But, most often, the two will prevail and be able to subdue the instigator with minimum injury to themselves and the instigator. I have had situations where an angry instigator has said, "You know, if it was just you and me, I would kick your ass, but, since you have a friend, I'll have to catch you on another day." Thus, having two responders allowed the individual to back down with a reasonable excuse, avoiding a physical altercation — a good day for all. More two-man teams can be assigned to a case, based on the size of the site and the response time that can be tolerated. Response plans are designed to provide the response time that can be tolerated and defended for any particular situation. The more teams you have, the closer they will be when the action starts and the quicker their response time. We will discuss this more in the following section on site security.

In office settings, a space for interviews and termination meetings should be chosen to minimize the number of people in the area who would be aware of the meeting and traumatized by any action that could take place. Ideally, it would be a small conference room (small, to minimize the space to be controlled), on a ground floor (if removal were necessary it would not be down a staircase or in an elevator), near an exterior exit (so law enforcement could extract the instigator with minimum time on the scene and minimum observation by others) and near an office where the security team could be placed. The door would have no glass beside it or around it so that people walking by would not be able to see in and know what was going on. A covert wireless video camera would be placed inside the room (no audio if legal issues preclude it) so that the security team could monitor the activity in the room and the assessor could provide hand signals for desired response. The instigator would normally be asked to come to the room to meet with a company representative the day of the interview (no prior notice, if possible), and would meet with that representative and the assessor. If there were concern about the instigator carrying weapons, the security team would observe the individual coming to the meeting to see if they could detect any obvious "tells" (involuntary body movements that are made to accommodate the unusual presence of a weapon). If there were evidence of a possible weapon, an agreed-upon plan would need to be activated. This plan could be to admit instigators into the room without stopping them or it could be searching them by metal-detecting wand or hand search. It would be preferable not to search subjects, if safety permits because that would reveal the presence of the security team. Also, the search would elevate emotions that must be deflated before a productive interview can proceed.

Ideally, instigators are called to the interview room, interviewed at length, allowed to leave the premises under their own power and have no knowledge that there was even a security team present. The theory behind this is, if violence is committed by instigators to establish or reestablish control, which they perceive to be necessary, controlling their perception is one tool to mitigate violence. Therefore, if assessors or the security team interact with them with the outward expectation that they will control themselves and they perceive they have some control, it lowers the probability of violence. If we openly display security, that is, treat them as if we expect them to act inappropriately, we tend to lower their perception of control and possibly their inhibition to act violently. People have a tendency to live up to, or down to, our expectations of behavior, so, by our process, we want to show hope for the best, but we must be prepared with a plan for the worst. As they said in the movie *Road House*, "Be nice, until it's time not to be nice anymore."

If, during collateral witness interviews, there should be a significant concern that the instigator might attempt to disrupt the interview process, a response plan should be developed for this contingency, including a security team positioned for these interviews. The management plan would consist of an initial plan by the assessor and any co-interviewer of how to handle an instigator who interrupted their interview with witnesses. Normally, I suggest that they dismiss the witness being interviewed and interview the instigator right away. This allows them to interview instigators when they are agitated, which can be revealing, while not allowing them to continue to escalate in the workplace and possibly raise anxiety in the workforce or intimidate future witnesses. Once instigators in a workplace setting have been interviewed, they are placed on "leave, pending the outcome of the investigation" and told to leave the premises. However, a secondary intervention plan would have to be developed stating when the security team should intervene and how. Away from the workplace setting, the assessor should have a plan for leaving at the close of the interview.

This secondary response plan, involving security team intervention, would be roughly the same with any instigator interview, regardless of how it came about. Any interviewee has the right to leave most interviews at any time he wishes, consequently, this secondary plan has to encompass what to do if instigators leave the room mid-interview, particularly if they are in emotional turmoil. It also has to address what to do if instigators stand up and begin to scream at assessors so that they believe they need help to control the subjects, or if they attempt to physically harm assessors or produce a weapon and position themselves to hurt anyone coming into the room.

If instigators "rabbit" from the room, the general strategy is to have the security team stay in proximity and monitor their progress until they stop or do something that alerts the team to the possibility that the instigators are about to physically harm others. If and when they stop, the security team calmly suggests that they need to leave the premises and remain "on leave" (if appropriate) until it is decided what the next steps (in the process) will be. If instigators become belligerent, they are talked with; if they become threatening, they are warned that the police will be called; if they start to act in a way that the security team believes poses a risk of physical harm to themselves or others, the security team takes whatever steps are necessary to stop the possibility of physical harm.

It is very important that the security team understand the difference between being disruptive and being physically harmful. If a person gets on top of a desk and begins to shout in the work area, I suggest that employees in the area be evacuated and the person talked down, not brought down. However, if the person makes any move to physically harm others, the security team reacts immediately to take the person into custody, calls law enforcement to take over the arrest and has the person processed appropriately. A verbal confrontation and defiance should be met with words, imminent or actual acts met with acts.

If the person becomes emotionally and verbally aggressive inside the interview space and help is called for by the assessor, my first suggested intervention is distraction. A security team member comes to the door, opens it quickly and says, "Oh, I didn't know this conference room was being used, how long will you be?" This distraction will break the instigators' momentum, allowing the assessors time to address the question and then, when the door is closed, suggest to the instigators that they would be willing to listen, but not be shouted at. In many cases, instigators will sit down and resume the conversation in a more controlled manner.

If the instigator gets angry with the interruption and verbally attacks the security team member who looked into the room, the team member who opened the door can make the choice to step into the room, leaving the door open and ask, "What is going on here?" The second team member should approach the room and be outside the door, but out of sight until needed. If the person can be talked down and the assessor signals they will resume, the team member can leave the room and resume observation. If the instigator remains agitated and the assessor signals that the meeting is over, the instigator can be asked to leave and the team member, with his backup, can escort the person from the site, if necessary. Normally, under these circumstances, I would not let instigators roam the site, but would ask them what they need from their workspace to go home right now and have someone who is "on call" (e.g., a human resource or security person sitting by his phone extension during the interview), get the property and bring it to the interview room. Then the individuals are escorted out the nearest door and brought to the general area of their vehicle and allowed to leave. As the vehicle is approached, I usually inform them that they should not return to any organization location until requested to do by the organization (trespass language for that jurisdiction) and inform them that if they have any questions they can contact X, who is the person designated to communicate with them.

If the instigator becomes physically aggressive in the interview room, the security team responds by coming immediately into the room, taking verbal control or physical control of the instigator, ending the interview and escorting the instigator from the site, using the same procedures outlined above. In the case of a need to physically control the subject, the security team should have a plan about how they will subdue the subject and how the assessor and witness should get out of the way and out of the room to provide more space for action; they should educate the assessor and witness about this plan before the interview begins. Normally, I suggest that one security team member take initial responsibility for physical contact while the second team member makes sure the assessor and witness get out of the room. The second person then engages when they see an appropriate opening. Certainly, the use of nonlethal weapons by the second team member (e.g., Air-Taser®, baton, etc.) would be an option.

If the instigator produced a weapon and threatened the assessor or witness and it was believed by the security team that they could respond, then the assessor and witness would need to go to their preassigned location in the room for this possibility (e.g., retreat to a particular corner, etc.) and the security team would have to enter and engage with firearms.

If the instigator produces a weapon and threatens the assessor or witness in a way that seems to preclude entry without significant loss of life, the security team would need to have a plan to close off departure from the room, evacuate that area of the building, establish communication between the instigator and the security team and wait for law enforcement to arrive with tactical support and hostage negotiators for situation resolution. The plan should be that armed instigators are not allowed to leave the interview room until they are under complete physical control sans weapon(s). This strategy contains the potential for harm to a small area and a small group of people. Don't forget that most ground-floor rooms have windows, and the outside perimeter may need to be cleared and controlled as well.

Concerning instigator interviews at the individual's residence or other space not controlled by the assessor and the security team (sometimes called a "knock and talk"), the security team should try to conduct some form of intelligence gathering concerning the location and make decisions about when and where to approach and how to handle similar concerns for safety. Restaurants are problematic because they can be noisy, distracting environments that are not conducive to long interviews and, if the situation should escalate, innocent third parties might be adversely affected. Meeting the instigators at their own living quarters increases their sense of control and can lower their anxiety, but it substantially increases the risk to the assessor because of the possibility of weapons access and other family members' becoming involved in the interview. I have conducted interviews at the instigator's place of work and those have been successful when I was able to show sensitivity to not embarrassing the instigator and minimizing the impact on his work environment. I have conducted interviews at Starbucks and other small coffee shops and in small, quiet bars, including bars in the lobbies of major hotels during the daytime. These venues are quieter, neutral, with less need by the sales staff to interrupt or be concerned about the length of time of the interview, have less third-party exposure because of smaller numbers of people and have an increased safety factor away from weapons that might be stashed in the residence or vehicle. However, based on need, we have also conducted interviews in living rooms, back yards, front yards and on front porches.

The majority of off-site interviews are conducted in a two-person format, with the assessor and a security person, and are backed up by a second security person in sight of the first watching for anyone approaching and for additional support as needed. If assessors are inside a business or residence, the placement of the second security person can be problematic, but if they are outside in the car, they are useless.[7] In these situations, safety must be balanced with information gathering and the assessor must work harder to establish rapport and have the instigator forget about the additional people and what they imply about the situation.

Site Security

A response plan for a fixed site is based on how much response time can be tolerated. There will never be enough budget and manpower to provide a completely staffed solution, so it is necessary to first identify the most likely points of access to the site and the most likely target and then place the primary response teams between those access points and the most likely target. We usually place the teams in unoccupied offices or conference rooms so they are less conspicuous, which keeps the organizational anxiety down. It is a myth that security makes people feel more comfortable, except for short periods of time. Over a period of a week or more, the presence of security, particularly armed security, just keeps reminding people they are at risk. Unarmed security and other individuals (e.g., receptionists, supervisory employees, etc.) can be used as "eyes and ears" to provide information on the approach of the instigator and then the trained protection personnel respond and engage with the instigator. The plan normally calls for instigators to be approached, identified and asked why they are there. Once that is understood, they are usually asked to leave the premises or are escorted to a safe location for further discussion, depending on what type of interaction is desired. If they refuse to cooperate, they are given the choice of either leaving or having law enforcement called (if the security element is law enforcement, then the option might be arrest for trespassing). If they attempt to harm others, they are subdued and removed to a holding space for transfer to jail. Certainly, if a subject arrives on the premises with an exposed weapon, containment is preferred, with shooting an option if the subject poses an immediate danger to the security personnel or protectees. Should the response team be called to the scene of an individual with a weapon, then dynamic two-man team movement through the space to identify the location of the instigator and contain the incident will be required. A number of firearm-training schools now provide this type of training for two-man teams, including Training Team (TFTT), Thunder Ranch and others.

For site security that is positioned at certain venues for a short period of time, the security team needs to incorporate dynamic security personnel assigned to the known targets, if any, and some two-man team elements in the areas of the site where the targets will be stationary for longer periods of time (e.g., meetings, dinners, receptions, etc.). Having this combination of a person or people with the targets who link up with people at a more stationary site who have checked the site, identified the access points and evacuation paths and located the most advantageous place for the targets to be in, is a tremendous advantage. However, this falls into the area of executive protection, which requires training in movement, communications and special response for open, dynamic situations.

Summary

Security, as a part of violence assessment and intervention, provides a framework of safety against violence for both assessors and victims. It is designed to keep people physically safe from violence as the assessment personnel assess, intervene and resolve potentially violent situations. It provides security training for participants, site hardening against risks, monitoring of behavior for assessment and intervention and direct response to confrontational situations. Security provides the barrier to prevent violence if assessment and intervention fail.

Endnotes

1. Lack, Richard W. (Ed.), in *Safety, Health and Asset Protection, 2nd Edition,* Chapter 32, Security, Boca Raton, FL: Lewis Publishers, p. 555 (2002).
2. July 1, 1993, Gian Luigi Ferri entered 101 California Street, San Francisco and began killing people in the law firm of Petit and Martin. The incident started at 2:55 P.M. and eventually migrated from floor 34 to floors 33 and 32. Ferri killed himself in the stairwell between floors 29 and 30 before law enforcement could locate him. Eight people, including Ferri, were killed and six were wounded.
3. A safe room is designed to hold someone at bay for a short period of time until a responding force can arrive. In the case of office buildings, a basic safe room means a room with no glass windows, a solid-core door with a peephole and a deadbolt lock with throw inside the room, and a means of communication with the outside, like a telephone. People are trained to go into the room, remain quiet and not let anyone in unless they recognize them and are sure that person is not being held hostage as a means to get the door open.
4. The Door Spy, model DS-6, by Rudolph-Desco Company, Englewood Cliffs, NJ. This model provides separate views straight ahead, on each side and directly at the base of the door. It is rated by Underwriters Laboratories for use in fire-rated doors and has an exterior that can be painted.
5. See Chapter 10 for more information on the legal concept of Duty to Warn.
6. See Chapter 7 for more information on Tarasoff.
7. There was a tragic example of this in Richmond, CA where, on April 27, 1995, a Housing Authority worker was being terminated from his job and law enforcement was called to stand by. They were posted outside the Housing Authority office when the subject went into the bathroom during the termination and returned with a gun, shooting both individuals in the meeting to death. Law enforcement officers then went into the building and arrested the person.

The Laws of Violence Risk Assessment and Intervention

10

Introduction

This chapter will address practical aspects and issues presented by the various laws that one may encounter in any violence assessment. It focuses on U.S. law, but the concepts for certain sections apply internationally. The authors are not lawyers, so none of the information in this chapter should be interpreted as legal advice. Also, the law continues to evolve constantly and some of the information presented could be outdated already in the weeks or months surrounding publication. Both of these considerations are sufficient reason to have competent legal counsel available for consultation. In some cases, especially the more serious ones, there may be a need for two types of legal counsel: one who specializes in criminal law and one who specializes in civil law.

On the criminal law side, an experienced prosecutor in the jurisdiction of the case would be ideal. This individual would be able to provide legal advice during a criminal investigation and prosecution, but also might personally know the judges who would be ruling on search warrants, bail hearings and other important procedural matters, which would allow effective case presentation at critical junctures. On the civil side, our experience is that a skilled employment law attorney, who has experience in seeking restraining orders and litigating (not just settling) claims of harassment, discrimination, sexual harassment, age discrimination, wrongful termination, defamation, invasion of privacy and "whistle-blower" (claims of violation of public policy with retaliation for reporting) cases, is the best counsel a company or organization can have when cases involve either a perpetrator or a victim who is an employee of the organization requesting the violence assessment. A similarly experienced family-law specialist could be invaluable in matters involving intimate relationships. Legal counsel should have a personality that works well in a team environment and a strong understanding that their role is a critical, but not central, part of keeping the victim safe. The law is a socially acceptable form of confrontation and it works when all parties agree to abide by its rules, which may not be the case with perpetrators who pose a high risk of violence. Consequently, the best practice is that attorneys must, like all members of a violence assessment team, realize that, at certain times in the process, they will be leading the group — but only at certain times and not all the time. Lawyers sometimes forget that it is better to be sued than killed, and the fear of getting killed should supersede the fear of being sued.

Now that all these caveats are in place, let's get to work. We will discuss how specific laws or concepts of the law might be involved in cases, as well as some case management considerations that are important to keep in mind. We expect that if you are interested in any of these areas, you will conduct your own research and seek out appropriate people with whom to discuss your interests.

Federal Law or Regulation[1]

In the United States, it is generally understood that when there is a conflict between federal and state law, federal law supersedes state law. States are allowed to make their laws more restrictive, but they cannot be in conflict by being more liberal than federal laws in the same areas. It is also understood that the Rules of Evidence are different in federal and state law. What this means for the violence assessor and case manager is that there is a need to "shop venue" when looking at any case in which it may be possible to use either federal or state law to intervene in a case. This requires an intimate knowledge of both the applicable federal laws and state laws so that one can be flexible in how to proceed with the case, depending on the options the case facts open up.

An example of this would be the use and enforcement of restraining orders. A stalking and threats case had occurred by telephone from Texas to California. Via voicemails captured on a California company phone system, the individual in Texas had repeatedly threatened to harm the victim. After a violence assessment had been conducted, the victim's company sought a "corporate restraining order" in California and served it on the individual in Texas. At the beginning of the 1990s, any state-issued restraining order would have had limited or no value in a case such as this because most state courts would have been neither willing nor able to enforce a state court order on an individual in another state, unless that individual came within the jurisdiction of the court, meaning, in this case, traveling to California. However, this order was issued after federal law had been modified to allow for interstate enforcement of restraining orders. Consequently, if this individual, as he was informed at the time of the service of the order, chose to violate the order, he could be prosecuted under federal law. This was sufficiently worrisome to the perpetrator to cause him to cease his behavior, an obsessional pattern of behavior that had plagued this victim for more than 10 years. This knowledge and use of state and federal laws to patch together an effective intervention strategy for a particular case is exactly what we should strive to provide for the victims we serve.

Violence Against Women Act (1994, Amended in 1998 and 2000)

This was a foundational law in the area of violence intervention. It initially contained language that created an office in the U.S. government that would be responsible for conducting research into issues involving domestic violence, restraining orders, stalking and related areas such as civil restitution for violence, etc. Incorporated into this act and its following amendments are several sections that are of special importance for violence assessors and preventors to know. These are sections of Title 18 of the United States Code (U.S.C.), specifically: 18 U.S.C. § 2261 (Interstate Domestic Violence), 18 U.S.C. § 2261A (Interstate Stalking), 18 U.S.C. § 2262 (Interstate Violation of Protection Order) and 18 U.S.C. 2265 (a) (A Full Faith and Credit of Restraining Orders). These provisions and their subsections provide very powerful tools to use in the United States for the prevention of violence. Following is a brief outline of each of these sections and discussion of case management issues. An Assistant U.S. Attorney (AUSA) is assigned in each U.S. Attorney's office to be the Violence Against Women Act (VAWA) specialist. These individuals can be valuable sources of both knowledge on these sections of the law and how the U.S. District Court in their area has interpreted these laws in their judicial districts. Another valuable resource in each judicial district is the U.S. Marshal's Service office. The marshals are responsible for the safety of the federal judiciary, which can provide them some unique insights, and we have found them to be very practical, professional law enforcement personnel who are highly motivated to help in any way they can.

18 U.S.C. § 2261 (Interstate Domestic Violence)

There are two possible ways to activate this statute, either by traveling in interstate or foreign commerce (or entering or leaving Indian country), "with the intent to kill, injure, harass or intimidate a spouse or intimate partner" or in causing a partner to travel in interstate or foreign commerce (or to enter or leave Indian country) "by force, coercion, duress or fraud" and then committing or attempting to commit a crime of violence against that spouse or intimate partner. In other words, if the perpetrator approaches a spouse or intimate partner across a state or international border or causes them to travel across a state or international border, regardless of whether they are driving them away or enticing them to come to them, and then attempts to or does commit a "crime of violence" against that victim, it is punishable by fine and:

(b)(1) for life or any term of years, if death of the victim results
(b)(2) for no more than 20 years if permanent disfigurement or life threatening bodily injury to the victim results
(b)(3) for not more than 10 years, if serious bodily injury to the victim results or if the offender uses a dangerous weapon during the offense
(b)(4) ... special maritime or territorial jurisdiction applications ...
(b)(5) for not more than 5 years, in any other case or both fined and imprisoned (U.S.C. § 2261)

Those reading this who have experience in dealing with the criminal justice process will find this law very interesting, because if the individuals have been married, have cohabitated "as a spouse" or had a child together and cross a state, territorial, commonwealth, District of Columbia or international borders, separately or together and a "crime of violence" is attempted or committed, the law applies and the penalties are generally much stiffer than many state penalties are for the same acts. This allows us to take a look at the case facts and determine whether the state laws involved or the federal laws are more applicable or *even if both laws apply simultaneously.* In some cases, you can pursue prosecution for both the state and federal law violations simultaneously, keeping the perpetrator in custody in either the state or federal system, possibly without bail in one system, while the cases are being brought to trial. This may provide a very important window of safety for victims by allowing them to increase their security, while allowing further evaluation of perpetrators with a goal of learning what, if any, behavioral levers we can use to redirect them away from the victim.

18 U.S.C. section 2263 deals specifically with the pretrial release of a defendant and the fact that an alleged victim of a defendant charged under sections in this chapter (Chapter 110A) "shall be given an opportunity to be heard regarding the danger posed by the defendant" when considering release or conditions of release. Careful consideration should be taken by victims about whether to exercise this right. A personal appearance by victims, in sight or hearing of perpetrators, may energize the latter and encourage them to continue their behavior, not stop it. Certain obsessed individuals would consider any action on the part of their victims as confirmation that the victims care for them or love them. Some perpetrators are capable of sitting in court and, when victims plead their fear, they actually hear words of endearment rather than the actual words being said on the record. Other

perpetrators may be sexually or emotionally stimulated by hearing that their victims are afraid of them, thinking that it makes them more powerful. Consequently, before testifying under this section, a thorough assessment of the perpetrators, their behavior and their possible reaction to this testimony should be completed before the victims choose to exercise this option.

18 U.S.C. § 2261A (Interstate Stalking)

This section states that

> ...whoever travels in interstate or foreign commerce or within the special maritime and territorial jurisdiction of the United States, ... with the intent to kill, injure, harass or intimidate another person and in the course of or as a result of, such travel places that person in reasonable fear of the death of or serious bodily injury to that person, a member of the immediate family (as defined in section 115) of that person or the spouse or intimate partner of that person; or (2) with the intent (A) to kill or injure that person in another State or tribal jurisdiction or within the special maritime and territorial jurisdiction of the United States; or (B) to place a person in another State ... in reasonable fear of the death of or serious bodily injury to ... that person; ... a member of the immediate family (as defined in section 115) of that person; or ... a spouse or intimate partner of that person, uses the mail or any facility of interstate or foreign commerce to engage in a course of conduct that places that person in reasonable fear of the death of or serious bodily injury to any of the persons described ... shall be punished as provided for ... in section 2261(b).

This section provides penalties similar to those mentioned under Interstate Domestic Violence for acts that are caused by individuals when they travel or use the mail or any facility of interstate or foreign commerce (e.g., phones, cell phones, pagers, e-mail, private mailing services, etc.) to kill, injure, harass, intimidate or to place a person in reasonable fear of death or serious bodily injury to that victim or to certain people close to them. This language moves away from just the domestic violence relationship by expanding the definition of the victims and the behaviors that trigger the statute. In many cases, both sections 2261 and 2261A can be charged, which can increase the time that the perpetrator may be held in prison.

18 U.S.C. § 2262 (Interstate Violation of Protection Order)

This law is based on language similar to the stalking law, substituting behavior that violates a protective order for behavior of stalking. There are two offenses in this law as well, one involving the travel or conduct of the offender and one involving the causing of travel of the victim. The penalties are identical to the penalties for violating section 2261. An interesting aspect of this law is that it includes violations involving contact, harassment and physical proximity. This means that the law recognizes some of the subtler behaviors that individuals use, short of threats and violence, to destroy the peace of mind of victims. This law is enforceable when the conduct would violate the order in the jurisdiction that it was issued in, not the jurisdiction that it occurs in. In some cases, the fact that the behavior would not constitute a crime or violation of a restraining order where it occurs, but does in the issuing jurisdiction, means that victims can be protected in places where local enforcement would not have been possible. This provision is strengthened by the advent of the full faith and credit provision discussed next.

18 U.S.C. 2265 (a) (A Full Faith and Credit of Restraining Orders)

This section is very important for the protection of victims. It states that any protection order that is issued by any court of one State or Indian tribe, that is consistent with two provisions, "shall be accorded full faith and credit by the court of another State or Indian tribe ... and enforced as if it were the order of the enforcing State or tribe." The two provisions that have to be met are that the state or tribal court that issued the order had "jurisdiction over the parties and matter under the law of such State or Indian tribe; and reasonable notice and opportunity to be heard is given the person against whom the order is sought sufficient to protect that person's right to due process." It goes on to state that, in the case of *ex parte* orders, notice and opportunity to be heard had to have met the requirements of the state or tribe issuing the order "sufficient to protect the respondent's due process rights." From a practical perspective, this means that victims who are traveling outside the state or tribal area that issued a protective order should carry a copy of the papers filed to obtain the order, showing the hearing dates and the proof of service for their orders. This will allow them to provide those papers quickly to law enforcement to substantiate their claim that their order has been violated.

The law then addresses the idea that a protection order is not entitled to full faith and credit if an order has been issued by a state or tribal court against someone who has "petitioned, filed a complaint or otherwise filed a written pleading for protection against abuse by a spouse or intimate partner," "if no cross or counter petition, complaint or other written pleading was filed seeking such a protection order; or a cross or counter petition has been filed and the court did not make specific findings that each party was entitled to such an order." In other words, no full faith and credit are provided if someone obtains an order against a person who has prior claims of spousal or intimate partner abuse against the order seeker, when the victim of the prior claimed abuse did not have the opportunity to contest the order or the court did not make a specific finding concerning who, if anyone, should be entitled to the order. This provision, though difficult to sort out in the streets of another state, recognizes that sometimes orders are sought by harassers to further harass their victims and until a court sorts out the claims and counterclaims, that type of order should not be granted the enforceability as a standard order.

Fair Credit Reporting Act (FCRA)

This act, which is found at 15 U.S.C. 1681-1681u, establishes rules of conduct for all investigations conducted by third parties that affect the rights of consumers, including the granting of credit, issuance of insurance and obtaining or being retained in a job. This law, which originally had a very narrow scope, was changed in 1996, thus creating a huge impact on the way investigations could be conducted, so the rights of consumers could be protected. Changes to the law became effective on March 31, 2004, when H.R. 2622, the Fair and Accurate Credit Transactions Act of 2003 (FACTA), took effect. In relation to violence assessments, this law has the most bearing when the assessment is being done by an employer on his employee and the gathering of information during the process is *partially or wholly conducted by a third party* (nonemployee of that employer) and the results of the assessment *could have* an "adverse impact" (e.g., reduced compensation, reduced ability to be promoted, loss of business reputation, loss of employment, etc.) on that person's employment. Since it is very difficult, if not impossible, to conceive that a valid violence assessment, at its outset, would not have a potential to create an adverse impact, it would fall under this law. This law would not pertain to the assessment of any third party (nonemployee) to the company or enterprise or an assessment for a private person on another person where no employment relationship existed.

This law normally requires prior notification to consumers (targets of the assessment), when it could have an adverse impact and requires their permission to proceed with the assessment (investigation). It also requires that a copy of the report, whether verbal or written, generated by the process be provided to the consumer (employee) before any adverse action is taken. Given that many violence assessments are being conducted on individuals who have exhibited volatile and aggressive behavior that triggered the assessment, prior notice and consent are not usually viable options. Investigations involving the possibility of misconduct, such as threats of violence, were the reason for the modification of the law. Under FACTA, Section 603 of the law was amended to exclude "communications" that are made to an employer in connection with an investigation that concerns either suspected misconduct related to employment, or compliance with federal, state or local laws and regulations, or any pre-existing written policies of the employer. Additionally, the communication cannot have been made for the purposes of investigating creditworthiness, credit standing, or credit capacity and the communication is not provided to anyone except the employer or agent of the employer, federal or state officer, agency or department or any officer, agencyor department of a unit of general local government, etc. If the investigation of potential misconduct (i.e., violence risk assessment) by a third party meets the above requirements, then the employer does not have to disclose the nature or scope of the investigation to the person under investigation, have the employee authorize the investigation in writing, provide a copy of the investigation report to the employee before taking adverse action or provide detailed information about the investigation, investigation's results, or the employee's rights under the FCRA. The employer does have to provide "a summary containing the nature and substance of the communication upon which the adverse action is based," but it does not have to provide the summary until and unless some adverse action is taken based on the investigation and the employer does not have to identify the sources of information (including witnesses) the investigation used, if it obtained the information only for the purpose of the investigation (assessment). It is still our strong recommendation that employers, working with employment counsel, review and consider all the relevant federal and state laws regarding their responsibilities to their employees and make an informed decision about how to proceed.

A series of actions, when taken in concert, have served as an additional hedge against claims of wrongdoing on this law in assessment cases. This packet of actions is not meant as a complete shield from all claims under this law and has not been tested before the Federal Trade Commission (FTC). It is meant to possibly further lessen legal exposure under this law while maximizing the ability to conduct a valid assessment, which is viewed by most people as the higher priority and the greater exposure. The workaround is as follows: If the employer retains a third-party violence assessor or third parties in the assessment process, such as outside legal counsel, investigators or investigative resources such as databases, then the

1. Organizational representatives (employees) conduct initial interviews of knowledgeable parties and provide that information to the assessor.
2. Violence assessors conduct a background investigation of the aggressor, without notifying the client that they are doing so. Assessors use that report for the purpose of enhancing their assessment opinion, but share no specific information on the material discovered with the client. Although assessors could share the information with another third party (e.g., outside counsel) if so desired, as long as clients (employers) are provided no information from any background, they could not use that information for any adverse employment decision.
3. Assessors conduct a direct interview with any collateral witness or the aggressor; an employee of the organization is also present at

the interview. The employee takes notes of the interview that would be used as the basis of any adverse employment action and the assessor takes notes for the purposes of his assessment. Assessor's notes are never provided to the client.

4. Assessors deliver their opinion of risk with no suggestion or guidance to the client about what type of employment action to take in relation to the individual and do not specifically mention any information that was not provided by witnesses or aggressors in the presence of an organizational representative.

It should be noted that many states have their own version of the FCRA, such as California's ICRAA, which may have slightly different rules that have to be managed for legal exposure, while also attempting to accommodate the federal law. Care should be taken to craft an assessment and intervention process that threads a path that creates the least disturbance through these legal thickets. This is important not just because no entity likes getting sued, but, from a violence management perspective, assessors and organizations should recognize that if the rights of aggressors are trampled, such treatment can become a validation or rationalization for them that the only way of "protecting" themselves is by the use of violence. Thus, if we are careful to maintain our efforts to protect the rights of aggressors while conducting the assessment and intervention, we may be lessening the available emotional or psychological fuel they could use to launch themselves into a more violent trajectory.

Americans with Disabilities Act (ADA)

This act is often discussed in the violence assessment process because of its requirements to make reasonable accommodation for an individual's disabilities. Many of the behaviors that lead to violence assessments in the workplace initially are thought to have some connection to medical conditions (psychological, emotional or physical) that may cause the behavior of concern. The good news is that, even though it will always be important to consider this law in relation to any case in an employment setting, it does not shield people whose behavior meets a certain level of harassment, threats or violence regardless of their medical condition. The U.S. Equal Employment Opportunity Commission (EEOC) issued Enforcement Guidance on the Americans with Disabilities Act and Psychiatric Disabilities and placed a copy of it on its Web site on February 22, 2002. This document is one example of a long stream of material that provides guidance on how the ADA applies to given circumstances. That document addresses a series of compliance issues in a question-and-answer format. Question 32 asks: "How should an employer deal with an employee with a disability who is engaging in misconduct because s/he is not taking his/her medication?" The answer is, "The employer should focus on the employee's conduct and explain to the employee the consequences of continued misconduct in terms of uniform disciplinary procedures. It is the employee's responsibility to decide about medication and to consider the consequences of not taking medication." Footnote 72 of the document goes on to state: "If the employee requests reasonable accommodation in order to address the misconduct, the employer must grant the request, subject to undue hardship." This shows an example of the reasoning of the EEOC as it interprets the ADA. The EEO believes that misconduct is misconduct and can be disciplined as such, as long as the discipline is uniformly applied in the workplace. However, if a reasonable accommodation is requested to address the underlying cause of the misconduct, which may reasonably be understood to be based in a circumstance related to a disability, then reasonable accommodation is warranted.

The next section of this document, after question 32, titled "Direct Threat," goes into the regulations concerning dealing with a "direct threat," which is defined as "a significant risk of substantial harm to the health and safety of the individual or others that cannot be eliminated or reduced by reasonable accommodation." The footnote (75) goes on to cite 29 C.F.R. § 1630.2(r) (1996) and states: "To determine whether an individual would pose a direct threat, the factors to be considered include: (1) duration of the risk; (2) nature and severity of the potential harm; (3) likelihood that the potential harm will occur; and (4) imminence of the potential harm." This section then goes on to state: "The determination that an individual poses a 'direct threat' must be based on an individualized assessment of the individual's present ability to safely perform the functions of the job, considering a reasonable medical judgment relying on the most current medical knowledge or the best available objective evidence." It concludes by pointing out that: "an individual does not pose a 'direct threat' simply by virtue of having a history of psychiatric disability or being treated for a psychiatric disability."

From a practitioner's perspective, this "individualized assessment" is exactly what we are concerned with in this book. Rather than just looking at the psychiatric condition and the professional literature's quantification of violence risk for that condition, the process of assessment looks at the behavior, the motivations or causes of the behavior, the likelihood that it could lead to substantial risk and the nature, severity and imminence of the potential harm. A valuable book on the specific subject of "fitness for duty" evaluations has recently been written by Anthony V. Stone[2] and, if you are interested in this topic, we encourage you to read this book. Remember, people have the responsibility to manage their conduct to the level required of all employees. A disability does not give someone a "magic card" that absolves him from responsibility for his own conduct.

Title VII: (42 U.S.C. § 2000e)

Title VII of the Civil Rights Act of 1964 prohibits employment discrimination based on race, color, religion, sex and national origin.[3] In a violence assessment context, this law is often involved in cases where the aggressors claim that the cause of their inappropriate behavior is discrimination on the part of the victim population. Violations of this law are also regularly claimed when individuals have been terminated and they file a wrongful termination claim, stating that they were not fired because of their actions, but because of some protected attribute. The important thing to remember as a practitioner is to make certain that you stick to assessing the behavior of the individual. If you stay focused on the behavior, not being influenced by any of the protected attributes, you will be able to defend yourself against any claims of discrimination. If you are not an employee of the entity that has asked you to do the assessment, remember that you should not be involved in guiding or directing any employment outcome related to your assessment, but you can provide information about how you believe the person might act if certain employment actions are taken. This also will fortify you against claims of discrimination. Certainly, employers should always consider the employment action they are planning to take in the context of whether it is similar to or different from what they have done in the past under similar circumstances, and whether their action is in line with their employment policies and conduct rules. If there is a change in this case, it should be clearly documented as to why they made their decision, so that a claim of discrimination can be successfully defended. Concentrating on behavior will inoculate you from most claims under this section of the law.

Occupational Safety and Health Act of 1970 (OSHA)

This law[4] was passed to form the Occupational and Health Administration and create the ability for the federal government to aid the states in enhancing worker safety. Over the years, OSHA has become involved in a variety of issues related to violence in the workplace.[5] The first duty cited under this law (29 U.S.C. § 654) is: "Each employer shall furnish to each of his employees employment and a place of employment which is free from recognized hazards that are causing or are likely to cause death or serious physical harm to his employees; ...." In the area of violence assessment and threat management, this clause has been interpreted as a mandate that requires employers to recognize and intervene to protect their employees from foreseeable acts of violence. If employers who fall under OSHA do not maintain employee safety, they can be cited and fined. In the early 1990s, as employers were waking up to the issue of violence in the workplace, this law was a major factor cited by legal staff and other employment professionals to acquire the resources necessary to begin the process of violence assessment program development and implementation. By the beginning of this century, most businesses in the United States had moved beyond the need to be reminded of their obligations in the area of violence assessment and management. Consequently, this law will continue to be relevant to most practitioners only in the most egregious cases of violence, when the employer has ignored repeated notifications of the possibility of violence or did an inadequate job of managing an incident. Most, if not all, states also have their own versions of this act and employers can also be subject to citations and fines from their state agencies for negligence in managing the threat of violence or acts of violence in the workplace.

Family Educational Rights and Privacy Act (FERPA)

This law (20 U.S.C. § 1232g; 34 CFR Part 99) came to prominent notice in relation to violence risk assessment during the post-incident assessment of the Virginia Tech school shooting which occurred on April 16, 2007 in the United States. A total of 33 died, including the perpetrator, and 23 were injured. Very few, if any, readers of this book will need to be briefed on this shooting, but one of the outcomes of the incident analysis was an exposure of the common beliefs that FERPA and the Health Insurance Portability and Accountability Act (HIPPA) precluded organizations, particularly schools, from sharing information that could be used as the basis for reporting behavior of concern involving students to others. Post-incident, this was discussed in depth and the results were prominently mentioned in the report complied on the incident for the governor of Virginia.* The upshot of this was that we learned that nothing in FERPA precludes anyone in an educational institution from reporting his or her behavioral observations and interactions with any student to others who have a reasonable interest in knowing those behaviors and interactions, including persons designated in an educational environment to receive that information for safety reasons (e.g., designated violence risk assessment personnel, campus administrators, law enforcement, etc.). Also, since FERPA preempts HIPPA when FERPA has applicable language, such as around medical records in counseling clinics on college and university campuses, there can be some appropriate sharing of information for safety-related reasons.† However, it is unclear at this time whether that allowance preempts applicable state laws around the privacy of medical records or is just another consideration that must be weighed in the development of an appropriate information sharing process for violence risk assessment. Rather than wait for an incident to bring these

* Virginia Tech Review Panel, 2007.
† 34 CFR Part 99.36.

matters forward for discussion and resolution, we would encourage the reader, if you are subject to FERPA, HIPPA or any other law, to work proactively with legal counsel to develop, train in and maintain a thoroughly vetted program of notification and information gathering and sharing that addresses all the laws and regulations that you are subject to as an organization. The time to struggle with this is not in the midst of a serious case.

Expert Witness Presentation of Violence Assessment in Court

This discussion is relevant to violence assessors because of our need, in some cases, to enter a courtroom and justify decisions that we have been a part of making, particularly those that affect someone's life or liberty. At the federal level, most of these discussions begin with Federal Rules of Evidence and move quickly to the *Daubert*[6] decision and keep going. We are going to stop at *Daubert* because it brings up the major issues we want to address about expert testimony. The *Daubert* decision looked at several things, but was centered around whether Rule 702 of the Federal Rules of Evidence superseded an earlier legal decision, *Frye*,[7] and the U.S. Supreme Court found that it did. The majority opinion, written by Justice Blackmun, does an excellent job of defining what the job of a trial judge is in determining whether an expert can testify and to what. It is interesting that, in our research of this decision, we discovered that much written on it actually appears to misstate the *Daubert* decision, making up certain requirements that need to be met in every case to meet the standard. It is best to do your own research in this area and, when working with attorneys in preparation for your testimony, to talk with them at length about the process and how they plan to approach the *voir dire*, the process that the judge will use to determine whether you will be *qualified* to present expert testimony in the matter being tried.

Rule of Evidence 702 states: "If scientific, technical or other specialized knowledge will assist the trier of fact to understand the evidence or to determine a fact in issue, a witness qualified as an expert by knowledge, skill, experience, training or education, may testify thereto in the form of an opinion or otherwise, if (1) the testimony is based upon sufficient facts or data, (2) the testimony is the product of reliable principles and methods and (3) the witness has applied the principles and methods reliably to the facts of the case." Rules of Evidence 703 and 704 go on to make clear that experts must have disclosed, prior to the trial, the facts and data they will be relying on to form their opinion and that there are certain areas where an opinion would not be admissible because such decisions that would have to be made by the "trier of fact (jury, or judge in a nonjury trial) alone."

The *Daubert* decision builds on Rule 702 and specifically states that first the judge has to, "pursuant to Rule 104(a)," determine "whether the expert is proposing to testify to (1) scientific knowledge that (2) will assist the trier of fact to understand or determine a fact in issue." The opinion then goes on to state that they would "not presume to set out a definitive checklist or test," but they do suggest several possibly relevant lines of inquiry, including (1) whether the scientific theory or technique has been tested, (2) whether the theory or technique has been subjected to peer review and publication, (3) whether the court has considered the "known or potential rate of error" of the theory or technique and (4) whether the theory or technique has a "general acceptance" in the scientific community that is interested in the particular specialized knowledge. Unfortunately, though this opinion clearly details how each of these criteria may not be relevant in a particular case, many commentaries on this decision have stated that these items are a checklist that needs to be met for evidence to be admissible.

In a violence assessment context, each case should be approached as if it would have to be defended in court. That means that each practitioner should be focused in his ongoing professional development to enhance his understanding of the field in a way that will strengthen his ability to be found an expert by the courts. This process would therefore include continually absorbing the scientific information available in all the various fields that are encompassed by threat and violence assessment. It also means, at this time, to meet the current generally accepted "standard" of the field, you should:

- Use an assessment protocol that includes, at a minimum, the review of all legally available public and private records that can provide information concerning the subject's past behavior and decisions.
- Conduct interviews with available collateral witnesses.
- Consider the use of an organized system of information analysis (e.g., HCR-20, SARA, PCL-R, etc.) to provide a different perspective on your data.
- Interview the subject of the assessment — if at all possible, from a safety and logistical perspective.

We recognize that this last item, the interviewing of the instigator directly, is a point of difference among some practitioners in the field. The authors of this book have had discussions about this at length. Cawood always starts from the premise that instigators have the most knowledge of whether, when and why they will act violently, so interviewing them provides the most direct information that can be acquired. Then, as he gathers information from collateral sources in any particular case, he begins to determine whether an interview of the instigator can be accomplished in a safe and cost-effective manner and whether the interview itself is likely to make the current situation worse. He does not want to take any step in the assessment process that is likely to make the situation more unsafe. So one must weigh all these factors to determine whether an interview of the instigator can or should be done and who should do it. After much discussion, Corcoran has been swayed toward this opinion, but still holds some reservations. For further discussion of this protocol, see Chapter 4, "Formula for Assessment," and Chapter 11, "Practical Ethical Issues."

Obviously, each state of the United States and every country with an adversarial court process will have its own specific rules of evidence that apply to the qualification of experts and the admission of expert testimony. However, a good grounding in the principles stated above will go a long way toward beginning the process of preparing to be an expert witness.

Protective and Restraining Orders

These orders, in all their various types, are a well-known, yet eternally debated intervention tool for a potentially violent situation. Currently, in the violence assessment and intervention community, there is much discussion about their use or misuse in various case scenarios. Complicating the discussion is that, to a large degree, the criminal justice community, not only in the United States but in many industrialized countries, recommends, in some cases forcefully, that all cases it encounters that present certain case facts, such as domestic or intimate violence, acquire such an order. In some cases, the presentation of this recommendation implies to victims that if the order is not obtained, follow-up law enforcement response for future requests for assistance will be delayed or not forthcoming at all. We recognize that this implication is false in the vast majority of the jurisdictions, but if victims perceive that this is the case, it still affects their decision making.

Protective and restraining orders are court orders that require the party who is the subject of the order, either individual or entity, to comply with listed behavioral guidance or face criminal penalties for violating a court order. Protective orders, in most jurisdictions, are issued in conjunction with another criminal matter under adjudication (e.g., assault, stalking, spousal battery, battery, etc.), and restraining orders are generally issued in a civil court, either as stand-alone cases in which harassment, threats or a credible fear for physical safety are alleged or as a part of other cases in which conduct of one party has led to a request for the order. An emergency protective order (EPO) is a variant of the protective order that allows an order to be issued in some jurisdictions after a law enforcement officer requests the order verbally and an on-call judge agrees to issue the order immediately, due to extreme circumstances.

All of these orders can have one or a variety of behavioral boundaries incorporated into them. These boundaries could include a "stay away" provision for a variety of settings including home, work, church, child-care sites, relatives' homes and other locations of regular attendance, a "no contact" provision for all forms of contact (e.g., direct, through a third party, electronic, through the mail, etc.), a weapon provision (e.g., no new acquisition, no possession, surrender of weapons, etc.), custody or visitation provisions, "kick out" orders for leaving a shared domicile, etc.

All the orders require that individuals who are subject to the order be, at some point, notified of the order (e.g., through a court proceeding in which they are in attendance, through a service of process or through contact with law enforcement) and that they will have an opportunity to contest the order and have it modified or removed. However, in many jurisdictions, the order remains valid during the period of contention, and until a formal ruling has been made. This ability to contest an order is a requirement for the federal enforcement of an order, as mentioned above.

In the case of civil orders, the normal procedure is that a person seeks an order by filing a request with the court. This order can be sought in two ways: first, *ex parte*, in which the party, for a variety of reasons, seeks the issuance of a temporary restraining order (TRO) prior to notice of the request for an order (service of process) being provided to the subject of the order or, second, in a regular fashion in which the persons are served with the court papers and appear at a court hearing if they wish to contest the order, with no TRO having been issued. There is normally a delay of several days, if not weeks, between the filing of the order and the hearing on the order. In California, it is normally in the 15-day range. In the vast majority of the cases we have worked in relation to violence assessment, the restraining orders are sought *ex parte* so that victims can get the protection of the order immediately and have an opportunity to serve the subjects without providing them the ability to flee the area to avoid service. After a hearing is held, the judge decides whether to issue a permanent restraining order or to vacate the order. In the case of issuance of the permanent order, the subjects of the order have to be informed of the result, either by appearing in court or by subsequent service of process. Then the order must be filed with the relevant law enforcement agencies so that it can be enforced. The order is usually valid for a period of 3 to 10 years, depending on jurisdiction and case circumstances, but some orders can be issued or renewed for a life-long term.

A variety of issues must be considered when the use of a protective or restraining order is being contemplated. The most important consideration is whether the violence assessment indicates that the order will significantly escalate the likelihood of violence, rather than have no effect or a deescalating effect. In most studies that have been conducted and reported in the last 10 years in the United States, the majority of the orders have helped control the behavior of the subject of the order eventually and have increased the victim's perceived sense of safety, as well as the actual safety of the victims who sought the order.[8] One study that did not find restraining orders to be of great benefit was conducted by Harrell, Smith and Newmark (1993).[9] In this study of domestic violence orders over a 1-year period, they found that 60% of the women reported violations of the order. It was also reported that women who had not obtained orders and those who had done so reportedly experienced similar levels of continued physical abuse. Grau, Fagan and Wexler (1984) reported similar results.[10] A more recent study of 2,691 abused women in Kings County in the state of Washington, conducted by University of Washington researchers and published in August 2002 in the *Journal of the American Medical Association,* found that women who received permanent protective orders, lasting a year or more, experienced 80% fewer physical assaults than women who did not seek an order or who had only temporary orders. In fact, physical violence increased toward women who did not seek any order during the period of the TRO, and it is speculated that this is because of the attempt to regain some control by the abuser over a woman who is breaking away. What is unclear is whether these results would be confirmed in populations of victims who had obtained the orders for reasons other than domestic violence (such as stalking, threats, intimidation and harassment) that were not based in a domestic relationship. Certainly, as these contrasting perspectives illustrate, no action in a violence intervention should be taken based on the statistical likelihood of any particular outcome, as each case is unique and all studies have a certain percentage of cases in which escalation has occurred. There have been many media accounts of victims who have obtained protective and restraining orders only to be killed in their homes, work sites or on the courthouse steps, which is exactly what we hope to avoid by doing violence assessment and intervention.

In general, we see protective and restraining orders being most valuable in two particular ranges of cases: (1) those assessed in the lowest 20% for potential physical violence and (2) those assessed in the top 20% of potential physical violence. In the first range, the lower 20%, we are not concerned at the moment with immediate escalation to physical violence, but, based on all the factors involved, we may recommend obtaining a protective or restraining order to test perpetrators' ability or willingness to control their behavior when official consequences can occur. The behavioral information learned during the process of obtaining the order plus the behavior that results after the order can provide a rich set of data to enhance the ongoing assessment and intervention strategy, assuming the behavior of concern does not stop immediately. In the second range, the upper 20%, when we recommend the orders, we do so with no expectation that the order will curb the potential for physical violence and we believe that the potential is so imminent that we have already implemented a protective (security) process that is comprehensive and can address the possibility that seeking the order could stimulate a retaliatory response. We seek the orders at this level for the purpose of showing "due diligence" on the part of victims in using all the remedies available to them, as well as the possibility that the order will provide enhanced law enforcement and court attention, if necessary. In all cases, but particularly the 60% of cases that fall between those two ranges on the assessment spectrum, we are very cautious when recommending seeking an order, due to the uncertainty of the behavior that can result.

Some of the factors that we consider prior to recommending seeking any order are:

- *Do we believe that the case facts would allow the issuance of the order?* We never recommend the pursuit of any order unless we are extremely comfortable that it will be granted. Seeking and failing to get an order can provide a host of negative consequences including:
  1. empowerment of the perpetrators, since they have "won" against the victim or "beaten" the court system
  2. increasing the victims' fear that they have no means of protecting themselves — particularly if they had to testify as a part of the process of seeking the order
  3. the potential exposure of entities (e.g., employers, victim organizations, etc.) or individuals (e.g., family members, co-workers, friends, etc.) who assisted in the process and now might become additional targets of the perpetrator without the benefit of protection from the order, possibly removing these supports as potential sources of safety for the victim, the revealing of intervention strategy, etc.
- *Has the person been subject to an order in the past and what behavior has resulted from the implementation of the order?* Certainly, if people have been subject to past orders and there has been a series of violations, seeking the order would be of limited value because we should have no expectation, based on past behavior, that the order would be effective. However, if they stopped the behavior after the past order was issued, this increases the probability that an order could work in the case at hand.
- *If the order were issued, do we have a high degree of confidence that the protectee(s) and the law enforcement jurisdictions involved would follow up on any violations of the order and arrest the individual for those violations?* If we do not believe that the protectee(s) of the order will document and report violations in a timely manner or that the law enforcement jurisdictions involved will arrest for violations of the order, then we are very hesitant to recommend an order be sought. This is because both of these elements, reporting and an active law enforcement response, are required to provide the enforcement of the order. The threat and reality of order enforcement is required to provide the visceral and real behavioral constraint the

order is meant to instill in the perpetrator. Repeated violations with no significant consequences strongly increase the probability that the perpetrator will perceive that the order has no power. Therefore, it becomes useless as a deterrent to future inappropriate behavior and may actually empower perpetrators by allowing them to believe that they are more powerful than a court order and therefore the court. Actions speak louder than words; consequently, arrest has more effect than asking perpetrators to stop their behavior.

- *Have perpetrators told victims that seeking an order will have no value in stopping their behavior?* In cases where this has been stated, we are always concerned that seeking the order may cause perpetrators to react just to show that they are not making idle boasts. Therefore, seeking the order could have an escalating effect because such people feel a need to protect their image of themselves as a "truthful person." As a part of the violence assessment, answers to questions of these persons' prior behavior when having stated they will act in a certain way if particular situations arise would be helpful to evaluate here, also — the value they have placed in the past on being perceived as "persons of their word."

- *What will the effect be on the other stabilizers in the perpetrator's life, if we seek and obtain the order?* This question addresses the public nature of these orders and the impact they can have on a person's family relationships, employment opportunities and future rights as a citizen. Many employers are now conducting background investigations of prospective employees and the presence of a restraining or protective order is a significant hurdle for an individual to overcome in being hired these days. Is the value of the order judged to enhance the safety of our victim to a greater degree than the reaction the order may cause if it becomes more difficult for the perpetrator to get a job or change jobs? (In other words, if the order means the perpetrator will never be gainfully employed, will that increase the risk to the victim?) Our goal is to enhance the safety of the victim, which, when we take any particular step, requires us to consider the entire dynamic, not just the perspective of the victim. Safety of the victim should be our first priority and, if the seeking of an order or any other intervention is considered with the impact it will have on the entire dynamic, we will be meeting our most important obligation.

- *Can someone else get the order and have our victim as a secondary beneficiary?* This strategy is often considered when there are multiple victims of a perpetrator, but the violence assessor is not responsible for all of them. The idea is that, by not having our protectees as the people or entities seeking the order, they may not be perceived as directly responsible for action. Therefore, we increase the possibility that they would be a secondary rather than a primary target for any escalated behavior caused by the order, while still receiving the benefit of the order. We recently had a case in Oregon that illustrates this idea. An individual who had been sent to prison for threatening federal officers was being released from prison and, rather than seeking a separate restraining protective order for our protectees, the U.S. Attorney sought a protective order listing our protectees and over three dozen other persons to be protected. Since it was the government seeking the order, it appeared that it was deciding to take this action on its own, while we received the benefit of the order. If we had decided to seek our own separate order, we would have created an individual dynamic with the perpetrator that would have increased his focus on our protectees — not a good thing, especially when, as in this case, the perpetrator is a criminal psychopath.

- *Will the order strengthen, in the mind of the perpetrator, the bond between the perpetrator and the protectee?* When an order is obtained, it links the protectee and subject of the order together for 3 or more years. In some cases, this linkage serves as a constant reminder to the perpetrators that the protectees have impacted their lives. This might continue to feed an obsession, instead of allowing it to end. We were consulted on a case in California involving a young man who was obsessed with Chelsea Clinton while she attended Stanford University. When contacted by the Secret Service, he stated that if they did not get a restraining order against him, he would get on a bus and come to Stanford to marry Chelsea. We were contacted concerning certain restraining order questions and we counseled that, given the case facts, it was possible that the perpetrator was requesting the order to "prove" a linkage to the victim and therefore the order would fuel his obsession with her. We suggested that an order not be sought until he proved by his actions he was willing to come to Stanford without "being kept away." A useful question in pursuing this question of linkage is whether perpetrators have been known to seek or obtain objects related to the victim as a way of fueling their obsessions. If so, what could be more powerful than an acknowledgment in a court of law that there is a connection between them?

Anti-Stalking Law

The first anti-stalking law was passed in California in 1990, Section 646.9 of the California Penal Code. By September 1993, all 50 states and the District of Columbia had some form of anti-stalking law.[11] In 1996, the U.S. Congress passed the federal stalking law, which was previously discussed in this chapter.[12] These laws were enacted because individuals were engaging in courses of conduct that were causing victims to fear for their safety and the safety of their families before restraining or protective orders had been obtained and violated. Therefore, these laws were meant to provide an additional tool to stop the escalation of behavior prior to violence being committed. In most jurisdictions, these laws require a series of acts (following, harassment, threats, etc.) carried out over a period of time less than 24 hours, that cause victims to fear for their safety or the safety of their families. In many states and other jurisdictions, the laws have been fine-tuned since their inception to incorporate new technology that stalkers use including pagers, cell phones, e-mail and other forms of electronic communication. Many of the laws have provisions for various levels of behavior to trigger various penalties. The important questions for all violence assessors to ask with all laws such as this are:

1. What are the various provisions of the current statute in the various jurisdictions where the case may reside?
2. Which jurisdiction is most likely to provide the level of prosecution believed to be necessary to increase the safety of your victim?
3. Will prosecution under this law increase or decrease the safety of the victim? In other words, how do we believe the perpetrator will act when arrested and convicted under this law and will that benefit or harm the victim's chances of long-term safety?

Other Statutes

Myriad other criminal and civil laws could be relevant to violence assessment and intervention. These include harassment statutes; trespass laws; terroristic-threat statutes; laws related to the intimidation of witnesses and victims; the use of electronic means to intimidate, harass and threaten; and the use of interstate services, including the mail, to intimidate, harass, threaten or harm another, etc. The more knowledgeable one is about the various laws and their applications, the more tools are available to victims to help divert an individual from harming them. Remember, a law or penalty will not stop a person from acting in a violent way if he or she is intent upon doing so. But the law can be used to make it more inconvenient for people to act and the distraction, obstruction or delay that enforcement of the law may create can cause them to choose to divert their path from violence or redirect their behavior away from the current victim. Compendiums of laws related to stalking or other threat crimes are available at the federal level and in many states or jurisdictions, which can simplify the process of learning about these types of laws. Many abused-women's organizations and the legal staffs that work with them have put together such materials in any area where a case may be located. It is always a good idea to educate yourself on the law, rather than relying on others who may not be as knowledgeable about how to use it, from a behavioral perspective, in the intervention process. As an example, the type of legal compendium I am suggesting has been issued by the District Attorney's Office for the County of Los Angeles concerning California law, titled *2002 Stalking and Criminal Threats,* as part of its Stalking and Threat Assessment Team, Target Crime Series. It covers the penal, elections, government and motor vehicle codes, protective orders and process, restraining orders and process and other miscellaneous and important legal tools for use in cases involving the potential for violence. All practitioners should have a reference like this available to them and keep it updated for their use in any jurisdiction that they work in regularly.

Other Concepts

Duty to Warn

This legal concept is embedded in every workplace violence-related case. It involves the idea that, if people have not been told about serious or hidden dangers and get hurt, those who knew about the dangers can be held responsible, either civilly or criminally.[13] An evaluation of possible violence in the workplace will require a discussion of who needs to be informed under the duty-to-warn concept and what they need to be told. I envision concentric circles of notification. Actual victims or directly named potential victims are in the centermost circle. Members of the immediate, physical workgroup of those victims are in the next circle out. Members of the workgroups on the same floor or in the same building as the victims are in the next circle out. Any employees on the same corporate campus are in the next circle out. Finally, all the employees in the entire company are in the last circle. Depending on the level of risk, visitors to the work site, such as customers, vendors, subcontractors, etc., may need to be considered as part of this process as well. The higher the assessed probability of physical harm, the more important the need to consider notification.

The important issues with duty to warn are "nesting messages," considerations of privacy, confidentiality and defamation, and recognizing that the duty to warn needs to be balanced with the reality that information can increase anxiety in the workforce and misjudging that balance point may cause more harm, in some cases physical harm, than not saying anything at all.

The concept of "nesting messages" comes from mathematics where you "nest" equations inside one another. This concept, like concentric circles, reinforces the idea that certain issues are separate but interdependent. However, the math equation has to be solved in the right sequence (inner equation outward) to correctly solve the overall equation. These concepts of individual dynamics coupled with interdependence and solving from the inner circle outward are central to an effective duty-to-warn strategy.

The potential or actual direct victims of physical violence have the most rights and the employer (and society in terms of victim's rights laws) has the greatest obligation to provide identified victims with information that will allow them to take measures to protect their own safety. Therefore, violence assessors, when they interview the potential or actual victim, should have a plan for how they will communicate an understanding of how this interview fits into the process of violence assessment, what that process entails, who will communicate with the victim as the process continues, what it will be possible to communicate versus what is privileged or falls under privacy or other restrictions and how that victim can communicate with the violence assessor when new instigator behavior comes to the attention of the victim. This communication during the initial interview constitutes that first step in documenting actions that fulfill duty-to-warn obligations.

If this first step is not appropriately handled and, in some cases, even when it is, the victims, often the violence assessor's best source of ongoing behavioral information, begin to withdraw from the process and start taking their own actions, actions that can be very disruptive to managing a violence situation. They may decide to begin their own investigation, inflame the situation by talking to other people, begin a secondary legal process for restraining or protective orders without understanding the consequences that could occur, hire their own security who may not understand how to best protect them or take other actions that become counterproductive. If their actions affect only their own safety, it is one thing. But in most violence assessment cases, the safety of others is involved as well — children, family members and co-workers. If the violence assessor or violence assessment team keeps in regular contact with the victims and continues to provide updates on the process and the assessment, we can minimize possible disruptive behaviors while continuing to meet our obligations.

The next part of the process is deciding what information needs to be shared with members of the other concentric circles and when. Crafting of these other messages should recognize that members of each of the circles will most likely talk to one another, regardless of requests for confidentiality. The messages must be congruent, even though they will not be identical. Our obligations to each of these groups is different, which, in general, means that we have to provide less specific process and assessment information to each circle as we move outward. The information we give each circle should be an extension of the information from the middle, or more disruption will occur. In plain language, if anyone in the process is given information that is not a "watered-down" version of the inner circle information, but is obviously contradictory to what other people have been told, they all begin to distrust the process and start their own less-educated process, leading to disruption and possible disaster. As an example, we cannot tell victims that we have great concern about their safety at a specific moment and communicate to the general workforce, in that same moment, that there is no immediate cause for concern.

The question of when the information is communicated can help, in some cases, solve the "what is said" concern. As stated already, the process of duty to warn starts immediately with the victims or directly identified potential victims, but generally all other circles are only provided information on a "need to know" basis until the initial assessment process has been completed and the intervention plan has been formed. Need to know, prior to these steps being taken, is driven by people who approach and ask what is going on because they have heard rumors in cases in which additional protective measures have been rapidly introduced to the environment, thus raising concerns. In the case of people coming forward based on rumors, it is suggested that those people be used to identify sources of leakage and given general messages deflecting them for the moment. This might be reflected in a conversation like:

> "John, I wanted to stop by and ask you what the heck all the activity in the conference room is about. The rumor is that someone is going to come in and kill us."
> "How many people are talking, Randy?"
> "Quite a few."
> "Why do people think the activity in the conference room is violence related?"
> "I don't know specifically, but after you interviewed Patrick, he came out and talked to a few people and it picked up from there."
> "Well, I can't share with you right now exactly what is going on in the conference room, but I can tell you that if I believed anyone was going to come into the company right now and hurt anyone, I would be certain to let all of you know that. I appreciate your letting me know what is going on in the rumor mill and will commit to you that, when we get farther along in understanding the issue we are assessing, we will get people together and let you all know what we can."

After that conversation, John should inform the violence assessor or violence assessment team about the conversation and a member of the team should quickly re-interview Patrick and ascertain whom he has talked to and what was said. This information may accelerate the process of providing information to the workgroup to get ahead of the rumor mill and decrease organizational anxiety.

If additional protective measures, due to immediate concerns for safety, are instituted rapidly in an environment, then an equally rapid communication with the group affected is important to minimize disruption. Such a communication needs to address the reality of what is being done, but temper the speculation until thorough assessment and intervention planning can be accomplished. Such a message might come in an e-mail with a subject line like "Enhanced Security" and a message of:

> Starting on Monday, the company has decided to enhance the security of the site by closing doors that have been propped open, placing new emphasis on the wearing of badges and increasing the use of security personnel in public areas. We have taken these steps because a situation has come to our attention that we are currently assessing and in an abundance of caution we decided that it was appropriate to increase security. However, we also believe that these efforts reinforce the idea that the safety of the workplace is important to everyone at ... Company and hope these measures refresh everyone's awareness of their responsibility to participate in helping increase that safety. We will keep you informed as we move ahead and thank you for your understanding and participation in increasing safety at ... Company.

An e-mail like this tells a limited version of the truth, wraps in some other focus (general safety) to soften the message of concern and explains some of the more visible steps that the company has taken to enhance security. This will cause 95% of any work group to move on to their real work, while 5% will contact someone for more information, where they should receive an interaction such as that scripted above between John and Randy.

It is important to note here that anything you communicate, whether orally or in writing, might not only be used against you later in court but, more importantly, could be heard by or communicated to the instigator and cause a reaction. Violence assessors and violence assessment teams should always carefully craft their questions (since all questions provide knowledge of what the assessor is interested in) and any information they give anyone in the process, to take into account what the instigators' reaction might be if they heard that piece of information at the time of the assessment. This care in handling information and possible behavioral reactions to it, from both the instigator and the other interested parties, will pay handsome dividends in successfully preventing violence, reducing victim and organizational anxiety and meeting legal obligations.

Tarasoff Warning

A "Tarasoff" is a specific type of warning provided by mental health professionals who are told by patients that the patients plan to harm a named person or target and the mental health professionals believe, in their judgment, that the threat is credible. This warning and its various requirements arise out of case law, specifically, *Tarasoff v. Regents of University of California*,[14]

and follow on decisions further refining this decision and laws and regulations that have been promulgated to encode this legal decision. I will not give
a full explanation of this, as it is readily available in other publications and
on the World Wide Web, but from a practitioner's perspective, several points
should be noted about this type of warning:

- When a client or other party receives this warning it establishes,
  from a legal/organizational perspective, a very high immediate level
  of presumed risk, which should trigger an immediate assessment
  process with discussion of a security plan for physical protection.
  Whoever is receiving the warning — the potential victim, the victim's employer or law enforcement in the state of the victim (a state
  Department of Justice) or local jurisdiction, depending on how this
  decision has been encoded into the laws or regulations of the mental
  health professional who is providing the warning — is being told
  that, in the mind of the person providing the warning, this is a credible threat. So it is essential that persons receiving the Tarasoff begin
  their own process of assessment and intervention. The reporting
  party is not obligated to do anything but provide notification; consequently, safe management (e.g., assessment and intervention) is the
  responsibility of the victims and those responsible for protecting the
  victims. Until further information is gained and evaluated, high risk
  should be presumed for the protection of the victim. Not responding
  accordingly will raise liability problems if an action should occur
  and appropriate defensive actions were not taken in an attempt to
  protect, as required by law or regulation.
- In the majority of Tarasoff warnings I have been asked to respond to,
  mental health practitioners who issued the warnings had no grounding in the literature of violence assessment and therefore were making a "gut-level" decision because the patient's statements scared them
  and they, in turn, were covering their legal obligations. They have no
  obligation and, in most cases, no legal right to share the details of the
  specific behavior threatened or reasons that they consider the information to constitute a credible threat. They just have the obligation
  to notify the victim and law enforcement in the appropriate jurisdiction. Therefore, you should not expect to be able to call the mental
  health professional back and get details for your assessment. If that
  happens it is wonderful, but in most cases, all you may be able to get is
  confirmation that the Tarasoff was provided and information about
  who, other than your known victims, might also have been notified.
- Because of the nature of the Tarasoff warning, its limitations and
  what obligations it sets in motion, it is very important that a wide

range of personnel in organizations you work in or work with be trained to identify and route these warnings to the appropriate internal personnel immediately upon receipt. These contact personnel could be switchboard operators, receptionists, desk personnel in law enforcement, human resource or personnel employees or managers or supervisors in any organization. They should be trained in their obligations under the law and organizational policy as they pertain to these warnings and whom they should notify that they have received one. Ideally, what would occur is that a call would come in and the person who receives it could identify that it qualifies as a Tarasoff, ask the caller if this is a Tarasoff warning and then transfer the caller to the appropriate intake personnel designated to receive the call. These individuals should be trained not only to capture all the information that the caller provides, but also to attempt to probe to gain specific information about when the threateners made these statements, what specific type of violence they mentioned and when they said they would act out this threat. It is possible that, in the heat of the moment of notification, callers will reveal information that they would not otherwise reveal, particularly after their anxiety recedes and they think about their other legal obligations. It is best to train people to take advantage of these opportunities, just as we train them to talk to people who call in bomb threats.

Privilege, Confidentiality, Privacy and Defamation

I address these concepts together because they all deal with appropriate handling of communicated information in the violence assessment and intervention process. As noted above, this can have both legal and behavioral (physical) consequences.

The issue of *privilege*, meaning legal privileges in the nondisclosure of certain communications, both orally and in writing, arises in most violence assessment situations. The practitioner should always consider this issue as the assessment and intervention process moves along. If assessment and intervention work is done under the direction of legal counsel, in anticipation of civil litigation alleging various torts (negligence, wrongful termination, discrimination, harassment, invasion of privacy, defamation, etc.), various protections against release of information can be claimed, including work product privilege. This means that if legal counsel is present on conference calls or in assessment team meetings, most of those discussions can be privileged against certain types of release. When certain types of reports are released and work product privilege is claimed at the beginning of the document, they also can be shielded. These protections can be activated by someone bringing this to everyone's attention during a meeting or call or noting it on a document with a statement such as:

This is a confidential communication. This report and all information contained herein have been completed at the direction of legal counsel. It is to be considered as being of a confidential and privileged nature and subject to the attorney–client privilege and work product doctrine.

Sometimes this protection should not be sought because the document would be released to parties who would raise the question of whether the privilege has been waived by claiming it and then breaking it. An example would be trying to privilege a report given to a threatener under the Fair Credit Reporting Act. If that report were privileged and then released to the threatener, who then sued for wrongful termination, the issue could be raised that release of the document outside of the company waives the privilege as well as the privilege to all other parts of the process, including discussions, that led to the report. Because of this, legal counsel should be intimately involved in making these decisions at every step of the way. Not only will care in managing this issue potentially save tens or hundreds of thousands of dollars in legal fees and settlements in some cases, but not revealing certain evolving discussions and perceptions of an organization toward an instigator can also reduce the "narcissistic wounding"[15] that an instigator could feel when these discussions or thoughts are revealed, lowering the likelihood of ongoing violence.

Confidentiality is an issue that every victim, actual or potential, and every witness interviewed either raises or thinks about. They wonder who will know what they have said, including the instigator, and how will they be thought of or what might be done to them because of it. In addition to the legal issues of maintaining the confidentiality of investigations, once again there is the reality that if we do not appropriately address this issue, victims and witnesses will withhold certain key information from us and jeopardize the assessment and intervention process. During my interviews with both victims and witnesses, I make certain to address this issue at some point during the interview. I usually will say something like:

I am sure you are concerned about who will know what you tell me and how the information will be handled. First, the information you provide will be shared with only a small group of people in the organization who need to know the information for the purposes of the assessment and any intervention that the assessment drives. We are not telling people we interview, including the instigator (assuming we are interviewing the instigator in that particular case), exactly what any individual person said or didn't say. However, you can assume, as we do, that each person may make assumptions about who might have known or said certain things. We are asking each person we interview, as we are asking you, not to discuss the questions and answers given in this interview with anyone else in the process, because that may influence the information we get and therefore the results of the investigation. At some point in the future, if any action is taken that leads to consequences that involve a legal process (e.g., arrest, employment action, etc.), the information you provided may have to be released as a part of that legal process.

A statement like this wraps several important concepts together for both the organization that is conducting the assessment process and the interviewee. It explains that confidentiality will be maintained, but there are limits to that confidentiality. It foreshadows that some information may later appear to have leaked from the process, but it was just people drawing their own conclusions. Finally, it requests that the interviewee maintain confidentiality and explains why that is important.

Sometimes a victim or witness will come forward and start a conversation with the statement, "Before I tell you anything, you have to promise me that you will not tell anyone else about this." The person says this because he or she is frightened or very concerned and wants reassurance. In most cases, that type of absolute confidentiality is not possible, due to other superseding duties on the part of the listeners (e.g., their roles as a police officer, doctor, manager, supervisor, etc.). So the listeners should not promise what they cannot deliver, but can say something like:

Obviously, you are very concerned or you would not want to tell me. Why don't you tell me what is going on and then we can discuss what to do about it.

If the person continues to press for some kind of promise, the listener could state:

I can see that this really concerns you. I would like to promise I will not tell anyone else, but I can't. If you say certain things, I have a responsibility (to the community, the organization, your co-workers, etc.) to let certain people know so we can take steps to keep you and others safe. But, as I said before, we can talk about what we might do, after I know what you are so concerned about.

This type of acknowledgment of their concern, but with honest and realistic boundaries to confidentiality, will usually allow the person to feel comfortable enough to move forward, without binding the listeners to an inappropriate and indefensible course of action — indefensible, either because they have to break their word in fulfilling their more significant obligations or because they maintain the confidence and others are hurt because of it.

Privacy is a hot topic right now for much of the United States, post-9/11. The question is how much individual privacy we can maintain while still allowing us to gain information to thwart further terroristic acts. In the area of violence assessment and intervention, including counterterrorism, this has always been an issue to address. Several states, like California,[16] include a clause in their state constitutions mentioning the preservation of individual privacy. Invasion of privacy is a tort action and can be classified into several categories, including intrusion, publication of private facts, false light and misappropriation. For the purposes of violence assessment and intervention, the important thing to remember is that you should not share what you learn about any individuals or their actions with anyone who does not have a legitimate, defensible reason to know that information. In the case of organizations, that means those individuals who have been designated to know sensitive personal information, like attorneys, appropriate human resource or personnel staff and only the appropriate level and number of management to meet the needs of safety. Disclosure to these people only will help protect you from claims. In line with this, all written reports and other documentation should be designated confidential and maintained in a way that shows an effort has been made not to have that information shared outside the appropriate circle.

Another area of invasion of privacy that needs to be addressed is background investigations that accompany violence assessments. It will be difficult for the average citizen, including employees of any organization, to claim invasion of privacy if background investigations are conducted in a legal manner, with care taken during the interviews to avoid inappropriate disclosure of personal information about the subject of the investigation. Employers engaged in investigations for the purposes of violence assessments and who follow legal information-gathering processes should be able to defend against most, if not all, claims of invasion of privacy. Surveillance of the subject by private organizations while not on a company site, even though a legitimate investigative tool, may be found to be an invasion of privacy under some circumstances. Surveillance by law enforcement can bring charges of harassment. Chapter 6 addresses the other risks associated with surveillance as a security tool in violence case interventions.

Defamation is defined by the fifth edition of *Black's Law Dictionary* as "holding up of a person to ridicule, scorn or contempt in a respectable and considerable part of the community." It can occur either in written form (libel) or oral form (slander). The absolute defense against a claim of defamation is the fact that what was written or said is proven to be the truth. However, using that defense in a violence assessment case, though legally powerful, may not stop an act of aggression from occurring for a variety of emotional and psychological reasons. Calling a criminal psychopath a criminal psychopath in an inappropriate setting may trigger a violent event where none would have otherwise occurred. Being truthful does not always provide safety. Guarding against this claim, for both legal and behavioral reasons, is as simple as not saying anything to anyone who should not know about the information and not providing anything in writing to anyone who should not have it. Basically, the same guidelines that apply for confidentiality and privacy concerns also apply in this area. So take them to heart and make them operational in your assessments and interventions.

A good World Wide Web source for U.S. law is the Legal Information Institute site at www.4.law.cornell.edu. It allows access to the current law, as well as parallel authorities and topical references.

Summary

Knowledge of the law is a powerful tool in violence intervention. But, like all powerful tools, it must be intimately understood from a practical level, not just a theoretical one. Use the right laws at the right time, but always have other contingencies to protect physical safety.

Endnotes

1. See 18 U.S.C., Part 1, Chapter 110A, Sec. 2266 for the United States Code definitions of these terms and others used in the sections mentioned in this chapter.
2. Stone, Anthony V., *Fitness for duty: Principles, methods and legal Issues*, CRC Press LLC, Boca Raton, FL, 2000.
3. A copy of the act itself can be found on the EEOC web site at www.eeoc.gov/laws/vii.html.
4. 29 U.S.C § 650 et seq.
5. Guidelines for Preventing Workplace Violence for Health Care and Social Service Workers — OSHA 3148-1996 and Recommendations for Workplace Violence Prevention Programs in Late-Night Retail Establishments, to name the two most prominent
6. *Daubert v. Merrell Dow Pharmaceuticals* (92-102), 509 U.S. 579 (1993).
7. *Frye v. United States*, 54 App. D. C. 46, 293 F. 1013, No. 3968.
8. An example of this is found in Chapter 5 of *Domestic Violence and Stalking: The Second Annual Report to Congress under the Violence against Women Act*, which summarizes a report, "Civil Protection Orders: The Benefits and Limitations for Victims of Domestic Violence" issued by the National Center for State Courts. It goes into very great detail concerning these issues for three separate jurisdictions in the United States.
9. Harrell, Adell, Barbara Smith and Lisa Newmark. 1993. *Court processing and the effects of restraining orders for domestic violence victims*. Final Report to the State Justice Institute, Washington, D.C.: The Urban Institute.
10. Grau,. J., Fagan J. and Wexler, S. 1984. Restraining orders for battered women: issues of access and advocacy. *Women and Politics* 4,13–28.
11. National Center for Victims of Crime, Legislative Database.
12. *National Defense Authorization Act for Fiscal Year 1997*, Public Law 104-201, § 1069.
13. See California Penal Code section 387, titled Failing to Disclose Serious Concealed Danger, but in California referred to by some as the "Be a Manager and Go to Jail" law.
14. 17 Cal. 3d 425, 551 P.2d 334, 131 Cal. Reporter 14 (Cal. 1976).

15. See Chapter 2, but also see an article by Roy F. Baumeister, Violent pride: Do people turn violent because of self-hate or self-love? published in the April 2001 edition of *Scientific American*, p. 96. This article is fascinating in reinforcing the idea that I heard from Dr. J. Reid Meloy that wounding a narcissist may be one of the most significant triggers for violence we can identify.
16. California Constitution, Article 1, Declaration of Rights. Section 1. "All people are by nature free and independent and have inalienable rights. Among these are enjoying and defending life and liberty, acquiring, possessing and protecting property and pursuing and obtaining safety, happiness and privacy."

Practical Ethical Issues

11

The purpose of violence risk assessment is to provide an accurate assessment of the risk of physical harm that a person may pose to a particular target or a population, in a particular period of time. Given that the work involves not just analyzing past behavior, but projecting into a *possible* future, the work poses some interesting ethical issues. We will outline some of these issues by working through the stages of a typical violence risk assessment and intervention, as we typically conduct them, and illustrating some ethical issues that could be involved. This exploration is not meant to be a definitive treatise on the topic, but given the importance of the topic and the lack of writing on this area of ethics, we hope that this chapter will provide some ideas that may be of benefit, should the reader encounter similar practice issues.

First, the overall concept of violence risk assessment raises an immediate potential ethical issue involving competence. Violence risk assessors are being asked to provide an opinion that may have a profound effect on an individual's future opportunities and civil rights, without the ability to know, for certain, what the future actually holds. Other professions are asked to project into the future and prognosticate about what might occur; however, the results of the projections of weathermen or stock traders, though they may have some health or financial consequences, rarely result in incarcerating someone or releasing him or her back to the community, taking away someone's job, taking away someone's right to go certain places, putting a person involuntarily into a mental health facility or forcing him or her to take medication. What is the level of accuracy that should be required for the process, recognizing that actual accuracy can only be retrospectively known in any given case, if at all? Who should be able to do this work? What type of training should they have? Right now certain psychiatrists, psychologists, police officers, Secret Service agents, Special Agents of the F.B.I. Behavioral Analysis Unit (BAU) and private sector practitioners all conduct violence risk assessments and interventions and have been qualified as experts in threat assessment or violence risk assessment in federal and state courts in the United States and other courts throughout the world. So, in specific cases, the courts have determined that a wide range of individuals can do this type of work, but, as an individual practitioner, how do you determine your own competence to do this work? It is assumed by many of our clients, and in many courts, that simply being a practicing psychologist or psychiatrist qualifies one to provide valid violence risk assessments. However, we have found that to be untrue. One of the co-authors of this book spends about 10% of his work time contacting psychologists and psychiatrists who have conducted violence risk assessments as a part of a "Fitness for Duty" request by employer clients. In about 65% of those contacts, he has found that the methodology used to determine future violence risk does not meet the current professional level of practice. The responding psychologists and psychiatrists are limiting the validity of their assessments by only interviewing the subjects and providing them some psychological test that has not been designed or tested for violence use (e.g., MMPI-2, WAIS, etc.), while not seeking and gathering any collateral information that would test the veracity of what they are being told and using tools that have been empirically tested for validity in violence cases (e.g., HCR-20, SARA, VRAG, COVR, etc.). As stated in *Ethical Practice in Forensic Psychology*, "The use of a multisource, multimethod assessment strategy to gather and review reliable and relevant information is a valuable approach to competent forensic assessment …".[1] Also, the use of incomplete processes and inappropriate tests would seem to violate the American Psychological Association (APA) Ethics Code 2002.[2] General Principle D: Justice states, "Psychologists exercise reasonable judgment and take precautions to ensure … the boundaries of their competence, and the limitations of their expertise do not lead to or condone unjust practices." Section 2.04 Bases for Scientific and Professional Judgments in the APA Ethics Code states, "Psychologists' work is based upon established scientific and professional knowledge of the discipline." Section 9.08(b) Obsolete Tests and Outdated Test Results states, "Psychologists do not base decisions or recommendations on tests and measures that are … not useful for the current purpose." The Specialty Guidelines for Forensic Psychologists[3] states, "Forensic psychologists provide services only in areas of psychology in which they have specialized knowledge, skill, experience, and education."[4]

But what about the ethics of other practice professionals that regularly make violence risk assessment and intervention decisions, including psychiatrists, police officers, security practitioners, human resource professionals, and attorneys? Psychiatrists, being medical doctors, are bound by several ethics codes, but the central one in the United States would appear to be the Principles of Medical Ethics of the American Medical Association.[5] Section 1 of this document states, "A physician shall be dedicated to providing competent medical service…." Section 2 goes on to state, "A physician shall deal honestly with patients and colleagues, and strive to expose those physicians deficient in character or competence, or who engage in fraud or deception." Police officers have quite a number of ethics codes available to them. Two prominent ones are the codes published by the International Association of Chiefs of Police (IACP) and Interpol's Code of Conduct for Law Enforcement Officers. Both of these codes speak to "competence." The IACP Law Enforcement Code of Ethics states, "I know that I alone am responsible for my own standard of professional performance and will take every reasonable opportunity to enhance and improve my level of knowledge and competence." Interpol's document states under Section 4: Performance of Duties, that law enforcement officers "... should sustain and, where possible, improve their professional knowledge and competence." ASIS International, the largest professional organization in the world representing security personnel, states in its Code of Ethics, under Article IV, "A member shall be competent in discharging professional responsibilities." The Society of Human Resource Management (SHRM), the largest organization in the world representing human resource professionals, states in its Code of Ethics, as a Core Principle under the Professional Development section, "As professionals we must strive to meet the highest standards of competence and commit to strengthen our competencies on a continuous basis." Last, the American Bar Association (ABA) publishes its *Model Rules of Professional Conduct*[6]; unlike the other codes of ethics that run from 1 page to about 22 pages, this document runs more than 187 pages when the Preamble and Appendices are included. In the Preamble of this document, under paragraph 4, it states, "In all professional functions a lawyer should be competent ...." However, in the Comment section of Rule 1.16 it appears to define and limit competency to the area of representation, not providing advice on violence risk as a member of an incident management team. Misconduct, under Rule 8.4, makes no mention of providing uneducated or untrained opinions.

So, where does this leave us? Each profession that can participate on an incident management team seems to believe that ethical conduct is an essential area of practice and most professions broadly define a requirement to understand the limits of one's own competency and require practice within those limitations, while aspiring to enhance competency as a part of ongoing professional development. Therefore, each participant on an incident management team or threat evaluation team should be careful to stay within the competency boundaries of his or her education and experience. Given appropriate education and experience, no professional is unethical in providing violence risk assessments or interventions, regardless of the core profession. Conversely, if a professional has not obtained appropriate education and experience, regardless of his core profession, his conduct would be unethical if he attempted to provide unassisted violence risk assessments or interventions.

Another question is what type of assessment process guideline should practitioners follow to qualify as competent practice? This issue of assessment protocol has been addressed by the Association of Threat Assessment Professionals in its Risk Assessment Guideline Elements for Violence (RAGE-V),[7] which was released in September 2006. This document, which provides practice advisories in the areas of psychology, law and information gathering, discusses each of these elements that are intertwined in violence risk assessment and provides a process flow chart for consideration in every case. This tool recognizes the wide variety of contexts in which violence risk assessments take place (e.g., in open environments, incarceration, medical facilities, mental health facilities, employment settings, etc.) and also that, in any given case, at any particular time, based on the rights and privileges of both the assessor and the subject of the assessment, only certain information will be available for use in any given assessment.

As for the issues raised in a particular violence risk assessment and management, we can break down the issues into distinct operational modules, some of which will have overlapping ethical issues. The distinct operational modules we will explore in this chapter are case intake, information gathering, primary assessment, initial intervention, case monitoring and re-assessment and intervention.

The ethical issues that can arise associated with case intake are fairly straightforward, including competence, financial arrangements, multiple relationships and conflicts of interest. Are you competent (qualified) to conduct the assessment that is being requested? One way to practically deal with this issue is to talk with the referring client, in some depth, and at no charge, before accepting the case. This allows time to determine enough of the case facts to make a reasonable determination of your competence to make this type of assessment and also whether a practitioner has adquate time to manage the case inside the expectations of the client. If we do not feel it is within our sphere of competence, or we cannot reach an agreement with the client regarding the time period to complete the assessment, we suggest other competent practitioners to work with them on this particular case. This initial screening, without cost to the potential client, not only can provide them some value, but also allows us the ability to appropriately control whether we should engage in the matter or not.

If we can all agree on competence and time frames, then we move on to a discussion of case process and financial arrangements. Here, again, the potential client may not understand the depth of information that is required to provide a valid assessment, such as outlined in the RAGE-V, and/or the client may not have the budget to allow for appropriate completion of the assessment. Both of these issues could pose ethical challenges if pressure from an uninformed client inappropriately truncates a valid process or the process is compromised by lack of appropriate financial resources. We have taken on cases pro bono due to lack of budget for certain non-profit organi-zations or low income individuals; however, if we all cannot agree on process, then it is inappropriate to move forward and compromise the validity of the assessment. This is in line with Section VI, subsection (C) of the Specialty Guidelines for Forensic Psychologists that states, "In providing forensic psy-chological services, forensic psychologists take special care to avoid undue influence upon their methods, procedures, and products, such as might ema-nate from the party ... by financial compensation or other gains."[8]

The last issues of multiple relationships or conflicts of interest have cropped up occasionally in our individual practices, but they are very rare. More often we are asked, as mentioned above, to review the methodology of other assessors after they have provided their assessment and these ethical issues are revealed during our review. A co-author recently had a case in which a client referred an employee for a "Fitness for Duty" evaluation to determine dangerousness to self and others. A clinical psychologist accepted the assignment, but did not disclose to the client that he had a prior therapeu-tic relationship with the subject and he went ahead with the assessment. This practitioner conducted an interview with the subject of the assessment and had the subject take an MMPI-2, but conducted no collateral information gathering, and relied on information from his prior therapeutic relationship to provide "context" to the current actions of the subject. Only when we were asked to review the matter did the psychologist, after initial resistance to our involvement, even though the subject wanted him to share his findings, reveal the prior relationship. This conduct seems to potentially violate both sections 3.09 (Cooperation with Other Professionals) and 3.05 (Multiple Relationships) of the APA Ethics Code 2002. It was obvious during our interview with the psychologist that he wanted to convince me that the employee was safe to return to work and provided his information in a way that attempted to "sell" us on his opinion. Ultimately, we completed the assessment and agreed that the subject could be safely returned to work, but the conduct of the psycholo-gist severely damaged his credibility with the client.

Moving on to the next module, information gathering, we run into the ethical issues surrounding due diligence, ethical information gathering and informed consent. The issue of due diligence really concerns how much information is required to be able to provide a valid risk assessment. This effectively breaks down into two issues: (1) how much information should be sought in a given case and (2) from what sources. Then, if certain infor-mation is not available due to legal issues, temporal issues or source resis-tance, at what point does the practitioner decide the assessment cannot be appropriately completed and suspend or end the assessment? In our case load, we routinely pursue information from public records (civil, criminal and financial), collateral sources that we have ready access to (e.g., co-work-ers, supervisors, managers, etc.), and we make active attempts to interview the subject of the assessment, unless we judge that pursuit of the subject's interview will increase the risk of harm to the client or his employees. Most often the issue of non-interview of the subject of the assessment arises when the subject is a non-employee, third-party stalker or outsider who has threatened an employee or employees and that person's behavior has demonstrated that interaction with a third party to the case (e.g., law enforcement, family members, friends, etc.) has caused inappropriate escalating behavior. If that is the case, we do not pursue an interview with the subject because "first you do no harm." This judgment seems to fall in line with the Forensic Specialty Guidelines, Section VI (H), under the "… possible or feasible …" exception.[9] Taking all the mentioned factors into consideration, it is rare that we are not able to *eventually* amass enough information to provide a valid, defensible assessment. However, when certain gaps exist in the data, we always disclose those gaps to our clients and provide an assessment that is bounded by the available data. This ensures that we do not "overdrive" the data and provide a weakly grounded assessment. In those rare cases that not enough data are available, we refrain from providing an assessment and encourage our clients to pursue, or allow us to pursue, additional data gathering, while taking a conservative approach to the protection of potentially at-risk personnel.

Ethical information gathering means the use of legal and appropriate means to gather information. Depending on our client and the particular case, we have access to a different array of information each time. Working for a private corporation will mean access to public records, internal corporate records and its personnel. Working with law enforcement will mean additional access to a wide array of records that are not public and concerns about how we approach witnesses and subjects of assessment, so that we are careful not to allow our role to become coercive under "color of authority." Ethical issues also arise when working in one sphere and we have access to the other sphere, through contacts and relationships. It is critical, not only on an ethical basis, but also on a legal basis, that assessors not "mix the streams" and place both themselves and their clients in jeopardy due to unethical and illegal information-gathering attempts. It is tempting in some cases, particularly when it appears that great harm could be an outcome, to "cut corners" or rationalize the decision to seek illegal or inappropriate information because "the ends (safety) justify the means." However, in our experience, that has never turned out to be an appropriate prism to determine what should be done. More often than not "you pay now or you pay later, but you always pay more later," meaning that unethical and inappropriate conduct comes back in a case to cause additional risk or harm that overwhelms the value of the information inappropriately obtained or action inappropriately taken.

Informed consent is the last issue we would like to cover in this module. In our practices, this issue is more nuanced and can be difficult to sort out.

Neither one of us is currently a licensed mental health practitioner, police officer or attorney, therefore we have no legal or ethical requirement to disclose our backgrounds, or a variety of other information that may fall under an informed consent. Our clients are aware of our backgrounds, experience, costs, methods, confidentiality practices, report style, etc., but, with victims, witnesses and subjects of assessment, we make an individual determination on what we disclose about ourselves, our role and the process of the assessment on an interview-by-interview basis. We also believe in, and conduct our work, ethically. Therefore, we disclose at the outset whom we are working for and the general purpose of our involvement. But, most often, the rest of the details are vague at the beginning of the interview. What the outcome of the overall process could be and what level of confidentiality is applicable to the interview are usually covered later in the interview, unless directly asked by the interviewee earlier. The purpose of this style is to test suspiciousness, compliance, cognition and the emotion of the interviewee at the outset, without jeopardizing rapport by placing potential "barriers" between ourselves and the interviewee.

The area of primary assessment contains several ethical challenges. As explored above, the areas of competence, training and protocol all can raise ethical issues. In addition is the area of reporting, including duty to warn and confidentiality.

Reporting contains several potential ethical pitfalls. We want to provide the client a well-anchored opinion that encompasses the sources of information and the methods we used, but do not want to expose so much of the underlying process that the interview questions or the assessment process is compromised for future use in the same organization or with the same population. This practice falls in line with the APA Ethics Code 2002, sections 9.10 Explaining Assessment Results and 9.11 Maintaining Test Security. There is also the issue in reporting of privacy and confidentiality in the gathering of information during the assessment process and the desemination of the assessment results. In terms of information gathering, this issue is covered under the "informed consent" section above for assessor seeking information from instigator; however, what about information available from mental health practitioners and other sources of information that believe they cannot release that information because of confidentiality provisions or right to privacy? What is interesting to us is how often the holders of this information are misinformed concerning the sharing of information with appropriate receivers, thus contributing to a weaker assessment process and creating a potential liability issue. We need look no farther than the Virginia Tech shooting in 2007, where a misinterpretation of FERPA led to critical information not being shared with those who could have intervened. It would behoove practitioners to acquaint themselves with the actual rules and regulations pertaining to confidentiality and privacy and actively look for ways to release information for the safety of others, rather than to obstruct that information from being released. In regard to the reporting of assessment results, it is important that the practitioners understand who their audience is for their reports and then to provide the information necessary to anchor their opinions, while remembering that all the information obtained during the assessment process is rarely required or desired to anchor their opinions. Consequently, in the reporting of results maintaining confidentiality and privacy of the assessed person careful consideration should be given to limit the amount of sensitive information that is released. This is particularly true in cases where the audience of the assessment is not actually clear, but can reasonably be expected to extend beyond the initial group the assessor is interacting with. There might be considerable value in openly discussing the need to maintain confidentiality and privacy of the process with each known recipient and the fact that they are responsible for any appropriate transfer of this information to others.

In the area of duty to warn, the Tarasoff expectations would appear to apply; however, neither of us is a licensed psychologist or mental health practitioner and, therefore, has the same obligations. Our clients are usually the employer of the victim or potential victim(s), and they may have a duty to warn under civil law precedents. However, in states outside of California, their duty is less clear than in California, where the expectation is firmly rooted in case law. From an ethical perspective, we believe that fully informing the potential victims of the possible risk is the right thing to do, so they can take appropriate steps to protect themselves. However, what about those cases in which it is clear that victims are likely to take actions that would increase the risk, not only to themselves, but to others? This is particularly true in domestic violence cases in which the victims may believe that only by "siding" with the abuser can they remain safe, so they deflect the blame for their actions onto the employer or others, hoping that the abusers, if they get angry, blame the employer or others for the event. The argument could be made in this case that the potential victims know their risk, because they are living with, or interacting with, the person and therefore do not need to be informed, unlike the Tarasoff case in which the victim was unaware of the risk. However, it has been our experience in many cases of domestic abuse that the victim is unaware of the abuser's behavior prior to the relationship and therefore did not enter the relationship with any real knowledge of the risk that the relationship might bring them. This new knowledge of a previous pattern of aggressive behavior, coupled with valid violent risk assessment, might be of great value to them, but if they shared it with the abuser it might increase the risk to the employer and the victim's co-workers. So to whom do we owe the duty, the potential or actual victim or the employer and the other employees? Practically, we decide this issue based on who our client is and on a "first you do no harm" basis, meaning that we attempt to provide appropriate duty-to-warn notification for each individual case, balancing out all these elements, so that we protect the maximum number of our client's employees, which includes the potential or actual victim. In some cases, that means being circumspect on providing the exact information we may have on a threatener or abuser, so that information cannot be inappropriately communicated and trigger an aggressive response from the person of concern. This also falls in line with the APA Ethics Code 2002, Section 9.10, Explaining Assessment Results, as this type of assessment could be classified as organizational consulting, security screening or a forensic evaluation, depending on the given client and/or case being assessed.

All forms of interaction with the subject of concern are an intervention. Contact with the subject, either directly or indirectly, changes the subject's perception of his or her world and therefore alters possible future choices on his part. Perception is the source of action. Interviews, phone calls, letters, court orders, detentions, etc. all are forms of intervention. Our practical approach is to use the least intrusive intervention we can, given the velocity and trajectory of the case, so that our attempted intervention does not cause the very act to occur that we are trying to prevent. This is why "zero tolerance" policies for violence are counterproductive. "Zero tolerance" is interpreted by most people as "zero judgment." So why should the subject of concern use judgment if we are not using any? A school expels a student for bringing a paring knife to school to cut an apple. Fellow students believe this is unfair and it increases their resistance to report real behavior of concern. In an actual case of ours, a student was expelled for writing on his desk "I will blow up the school tomorrow." The school never asked him what he meant; sent him home alone; since both his parents worked during the day; acknowledged that they could not really stop him from coming back on campus if he wanted to commit harm; and, under the rules of the Board of Education, would have to take him back as a student in 6 months time. Then, they asked us if they had done the right thing! We find most often that if we can provide people of concern an opportunity to tell their story and, then, we take action based on all the information available, the person of concern may not agree with our client's ultimate decision, but he or she appreciates having been heard and it lessens his or her need to use violence to make his or her point. We, therefore, eliminate one avoidable error and if they act out anyway, after being listened to, then we have increased the defense against claims of negligence. Again, "first we do no harm."

Case monitoring, re-assessment and follow-up intervention are the parts of the management process that most often break down. It is relatively easy to do an initial or primary assessment and intervention. All the stakeholders are attentive, resources are available and case momentum carries the process along through the initial intervention. Then, the case stabilizes, the subject of concern is placated, deflected, detained or medicated and the immediate risk is diminished. Now, who is paying attention to new behaviors a week, month or year from now? Do they report the new behavior? Is it reassessed? Is a new intervention initiated, if necessary? Failures like this are seen on a regular basis. A fired worker comes back and kills his co-workers, after emailing that "this matter isn't over until I say it's over," but no additional assessment is done or intervention made before the act. An individual gets a restraining order, the person of concern violates it, but the police do not find and arrest the violator, so the behavior escalates and, eventually, the protectee is hurt or killed. Or, the person is arrested for violation of the restraining order and stalking, but the prosecutor does not believe that there is enough evidence of a continued pattern of harassment or violation, so he or she is not charged, and the behavior continues until the person escalates to physical violence. All of these failures in the process occur, in most cases, due to waiting passively for behavior to be reported, or by failures of public entities (e.g., law enforcement, prosecutors or the courts) to enforce the laws as written, instead of establishing active monitoring that seeks new behavioral information and effectively responding to that new behavioral information. These failures do connect to ethics in that professionals know that the process breaks down and where it, most often, breaks down. Therefore, this knowledge ethically obligates them to make certain that their actions reinforce best practices and minimize the possibility of harm to others by taking the extra steps necessary to continually manage the process until safety is achieved to the degree humanly possible. The APA Ethics 2002, General Principle B: Fidelity and Responsibility, certainly anchors this concept when it states that psychologists "are aware of their professional ... responsibilities to society and to the specific communities in which they work. Psychologists uphold professional standards of conduct, clarify their professional roles and obligations, accept appropriate responsibility for their behavior ...." This is certainly an aspirational goal all violence risk assessors should strive to achieve.

In conclusion, we have explored a wide range of ethical issues that we associate with the work we do in violence risk assessment and intervention and, briefly, outlined the practical way in which we try to manage those issues in our practices. A continued effort to provide ethically based violence risk assessments and interventions is not just a good aspirational goal, but practically guides good process that provides more accurate assessments and, therefore, safer intervention outcomes, while minimizing the likelihood that the assessor will use inappropriate methodology that will further legitimize the instigator to escalate his behavior and couch it as a defensive response to an inappropriate act against him. "First we do no harm."

Endnotes

1. Bush, Connell, & Denny, 2006, p. 50.
2. American Psychological Association, 2002.
3. Committee on Ethical Guidelines of Division 41, 1991.
4. Ibid., Section III(Λ.) Competence, p. 658.
5. American Medical Association: Code of Medical Ethics, in *Current opinions with annotations of the Council on Ethical and Judicial Affairs*, American Medical Association, 2000.
6. Originally adopted in 1983, the latest version was published in 2007. ISBN: 1-59031-873-0.
7. ATAP, 2006. See Appendix to Chapter 5, "Assessment Tools."
8. Committee on Ethical Guidelines of Division 41, 1991, p. 661.
9. Ibid., p. 663.

Consultation Issues

12

Introduction

While there are many times you will want to consult with an outside expert on the best approaches to handle given situations, there are some times where it would not only be most appropriate, but bordering on negligence if you did not. We would like to believe there can never be a time where others could demean you for asking for assistance or assurances of proceeding properly, but both authors have seen where an organization has limited this ability for its in-house experts for a variety of political, economic or emotional reasons. This chapter may appear to address some of the more obvious times where consultation is necessary. However, the ramifications that surround managing these incidents without a full understanding of how convoluted many of these cases become, the ethical considerations for the safety and security of those directly and indirectly involved in an incident and the potential legal accountabilities that are becoming more evident and applied preclude not discussing this topic so any assessor will better understand these important considerations and can share these concerns with everyone else during the "do we really need them" process.

In the Beginning

Two essential principles for dealing with a crisis or situation requiring an assessment for the potential of violence are critical. First, planning to prevent a crisis may seem useless by some and overkill by others. Very few get past the "good idea" stage unless you are thoroughly prepared from the beginning when given the opportunity to design or implement a violence prevention program. Second, once into a crisis you really don't have any other option but to get yourself out of it.

Preparation is emphatically critical as long as you understand two more things. First, whatever you plan for, and however you plan for it to occur, will never happen. But second, and much more important, because you have stimulated the process of preparation in that "computer" brain of yours and hopefully in those around you, you will find answers or solutions much more quickly than if you had never prepared. Reaching these conclusions pulls from myriad old memories and experiences and, in a sense, preparation is the "primer" to get you propelled toward resolve.

In any organization, it is almost a given that a crisis will occur. It may not be life-threatening but the law of diminishing returns suggests it may eventually become so. It might be the attractive nuisance of the building that emits strange noises next to the local school. Even though it's posted with "No Trespassing" signs and there is a 10-foot chain-link fence all around it, a local youth tries to climb over the fence, falls and breaks his leg. Perhaps the insecurities of a newly hired employee, the jealous husband of a female employee or a disgruntled vendor who recently lost his contract with your company might lead to possible retaliatory acts. Or the cause of the crisis might simply be a natural act, such as a fire, an earthquake or a tornado — all of which can cause tremendous damage as well as personal injuries.

Therefore, preparation is important in addressing a crisis. It is, in essence, the first step toward resolution — assessing the risks to prevent the catastrophe. Thus, the first question for those conducting assessments must be whether they are qualified to conduct these evaluations to determine the violence potential of an individual. Most likely the types of circumstances previously described can never be controlled. Some of them are the unfortunate constant of a particular organization, while others are acts of nature. But, through training as well as appropriate policies and procedures, you can control those issues that contribute to the potential risk of the occurrence of violence. You can also control the proposed necessary responses to mitigate further problems — but only if you are prepared yourself, through understanding the process and necessity of a complete assessment, which often means the use of a consultant.

For example, it is an unfortunate truism at the time of this writing that domestic violence is all too common in the workplace. Thus, it is highly likely that your organization may have such a problem and, since it generally begins outside the workplace, there is little you can do to control this issue. But how far it goes and whether it becomes a crisis depend on what measures have already been put into place. What training has been offered to supervisors on what to look for and how to approach an employee they feel may be having some problems at home? What is your policy at work concerning the reporting of potential "family" problems coming into the workplace? Who has been identified to contact when this concern arises, both internally as well as externally?

It is this type of "prevention" that supports a strong deterrence to a crisis. It is the first step in dealing with a crisis, and it is one that generally requires consultation, perhaps for the initial evaluation or perhaps for the training. If you take on this challenge yourself and cannot show adequate background and experience in dealing with what you are offering, you (which also means your organization) may become liable for negligence because of not adequately knowing how to stop the crisis that occurs.

Both authors have been approached numerous times, especially at training seminars, by individuals in human resources, security, facilities management, etc., asking, "I see the value of this but how do I get my administration to see it as well?" Often this comes down very simply to a dollars-and-cents issue — the cost of implementing the necessary training (bringing in a consultant, time off for employees, etc.), the distraction from the usual routine that personnel will now be subjected to or the "it won't happen here" attitude. Again, the value of preparation is evident. A little research into regulatory agencies and case law (look up what OSHA recommends, contact the corporate attorney, etc.) should help show liability concerns. And again, a consultation with a qualified expert may prove useful. Then present facts — what are the realities of violence occurring and, if it does, what are the costs of dealing with the issue as well as the aftermath versus a preventive program?

Once the preparation is in place, it is necessary to plan for when the procedure doesn't work. Remember, the first axiom of preparation is that whatever you planned generally won't happen. Accordingly, you must now prepare for the myriad other things that can happen when disaster strikes. Not only must you look at how you will respond to the event, but you must also include how you are going to communicate to others and, of course, to whom you are going to communicate. What do you have in place that will allow you to slip from talking on one two-way radio to another when utilization of such a device might only make matters worse (transmitting radio waves after a reported bomb threat, for example)? Who else has been designated to talk to the press when you have a domestic-violence-turned-hostage situation or murder/suicide and your main press-information person is on vacation?

Drills will always, *always*, help exercise concepts and quickly point out deficiencies, so this would be an obvious "must do" regime. But until you have tested all these issues, appointed who is going to be doing what and when, who are the backups for each of these positions and what are the backup means of communications, consideration might be given to looking for outside consultation for establishing all this.

Putting It Together

Before deciding whom to call, it is necessary to determine why and when you should call others, as well as what it is you really need them to do. To do this, you must understand their role. It is also a good idea during the preparation stage of this step that you confirm that consultants are qualified, that they can do what they say they can, that they understand their role in the process for you or your organization and that they are willing to stand behind their work (write a report, go to court, etc.). The following section explains how to put together a good violence prevention program for your organization and with whom you may want to consult at various times before, during and after an incident.

Assembling a Violence Prevention Team

We recognize the need for fewer people in an organization and that means that those who are left are expected to wear more than one hat. But, when it comes down to actually running or overseeing the program, one person should be in charge. However, as the reader must have determined from reading previous material in this text, the call on whether someone has the potential for violence should probably not be made by one person alone — often not even by one outside expert. Hence, in any organization, a resource and monitoring team should be put together for the program. The intent is to bring more talent and experience into the pool of the decision-making process, as well as make the job of an assessment more manageable and realistic. Therefore, the size of the team is not as critical as the function, which is described in the following paragraphs.

Basically, this group would:

- Establish safe and secure ways to report threats (e.g., internal or external anonymous hotline).
- Set a clear policy encouraging reporting.
- Decide when and if outside consultation should be made.
- Mandate appropriate training and either supply the training or have qualified personnel present training.
- Clearly define disciplinary actions for incidents.
- Determine how best to utilize EAPs (employee assistant programs), mental health services, fit-for-duty evaluations, etc.
- If warranted, establish guidelines for first responders to an incident, which may include calling local law enforcement.

Group Members and Their Functions

First Team Member (The Leader)

This designee should be skilled in handling people, have superb communication skills and be able to take responsibility for the implementation of appropriate training to all supervisory personnel. The most important qualification for this individual is the ability and authority to make decisions or be able to contact someone who can make decisions *immediately*. Potentials for violence will not wait for a committee.

While most organizations designate a human resources or personnel department supervisor for this position, you can select whoever you feel most meets these qualifications. This person must also have an alternate designee and one or the other should be available or at least on call 24 hours a day. This person should also be readily available to all personnel.

Duties: To collect all initial information about the incident; confer with the individual's immediate supervisor; review the individual's personnel file specifically in reference to performance appraisals; and determine what, if any, further action is necessary.

Second Team Member (The Attorney)

The next most important individuals on these teams are labor law attorneys. They should be brought into the discussion of the facts as soon as possible for guidance, but, more importantly, for the issues of confidentiality, procedure and liability or negligence issues. Hence, all verbal and written communication between those involved, if done under the cloak of attorney–client privilege, or if considered attorney work-product, may be nondiscoverable for court or other legal proceedings. These individuals need not be on site. But care must be taken that these people are not just "corporate" attorneys, as they must have a sound understanding of labor law and ADA rulings, as well as numerous other employment law, privacy law and regulatory agency issues.

Duties: To supply necessary legal information and protect the confidentiality of any inquiry or scrutiny of the individual. Also, these designees should review all data received and direct the relevant information to the appropriate individuals to maintain the attorney–client privilege. Appropriate training for periodic necessary legal updates would be an additional role for these people.

Third Team Member (The Boss)

The next member of these groups who should be consulted and informed on all matters are high ranking management persons who should be designated chairpersons. It should be their responsibility to oversee all of these incidents brought to their attention via the team members. Again, it is important to have viable and available alternates to these people so that someone at this level is available 24 hours per day, 7 days a week.

Duties: The primary function is to offer insight into the overall organization's feelings of the proceedings; coordinate all team member activities; decide who else needs to be contacted about the matter, including but not limited to outside resources; and conduct debriefings of all incidents with all parties involved to determine whether additional steps should be taken. These people should also prepare for dealing with the press, either directly or through a designee.

First Optional Team Member (Security)

This should be a safety or security designee at the basic equivalent level of the manager of the team. This individual should be generally familiar with local laws and OSHA regulations that the group may want to consider before taking specific action. This person would also generally have direct control and training over those individuals detailed with the role of first responder in times of crisis within the organization, unless, of course, this task is turned over to an outside resource.

Duties: Security's main concerns are to prepare appropriate security procedures for dealing with the possible instigator or lessening fears of co-workers and to oversee those members of the organization who may be called upon as first responders, which includes ensuring their continued specialized training. Also, they should be ultimately responsible for the delineation of what is necessary for the safety and security of the organization, which may include conducting site surveys and offering recommendations to make them safe and secure.

Second Optional Team Member
(The Violence Assessment Professional)

Behavioralists, occupational psychologists or forensic psychologists or psychiatrists who have sufficient background, training and experience in dealing with human behavior, especially in the workplace arena, are the final members to consider as part of these groups. Actual hands-on field experience in negotiations and handling such situations or individuals is a considerable plus. These individuals must also be people who can fully explain their findings in a manner that is understandable and useful to the rest of the team and are willing to stand behind their findings, even if they may develop into legal proceedings.

However, the matter of confidentiality must be broached and clarified with these individuals prior to utilization, as most clinicians have an ethical duty not to breach the doctor–patient confidentiality pact. If clinicians are used to interview subjects, unless there is a finding of a potential threat or they feel someone is in danger, information revealed to them might not be revealed to the organization, unless the appropriate releases are sought from the interviewees prior to the beginning of the interview process. It is therefore possible that valuable information might not be shared with the organization's assessment team to best decide how to proceed in this matter, unless the team acquiesces entirely to the mental health providers' findings and direction (in which case, it would seem unnecessary to put together such a team). Therefore, qualified people who are not licensed clinicians may be of greater value in any situation in which seeking or obtaining consent for the release of information could be a barrier to completing the assessment interviews.

Duties: The mental health professionals' sole purpose is to provide valuable insight as to the probability of continued behavior so that a better determination can be made by the team for the most prudent course of action. If appropriately qualified, they can render an opinion of the potential for violence. This should be followed by probable future behaviors and specific recommendations on how to handle the incident and the individual. The ability to respond either in person or via phone 24 hours a day to advise on immediate handling or negotiations with a subject is advisable. (A written evaluation and assessment from this team member can prove invaluable for certain legal actions that may be initiated.)

Other Optional Team Members

EAP   Many organizations have an employee assistance program already in place for their members. This service can play a vital role in the overall well-being and achievements of the organizations, but care must be taken when considering this service as a viable team member, as most organizations consider the EAP to be a mental health service. Hence, the authors have observed several mental health professionals who happen to work for the EAP represent themselves as capable of conducting violence potential assessments when they really have little more than counseling experience behind them. At the same time, because of the increasing demand for expert professional assistance in dealing with these types of issues in today's workplace, more EAPs are beginning to place qualified and experienced specialists on staff.

If the EAP is used for violence assessment, another issue to address is conflicting perception of duties. Employees referred to an EAP expect confidentiality; however, in the case of a violence-related issue, a Tarasoff warning (see Chapter 10 for more information) could be issued if the EAP violence assessor determines that the employee is an immediate risk. This decision could lead to termination. Employees may shy away from using the EAP because their perception is that a visit to the EAP could mean getting fired. The organization cannot share with the employees the real reason for the termination (confidentiality and privacy) and, because the role of the EAP in helping people was confused with the role as a violence assessor, a mixed message results that can cause harmful disruption of an important helping process.

On the other hand, the EAP is probably one of the most underutilized services for exactly its specialty — counseling after the event. Critical incident debriefing requires crucial training and experience to convey caring and appropriate concern as well as assistance after times of violence or other critical incidents. EAPs are generally fully prepared for such situations. However, this needs to be verified, as this author witnessed an international company experience an employee mass murder, and the EAP representative told the client they had no one to respond, as it was a weekend, but they would be there first thing Monday morning.

EAPs can be valuable resources for other issues that mitigate the violence potential. Truly, they are more than mental health professionals, as their primary role in any organization is to assist employees who are having difficult times. While this is generally associated with behavioral problems in the workplace that may include drug or alcohol abuse, sexual harassment and other inappropriate activities, sometimes it is dealing with an employee's financial difficulties or outside family problems. Hence, a good EAP resource can offer some valuable insights into the best approaches to potentially violent situations, as well as quick and shrewd methods of correcting problem circumstances that may lessen violence potentials.

Media Representative   I served as a press information officer (PIO) for a moderate-sized police department for approximately 3 years. The common perception by the police in this case was that the press was biased against them and viewed them in a negative light. They realized the importance of trying to liaise with the press and hence attempted to create this position. It was also created because they wanted to have one person to focus on these individuals and vice versa. The press could be told to contact the one person who was their main contact for any and all information so the police would be left alone to do their work. The police also hoped that having one person dealing with the press would allow them to have a better handle on what the press was actually trying to find out so that appropriate steps could be taken to protect valuable evidence while, at the same time, trying to steer the press toward other options.

But isn't this exactly what any organization would want to do? No one wants to have "strangers" trampling all over their property (the organization) after a crisis. No one wants the press to make public those things that may prove embarrassing. Yet the press has a job to do, protected by certain constitutional rights, and can often play a pivotal role in broadcasting important information that can only be of benefit to the organization. Reporters are going to do their job whether you talk to them or not, so why not have a designated individual who can be "point" for events in the hope of establishing some link of cooperation and assistance?

The way the media goes about gathering the information depends chiefly on which medium of communication they represent. Television may be the most difficult because the reporters need lead time consideration if you want to make a statement and, when they are on the scene for immediate broadcast, they need sound bites with quick, concise statements. Radio also needs quotes, so a spokesperson who is especially articulate and knowledgeable is preferred. And, because radio has more frequent, continual broadcasts than television, more frequent updates are necessary. Finally, the print or newspaper people need more in-depth information than either radio or television.

They need media releases and printable quotations and, since they have deadlines to meet for all this plus background information, they tend to look for more people to interview as well as ask more questions.

An organization should then be prepared to handle these needs, hopefully through prearranged meetings and liaison with the local media. Most organizations have neither the time nor the manpower to focus on this venue. But, for a team that may have to deal with a potentially violent ordeal, preparation seems only logical in this area because the media will certainly want to cover the event if it becomes violent. Therefore, at least designate a specific press area where the press members are safe, out of the area of operation, but where they can observe and film or photograph that which is reasonable (although it is generally private property, any concession that would allow them to obtain what they need will go a long way toward building a positive relationship). Remember, they need timely and accurate information, preferably in a written press release, and they want to be able to interview appropriate personnel during the event.

Having press or public information representative designees on teams may not be practical, but the tasks they would be expected to perform are legitimate concerns. Preparation then, once again, becomes the key to success in this endeavor. Do not overlook this position, if not from an actual body being assigned or, if not contracting for such services from an outside consultant, then by designating someone on the team to be prepared for the eventual media blitz if and when a critical incident occurs.

When this team has been created, it is now time to put into words what the program is. However, this cannot be accurate or suitable for any organization unless the team understands what really needs to be addressed and how it should be implemented. Hence, the next step is training.

Training the Decision-Making Team

The organization should have policies and procedures in place to handle potentially violent situations. Unfortunately, simply copying the sample policy that can be downloaded from the OSHA web site is not enough, although it is an excellent start and certainly better than nothing. Before you can design a policy or procedures plan, you have to show why you need the things you say and why others are expected to do certain things. How do you know this without training?

We recommend that all decision makers within an organization go through this initial training but we are realistic enough to understand that only the team will do so, and, in some instances, the "team" might just be you. Either way, this training should be something you feel is appropriate for you and your organization and is presented by a qualified person or group. How long it should take and what specific areas it should cover are variables that differ with every industry and organization. Your guide for what level of training is necessary is whatever level makes you feel very comfortable in answering why you did what you did, if you are asked in a court of law after an employee in your organization has been killed by another employee. We readily agree with one of our colleagues, who compared the odds of someone's being a victim to violence, especially in the workplace, as about as likely as being bitten by a shark when swimming in the ocean and then, upon limping out of the water, being hit by lightning. But, if it should happen to you, those odds don't really mean much.

Once you, and preferably all those who are going to be charged with putting together the policy and procedures, have received this education, it is important to apply it to the specifics of your organization. This may be addressed by a consultant brought in specifically for training in your organization — at least, one would hope the trainers were qualified and sufficiently experienced to design the program for their audience. But one additional step would be for you to confirm with others in your field (similar or same businesses, associations, groups, etc.) what they are doing or have done. In a lot of instances, you may find they have done very little, if anything at all. Nevertheless, it is important that you look into this matter to determine what the industry standard is and whether you have met or exceeded this standard.

Once training is obtained, the team should be ready to tackle the next phase of designing and implementing policies and procedures for a violence prevention program.

Policy and Procedures

The main focus of the policy is to establish what you want and why you want it. It is not sufficient to indicate you decided to put together a workplace-violence-prevention policy because such events occur in our country. The policy must state why your specific organization has decided to implement this (there have been potentially violent instances in our industry) as well as why it is necessary for all within the organization to be aware of these policies and procedures (we value the safety of our employees) and follow their directions.

A policy does not have to be lengthy; it can vary from one paragraph to several pages. The procedures part may be longer, as this must go into more definite components of what to do and who to contact. And, while numerous books and articles in print show examples of these, we recommend visiting the OSHA web site and utilizing its examples. Much like the issue raised about the training of decision makers, it is necessary to be able to explain why your policy and procedures documents state certain things and give specific directions.

For example, it is necessary to have the specific names and ways of contacting the organization's team members and their back-ups listed in the procedures document and available to all personnel. This will require someone to keep the document current, an important element of consideration for any preventive program. It is also advisable to list inappropriate behaviors and consequences for such behavior so there can be no claim of ignorance of the protocol. The consequences can be worded in a general way, such as, "This offense may include disciplinary action, up to and including termination."

Because of many considerations when putting this together, you may want to refer to the guidelines of an expert in this field to assist you in designing such a document, for this is the basis of your whole program. The cost for such advice, especially if you have already gone through the training, should be minimal and it certainly helps in the mitigation of legal liability issues. Besides, bringing in someone from the outside who can look at your framework from the "big-picture" angle may give you some excellent insights on how to make the program even more successful.

Training

The entire organization must understand the nature of the program, its purpose and how it works. There is no better way of accomplishing this understanding than through training. If the team feels comfortable in supplying this to the other members of the organization, then they should do so. There is always the use of the outside consultant to do this as well, but we recommend a combination of the two for the most effective program. Regardless how much expertise the outside consultant may have, the organization does not know this person and oftentimes the training is not accepted as readily if it comes from within the organization. Ideally, the consultant would instruct on those issues of general concern and liability and the members of the organization's team involved in the training would go over the policies and procedures and would correlate other areas of the training to the specifics of the organization.

It is also recommended that supervisors receive a different level of training from the line personnel's, as there is a higher level of duty expected from supervisors to act upon issues as they are the direct representatives of the company to the rest of the organization. Consultants are often called upon to instruct the majority of the supervisors and management personnel within an organization, and one class videotaped by the consultant and administered by in-house designees serves as a supplemental part of the training for others.

Hence, the use of consultants for this phase can be minimal, depending upon the need and casualness of the organization. What is most important is that all personnel within the organization understand what is expected of them, that it is their duty to become part of the solution instead of part of the problem and that they know what to do about an issue they have concerns about. Thus, in-house training is continual and essential, but should only be conducted to the level of comfort and efficiency.

Acquiring the Consultant

It doesn't matter whether you are looking for a good labor or employment law attorney, a mental health professional, a security expert, a media liaison person or a violence assessment expert, the roles they play in the assessment process are all important. But you must first determine who is going to be the best consultant you can acquire. We discussed the concepts of making sure they are experienced and qualified and we outlined their basic roles and duties, but what else is important?

Background checks may be a consideration, but this is generally too impractical. Getting a referral from a trusted resource is usually effective. Asking a reputable organization, such as a local law enforcement agency or district attorney's office, may give you some leads, but, because they are public organizations, they are prevented from giving you anything more than just names and contact information, leaving you to still do your homework. Asking reputable groups such as the Association of Threat Assessment Professionals (ATAP) for a referral may prove helpful (located in most major cities), as these are mental health, legal, law enforcement and security people from around the world that deal mostly with these issues. And the fact that a consultant may have great credentials or may have written a book is not sufficient.

So the key is the preparation process, looking for the right consultants before there is a problem, interviewing them to make sure they fit your needs and the culture of the organization and, finally, a contract. The contract should be complete for your needs and the needs of the organization. The contract also puts the consultant on notice that you are a professional seeking professional assistance and will hold the consultant to the highest standard possible.

The contract should begin by simply outlining the job to be done (conduct an assessment to determine the potential of violence). The exact names of the parties involved are not usually included, for the service is to provide an assessment for the safety of all, establishing liaison with the media or providing legal guidance on issues of labor or employment law, etc. The idea is to identify and delineate the specific service for the organization, not just as it may involve one or two people. The contract should discuss fees and the payment of same. If there are different aspects of the services, these should be broken down and clearly defined, as well as listing the specific fees for each service (travel, room, background checks, handout material, etc.). The contract should outline severability (who can cancel the contract, when and how) and what happens if there is a disagreement (binding arbitration, jurisdiction of deciding court, etc.).

Public Entities

Local law enforcement individuals can be your most important associates. If there is a crisis, especially if it is a violent event, you or anyone in your organization will probably call 911 before doing anything else. It is, therefore, an excellent idea to get together with law enforcement prior to any event.

Often, such liaisons are successful primarily because neither entity has a truly clear understanding of what the other's role is until after they have met and conferred. The police are used to getting 911 calls and simply taking over and handling the situation. The organization is used to being in control and being able to tell outside resources what they expect them to do. But, if they start from the common goal shared by both, the ultimate safety for all personnel, then a successful game plan can be achieved.

Many police or sheriff's departments have crime prevention specialists. Many have developed some expertise in the workplace violence area, since such incidents occur and there are businesses in their jurisdictions. Even those who do not have that specific expertise understand why it is necessary to prevent violence before it occurs. Hence, asking these specialists to come and visit the organization to look at the physical construction of the site can be an excellent beginning.

Law enforcement has been a pioneer in the concept of crime prevention through environmental design (CPTED). Its premise is that the physical construction, the placement of lights, plants, desks, etc., can all contribute to the psychological component of the environment to promote good feelings of safety and increased productivity while, at the same time, discouraging crime and feelings of violence — sort of a corporate *feng shui*, if you will.

The benefits of using this system are that it can utilize the environment already in place, identify areas where significant problems could occur, demonstrate to personnel how they can take back some control over their environment and, since they already pay for the service through their taxes, there is no initial cost out of pocket. You now have the expertise of a qualified professional to show you how to make your organization safer and less vulnerable to violence.

Additionally, whether the local police force has such an expert on staff or not, getting anyone from the police department to respond for a meeting prior to an event can prove very constructive. The police realize that a violent event could occur at any place and at any time, so they welcome the opportunity to see what is in place should they have to respond during a crisis incident. They want to know the "lay of the land," who is in charge, how many people are on site at any given time and just exactly what the organization does (e.g., are there any hazards present). At the same time, this affords the organization the opportunity to confirm how and when the police would respond, what they will actually do and what they expect or need from the organization. In this way, realizing what the police will be able to do, the organization can also assess the best way to establish a first-responder group.

Finally, local law enforcement can be an invaluable source for information concerning crime and other such concerns in the organization's area. They can share the latest crime statistics so that steps can be taken to "harden" targets (a recent theft of car stereos in the area can alert employees to be more aware of who is in the company parking lot, for example). They can discuss crime demographics with the organization, which may help determine, because of projected crime rates or problems, if moving to another location would be more advantageous than expanding the current site. Also, they can often alert or share certain information with the organization concerning special problems with radical or fanatic groups that may be of interest.

Part of this law enforcement group, in a general sense, is those officers of the court and their investigators, such as the city or county district attorney's office. Often very knowledgeable in understanding potentials of violence from a workplace-violence perspective, a domestic-violence perspective and even a stalking perspective, the wealth of information they may be able to share can often prove extremely helpful. They are not as available to you as local law enforcement, for they are handling specific cases and will often refer you to the local police. But their expertise in handling numerous cases involving these matters makes them a tremendous asset and they should be asked for their advice and counsel. They cannot give you legal advice, but they can tell you very clearly what the law is, whether you have a violation of law and what would be the next best steps to take when you have a potentially violent situation.

One caution concerning the interaction with law enforcement: Recognize that law enforcement personnel are bound by the law and department policy to respond to certain situations in a certain prescribed way, regardless of the nuances of any particular situation. As mentioned in Chapter 10, in many jurisdictions if you tell law enforcement personnel that a person in a domestic relationship has been physically struck, they are obligated to take a report, attempt to confirm it and then make an arrest. This may not be in the best interest of the victim or victim's organization, depending on the assessment of the instigator's current mental or emotional state. So, prior to approaching law enforcement on any specific case, care should be taken to understand what law enforcement may be obligated to do or will do in that jurisdiction before making a report, and that may mean, in some cases, that no report will be made. Another alternative is to report another crime that has occurred and then establish the liaison under those circumstances. An example would be the above-referenced case, when, as often happens, the instigator has been making harassing and threatening calls to the victim's family members as well. Now the case can be reported to law enforcement as a "harassing calls" or "terroristic threats" case, depending on what is said and the laws of that jurisdiction. No one mentions the behavior that could lead to mandatory action that may not be desirable. As in all matters, judgment must be used about when and how to work with any resource, including law enforcement.

Guards

There can be no greater fear than having your life threatened and, from everything you see and feel, believing it. We have received more frantic calls from organizations where an instigator has just threatened to shoot a victim and, because there is a "history" between the two, everyone believes it can happen. The organization wants protection and it wants it right away. But whom do you call?

While not an easily believable concept in the beginning, we have experienced it for over three decades of service to our clients and we are comfortable in saying that, about 80% of the time, "guards" are not needed. Approximately 10% of the time, it is strongly recommended and the remaining 10% is up for grabs. Unfortunately, many others in this field, especially those whose primary economic profits come from protection contracts, do not share this feeling. Some are all too happy to supply personal protection agents for the client because that is what has been asked for and it is generally a good profit-making activity.

Naturally, when an active threat is made, it is difficult to convince anyone to slow down and conduct a violence assessment before bringing in protection. And often, supplying such personnel, while perhaps unnecessary from the standpoint of the actual potential for violence, goes a long way in calming fears and enabling employees get back to their business. So how do you know when to request this service, exactly what is it you need and where to find the right people for the job?

If you have the luxury of having security people as part of your organization, this should be discussed with them and they should already be doing their homework to provide the answers to these questions. If not, you are going to have to do the research. Start with those in the field you may already know through members of your assessment team, security companies or associates in other organizations who may have had occasion to need such assistance.

Do you want armed or unarmed guards? If someone is threatening to harm another and you are going to try to prevent this, the person to whom you entrust that job must have whatever is necessary to accomplish the goal. If such people do not have the tools and they get injured, you may be held liable for placing them in harm's way, because you knew the instigator was threatening injury to another. On the other hand, if the instigator has never shown any signs of violence before and has not really made a violent threat, you may just want someone to be present to give the appearance of security.

Unarmed guards, those you see standing at the entrance to a Wal-Mart, wandering around a McDonalds or sitting at the front podium of a business meeting, have only one real responsibility — to observe and report. They are not there to intervene if there is an altercation. They are not there to neutralize an aggressive act. They are there to observe what is happening and, if something threatening occurs, to report it to the appropriate person. Expecting any more from them, when they average little more than minimum wage, is unwise. This is why, if you consider hiring a guard service for any reason, the service and performance really depend more on the company than the actual guards because the guard companies all pull from the same pool of people living in your area.

If you have decided you want to have armed guards, but you really don't want them to look like something out of the Old West with a sidearm on their hip — even the clean, crisp uniformed appearance of a professional off-duty police officer is a little much for your conservative office location. The need is for a well-groomed person who dresses to fit into the environment and is armed, but in such a way that you cannot tell where the weapon is actually carried. Armed guards should be big enough to look like they can take care of themselves in any struggle, yet present themselves as sociable, calm and professional.

Nothing can substitute for experience in choosing qualified personnel, and, although we are always looking for new people because you can never know too many in this field, we seem to keep coming back to the same ones we have used and trusted in the past. Our guideline is that they ultimately represent us, so we will not recommend anything less than those we know who are capable and will act professionally.

Without a referral source running interference for you, keep in mind that you are not simply looking for off-duty police officers because they can carry a gun and are often inexpensive. There are several reasons, from the type of training they receive to their in-field experiences, that prevent us from strongly recommending off-duty police officers for these types of assignments. But this is not necessarily a given because some of our best and most reliable protection personnel are retired police officers. But the primary concept you should keep in mind is that, while you want people who are professional in demeanor as well as qualified, their primary mindset must be that they are willing and able to do whatever is necessary to neutralize the level of aggression they encounter. This, hopefully, means nothing more than confronting a hostile instigator and convincing him to go away, but, if placed in a life-threatening situation, they cannot hesitate. They must be prepared to take another's life.

It is because of this you must be prepared to pay (actually more due to insurance coverage, workmen's compensation and other administrative costs) anywhere from $55 to $125 per hour, per person. That per-person concept is very important for it is rare that a protection assignment, especially if there has been threatened violence, will be handled by fewer than two people on duty at any one time. The object is to prevent violence and the presence of two people is certainly more psychologically intimidating than one.

Even if you decide to acquire the protection agents up front, assessment must still be conducted. If assessment is not done, when does the security coverage stop? If you stop it on a whim, with no assessment to support the decision, and an incident then occurs, the standard of protection you have set by placing security personnel on site will be the standard that proves negligence for having removed them prematurely. Thus, another consideration when considering hiring protection agents is how far to go in providing protection for your employees. Consider this: If you think the situation is dangerous enough to hire an armed presence because Larry has threatened to shoot Carol, at what point is Carol out of danger? She is your employee and if you hadn't hired Larry, Carol would never have met him, so do you have to accept part of the liability for placing Carol in harm's way? If so, are you required to provide Carol with personal protection 24 hours a day — even at her home? These are questions you need to consider before they actually come up and thus, consulting with the appropriate experts may prove helpful (attorney, violence assessment expert, etc.).

You must also decide who is to be protected — just the victim or all the employees within the organization? If the threat is made by more than one person and there is more than one way to gain access to the site, you may need more than just two protection specialists.

Finally, what is your liability if the instigator shoots someone and is about to shoot another; the protection agent fires but misses and kills an innocent bystander? A "good shoot" is one justified by legal standards; most jurisdictions agree the instigator would be the one charged with the killing of the bystander. However, what about your civil liability? You knew there was this potential for violence, unless you found out differently from an assessment, so, it might be argued, shouldn't you have taken the precaution of warning visitors? These are necessary points to clear up prior to the event.

Other considerations concern the training and qualifications of these individuals and will not be hashed out here. Suffice to say, numerous reflections must be discussed with all involved. The odds are you will never have the need for this service, but if you do, last-minute phone calls may prove more stressful than dealing with the instigator.

Case History

The following scenario patterns many cases we have been involved in. The discussion may seem to digress a bit from the main focus of this chapter, but it does serve to demonstrate many of the usual issues that need addressing when deciding how best to proceed in handling such a case. It shows how a case, without the presentation of any real violence, can benefit tremendously by use of the proper consultants.

Pete is a 32-year-old man who has been working for a company for a little over 8 years. He is a mechanic by trade, but drives a forklift for this company. Everyone describes Pete as a "hothead" at times, moody and just generally hard to get along with. He recently claimed to have hurt his back on the job and so is off work, but because he has abused his sick leave in the past, he is about to run out of this, vacation and other paid leave he can take. Ted, Pete's immediate supervisor, has just been informed by human resources that this is the case and he must now call Pete to determine his status — something Ted is not looking forward to, as he and Pete have had numerous run-ins over the last couple of months. In fact, just prior to Pete's going off on this job injury, Ted had given him a written reprimand for not doing what he was told to do and arguing with his co-workers over an assignment.

When Ted telephones Pete to tell him of his status he can tell Pete is under the influence of something — and it is only 10:00 A.M. Pete says he doesn't have to come back to work because he has a doctor's note. Ted keeps telling him no one knows about that and if Pete doesn't come back to work by Friday he will be terminated. Pete replies, "F... you. You've been after me since I started working there. You can't fire me if you're dead!" and he hangs up on Ted.

Was this a threat or merely a statement of fact? Certainly Ted believes it's a threat; he tells the human resources people, they contact the company's attorney and the decision is made to have security contact Pete to explore his statement. For the sake of this scenario, let's assume the company's assessor has done everything right up to this point, following the guidelines of the assessment process we have been discussing in this text, including utilizing some of the tools in Chapter 4, such as the Assessment Grid. Following the Response Grid in the same chapter, you have initiated a criminal background check, you've conducted appropriate interviews with Ted and others and you have reviewed Pete's personnel file. Not surprisingly, there are numerous discipline notations (including a 2-week suspension for insubordination) and performance problems noted in his file and his criminal record includes convictions for driving under the influence (one) and public intoxication (two).

The interviews produce important background information. You confirm there are no organizational problems and there are no apparent personnel problems other than with Pete. Everyone tells you Pete has a quick temper, that he walks and talks like he is really tough and everyone just better keep their distance — which they do anyway. Everyone seems to agree Pete is a loner, and when he does interact with people, it is to try to con them into doing something that would benefit him. You also learn from a couple of his co-workers that Pete mentioned he once threatened to stab another kid when he was 14 because he caught him cheating on his share of the marijuana they were selling to classmates. Everyone seems to agree that Pete smokes marijuana, snorts cocaine, seems to love to get drunk and then threaten to beat up those in authority — as long as they are not present.

In addition, his supervisor tells you he is fearful of Pete and believes Pete wants to kill him. You know this supervisor and his reputation in the company; there is no indication he is unreasonable or has any problems with others. And finally, human resources tells you, through the privileged communication of the attorney, they would just as soon never have to see Pete again. Your "homework" done, you are faced with just one last question. What is the best way to contact Pete — or should you?

Here is where a consultation with a violence assessment specialist or someone who is versed in understanding human behavior and also has the experience of dealing with potentially violent people becomes valuable — not only because of the ability to assess the violence potential, but to address the question of approaching Pete and how to do it in the safest fashion. It is also a good time to consult with a labor law attorney concerning the Americans with Disabilities Act (ADA) issues, workmen's compensation, the Family and Medical Leave Act (FMLA) and other legal concerns. This will also allow you to speak quite frankly about what you have, what you want to do versus what you are legally required to do and what the legal ramifications are, if any, of one set of actions versus another.

The advantage of psychologist consultants is that they could advise you that Pete is probably an antisocial personality. This comes from common psychological concepts that have been researched and developed over many years. Why is this important and what does that mean for you? It offers insight into the behavioral aspects on how best to approach Pete or someone like Pete as we have identified a likely personality trait that has some consistent expectations. It is important to note that it suggests *some* consistent expectations, because there are many variations even in this psychological category — some very extreme. For example, it could be said that Jeffrey Dahmer was antisocial, which is putting it mildly. But, at the other extreme, you may have a neighbor who is described as antisocial but has never committed a crime in his life.

So, assessing Pete a bit more, it can be suggested that his "tough-guy" role is probably not only something he is comfortable with, but also perceived by Pete as the only way to get what he wants — or at least to guarantee that no one will take advantage of him. This also tells us his general demeanor is his crutch, his mask, his security blanket; call it what you like, it is critical to him. Is this the kind of person you can approach and not expect him to get angry? And what does his anger really mean? Will contacting him push him over the edge where he may harm someone?

Actually, from a clinical perspective, you need more information before attempting to answer these questions. Thus, this may be a consideration as to whether you use clinical psychologists in such a matter, although they are often called upon to assist in these types of cases and explain many questionable behaviors. However, the best resolution can only be achieved after talking to Pete.

It is possible to effect an assessment without talking to the instigator — in essence, in this case, a probable character disorder was chosen to label Pete. From that label, reasonable assumptions can be made about his behavior. One can certainly make an educated guess about likely conduct and, at the very least, if a certain action occurs, because it has been determined that Pete is an antisocial personality, reasonable recommendations can be made of the best manner in which to respond to that action to either mitigate a volatile act or direct him toward a more reasonable action. But, in this case, not only are there obvious ADA issues to consider, but we also want to be sure Pete is left intact. You are not a therapist and it is not your job to help Pete change his character disorder. You want Pete to feel good about his position of control while at the same time convince him continued employment with this company is not reasonable or in his best interest. This will require a direct interview with Pete.

It is also important to learn the breadth of the focus of Pete's anger. The more narrow the focus (he wants to harm only Ted) the more ascertaining his specific thought process to accomplish this harm becomes in determining his true potential for violence. If it is discovered he has narrowed his focus and devised specific plans for harming Ted, it may be necessary to attempt to broaden his focus, if possible, by talking to him. The same principle is applied when negotiating with those attempting to commit suicide. If there is one basic human emotion all humans share it is a desire to feel in control — at least over our own lives. The ultimate control one has is whether to kill oneself. While perhaps not as dramatic in this case with Pete, the same rule of trying to broaden those areas of control so that other alternatives not only seem realistic but attainable — to him, not to you — can make the difference between Pete's acting out his threats and not. Additionally, even if not successful in this endeavor to help Pete see viable alternatives, you now have valuable insight into his process, his motivations and his reality for a better determination of the true potential of violence. Therefore, it is not only necessary to talk to Pete, but the insights gained from a consultation with an expert will allow you to be better prepared for what to expect, how to respond and what should be your main areas of focus or concern during the interview.

Another concern is where to conduct this interview. Over the phone is out, as this allows Pete total control and he may not even answer the phone. Calling Pete into the workplace is going to remind him of the anger he still has for certain people, so this might be a disadvantage. Pete would feel compelled to demonstrate he is in control right away, which can be stressful for all. And, if you ask him to come in and he says no, what do you do?

Going to his home is another option. Many would disagree with this approach, but Pete will feel in control in this environment. Naturally, safety becomes a concern because going alone does not sound safe. What if Pete should turn violent? It is necessary to consider being prepared to use whatever force is required to neutralize his aggression. This would be a good time to consult a security expert or even local law enforcement to discuss the feasibility of this plan and to solicit one of them to accompany you. Of course, you would still want to get a sense from the attorney what your liabilities are (for example, if Pete becomes violent, can he claim your presence was the catalyst?). A behavioralist can offer opinions to this because a home visit would give some tremendous insight into Pete's environment, his perceptions of his power, how he operates to maintain control and how he reacts toward the introduction of another element he would perceive as a threat — his perception will tell him your visit is obviously meant to take back control. However, for a case such as this, most expert consultants would probably recommend against this option. Unless you have a lot of experience, it could get too complicated.

What about a neutral area? Many experts prefer this, setting up a meeting at a hotel or even a coffee shop. While the issue of safety may be more easily dealt with in this environment, it is an unknown whether it will be comfortable for Pete — probably not. But it is an option, if you feel you simply do not want Pete back on the premises.

This would be an excellent time to turn to your team for discussion and advice. The recommendation would probably be that Pete should be called into work just as you would any other employee. Remember, he is still an employee you have some control over and you don't want to change any organizational procedures if you don't have to. You can make the interview area safe (hidden cameras, monitoring devices, others standing by, etc.) and hold it in any room you want (a room away from Pete's co-workers, a room where you can make a quick exit, a room far away from his possible targets, etc.). Remember, even though he will approach you with the concept of wanting to take control, he still has many years of accumulated behavior at the site where he has felt power, so he will actually be fairly comfortable. In fact, this is almost an invitation for him to feel he can come in and clearly demonstrate he is in control and is going to take back his position of power.

Now you need to put on a negotiator's hat and plan your discussion with Pete. Psychologists, behavioralists, security persons, EAP staff and many other workplace-violence experts may be good to bring in for discussion on what might be the best way of talking to Pete. However, one of the best resources may be experienced negotiators from a local police department, providing they have many years of experience. Talking and negotiating with the Petes of this world are not uncommon events for these people.

A hostage or crisis negotiator would tell you the following: With antisocial personalities three main rules are consistent:

1. Since we know Pete's primary motivation is for power and control, the word or concept you want to stay away from is "no." If you use the "no" in the conversation, you are taking away from him the very things he is trying to achieve — power and control.
2. Since antisocial personalities are rebellious and antiauthority, the last thing you should try to use on him is the nice-guy routine. He is not going to listen to your rapport-building chatter and could care less about your concerns for his welfare. Remember, you found that Pete was mostly a loner and about the only time he got close to people was when he was trying to use them. So, like most other antisocial individuals, Pete is not prone to form attachments with others and thus is not about to start with you. The antisocial personality generally has a complete inability to understand aspects of attachment or empathy.
3. Since Pete wants to feel power and control, do not present a powerful and controlling presence. This is not the time to show that you are in charge. Thus, never be confronting, although there may be many good facts you could use to be so. Instead, use the infamous "Colombo" approach. Demonstrate that you can listen well, but you need direction and assistance, hence you seem to fall right into his game of manipulation and conning. You ask him to repeat his thoughts or demands, "to be sure you've got it right." This ruse also helps you play dumb regarding what might happen, perhaps saying, "Gee, I don't know how that's going to work. You know how management can be sometimes. But it sounds reasonable so let me go and check," clearly lets Pete feel you may be on his side without demonstrating you want to be his friend.

This also gives you the opportunity to stop the discussion for a while if you feel it is appropriate as you can now claim you need to go and consult with others. You will generally do this when you sense that Pete needs time to collect his thoughts or develop his game plan to better "con" you. Sometimes you might want to do this when he is coming on too strong because this lets him believe you are a simple person who cannot take a lot and thus you are even more "manageable" than he first surmised.

This brings up a final rule every negotiator lives by that is true for any personality you may face. *You are not the final word* ... even if you are. In this case, this really works to your advantage if you can convince Pete that you and he are working on resolving this problem through his controlling con of you.

Human behavior does require some study. But, once understood, the "read" on an action, a behavior or a statement can take you to an even stronger point of negotiation or, at least, understanding. Thus, you may even want to consider asking a consultant to conduct the interview with Pete. Anyone skilled in these types of cases would want to start pushing Pete a bit to test his potential toward violence.

For example, using Pete's "faults" for the interview process would mean trying to get him to see that his current status and way of handling things are not in his best interest nor will they gain him control. Thus, after a brief introduction of who you are and your purpose (in this case, to determine the true nature of the conflict and how to resolve it) you might begin by asking Pete simply to tell you what is going on and why he thinks the situation has reached this stage. Obviously, Pete will relate a story that makes him look good, an innocent victim and how others in control (supervisor, etc.) are out to get him. This allows him to spin his web of deceit and rationalization in his attempt to con you into control.

In so doing, you can point to many of his details as possible shortcomings for him to achieve the power you know he wants ("I know how management seems to think they can just make these crazy demands of us all. But do you think by not doing that task it will really cause them to back off?"). This is a way of suggesting he may not really be achieving the power he is looking for without challenging his obvious perception of being in control by simply not doing what he is told.

On the other hand, you must also be careful not to try to trick such a person. Pete and those like him have years and years of experience at this game and they can spot someone trying to con them a mile away. At the same time, realize that if he senses you are not responsive to his con, he may tire of you and begin raising the stakes. These personalities generally need a fair amount of stimulation. Hence, if you do not keep him involved in this process, he may decide to make up a whole new scenario to make things more interesting. (For example, "Well, if Ted hadn't propositioned me last year, this whole thing would never have happened. Naturally, I couldn't tell anyone about this earlier because he's my boss, but I'm just not into guys.")

It is also important to remember the Petes of this world cannot focus on long-term concepts of gratification, such as suggesting that his present behavior is unlikely to get him a raise next year. They are into satisfying the impulses of the here and now. They did not grow up in an environment where they could learn how to model their "parent-self" (what psychologist refer to as the superego). Hence, they are dealing with the instant-gratification demands of their little kid (the id). And what we know of the little kid is that it basically really understands only two things very clearly — pain and pleasure. Pete is going to be able to focus only on short-term concepts; consequences are too subjective, too far away. The best results are achieved by getting Pete to find an immediate resolution with an obvious concrete negative consequence if the resolution is not achieved ("If you resigned today, you would take away their ability to fire you.").

You are also not going to intimidate or cause Pete to feel anxious about his position or his actions. Antisocial personalities have no fear of hurting others, disappointing someone or feelings of guilt, shame or embarrassment for what they have done to others. And, since anxiety requires a capacity for empathy, the antisocial generally cannot feel anxious. Thus threats that he could be fired would have little effect on Pete. About the only anxiety Pete might ever feel is the fear of getting caught for committing some illegal act, but even this is transitory.

It is also interesting to note that these personalities have no real life goals; they live for immediate gratification, so how can they have any goals? Thus. appealing to their future is not only a waste of time but may steer you into a whole line of useless discourse. If Pete decided to run with this, he would lie and rationalize something socially acceptable he believed you wanted to hear. If you buy into this, he might try to rationalize and con you into seeing how, since he is now the persecuted victim in this case, he should be allowed certain rewards and fewer punishments for his actions.

What are antisocials looking for, beyond the obvious need to feel they have the power or are in control? They need to feel strong and self-sufficient. Since others are obviously out for their own power and control, then this additional need the antisocial has means he must do unto others before they do unto him. People who do not believe in this principle are weak and deserve what they get. Thus, in talking with Pete, allowing him to feel he is directing his opportunities in the process becomes an important element.

Continuing with a whole-case scenario here would take another chapter, as there are too many variables for how this discussion might bob and weave. But, with the information shared thus far, it is evident this meeting will take some time. It will go back and forth, with concepts of power and control. The end should be getting Pete to see how his resignation would be in his best interest (he is in control of his future; he has shown them they cannot control him; he has prevented them from firing him, etc.). It may mean a corporate compromise that is not always the most pleasant resolution, but there is no reason that it should not end with the ultimate goal of the company being achieved. But, if the goal of this discourse is to present a "changed" person who now will comply with management and supervisory orders, that simply will not happen.

It is also important to realize these types of individuals, where they have not crossed the line from being antisocial to being psychopathic, are rarely openly physical. One can never say "never" in any of these cases, but their business of deceit and exploitation requires such a level of con to prevent getting into trouble with the law that their restraint from violence becomes part of their interwoven character. In this case, Pete seems to be creating an assertive persona; he wants others to "feel" him and then back off. In this way, he has to form no attachments and is clearly in control. This confirms that Pete has no other history of violence or physical controls, unlike many antisocial personalities who, especially in domestic-violence cases, not only use physical violence to maintain their control, but also are actually proud of their physical prowess.

Although a bit lengthy, our point is nevertheless still germane. Determining the best approach to even the simplest of cases may actually be more convoluted than originally thought. Hence, proper selection of key consultants prior to events occurring cannot only save you time in trying to draw the right people together to make an assessment, but may prove to be the best way of deciding how to approach and handle someone to prevent further problems and perhaps solve the issues of concern to everyone's benefit.

After the Crisis

Crisis and trauma in the workplace are not uncommon, and much thought has been given by many on what to do when they occur. But what about later? Think about each of these types of situations and how they would affect you:

- A co-worker or someone you know is shot.
- A co-worker's family member is shot and killed.
- Your spouse comes into the workplace, accuses you of cheating and then shoots himself in front of your manager and several others.
- A female employee who has been telling you she has been getting an uneasy feeling from a male co-worker is raped one night in her home by that man.
- An employee is mugged one evening in the parking lot by a non-employee, and everyone has been telling you the lighting in the parking lot is bad.

Just as you would feel terrible following any one of these events, others may feel even worse, depending upon the relationship.

Much as you would respond to a family member in crisis, it is equally important to respond to an employee. Once any crisis or trauma occurs in the workplace, just as you would rush to the side of your significant other, rush to the side of those involved. If you have an EAP, use it. But be aware of how the EAP members operate because you don't want to call them only to have them tell you they cannot respond until a later time.

Local emergency responders (police and fire) can sometimes prove useful in these events as well. They often have specific persons, including chaplains and mental health professionals, on staff. Or they have their own consultants they contact for incidents who can reach out to quickly assist you. And, since they are used to the 24-hour–availability concept, they may prove beneficial in a late night or weekend situation.

What about the mess? A broken window or chair may be fixable in house, but who is responsible for cleaning up blood? After paramedics respond, they don't clean up the scene, so who will?

Professional companies specialize in these types of responses. Some are more used to dealing with water damage from floods or repairing windows after an earthquake or tornado. Such companies often can offer you assistance in cleaning up "the mess" and will do it quickly and professionally. You may want to contact your local emergency responders for ideas of whom to call. Whatever you do, have someone to call, someone you can reach 24/7.

Should you conduct your own debriefing? Violence assessors are often asked to talk to many employees about an event after it has occurred. Sometimes that involves a large group (the whole floor of a plant), sometimes just a particular department and sometimes just one individual. The psychological advantage to this approach is that the company is telling its employees that management is concerned enough to bring in an expert and will not try to hide from what has happened. It is important to have a high-ranking member of the organization present as well.

This debriefing should be arranged as quickly as possible. The literature suggests within the first 3 days is acceptable. Some even suggest it is better to hold off for a couple of weeks if necessary to give a clear, well-thought-out debriefing rather than a haphazard, disorganized one more quickly. It is important that the debriefing be distinct and well thought out, not disorganized. But we believe even going beyond a few hours is not the best. We have seen too many people become too entrenched with misinformation because the debriefing was put off to a later time. Rumors can't be stopped entirely, but you can mitigate their power if you set the record straight as soon as possible.

We recommend getting a consultant on board for this part of your process as soon as possible. Call in someone who can address what has occurred and at least discuss possible reasons for it. At the same time, this person should be someone who really understands what feelings are going to be experienced. It should be someone who can articulate what to expect over the next few days, weeks and perhaps even months — psychologically and perhaps even physiologically. You need someone who can suggest warning signs to look for in all parties and what to do once those signals are recognized, and someone who can show knowledge of what generally happens following these kinds of situations. And finally, these should be people who know their limits sufficiently to recognize when someone needs more assistance than they can give them, know this group of people or that person needs to be talked to again or has enough common sense to realize when they are talking and no one is listening and that something else must be done.

Terminations

Consider a troubled employee who has done many inappropriate things over the last few months. Fortunately, none of them is violent, but you have reached a point where termination not only seems appropriate, it's what you really want to do. Is it legal? Have you sufficient documentation? Have you considered ADA and FMLA rulings? Who should be consulted? A good starting point is a labor law attorney. Unfortunately, the in-house corporate attorney who is a whiz at contract law may not be the best option. You need people who know about all the rules, laws, regulatory agencies and union functions so they can advise you intelligently; you can talk to these people honestly about the case and, because of attorney–client privilege, your off-the-record comments are never discovered by others.

The way is clear, the decision made, the termination is ready to proceed. When should you do it, and where — morning, afternoon, Monday, Friday, in the boss's office, in the troubled employee's cubicle, at a local Denny's? Who should be present — you, the boss, human resources, a mental health professional, a police officer? There is no definite answer to any of these questions, hence the need to consult with an expert. Every case is different. The assessment process for a termination is as important in determining when and how to terminate as it is in determining the potential of violence.

You may have the luxury of handling a termination face to face in a comfortable boardroom with covert surveillance cameras monitored by armed associates or you may end up calling a person on the phone after he just arrived at work to tell him to go home because he was fired. Which way is better? There does not seem to be an established protocol per se. But there are many considerations before deciding when and how to terminate.

In general, it is preferable to terminate early in the week as opposed to later. Regardless how prepared someone is for termination, no matter how many warnings he has been given, no matter how many times he has been talked to about his inappropriate behavior, when he is finally told he is terminated he seems to go into shock. Some become irate and some keep asking if you're serious, but most simply act surprised. And when they get to this state, they are not hearing all you have to say.

Think of it as a death. Regardless how mad or angry you might get with a friend or relative, if you have a relationship with them and they die, you go through several stages of grief. Anyone who puts in time at work has developed a certain relationship with the workplace, if not with other employees. What is the first thing you feel when you learn of someone's death? You may feel shock, surprise, disbelief, etc., but certainly not complacency. This, then, is what the terminated employee is going through.

Consequently, after the numbness wears off, there are usually many questions or negotiations these employees may want to go through. If you fire them on a Friday and they want an answer to what they believe is a very important question on Saturday but no one is available to give that answer, odds are, by Monday, these terminated employees are going to be so obsessed and frustrated over this issue they may decide to try and take it out physically on someone at the company. If they were terminated on Monday, they would be able to reach someone Tuesday or Wednesday to ask their questions or begin their pleas or, quite possibly, get their tirades off their chest ... all of which can prove very helpful in your continual attempt to assess the potential for violence.

Who should be carrying out this termination? If possible, the immediate supervisor should not be part of the team or the person to terminate an employee. The employee will probably believe this supervisor has been out to get him all along and now he is getting his way. Hence, the employee will never believe the supervisor did not have a lot to do with the firing. Also, even if the supervisor feels he has a good relationship with the employee, it is still more likely the employee will believe this is just one person's opinion (the supervisor) and thus, unfair.

The best person to do the actual termination would be that person who is at least one step above the immediate supervisor's position. Psychologically, this tells the employee the problem has been discussed with others with more power than the supervisor and it has still been decided he is to be terminated. This also helps take the immediate supervisor out of the main focus of the employee because now another person has been brought in to do the actual firing. This lessens the narrowing of focus these employees seem to go through, as the one person who may have caused the problem is now removed somewhat from the equation. This then helps mitigate the employee's potential for violence.

Specifically, who should do the actual termination? Should it be someone from human resources? Should it be a manager? Should it be an outside consultant? We have often been brought in as representatives of "corporate," or "the home office," or even quite simply as "outside consultants." This not only helps to make the employee feel this case has been run all the way up the corporate ladder but also diffuses a lot of anger, because now complete strangers are doing the termination.

There are many possibilities and you should conduct an assessment to decide the who, where and how. In general, don't do anything too out of the ordinary. Usually try to have more than one person conduct the interview, which should not take more than about 10–15 minutes. Design and stick to a script. First acknowledge those areas where the employee may have done good work (praise helps them want to listen more attentively in the hopes of getting more) but then clearly detail the problems as well as the directed corrections and their outcomes. Remember to base your comments on behavior and performance, not personalities. End the meeting with preparation of final payments, if possible, as well as the name of one person the employee may contact if there are any future questions.

Now comes the moment of truth — getting the employee out of the office. Should security escort him? Should there be a squad car waiting outside for him? Should he simply be allowed to get up and walk out on his own? Again, there are too many variables and no right answer. Remember, no one likes to be embarrassed or feel he is being ridiculed. We have personally walked employees to their desks and then to their cars. We have had associates in plain clothes do the same. And we have had uniformed police officers right outside the door escort terminated employees to their cars, where a consensual search revealed a loaded handgun — and they were subsequently arrested. But in these and all cases, the first consideration was how best to help the employee save face.

We have done terminations away from the office and told the employee his personal property would be mailed to him. We have done them at night or early in the morning when almost no one is around so that very few people see the exit. We have also had an entire floor emptied out during the time we were conducting the exit interview so when we were done, there was no one who would see the employee as he was escorted to his desk and then to his car.

Two other points are worth mentioning. Remember, termination means you no longer have any rights or controls over this employee. We can relate many horror stories where an employer has recently fired an employee who has now begun a threatening campaign and the employer calls us, thinking we can simply wave a magic wand and get the employee to stop. That is impossible, and is why we always recommend putting the person on leave (paid, unpaid, administrative, whatever) until an assessment can be made. For those who strongly believe it is critical to talk to the identified problem employee to conduct an assessment, terminating him or her prior to an assessment only makes this process more difficult and often impossible.

The other issue is one of surveillance, both during the process of the termination through the use of covert cameras and people following and watching the employee as he moves about his daily routine. Again, there are many pros and cons. One should first realize surveillance in the field, even when conducted with numerous agents and vehicles, often ends up losing the subject. It is very costly for the private sector and often produces minimal results. It also runs the risk of inflaming the subject if he sees people following him.

On the other hand, field surveillance can provide a bounty of intelligence. It has helped us develop our profile and thus our assessment almost every time we have been able to use it. The covert cameras in the room where the termination is to be conducted are a positive influence. They help the party doing the termination feel more comfortable by showing help is monitoring the event and the events recorded may prove useful for future use — either for intelligence by reviewing wording and behavior or for behind-the-scenes legal negotiations.

Finally, what if the individual simply does not get the picture and continues to call, to show up at the work site and to contact other employees. Our advice is to start with a firm warning to cease and desist or there could be legal consequences. We often go to the attorney again and have a letter drafted stating exactly the same thing, threatening the ex-employee with legal action but now on an "officer of the courts" letterhead. However, just as it is never wise to threaten your children with something you would never actually do, don't tell this former employee something you have no intention of following through on. You must follow up on everything you say. This just again substantiates the importance of the violence assessment so you know how best to approach this person and what is more likely to work than not. In many cases, a restraining order is necessary — individual or corporate. Sometimes just getting the local police to talk to the ex-employee is enough; other times you may have to file a crime report that could cause the person to be arrested. Consider the facts, consider your alternatives, talk to a consultant and be ready to back up your words with actions.

Summary

We purposely did not make this chapter a simple listing of consultant types or personnel because there is insufficient literature on the use of consultants in such cases, except in the mental health field. But just as the purpose of this book is to get you to think, not to set ourselves up as the final word, we tried to give you examples of many of the practical problems we have been exposed to that have convinced us a consultation with another expert was a wise investment. We hope this has stimulated the same thoughts in you and that you got valuable new ideas of when and why to turn to a consultant or at least to reach out for advice.

Consultation issues are many and varied. No one has all the answers and no one answer is always correct. But when faced with the barrister in that daunting black robe who may ask you one day why you did what you did, you're going to feel better if you can say, "I consulted with X and Y and, based on their expert opinions as well as my own research and experience, I did what I did." That certainly sounds better than saying, "Well, I thought it was the best thing to do at the time."

References

American Bar Association. (2007). *Model rules of professional conduct.* Chicago, IL.

American Medical Association. (2000). *Code of medical ethics.* Chicago, IL.

American Psychological Association. (2002). Ethical principles of psychologist and code of conduct [Electronic version].

American Psychological Association (2004), Warning Signs of Youth Violence. Available at http://apahelpcenter.org/featuredtopics/feature.php?id=38.

ASIS International. *Code of ethics.* Policy and Procedures Manual. Alexandria, VA.

ATAP. (2006). *Risk assessment guidelines elements for violence (RAGE-V).* Los Angeles, CA: Association of Threat Assessment Professionals.

Banks, S., Robbins, P. C., Silver, E., Yesselinov, R., Steadman, H. J., Monahan, J. et al. (2004, June 1). A multiple-models approach to violence risk assessment among people with mental disorders. *Criminal Justice and Behavior, 31*(3), 324–340.

Barish, R. C. (2001). Legislation and regulations addressing workplace violence in the United States and British Columbia. *American Journal of Preventive Medicine, 20,* 149–154.

Barling, J. (1996). The predication, experiences, and consequences of workplace violence. In G. R. VandenBos & E. Q. Bulatao (Eds.), *Violence on the job: Identifying risks and developing solutions* (pp. 29–49). Washington, DC: American Psychological Association.

Baron, R. A., & Neuman, J. H. (1996). Workplace violence and workplace aggression: Evidence on their relative frequency and potential causes. *Aggressive Behavior, 22,* 161–173.

Bennett, J. B., & Lehman, W. E. K. (1996). Alcohol, antagonism, and witnessing violence in the workplace: Drinking climates and social alienation-integration. In G. R. VandenBos & E. Q. Bulatao (Eds.), *Violence on the job: Identifying risks and developing solutions* (pp. 105–152). Washington, DC: American Psychological Association.

Bies, R. J., Tripp, T. M., & Kramer, R. M. (1997). At the breaking point: Cognitive and social dynamics of revenge in organizations. In R. A. Giacalone & J. Greenberg (Eds.), *Antisocial behavior in organizations* (pp. 18–36). London: Sage Publications.

Björkqvist, K., Österman, K., & Hjelt-Bäck, M. (1994). Aggression among university employees. *Aggressive Behavior, 20,* 173–184.

Bolton, R. (1979). Differential aggressiveness and litigiousness: Social support and social status hypotheses. *Aggressive Behavior, 5,* 233–255.

Borum, R. (1996, September). Improving the clinical practice of violence risk assessment: Technology, guidelines, and training, *American Psychologist,* pp. 945–956.

Borum, R. (2000). Assessing violence risk among youth. *Journal of Clinical Psychology, 56,* 1263–1288.

Borum, R., & Reddy, M. (2001). Assessing violence risk in Tarasoff situations: A fact-based model inquiry. *Behavioral Sciences and the Law, 19,* 375–385.

Borum, R., Fein, R., Vossekuil, B., and Berglund, J. (1999). Threat assessment: Defining an approach for evaluating risk of targeted violence. *Behavioral Sciences and the Law, 17,* 323–337.

Boye, M. W., & Jones, J. W. (1997). Organizational culture and employee counter-productivity. In R. A. Giacalone & J. Greenberg (Eds.), *Antisocial behavior in organizations* (pp. 172–184). London: Sage Publications.

Bush, S. S., Connell, M. A., & Denny, R. L. (2006). *Ethical practice in forensic psychology, a systematic model for decision making.* Washington, DC: American Psychological Association.

Calhoun, F. S. (1996). *Hunters and howlers.* Alexandria, VA: United States Marshals Service.

Calhoun, F. S., & Weston, S. W. (2000). *Defusing the risk to judicial officials.* Alexandria, VA: National Sheriffs' Association.

Calhoun, F.S., & Weston, S.W. (2003). *Contemporary threat management: A practical guide for identifying, assessing and managing individuals of violent intent.* San Diego, CA: Specialized Training Services.

Carll, E. K. (1999). Workplace and community violence. In E. K. Carll (Ed.), *Violence in our lives* (pp. 4–23). Boston, MA: Allyn & Bacon.

Cole, L., Grubb, P. L., Sauter, S. L., Swanson, N. G., & Lawless, P. (1997). Psychosocial correlates of harassment, threats and fear of violence in the workplace. *Scandinavian Journal of Work, Environment & Health, 23,* 450–457.

Committee on Ethical Guidelines of Division 41. (1991). Speciality guidelines for forensic psychologists. *Law and Human Behavior, 15*(6), 655–665.

Corcoran, M., & Cawood, J. (2003). *Violence assessment and intervention: The practitioner's handbook.* Boca Raton, FL: CRC Press.

Cornell, D.G., Warren, J., Hawk, G., & Stafford, E. (1996). Psychopathy in instrumental and reactive violent offenders. *Journal of Consulting and Clinical Psychology, 64*(4), 783–790.

Criminal Justice Information Services Division. (2007). Federal Bureau of Investigation, "School violence." http://www.fbi.gov/ucr/schoolviolence/2007/.

Crocker, A. G., Mueser, K. T., Drake, R. E., Clark, R. E., McHugo, G. J., Ackerson, T. H., et al. (2005, August 1). Antisocial personality, psychopathy, and violence in persons with dual diagnosis: A longitudinal analysis. *Criminal Justice and Behavior, 32*(4), 452–476.

Dahlberg, C., Toal, S.B., & Behrens, C.B. (Eds). (1998). *Measuring violence-related attitudes, beliefs, and behaviors among youths: A compendium of assessment tools.* Atlanta, GA: Centers for Disease Control and Prevention, National Center for Injury Prevention and Control.

Davis, R.C., & Smith, B. (1995). Domestic violence reforms: Empty promises or fulfilled expectations? *Crime and Delinquency, 41,* 541–552.

Davis, R. C., Smith, B. E., & Nickles, L. B. (1998). The deterrent effect of prosecuting domestic violence misdemeanors. *Crime & Delinquency, 44,* 434–442.

Dolan, M., & Doyle, M. (2000). Violence risk prediction: Clinical and actuarial measures and the role of psychopathy checklist. *British Journal of Psychiatry, 177,* 303–311.

Donlan, M. C., & Rennie, C. E. (2008). The structured assessment of violence risk in youth as a predictor of recidivism in a United Kingdom cohort of adolescent offenders with conduct disorder. *Psychological Assessment, 20*(1), 35–46.

Douglas, K. S., & Kropp, P. R. (2002, October 1). A prevention-based paradigm for violence risk assessment. *Criminal Justice and Behavior, 29*(5), 617–658.

Douglas, S. C., & Martinko, M. J. (2001). Exploring the role of individual differences in the prediction of workplace aggression. *Journal of Applied Psychology, 86*, 547–559.

Douglas, K. S., Yeomans, M., & Boer, D. (2005, October 1). Comparative validity analysis of multiple measures of violence risk in a sample of criminal offenders. *Criminal Justice and Behavior, 32*(5), 479–510.

Dwyer, K., Osher, D., & Warger, C. (1998). Early warning, timely response: A guide to safe schools. Washington, DC: U.S. Department of Education.

Ekman, P. (2003). *Emotions revealed — recognizing faces and feelings to improve communication and emotional life.* New York: Henry Holt and Company Time Books.

Farrington, D. P. (1994). The causes and prevention of offending, with special reference to violence. In J. Shepherd (Ed.), *Violence in health care: A practical guide to coping with violence and caring for victims* (pp. 149–180). New York: Oxford University Press.

Fast, J. (1991). *Body language in the workplace.* London: Penguin Books.

Fein, R. A., & Vossekuil, B. (1998). *Protective intelligence and threat assessment investigations: A guide for state and local law enforcement officials* (NCJ 170612). Washington, DC: National Institute of Justice.

Fein, R. A., Vossekuil, B., & Holden, G. A. (1995, September). *Threat assessment: An approach to prevent targeted violence.* National Institute of Justice Research in Action (NCJ 155000). Washington, DC: U.S. Department of Justice.

Fisher, R. P., & Geilselman, R. E. (1992). *Memory-enhancing techniques for investigative interviewing: The cognitive interview.* Springfield, IL: Charles C Thomas.

Folger, R., & Baron, R. A. (1996). Violence and hostility at work: A model of reactions to perceived injustice. In G. R. VandenBos & E. Q. Bulatao (Eds.), *Violence on the job: Identifying risks and developing solutions* (pp. 51–85). Washington, DC: American Psychological Association.

Furlong, M., & Morrison, G., (2000), The school in school violence: Definitions and facts. *Journal of Emotional and Behavioral Disorders, 8*, 71–82.

Gall, T. L., Lucas, D. M., Kratcoski, P. C., & Kratcoski, L. D. (Eds.). (1996). *Statistics on weapons and violence.* New York: Gale Research.

Garrity, C., Jens, K., Porter, W., Sager, N., & Short-Camilli, C. (2000). *Bully proofing your school,* 2nd ed. Longmont, CO: Sopris West.

Goleman, D. (1995). *Emotional intelligence.* New York: Bantam Books.

Grann, M., & Wedin, I. (2002). Risk factors for recidivisim among spousal assault and spousal homicide offenders. *Psychology, Crime & Law, 8*(1), 5–23.

Greenberg, L., & Barling, J. (1999). Predicting employee aggression against coworkers, subordinates and supervisors: The roles of person behaviors and perceived workplace factors. *Journal of Organizational Behavior, 20*, 897–913.

Grossman, D., Lt. Col. (ret.). (1996). *On killing: The psychological cost of learning to kill in war and society.* New York: Little, Brown, and Company Back Bay Books.

Hare, R.D. (1993). *Without conscience — the disturbing world of the psychopaths among us.* New York: Pocket Books (Simon & Schuster).

Harris, G.T., Rice, M.E., & Cormier, C.A. (1991). Psychopathy and violent recidivism. *Law and Human Behavior, 15*, 625–637.

Hemphill, J. F., & Hare, R. D. (2004, April 1). Some misconceptions about the Hare PCL-R and risk assessment: A reply to Gendreau, Goggin, and Smith. *Criminal Justice and Behavior, 31*(2), 203–243.

Hilton, N. Z., Harris, G. T., Rawson, K., & Beach, C. A. (2005, February 1). Communicating violence risk information to forensic decision makers. *Criminal Justice and Behavior, 32*(1), 97–116.

Hurrell, J. J., Worthington, K. A., & Driscoll, R. J. (1996). Job stress, danger and workplace violence: Analysis of assault experiences of state employees. In G. R. VandenBos & E. Q. Bulatao (Eds.), *Violence on the job: Identifying risks and developing solutions* (pp. 163–170). Washington, DC: American Psychological Association.

International Association of Chiefs of Police. (1989). *Law enforcement code of ethics.* Alexandria, VA.

International Association of Chiefs of Police. (1999). *Guidelines for preventing and responding to school violence.* Alexandria, VA.

Interpol. (2008). Code of conduct. Retrieved from http://www.interpol.int/Public/Corruption/1GEC/Codes/default.asp.

Kaplan, S. G., & Wheeler, E. G. (1983). Survival skills for working with potentially violent clients. *Social Casework, 64*, 339–346.

Koerin, B. (1978, January 1). Violent crime: Prediction and control. *Crime & Delinquency,* 49–58.

Kroner, D. G., & Mills, J. F. (2001). The accuracy of five risk appraisal instruments in predicting institutional misconduct and new convictions. *Criminal Justice and Behavior, 28,* 471–489.

Kropp, P. R. (2004, June 1). Some questions regarding spousal assault risk assessment. *Violence against Women, 10*(6), 676–697.

Kropp, P. R., & Hart, S. D. (2000). The spousal assault risk assessment (SARA) guide: Reliability and validity in adult male offenders. *Law and Human Behavior, 24*(1), 101–118.

Kropp, P. R., Hart, S. D., & Lyon, D. R. (2002, October 1). Risk assessment of stalkers: Some problems and possible solutions. *Criminal Justice and Behavior, 29*(5), 590–616.

Labig, C. E. (1995). *Preventing violence in the workplace.* New York: American Management Association.

Lewis, G. W., & Zare, N. C. (1999). *Workplace hostility: Myth and reality.* Philadelphia, PA: Accelerated Development.

Loza, W., & Samia, H. (2006, June 1). Is schizoid personality a forerunner of homicidal or suicidal behavior? *International Journal of Offender Therapy and Comparative Criminology, 50*(3), 338–343.

Maggio, M. J. (1996). Keeping the workplace safe: A challenge for managers. *Federal Probation, 60,* 67–71.

Maiuro, R. D., Vitaliano, P. P., & Cahn, T. S. (1987). A brief measure for assessment of anger and aggression. *Journal of Interpersonal Violence, 2,* 166–178.

McClure, L. F. (1996). *Risky business: Managing employee violence in the workplace.* New York: The Haworth Press.

McGee, J., & DeBernardo, C. R. (1999, May/June). The classroom avenger: A behavioral profile of school based shootings. *The Forensic Examiner,* 16–18.

Mehrabian, A., & Epstein, N. (1972). A measure of emotional empathy. *Journal of Personality, 40,* 525–543.

Meloy, J. R. (Ed.) (1998). *The psychology of stalking: Clinical and forensic perspectives.* New York: Academic Press.

Meloy, J. R. (2000). *Violence risk and threat assessment: A practical guide for mental health and criminal justice professionals.* San Diego, CA: Specialized Training Services.

Meloy, J. R., Cowett, P. Y., Parker, S. B., Hofland, B., & Friedland, A. (1997). Domestic protection orders and the prediction of subsequent criminality and violence toward protectees. *Psychotherapy: Theory, Research, Practice, Training, 34,* 447–458.

Michie, C., & Cooke, D. J. (2006, December 1). The structure of violent behavior: A hierarchical model. *Criminal Justice and Behavior, 33*(6), 706–737.

Miller, G. R., & Stiff, J. B. (1993). *Deception communication.* Newbury Park, CA: Sage Publications.

Miller, M. J. (2001). *The prediction and assessment of violence in the workplace: A critical review.* Doctoral dissertation, United States International University. *Dissertation Abstracts International, 62,* 2070.

Mills, J. F., Jones, M. N., & Kroner, D. G. (2005, October 1). An examination of the generealizability of the LSI-R and VRAG probability bins. *Criminal Justice and Behavior, 32*(5), 565–585.

Milne, R., & Bull, R. (1999). *Investigative interviewing, psychology and practice.* Chichester, England: John Wiley & Sons.

Mohandie, K. (2000). *School violence threat management.* San Diego, CA: Specialized Training Services.

Monahan, J. (1981). *Predicting violent behavior: An assessment of clinical techniques.* London: Sage Publications.

Monahan, J., & Steadman, H. (2001). *Rethinking risk assessment — The MacArthur study of mental disorder and violence.* Oxford, UK: Oxford University Press.

Monahan, J., Steadman, H., Robbins, P., Appelbaum, P., Banks, S., Grisso, T., Heilbrun, K., Mulvey, E., Roth, L., & Silver, E. (2005). An actuarial model of violence risk assessment for persons with mental disorders. *Psychiatric Services, 56,* 810–815.

Moos, R. H. (1988). Psychosocial factors in the workplace. In S. Fisher & J. Reason (Eds.), *Handbook of life stress, cognition and health* (pp. 193–209). New York: John Wiley & Sons.

National Center for Education Statistics. (2005). Indicators of School Crime and Safety: 2005, NCJ 210697. Available at http://www.ojp.usdoj.gov/bjs/abstract/iscs05.htm.

Neuman, J. H., & Baron, R. A. (1997). Aggression in the workplace. In R. A. Giacalone & J. Greenberg (Eds.), *Antisocial behavior in organizations* (pp. 37–67). London: Sage Publications.

Neuman, J. H., & Baron, R. A. (1998). Workplace violence and workplace aggression: Evidence concerning specific forms, potential causes, and preferred targets. *Journal of Management, 24,* 391–419.

Peek-Asa, C., Runyan, C. W., & Zwerling, C. (2001). The role of surveillance and evaluation research in the reduction of violence against workers. *American Journal of Preventive Medicine, 20,* 141–148.

Philipse, M. W. G., Koeter, M. W. J., Staak, C. P. F. V. D., & Brink, W. V. D. (2005, December 1). Reliability and discrminant validity of dynamic reoffending risk indicators in forensic clinical practice. *Criminal Justice and Behavior, 32*(6), 643–664.

Privacy Rights Clearinghouse. (2006, June 1). FACTA, the Fair and Accurate Credit Transactions Act: Consumers win some, lose some. Retrieved from http://www.privacy.rights.org/fs/fs6a-facta.htm.

Quinsey, V. L., Jones, G. B., Book, A. S., & Barr, K. N. (2006, December 1). The dynamic prediction of antisocial behavior among forensic psychiatric patients: A prospective field study. *Journal of Interpersonal Violence, 21*(12), 1539–1565.

Reddy, M., Borum, R., Vossekuil, B., Fein, R., Berglund, J., & Modzeleski, W. (2000). Evaluating risk for targeted violence in schools: Comparing risk assessment, threat assessment and other approaches. Available at http://www.campbell.edu/faculty/gay/readings/school_violence/ntac_sch%20violence1.pdf.

Reid, J.E., Inbau, F.E., & Buckley, J.B. (1986). *Criminal interrogation and confessions.* Baltimore, MD: Williams & Wilkins.

Roehl, J., O'Sullivan, C., Webster, D., & Campbell, J. (2005, May). *Intimate partner violence risk assessment validation study: Final report* (NCJRS 209731). Washington, DC: U.S. Department of Justice.

Roehl, J., O'Sullivan, C., Webster, D., & Campbell, J. (2005, May). *Intimate partner violence risk assessment validation study: The RAVE study assessor summary and recommendations: Validation of tools for assessing risk from violent intimate partners* (NCJRS 209732). Washington, DC: U.S. Department of Justice.

Schacter, D. L. (1996). *Searching for memory: The brain, the mind and the past.* New York: Basic Books.

Silver, E., & Chow-Martin, L. (2002, October 1). A multiple models approach to assessing recidivism risk: Implications for judicial decision making. *Criminal Justice and Behavior, 29*(5), 538–568.

Silver, E., & Miller, L. L. (2002, January 1). A cautionary note on the use of actuarial risk assessment tools for social control. *Crime & Delinquency, 48*(1), 138–161.

Silver, E., Felson, R. B., & Vaneseltine, M. (2008, April 1). The relationship between mental health problems and violence among criminal offenders. *Criminal Justice and Behavior, 35*(4), 405–426.

Slora, K. B., Joy, D. S., Jones, J. W., & Terris, W. (1991). The prediction of on-the-job violence. In J. W. Jones (Ed.), *Preemployment honesty testing: Current research and future directions.* Westport, CT: Quorum Books.

Slora, K. B., Joy, D. S., & Terris, W. (1991). Personnel selection to control employee violence. *Journal of Business and Psychology, 3,* 417–426.

Society of Human Resource Management. (2008). *SHRM code of ethical and professional standards in human resource mangement* (Code of ethics).

Spector, P. E. (1997). The role of frustration in antisocial behavior at work. In R. A. Giacalone & J. Greenberg (Eds.), *Antisocial behavior in organizations* (pp. 1–17). London: Sage Publications.

Thistlethwaite, A., Wooldredge, J., & Gibbs, D. (1998). Severity of dispositions and domestic violence recidivism. *Crime and Delinquency, 44,* 388–398.

Thompson, G.J., & Jenkins, J.B. (1993). *Verbal judo.* New York: William Morrow and Company.

Tobin, T. J. (2001). Organizational determinants of violence in the workplace. *Aggression & Violent Behavior, 6,* 91–102.

Trafford, C., Gallichio, E., & Jones, P. (1995). Managing violence in the workplace. In P. Cotton (Ed.), *National Occupational Stress Conference: June 1994. Psychological health in the workplace: Understanding and managing occupational stress* (pp. 147–158). Brisbane, Australia: Australian Psychological Society.

Turner, J. T., & Gelles, M. G. (2003). *Threat assessment: A risk management approach.* Binghamton, NY: The Haworth Press.

Turvey, B. E. (1999). *The deductive method of criminal profiling.* In B. Turvey (Ed.), *Criminal profiling* (pp. 25–32). San Diego, CA: Academic Press.

Verlinden, S., Hersen, M., & Thomas, J. (2000). Risk factors in school shootings. *Clinical Psychology Review, 20,* 3–56.

Virginia Tech Review Panel. (2007, April 16). Mass Shootings at Virginia Tech Report of the Review Panel presented to Govenor Kaine Commonwealth of Virginia. Retrieved from http://www.governor.virginia.gov/TempContent/techpanelreport.cfm.

Vossekuil, B., Reddy, M., Fein, R., Borum, R., & Modzeleski, W. (2000). Safe school initiative: An interim report on the prevention of targeted violence in schools. Washington, DC: U.S. Secret Service, National Threat Assessment Center.

Walters, S.B. (1999). *Principles of kinesic interview and interrogation.* New York: CRC Press.

Waters, J. A., Lynn, R. I., & Morgan, K. J. (2002). Workplace violence: Prevention and intervention, theory and practice. In L. A. Rapp-Paglicci, A. R. Roberts, & J. S. Wodarski (Eds.), *Handbook of violence* (pp. 378–413). New York: John Wiley & Sons.

Weber, R. (1995). Suicide prevention at the workplace. In P. Cotton (Ed.), *National Occupational Stress Conference: June 1994. Psychological health in the workplace: Understanding and managing occupational stress* (pp. 171–182). Brisbane, Australia: Australian Psychological Society.

White, T. W. (1996). Research, practice, and legal issues regarding workplace violence: A note of caution. In G. R. VandenBos & E. Q. Bulatao (Eds.), *Violence on the job: Identifying risks and developing solutions* (pp. 87–100). Washington, DC: American Psychological Association.

Wilkinson, C. W. (2001). Violence prevention at work: A business perspective. *American Journal of Preventive Medicine, 20,* 155–160.

Williams, K. R., & Hawkins, R. (1989). Controlling male aggression in intimate relationships. *Law and Society Review, 23,* 591–612.

Wodarski, J. S., & Dulmus, C. N. (2002). Preventing workplace violence. In L. A. Rapp-Paglicci, A. R. Roberts, & J. S. Wodarski (Eds.), *Handbook of violence* (pp. 349–377). New York: John Wiley & Sons.

Yeschke, C. L. (2002). *The art of investigative interviewing.* Burlington, MA: Elsevier Science.

Index

Note: *n* refers to notes.

A

ABA (American Bar Association), 313
Abuse
    information gathering on, 47
    laws on, 284
    post-secondary school violence and,
        232–233
    questions about, 134
    risk and, 117
    romantically involved victims
        and, 195
Acceptance by instigators, 80
Accommodations to environments, 206
Active listening
    in interviews, 76
    telephone interviews and, 83
    victim's role and, 189, 191, 199
Actuarial methods, 151
ADA (Americans with Disabilities Act),
    287–288, 342
Advocates for victims and
    witnesses, 267
Affective sentiment, *see* Emotions
Aggression
    assessment grid and, 112–113, 126
    conflict and, 214–215
    security and, 273–275
    of victim, 197
Alarm systems, 261, 262–263, 278n4
Allaway, Edward Charles, 228–230
Altom, Jason, 231
American Bar Association (ABA), 313
American Medical Association
    Principles of Medical Ethics,
    312–313
American Psychological Association (APA)
    Ethics Code, 312, 315, 317,
    319, 320
Americans with Disabilities Act (ADA),
    287–288, 342

Anger
    case history, 339–347
    control and, 146
    in "Death of a Story" protocol, 79
    motivation and, 216
    post-secondary school violence and,
        223–224, 232–233, 238–239,
        250–251
    risk and, 113, 115, 116–117
    victim's role and, 196
Antisocial personality disorder (ASPD),
    110, 116, 339–347
Anxiety
    antisocial personality disorder and, 346
    control and, 147
    duty to warn and, 302
    interviews and, 19, 22
    organizational influences and, 206
APA (American Psychological Association)
    Ethics Code, 312, 315, 317, 319, 320
Appalachian Law School (VA), 237–238
Appearance of assessors, 68–69
Approach-behavior, 164
Armed personnel, 263
Arson, 134
ASIS International Code of Ethics, 313
ASPD (antisocial personality disorder),
    110, 116, 339–347
Assessment
    call (notice event) and, 3–5, 6, 45
    control vector analysis and, 147–149
    costs of, 105–106
    definition of, 161, 165
    environment and, 217
    ethical issues with, *see* Ethical issues
    guidelines for, *see* Risk Assessment
        Guideline Elements for Violence
        (RAGE-V)
    information gathering in, *see*
        Information gathering;
        Informative discussions
    laws of, *see* Laws of risk assessment and
        intervention